THE CELESTIAL BRIDES

THE VISIONS OF THE EASTERN PARADISE INFILTRATE THE MEDITERRANEAN AFTERLIFE

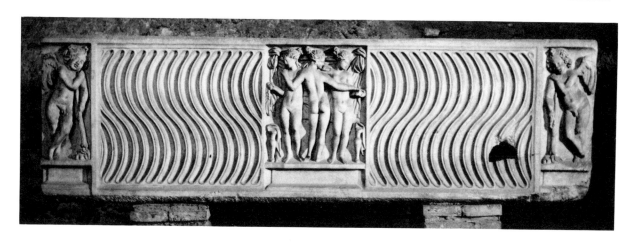

A STUDY IN MYTHOLOGY AND ARCHAEOLOGY

BY OCTAVIO ALVAREZ

INTRODUCTION BY MARIE DELCOURT

PREFACE BY JAN VAN DER MARCK

HERBERT REICHNER · PUBLISHER · STOCKBRIDGE · MASS.

Herbert Reichner, Scholarly Books Division

Stockbridge, Massachusetts 01262 U.S.A.

PRINTED IN THE UNITED STATES OF AMERICA BY WHITMAN PRESS, NEW HAMPSHIRE

CONTENTS

THE VARIOUS PARADISES

INDIA

THE TEMPLE GIRLS

THE TEMPLE SCULPTURES

I

APOTHEOSIS

THE SYMBOLS OF RESURRECTION

THE EGYPTIAN CONNECTION

TEFNUT AND ELEUSIS

EGYPT

FEMALES IN THE BEYOND

GIFTS OF THE DEAD

SUBJECTS SHOWN ON MIRRORS

PLAQUES

THE PLAQUES OF NAPLES

THE PLAQUES OF ATHENS

SEA SARCOPHAGI

152 ILLUSTRATIONS WITH CAPTIONS

ACKNOWLEDGEMENTS

RESPECTFUL THANKS FOR THEIR HELP IS HERE GIVEN TO THE FOLLOWING PERSONS:

IN ALPHABETICAL ORDER

Dr. Santosh K. Chawla
Professor Marie Delcourt
Professor Wentworth Eldredge
Professor Alfonso de Franciscis
Professor Dr. Ambros Pfiffig
Professor Dr. Hellmut Sichtermann
Dr. Jürgen Thimme
Direttore Generale
delle Antichità e Belle Arti
Ministero per i Beni Culturali, Rome

ACKNOWLEDGEMENTS

THE ILLUSTRATIONS ARE PUBLISHED COURTESY OF:

MUSEUMS (Illustration number):

Archaeological Museum, Ankara, Turkey-36
National Archaeological Museum, Athens, Greece-
    9, 10, 11, 12, 53, 117, 119, 120, 121
Museum of Fine Arts, Boston, Mass.-
    13 (Detail) Catherine Page Perkins Collection
    18 (Detail) H.L. Pierce Fund
    29 (Detail) Gift of Mrs. Gardner Brewer
    42 (Detail) Loaned by Boston Athenaeum
    51 and 52 Gift of E.P. Warren
    54 Francis Bartlett Donation
Brooklyn Museum, Brooklyn, N.Y.-37 (Detail)
Cleveland Museum of Art, Cleveland, Ohio-56 J.H. Wade Fund
Museum of Ancient Corinth, Corinth, Greece-
    122 American School of Classical Studies
Dartmouth College Museum and Galleries, Hanover, N.H.-143
Badisches Landesmuseum, Karlsruhe, Germany-55, 104
British Museum, London, Courtesy of the Trustees-39, 44, 57
Museo Archeologico Nazionale, Naples, Italy-
    6, 7, 8, 17, 22, 105, 106, 107, 108, 109, 110,
    111, 112, 113, 114, 115, 145
Metropolitan Museum of Art, New York, N.Y.-
    24 (Detail) Fletcher Fund, 1924
    27 Rogers Fund, 1947
    126 and 127 (Details) Cesnola Collection (Subscription) 1874-76
Museo Archeologico, Palestrina, Italy-16
Musée du Louvre, Paris, France-60
Philadelphia Museum of Art, Philadelphia, Penn.-
    2, 3 by purchase (Wyatt, Phot.)
Museo dei Conservatori, Rome, Italy-61, 138, 140, 149
Museo Nazionale Romano, Rome, Italy-21, 32
Villa Giulia, Rome, Italy-14, 15

ACKNOWLEDGEMENTS

PUBLISHERS (Illustration number):

Edition Leipzig, Verlag für Kunst und Wissenschaft, Leipzig (DDR)-62
De Gruyter & Co., Berlin, Germany-63 to 103
The Hamlyn Group, Feltham, Middlesex, England-45
La Guilde du Livre et Les Editions Clairfontaine, Lausanne, Switzerland-4
Verlag F. Bruckmann, München, Germany-50
Dover Publications, Inc., New York-38
Grove Press, New York-58
Tudor Publishing Co., New York-128

PHOTOGRAPHS (Illustration number):

Bildarchiv Foto Marburg, Germany-23
A. L. Syed, Palanput, India-1
Max-Pol Fouchet, Paris-4
Josephine Powell, Rome, Italy-5
Franz Mayer, Vienna, Austria-35
Octavio Alvarez-6, 7, 8, 17, 21, 22, 23, 32, 36, 105, 106, 107, 108, 109, 110, 111, 112, 113, 114,
    115, 122, 138, 140, 143, 145, 149
Andre Held, Ecublens, Switzerland-59
Fratelli Alinari, Florence, Italy-47, 62, 129, 133, 135, 142
Terry Gallowhur, Reading, Vermont-48
Deutsches Archaeologisches Institut, Rome-19, 20, 25, 26, 28, 30, 31, 33, 34, 40, 41, 43, 46, 49,
    116, 123, 124, 125, 130, 131, 132, 134, 136, 137, 139, 141, 144, 146, 147, 148, 150, 151, 152

VIGNETTES IN THE TEXT (Page numbers):

Dr. Santosh K. Chawla-5, 6, 7, 10, 29, 31, 33, 126, 156, 157, 172
F. Bruckmann Verlag, München-138, 139
Dover Publications Co. (Ernst Lehner), New York-36, 82, 90, 124, 193
De Gruyter & Co., Berlin-143, 168, 178
Hamlyn Group, Feltham, Middlesex, England-124, 236, 237
Editions E. Leroux, Paris-39, 43, 204, 205, 207, 209, 210
Metropolitan Museum of Art, New York-137
Verlag von Zabern, Mainz, Germany-140
Akademische Druck- & Verlagsanstalt, Graz, Austria-91, 92, 93, 97, 104, 105, 106, 107, 110

ANIMULA VAGULA, BLANDULA
HOSPES COMESQUE CORPORIS,
QUAE NUNC ABIBIS IN LOCA
PALLIDULA, RIGIDA, NUDULA,
NEC, UT SOLES, DABIS IOCOS

P. AELIUS HADRIANUS, IMP.

Soul, tender, vague and wandering
The body's guidance, guest and friend
To what strange regions dost thou tend
Death-pale, confined and naked thing
How will they wonted jestings end

Hadrian, Imperator

X

INTRODUCTION

Men have rarely resigned themselves to accept death as the total abolition of personal existence. Almost every culture has admitted the notion of an afterlife. Such an afterlife is sometimes seen as the unique privilege of those who were powerful during their earthly life; often this privilege is also available to everyone. But with the growth of moral thought, the afterlife has been increasingly understood as a state in which men would receive the reward for their good deeds and be punished for the wrongs they had committed. Such was the view of the Greeks. Whenever one examines the texts where they describe these two opposite conditions, however, one notices that, while the Greek poets left no striking image for the happiness of the blessed, they conceived of the most exquisite tortures for punishing the damned. When the living Ulysses descends into the world of the dead, he witnesses the impotent, exhausting efforts of Siphysus and Tantalus, the enemies of the gods. The heroes of this underworld should be as happy as the wicked are tormented, but this is clearly not the case, for the former greet Ulysses with lamentations about their present fate. They may still be lords and kings, but it is in a world without substance. "I would rather be a serf in the house of some poor farmer," says Achilles, "than lord over all these spent men."

From Homer to Dante, there has been more than one Descent into Hell where infernal punishments have been depicted in increasingly vivid colors. The bliss of paradise, however, remains extremely vague; poets speak merely of flowery meadows, of sweet music, and of joyful dances.

A rather short reference, unique to my knowledge, suggests a different picture. In the 'Republic' (363 C D) Plato recalls that the legendary poet Musaeus and his son, Eumolpus, hold out to the blessed, once they are established in the other world, "sumptuous banquets at which, crowned with wreaths, they will wallow everlastingly in their cups, as if the supreme reward for virtue were eternal drunkenness." This conception of paradisiacal felicity, apparently of popular origin, scandalizes the philosopher. We should like to know more about it, but our sources remain silent.

The paradise of the Germans, on the other hand, has been obligingly described by their poets: carousing and feasting for the warriors who are beloved of the gods, with furious new combats every evening, as if martial ardor were the very sign of rebirth.

But it is the Vedic paradise which offers the most complete rejuvenation. Here is how Hermann Oldenberg describes it in 'Die Religion des Vedas': A garden of Eden with never ending springs of milk and honey and with equally never ending games of love." The poems promise the chosen ones the joys of everlasting sexual activities: "Fire cannot burn their Linga. Much womenfolk is there for them in heaven . . . God Yama does not steal their semen."

While studying Etruscan tombs, Mr. Alvarez was struck by the discovery of an entirely similar inspiration: the representation of a return to a full life involving sexual along with all other activities, in a manner comparable, in fact, to what is promised by the Islamic doctrine of Afterlife. Guided by a keen intuition in mythology and by concrete knowledge of all forms of artistic rendering, Mr. Alvarez recognized in the funeral art of the Etruscans the disclosure of their conception of the thereafter, including the rejuvenation of the

Blessed in paradise. At the same time, his research on Greco-Roman funerary art was oriented along similar lines. He was especially interested in the immensely rich representations on those sarcophagi which exhibit subjects apparently without relation to death. The presence of such motives has remained largely unexplained, and Mr. Alvarez has rejected the traditional view that they serve simply to demonstrate the virtuosity of ancient artists. He has probed more deeply and asked whether these forms do not reveal conceptions similar to those which are exposed in Hindu and Etruscan art. To be sure, in Greco-Roman art the longing for a complete rejuvenation appears in a much more allusive manner, and understandably so, because the common religious beliefs which we know through the texts make no mention of an afterlife where the elect might experience the joys of love. But there may be a certain discrepancy between pure mythology and the funeral use of symbols. The sensualistic conception of the afterlife, which Plato criticizes and rejects, had already been brought to Italy by the Etruscans and may subsequently have permeated the Greco-Roman world from the East in late antiquity. Eastern ideas and cults were triumphant in their invasion of Greece, Italy, and even Roman Gaul; here they implanted themselves, despite their foreignness, especially among those who had not been moulded by classical philosophy.

Mr. Alvarez has undertaken a study in depth of the motives of funerary art. His study is based on three types of evidence, which all lead to the same result: mirrors and cistae made and found in the North of Italy, sarcophagi from Central Italy, plaques from South of Italy. Many documents which appear in this book have never been published or studied before. Mr. Alvarez unveils their symbolic value, revealing thereby in the declining Greco-Roman world a longing for an afterlife which would restore the Golden Age, the felicity, and the freedom of which mankind has always dreamed. Here love reigns supreme, in realistic terms, but without all that opposes or alters love on earth.

Here is a book overflowing with new ideas and rather amazing combinations, dove-tailing textual with archaeological evidences tending to demonstrate the gradual increasing manifestations of Eastern visions in Mediterranean funeral art. However bold its conclusions may appear, they are based on archaeological evidences. Whatever the author says, he learned from visual documentation. He also displays a compassionate understanding for the great problems of the creative artists and their dilemma in chosing between symbol-figures expressing perfectly new concepts and visions of foreign lands and cultures.

A part from the interest this book will have to students and experts of archaeology and mythology, it will stimulate new researches and insights. It should induce at least the resumption of the strange religious problem of the 'post mortem marriage,' so poorly attested by the literary texts, but well known in many folklores. A good book awakes sleeping curiosities.

MARIE DELCOURT
PROFESSOR EMERITUS CLASSICAL PHILOLOGY

PREFACE

Early twentieth century art historians, with more wishfulness than proof, tended to regard the Mediterranean world as self-contained and thus inviolate as Victorian parents assumed their daughters to be virtuous and virginal. They took a dim view of Josef Strzygowski, the Czech art historian who was offered a chair at the University of Vienna for his pioneering research into the Russian and Mideastern influences on Mediterranean art. In a burst of formalist outrage, the great Bernard Berenson branded his colleague Strzygowski the "Attila of Art History." Vienna had always been a buffer between Western Europe and the Ottoman Empire. Its intellectuals and artists were sensitized in the crucible of cultural contradictions and its scholars took a lead in the field of Asian studies. Paying tribute to the Indian genius for poetic thought, Strzygowski dedicated 'Die Krisis der Geisteswissenschaften' (1923) to Rabindranath Tagore.

The neo-Hegelian aesthetic and its formalist view of art can lead to untenable positions. In 'The Nude: a Study in Ideal Form' (1956), a series of lectures dedicated to Bernard Berenson, as distinguished an art historian as Kenneth Clark voiced the opinion that "sea-sarcophagi" derived their design from a single artist because they followed the same pattern all over the antique world. Although he considered their origin to be obscure, Sir Kenneth was struck by the Nereids' abandoned pose on some of those sarcophagi, so different from that of her more decorous sisters, and he speculated that there may have been a source for it in Oriental art. To him that pose, atypical for what in every other way seemed to be a Roman genre, indicated that the artist had stolen a glance at some work of art from the Orient. It did not occur to this formalist art historian that the genre as a whole might have Eastern roots.

Andreas Rumpf, the leading authority on sea sarcophagi, contends in 'Die Meerwesen auf den Antiken Sarkophagreliefs' (1969) that the frequently used motif of the Nereids embracing the sea bulls originates in the legend of Europa and the Bull. He cites no specific evidence for it and that legend, quite clearly, has no bearing on the cult of the dead. This and other attempts at linking the iconography of sea sarcophagi to Graeco-Roman mythology demonstrate a failure to interpret those fascinating but puzzling images in terms of anything outside the Mediterranean lore. Oddly enough, the mythology of other cultures was not considered.

In another passage of his book, Rumpf admits that the exotic ornaments on sarcophagi and chests may have been borrowed from Oriental rugs, but then he flatly states that there is no connection with the rites of burial and the concept of an afterlife in the way these funeral objects are decorated. He gives us no clue as to what the ancient craftsman might have had in mind. After having dismissed the conventional explanations for the imagery on sea sarcophagi (e.g., the return to the pool of nature or the voyage of the dead souls), Rumpf questions, with the exasperation of an archaeologist who would have preferred to describe only what he sees, whether there has to be an explanation at all for those Tritons, Nereids and Ichthyocentaurs. With more frustration than logic, he concludes that, even if they do have a religious meaning, that meaning must have been limited to Italy.

XVI

His own background has prepared this writer to favor the iconological over the formalist approach. The acquisition by the Dartmouth College Museum and Galleries of a sarcophagus panel, for centuries the pride of the Earls of Pembroke at Wilton House, and the questions raised by the style in which it is carved and the theme it portrays have made me an early initiate and subsequent subscriber to O.J. Alvarez's thesis that we are dealing, in this case, with a late Roman adaptation, no longer properly understood, of a Vedic vision of the Hereafter introduced to Italy by the Etruscans. With nothing more than graveyard artifacts as evidence, but with an intimate knowledge of Mediterranean and Asian myths, particularly those of origin and extinction, the author of 'The Celestial Brides' has advanced a theory that should be acceptable to philologists and archaeologists alike because it draws into sharp focus images the philologist is not usually familiar with and meanings never before made explicit in an archaeological context.

Mr. Alvarez's interpretation of sea sarcophagi is firmly anchored in the iconography of the mirrors found in northern Italian graves and the funeral plaques of the South. Those mirrors, gifts with which the deceased was to endear himself to the deities of the Beyond, carry images crucial to our understanding of the Etruscan concept of life after death. They also pose problems of interpretation that cannot be solved unless we look beyond familiar Graeco-Roman myths. The author of 'The Celestial Brides' proves to us in a manner that is free of defensive scholarship or argumentative reinterpretation of known facts, that the impetus for the Etruscan funeral art can be found in the Indian scriptures and that the vision opened up by the Sages of the Vedas was so compelling indeed that for centuries purveyors of graveyard artifacts continued to cater to an Oriental instead of a Graeco-Roman concept of the Hereafter.

To the Etruscans, the Souls' final abode was not Hades, as it is in Greek myth, nor that Nirwana or simple release from the burdens of existence, promised to the followers of Buddha. Instead, those early settlers of the Italian peninsula and their Roman successors had an earthy, materialistic concept of the Hereafter that matched their pragmatic view of religion. Theirs was an escape into the paradise of the senses as pictured by the Vedo-Brahmanic cult of the Indo-Aryans. Linking the two distant worlds were the Thracians, with their Oriental customs described by Herodotus, and the Ionians, with their Orphic roots. Corinth is thought to be the port of entry for these foreign ideas into the Mediterranean basin. Whatever immediacy existed between India and Etruria dates back, in all probability, to the middle of the first millennium B.C. Etruscan iconographic traditions related to the afterlife gelled, according to the author of 'The Celestial Brides', into a pattern that started as a vague hear-say coming from the East, but gradually and visibly absorbed more specific information, probably supplied by traders and preachers coming from the bordering Asiatic Orient.

In his essay 'Iconography and Iconology' (1939), Erwin Panofsky demonstrates that in the Middle Ages a dichotomy developed between the representational and textual traditions in art. Classical motifs were invested with a non-classical meaning and classical themes were expressed by non-classical figures in a non-classical setting. There is a parallel with what happened to those Eastern ideas in the hands of Etruscan and Roman craftsmen. The first settlers in Etruria may well have come from Asia, if not with actual cult objects or works of art, than at least with a memory of them and with a tradition of craftsmanship in the Oriental manner. Early stone carvings betray Asiatic features and a style and iconography that seem both foreign and primitive. But, as time goes on, the formal quality of those funeral decorations improved while their contents became more and more alienated from their original Asian roots. The fact that the Vedic visions were acted-out by Graeco-Roman protagonists, is one of the main theses of this book, which unlocks many of the great enigmas in funeral art. Once the sarcophagus, that ultimate vessel, had reached the height of its stylistic perfection it had shed every last trace of its original inspiration so its decorations became meaningless allegories, understood, one may assume, by the initiated, but abstruse to everybody else, then and now.

In Vedic mythology, the soul of the departed ascends to the blue yonder, called 'Svarga,' or "heavenly sea" where Indra reigns supreme. Indra is an Aryan god brought by the Indo-European warriors and he supplies life's most essential commodities, light and water. Enthroned on Mount Meru, north of the Himalayas, the center of the earth, he is surrounded by a court of deities, the centauric and musical Gandharvas and the Apsarases, their licentious paramours, who also become the heavenly brides, embracing the souls of the departed in their celestial spheres. While in the Graeco-Roman afterworld the shades are said to exist "without midriff," i.e., deprived of food and sex, in the mythic world of Indra they are given young and handsome bodies so they can enjoy the eternal pleasures.

Schopenhauer in his later years said that in the whole world there is no study so comforting and so elevating as that of the Upanishads. It has been the solace of my life, and shall be the solace in the time of my death. The nature of heaven, as we learn from Arthur B. Keith's 'The Religion and Philosophy of the Veda and Upanishads' (1925), is described in the Rigveda, the Mahabharata and the Samhitas. There is light, sun and every form of happiness. The spirits are so material that they not merely enjoy the most material things – the fruit of the lotus, milk and honey – but also delight in the pleasures of love, a clue to the corporeal state of their transcended being. The sound of singing and the music of flutes reverberate in Indra's Paradise. The spirits encounter wish-cows and yield to all desires and the ambiance is one of perfect harmony and joy unbounded. This picture of heaven, combining whatever pleasures the mind can conceive of on earth, is raised to an even higher level of visionary intensity by the priestly imagination of the Vedas.

"Within each person is his Un-manifest
all-pervading and unperceptible Self.
A man, after falling asunder of his body
is embodied again as immortal.
Whatever desires are difficult to satisfy
in the world of the living are given to him then.
The heavenly maidens shall wait for him then,
at his choosing to fulfill all his desires."
[Katha Upanishad II.3]

'Kama,' or pleasure, is an essential feature of the Indian concept of life as well as of that of the soul's transmigration following his earthly death. It is the faithful's celestial reward, recorded in scriptures and on temple sculptures. Recognized, by students of Indian art, for its sensuous and often overtly erotic nature, this portrayal of the soul's ascension and rebirth, as it changes into the reception of the Souls on Etruscan mirrors, cists and sarcophagi, is no longer understood in its original context and becomes the subject of homilies or mere formal analysis by Western archaeologists. Mr. Alvarez has probed beyond the formal and simply allegorical in his study of Etruscan mirrors, cists and sarcophagi, some of which have never been reproduced before, and he has shown that unveiling the meaning of their imagery is crucial to our understanding of Etruscan eschatology as rooted in the vision of the Vedas.

'The Celestial Brides' traces among other things, some very specific notions about life after death from India to the Eastern Mediterranean. In this fascinating book we find in the opening chapter a new interpretation of the Indian temple sculptures, which appeared inexplicable until now. The author describes the influx into Egypt of an Asian vision of the Hereafter as a pleasure paradise where the souls are received not anymore by the tragic death-god Osiris, but instead by the enchanting Hathor, divinity of eternal youth, beauty and love. The relation of the Egyptian Tefnut, to the religious mysteries at Eleusis, heretofore unexplored, may be the book's most far-reaching and compelling thesis. Mr. Alvarez deals with the "Symbols of Resurrection," amply documented by new source material. He touches on the delicate question of the "Apollonic Epiphany" of the soul's alter ego and its tender encounters in the Hereafter. To the enigma surrounding the "Gifts of the Dead" he offers a solution which makes perfect sense if we accept the origins of Etruscan funeral art. The key to our understanding of the mysterious sea sarcophagi lies in the author's establishing a connection between the Indian "Water Maidens" or Apsarases and the Water-Nymphs in Graeco-Roman mythology.

Intimate connections have been established between water, night, sleep and death. In 'Die Bedeutung des Wassers in Kunst and Leben der Alten' (1921), Martin Ninck has written: "An der Scheide von Tod und Leben, von Nacht und Tag fliesst der Toten-oder Traumstrom." But this is not its only symbolic connotation. At once purifying and giving new life, water has been considered germinative. Since prehistoric times, water, moon and woman were seen as forming the orbit of fertility both for man and the universe. The soul's longing for water in funeral representations may very well spring from that deep desire for reincarnation. "Water, thou art the source of all things and of all existence" says one Indian text, summing up a long Vedic tradition.

Vishnu slumbers on the World Serpent "Endless," Endymion is plunged into eternal sleep and Jonah is thrown back on the shores of life, all on or near the water. The sarcophagus is the vessel and death is man's ultimate voyage. Water, more than earth, air and fire, is the total element and a complete poetic reality: it has body, soul and voice as Gaston Bachelard has observed in 'L'Eau et les Rêves' (1942). It can be perceived as male or female. To the Ancients it was a male element: Aphrodite Anadyomene rose from the white foam produced by the severed genitals of Uranos, and the ocean is often referred to as the great spermatic pool of nature whence all life has sprung. Poets, on the other hand, see water in a female guise and the swan-turned-nymph is its prototypical embodiment. In 'Heinrich von Ofterdingen' (1802) Novalis evokes the image of waves turning into the limbs of lovely maidens, another favorite transformation. He relates how his hero descends into the water and experiences every wave as a tender bosom pressed against his eager body: "Die Flut schien eine Auflösung reizender Mädchen, die an dem Jünglinge sich augenblicklich verkörperten."

"Darkness was at first, by darkness hidden.
Of neither night nor day was any token.
Without distinctive marks, all there was water.
But the mighty waters contained the universal germ.
He of the powers surveyed the floods
containing all productive forces
of those he formed then Desire
as the beginning of all beginnings in the soul
and then made you, enjoyer of all desires."
[Rig Veda X.21]

'The Celestial Brides' presents the themes of love and death so dear to poets who since time immemorial have linked one inescapably to the other. But, in this book the sequence has been reversed and death has become the portal through which the soul enters the sphere of heavenly and lasting love. It is that "life after life," forever puzzling and uncertain, which generation after generation has summoned and evoked according to its most cherished religious and artistic visions. Blessed are those cultures fostering a belief that love triumphs over death and that souls upon entering the hereafter reincarnate to become actors on the stage of infinity, embracing love in its most marvelous mythical disguises.

Every work of art mediates between what inspired it and what we project into it. 'The Celestial Brides' has cast a new and unexpected light on our understanding of Etruscan and Roman eschatology. With that secret delight of the initiated we look at the Nereids, those fair virgins frolicking with the Tritons in the Mediterranean waves and we think of the Apsarases seducing their soul companions in Indra's heavenly sea. But, since the mind is irrepressibly turned toward the familiar, these age-old images will remain, uncorrupted by our greater knowledge, the lovely embodiments, by whatever name, of the Ancients' aspiration toward life eternal.

JAN VAN DER MARCK
DIRECTOR DARTMOUTH COLLEGE MUSEUM AND GALLERIES

THE VARIOUS PARADISES

THE BIRTH OF PARADISE
(The abstract thought)

The helpless human creature, a miserable worm during the inordinately long time of his infancy, of delayed maturing, with no fur to protect him from heat and cold, hampered by mediocre sight and hearing – (as compared to the animals who are out to get him) – with an almost useless nose, to pick up the scent of an approaching animal, with teeth that are useless in battle (as compared to the tiger or wolf) – with no horns, no claws to defend his life. This miserable misfit would never have made it in this world without that secret trick – the 'abstract thought' – which no other creature seems to possess, and of which a further consequence and outgrowth became the 'Abstract World.' The so-called 'a priori knowledge' that, for instance, two and two is four, without having to first ask nature to verify that abstract assumption with apples laid out and counted, this independence from the material verification through nature, gave man a 'free ticket' to speculate without regard for verification through material experience in other matters too. This then was his free ticket to abstract speculations of any kind, and his ticket into a non-existent world, a transcendental world, populated by Spirits.

As the material world appeared to obey and to submit to our 'a priori' percepts – (see the example of the apples) – this conceptual world of thoughts seemed thereby to be superior and to guide the material world. In the end we fell victims to our own 'a priori' speculations in assuming that we too are subject to a spiritual stratagem above us, in considering ourselves as material, and giving the supremacy over all material things to the spiritual. Man suspected this world, and the human condition, to be nothing but the material consequence of some 'Spirits,' in their highest echelon, being the gods.

1

The next step was then to imagine the circumstances in which those governing forces were living, and there we reverted to visions of power structures known to us from earthly experience, the life-style of those who were so powerful that they were above work and drudgery and any care for material things, but lived only for their sensual pleasures. This mode of circumstances became the pattern of the earliest visions of paradises. The word 'Paradise' is derived from the Avestan Pairidaeza which means 'Enclosure of Women'' – while "Eden" in Hebrew means "Delight" – hence: "Garden of Eden" means "Garden of Delights" – and taken together conveys the idea of DELIGHTS IN THE ENCLOSURE OF WOMEN – being a hint at the first and most opulent imaginations of Paradise which only later shifted towards leaner and more spiritual interpretations . . . as we shall see in the following.

THE INFINITE SPAN OF PARADISE
(Prehistory being the Model)

Today we deal with the idea of a split Paradise: one is that of Adam and Eve, at the dawn of time, the other is the post-mortem Paradise, which we hope to enter after leaving this earth.

But, interestingly, in the earliest thoughts of India, it is believed that the post-mortem Paradise is the very same as the premordial Paradise, and it is specifically said that the conditions in the realm of the Blessed in the great Above are those of the mythical dream-fantasy of a Prehistoric Herd, which peacefully roamed the hills of this earth, and where everybody made love to anybody, without restraint in the blissful innocence, which prevails in a herd of our brothers, the animals.

It is even more interesting to see that this connection between the two paradises, or their unity, must be very deeply rooted in the 'Collective Memory' of the human race, so that it surfaces since earliest times and in completely separated parts of the globe in certain festivals or ritualistic reunions, expressing the notion that the premordial condition is the model of the post-mortem paradise, and that the two states of paradise have a causal connection.

As an example of it we learn that on some of the Polynesian islands a cult sprang up in which the natives were instructed by their leader and prophet to destroy all their worldly possessions and so prepare for the coming of a paradisial condition. They were further ordered to abandon all existent rituals and taboos and to establish instead the paradisial status of the Prehistoric Herd. All members of that clan had to be completely naked and all females belong to all men and indiscriminate intercourse should be performed in the open, to return to the paradisial status of bliss eternal, which was believed to bring about immortality too, as one of the postulates of paradise.

In contrast to our idea of the "Day of Judgement" where on a certain day the dead shall rise and all of them would be summarily judged – the postulate of the East envisions that each person, after death, separately goes through the process of entering the realm of the Blessed. We therefore see a permanent and infinite procession of souls moving into the paradisical Above, which started at the beginning of time and is continuing into eternity. Left behind are only those who are condemned to reappear on earth in further incarnations.

THE PARADISE OF REASON
(The Immortals of the King)

The ancient kings had bodyguards, sometimes numbering 1,000 men. They were expected to give their lives for the protection of the king. In return, they were given enormous privileges of earthly kind. This was tempting enough to attract men to enlist in their ranks. But one was still not sure how those men of the guard would act in a real emergency and if, in fact, they would sacrifice their own lives – because, what earthly benefits can you give to a man to entice him to give up that life on earth, which was made so sweet and tempting for him? Well, obviously, you can not promise him earthly benefits to make him leave this world. But what else? You must make him even more attractive promises concerning his life after death when it was given to save the king. And so, the court-poets invented, with exuberant eloquence, descriptions of enormous suggestive power, and the priestship, on the side of the king, verified those inventions, easily taking advantage of the fact that nobody could testify to the contrary, and that any doubt in the word of the priest, 'the word of power,' was sacrilegious and a crime against religion punishable by death. And also, there was no choice between different religions, so that even the slightest questioning of religious matters was not in fashion. There were no different religions to choose from, but instead — that which the priest and the king proclaimed was the absolute and ultimate truth.

So it came about that the idea of Afterlife was expedient, or even necessary to be established, and that it was accepted, and the select few who were admitted to that marvelous other world were 'The Immortals of the King' — who were his bodyguard. (See Herodotus VII.211, also mentioned by Athenaeus in his Deipnosophistae XII.514, which refers to those bodyguards.) In the Indo-Mediterranean sphere they were sometimes called the Mazagrapati, with dignity accorded to them as if being already almost from another world.

They were called "The Immortals" because it was proclaimed that only and exclusively those who were killed to save the king were privileged to partake in the celestial eternity of bliss, and also, because they were replaced by equally costumed ones as fast as they were killed, so that they appeared to the attackers as forever arising anew, and therefore to be immortal.

> "A thousand Calasirians and a thousand Hermotybians
> served, in rotation, each year in the King's bodyguard and
> received during their service, in addition to the grant of
> twelve Arurae (about 10 acres) of land, a daily allowance of
> 5 mines (about 5 lb.) of bread, 2 mines (about 2lb.) of beef
> and 4 Arysterene (about 4 cups) of wine."
>
> [Herodotus II.168]

4

INDIA

THE PARADISE OF INDIA
(Eros in Paradise)

The main subject of this book is the flow of paradisial visions from the East to the Mediterranean. But before following this stream we may look at the Indian scene as a point of departure, to see that it is the increasing role of the Female Element in the Beyond, and Eros in Paradise, which can be traced in the Etrusco-Italian funeral art.

Parallel to the picture of a 'Celestial Ocean,' there is a vision of Paradise, in which a gigantic Mount Mehru, center of the universe, penetrates the Celestial Waters and thereby connects the aquatic scenery with a mountainous landscape. This paradise is called Uttarakurus – (meaning: North-Mountain) – and is thought to exist in the dramatic setting of the Himalayas where heaven and earth seem to fuse in brewing mist and clouds, as the realm of the gods, the Apsarases, and the souls of the blessed . . . "any mortal who tries to reach it will perish in the attempt" . . . and of which we have the following description:

> "THE BLESSED IN UTTARAKURUS HAVE A LIFE OF
> SENSUAL PLEASURES AND DRINK MILK FROM TREES.
> THEY ARE BORN AS TWINS OF OPPOSITE SEX, WHO
> FORM A COUPLE, JUST AS WAS THE CASE WITH
> PRIMITIVE MEN IN THE KRTAYUGA. ORIGINALLY ALL
> WOMEN HAD SEXUAL INTERCOURSE WITH
> WHOMSOEVER THEY PLEASED AND THIS CONDITION
> STILL PREVAILS IN UTTARAKURUS. ALL THE
> INHABITANTS THERE ARE GIVEN TO LOVE, YIELD TO
> ALL DESIRES AND HAVE ALL THEIR DESIRES
> FULFILLED, NONE WHOSE DESIRES ARE NOT FULFILLED."
> [Mahabharata VI.7, Adiparvan CXXII]

(Krtayuga is the prehistoric mythic Golden Age)

PARADISE

We have similar descriptions in the Ramayana IV. 43 and the very early Aitareya Brahmana VIII.14 and in the "Secret Teachings" of the Upanishadas as well as some references to such premordial and paradisial bliss in the Rig-Veda, while the very substance of that vision of paradise seems to reach back to the third millenium B.C. based on archaeological finds, carbondated as belonging to that epoch, which objects are then mentioned in those venerable texts.

GANDHARVAS

THE GANDHARVAS

The Gandharvas are glorified symbols of the male, the lure of masculinity. They are in their later form called 'The Musicians on the Court of Indra' – (as Gandharva actually means Music) – but music was understood as a means of bewitchment like the magical 'carmina' or the irresistible song of the Sirenes in Mediterranean lands.

The Gandharvas cast their masculine spell over the females by means of Music, or by Wealth or by pure Sensuality in the image of bounding man-horses.

Accordingly we find them sometimes depicted as musicians and sometimes as jewelled princes of fabulous wealth, but in their archaic form they are shown as sensual Centaurs in the premordial Ocean, their impressive manliness languidly embraced by the Apsarases, the Nymphs of the paradisial waters, who are their paramours.

1

APSARASES

THE APSARAS

One of the most important figures in the following discussion will be the Apsaras, also called Apsarases. The word Apsara means 'Those of the Waters' with reference to the Celestial Waters, the premordial Ocean, far above the sky, out of which all creation arises, but being at the same time also the paradise to which the blessed will return after their earthly departure.

Although the Apsaras were in their earliest version thought to be Nymphs of the Waters, they were later depicted as floating in the Clouds and therefore called "Cloud Maidens" but are in their last version involved in Earthly adventures, like bathing in pools and seducing glittering Kings and the dreamy Saints of the woods, and are even depicted in charming simple mortals in a spooky way, as reflected in many sagas – while being royal princesses as the daughters of Indra, which makes their amorous exploits still more glamorous, dazzling, and extravagant.

In whatever element they appear, they are the impersonations of sensual joy without attachments and without regrets. They are of heavenly beauty and eternal youth. They are forever passionate and their embrace is "ten-thousand times sweeter than any lust experienced on earth." They fulfill "a million times" all the desires of the blessed in paradise. Their voluptuous appeal is so irresistible that they are dispatched by Indra to earth to seduce saints who by their severe penance endanger his sovereignty. This interference by the Apsarases seems so unquestionably successful, that the holy scriptures affirm: "The Children born of those unions are of uncommon beauty and enlightenment."

The Apsarases are mostly shown in a stillness of felicity with a melting smile of readiness. Their costumes consist mainly of a very high hairdo resembling a cupola or crown, which is over and over beset with pearls and precious stones, ornaments, and even picture-like inserts, similar to the ex voti of holy shrines. It seems that all endearments people could think of, were heaped on those elaborate head-pieces. Another remarkable part of their makeup are tremendous round earrings which sometimes seem to defy gravity and at other times swing with the rhythm of their movement.

2

3

Otherwise the Apsaras are nude or sky-clad and only strewn with jewelry. Rows of pearls accentuate the curves of their bodies and some bands suggest that they were just loosened and falling away to indicate a consent to please, to be available. Sometimes the Apsarases wear artful drapes around their sex to frame it like curtains of a stage which are just raised, to theatralize its importance. In other cases they wear transparent tight clinging slacks with spiral stripes to accentuate the form and motion of the thighs.

The most remarkable feature of the Apsarases is their acrobatic agility and their quasi weightless skill with which they cling to their lovers, reminiscent of trapeze artists in flight, and it is this characteristic which makes them easiest to recognize in India's iconography. The reason for it seems to be a strange reversal: Because the earthly impersonatrices of the celestial Apsaras were mostly trained by the acrobats, the characteristic skills of those imitatrices were then back-projected into the Apsarases of the Above, who were therefore presented in acrobatic poses in the statuary of the temples.

TEMPLE GIRLS

THE EARTHLY REPLICA

As to the background of the girls who aim to be the earthly doubles of the celestial Apsaras:

The word Maithuna is used in the oldest holy scripture of the Veda for 'ritual coitus.' The temples were the place of those rituals. (The word Maithuna was in later and Buddhistic times after 500 B.C. used for the ritual union of the sexes in the then so-called "lower heavens" which were, in an effort at greater spirituality, said to be surmounted by a still higher heaven of pristine abstractions.) The venerable Vajasaneysamhita recognizes religious prostitution as a sanctified profession. Those girls had the title of Devadasi or Devaratial, meaning "Slaves of God." In western India they were called Bhavin, in sanscrit "handsome or wanton." In Marwar the temple-girls were called Bhagtan, meaning "She of a holy Man" because she was thought to be the sanctified earthly replica of a heavenly Apsara, bestowing the Smarasa or "State of Bliss" upon a man, who was elevated temporarily to holiness by that ritual.

Even Buddha is reported by one of his disciples to have said: "There is no Nirvana (state of wishless bliss) outside Samarasa."

On less ritualistic and more ceremonial occasions the girls were called Patra, which is Sanskrit for "Actor" because they impersonated on templestages figures of India's heaven in Maithunas with some divinities and appeared thereby elevated to transmit their blessings and the transcendental forces, so obviously received from the inflow into them by the heavenly emissaries, to earthly beings. It also was thought that the embrace with those semidivine servants of the Gods would wash away all sins.

"May the ascending radiance of heavenly splendor by the maker of days, be praised with the sweetness of words, mixed with the prose and the poems of the celestial singers, exalted by lutes, cimbals, the drums and the flutes, mow down and erase your sins of the day."

[Mayura, strophe 36, of his 100 strophes to Suryasataka, the Sungod]

As the creative force of the universe was symbolized by Siva, who in turn was symbolized by the mystic phallus as the Well: 'to bring into existence' – it seems natural to see that very symbol in the act of giving its creative energy to so many manifestations of nature which were represented by females, that is: 'receiving' symbol-figures – like the obviously 'heavenly' rain-storm coming from above, creating the earthly wells and waters, who were then represented as Water-Nymphs, the Naginis, shown to receive with piously folded hands the heavenly infusion, on their faces the smile of religious felicity – the same as other manifestations of the general creation of the plant or animal world, which were represented by female symbol-figures too, and are shown to conceive the divine influx in a state of grateful devotion. When dealing with such divine blessings as the fertile herds, the Sivatic spirit of procreation was often shown in the form of bounding male animals, with the earthly goddesses or patronesses of the species represented by the Patras in tender submission, and their Maithunas and Samarasas performed with the highly trained elegance of ballerinas.

देवदासी

DEVADASI

THE RECRUITMENT OF THE DEVADASI

The monks went through the land recruiting young, good looking and intelligent girls. Sometimes they were given to them by parents who had too many children to feed, as girls were generally considered of little or no value. The donation of a daughter to the temple was considered a good deed before the gods, a pious gesture, similar to the nobility in Europe who donated one of their children to the church, to become a priest or a nun. Or even with less finality, the parents of today are proud to have their child sing in the choir of the church – maybe less for religious convictions than because of their pride that their child had been "chosen." This same pride filled the Indian parents, and also the joy of knowing that their little daughter would from now on be well fed, well clothed and washed and would live forever under the protection of the temple and the secular lords to the pleasing of the divinities. The donation of children to the temples often was also the fulfillment of a sacred pledge to the gods, in the sense of an 'ex voto.'

> "He who piously dedicates to the sanctuary of the Sungod
> a bevy of courtesans, is permitted to enter the highest of
> heavens, where the most radiant one dwells."
>
> [Bhavisyapurana I.97]

The act of giving away a child is stunning to us and we may therefore think of comparisons in our culture. A certain parallel could be found in a girl joining the theatrical world, where the parents may feel in a similar way concerning the attraction of the aura of glamor surrounding her and the possibility of a rich marriage, as the bodily charms of their daughter will be displayed in the best light to so many of the upper-classes – when she will be speaking brilliant words which were composed by the most gifted writers – so as to endow her personality also with spiritual magnetism.

Concerning that last comparison, we must remember that the temple-girls too were often married by influential gentlemen, even princes, and that they too appeared in highly theatricalized settings representing semidivinities – (Apsarases) – with their prestige borrowed, for the moment. They too spoke words composed for them by great poets, seemingly now flowing from their perfumed lips. When the girls were not able to memorize them, they were spoken behind the scenes by a female "presenter" also called "lector" who was sometimes a male soprano with a far-off haunting voice as if coming from unearthly spheres, while the girl moved her mouth and supplied the appropriate gestures. The same technique was used in Egypt and Babylon and Japan in conjunction with liturgical ceremonies, where the texts were not spoken by the heavenly embodiments appearing on the stage, but by another person, invisible to the public, while the earthly replica of the epiphany went through the pantomime.

With all the traditional decorum of the sanctuaries and the supreme authority of the clergy we can understand that it was not difficult to recruit simple country-girls for the magnificent temples. Sometimes, too, an important man would buy a girl from peasants and give her to the temple, when he wanted to oblige the clergy to influence the people in a direction desired by him. The clergy could form the public opinion because they were the sole agency of information for the people. The clergy wanted the support of the princes or the wealthy, while the power-structure needed the clergy to guide the people. In this sense the monks were eager talent-scouts for recruiting pretty girls, as dancers for the temples or as gift-objects from the wealthy to the clergy. The more pretty girls there were in the temples, the more attraction there was for the great donors to visit the temple, as well as for the less exalted patrons to come there for their special kind of worship, which was to the profit of that sanctuary.

THE DESTINY OF THE DEVADASI

The monks trained the country-girls in the skills of dancing and the most elaborate arts of love. This was not considered to be degrading for the girls, as it was generally assumed that the mission of any female was to please the man, and their skill in doing so, as their legitimate means to advance in life. Therefore many sages wrote ponderous, and at times surprisingly cunning guides and now famous volumes of instructions on the techniques to enchant a man. Those manuals were written in a very scientific attitude, enumerating and cataloguing all things to be considered and to be done.

The aim of those schools conducted by the monks were spelled out in texts of which several still exist. According to them the purpose of the training was "to make the girls capable of being useful in a foreign land," which, however, did not include the learning of a foreign language, relying, as it seems, more on the silent language and gestures of love. The girls were then exported to the West, which was a serious and profitable business for the temples. Some of them were considered as veritable coins in trade between provinces, and according to Herodotus, certain numbers of them were stipulated as tax-contribution by several satrapies to central governments — together with a specified number of castrated boys, to be used in the temples.

Another group of customers for the trained girls were 'masters of the harem,' who were recruiting the finest pupils from the temple-schools for important personalities or princely courts. As they paid very high prices for girls with outstanding beauty and charms and elaborate skills, considerable attention was given to this very profitable branch of the trade. The 'masters of the harems' had the position comparable to theatrical agents with international connections and operations. A girl in the harem or on the court of a mighty man could become a politically very influential factor; they were at times in charge of the department of douannes or tax collectors, which made them very powerful and sometimes immensely wealthy. We know of courtesans or favorites who donated whole temples, or truly magnificent shrines with golden ornaments to existent sanctuaries. The names of some of those exalted donors are still inscribed on several temples, in devout praise by the monks for the generosity of their now famous alumna. Even her likeness as epitome of female charms and beauty, in an Apsara-like apotheosis, graced some of her temples in an honored niche and mothers prayed to her imploring the images of the sanctified Hetairae to become patroness and guide to their own children and bless them with similar graces and fabulous wealth.

Some of those great courtesans had in their palaces an army of guards and their own male harems and theatrical groups of entertainers and peculiar amusements in the way of love, comprising, as it seems, those combined employees, and being in this respect, too, the equal of the male lords and potentates. Judging from diverse literary sources, they seem to even have outdone their male counterparts concerning the capacity and inventiveness of extraordinary lovegames intermixed with beheadings.

Not all the temple-girls fared so well in foreign lands. Some of them, when they got older, were used as domestic help in Greece.

Others slipped into the entertainment world and some into temple-prostitution, but some married solid citizens, proved by several laws pertaining to their legal status. Lex Julia, for instance, states that such a girl when married by her owner, can not sue for divorce, when abandoned, etc. The Byzantine Empress Theodora, wife of Emperor Justinian, was an ex-dance-girl and sent 500 prostitutes from Constantinople into a rest-home on the other shore of the Bosphorus, but many committed suicide because of the totally unaccustomed lack of love. The destiny of the Temple girls appears less extraordinary when we learn that it was the normal procedure in the sphere between the Mediterranean and India that a girl assembled her dowery by giving herself to strangers before her marriage. To copulate with unknown men was considered one of the accepted chores of girls and did not involve love, nor lust on her part. As relatively late as 63 B.C. to 19 A.D. Strabo, whose uncle was high-priest of Comana, reports [XII, 3.36] "No custom is more widely spread than the providing for a guest a female companion, who is usually a wife or daughter of the host." Strabo [XI, 14.6] narrates concerning the temple of Anaitis in Acilisena that the girls had strangers for lovers to collect her dowery before they married in their hometown. The same is said of the girls of Ouled-Nail in North Africa. The Gipsies, who originally came from India, still use the same method of collecting their dowery, even when migrating to the lower reaches of the Danube. To collect small coins in this manner seems to those girls most acceptable, while doing even light work for a ten times higher price would be to them repugnant because subjecting them to servitude.

THE PROCEDURES

The temples with the most stunning dancers developed, at times, into truly artistic show places, where ballets and music were performed. The aristocracy, the rich, and the art-loving came to see it, similar to our operatic performers or benefit-shows. The money collected this way went to the temples.

The majority of shows, however, relied on the prolonged unveiling of the more exotic girls during their involvements with the demons and specters of Night and Solitude.

There were finally also the stagings of voluptuous girls to mime or actually perform mythological happenings between divinities in more improbable situations, re-enacted to show "the divine freedom from human restraint" in the paradisial spheres at the brewing dawn of creation.

There is, however, a new element in the Indian playacting: The magic of the priests, which can transform by their incantations practically everything into spiritual beings. Underlying here is the assumption of reincarnations. Religious cults gradually changed into magic, by which the priests could force and command the demons. The clergy drew great material advantages from that enormous power – which they allegedly possessed (even over Kings and Princes) – and threatened to turn the terrifying magic and demons against all who did not donate enough to the temple. The sanctuaries became remarkably money-conscious and amassed great wealth and still developed more stratagems to increase their income and influence over the people and their lords. By "priestly magic" the temple transformed a paying customer into a legendary figure, preferably a semi-divine prince, on a temporary basis. As such, he was made to meet in the dark sacrality of the temple, which was assumed to be extraterritorial, and an analogue of heaven, a temple-girl, who was also transformed, by extraordinary magic, into the replica of a mythological semi-divine, for that occasion. Out of the clouds of incense the girl then emerged as a celestial apparition to bestow upon her heavenly partner the blessings of youth and beauty. In addition to their soft agility those consecrated impersonatrices of paradisial bliss were dusted with gold and fragrant in their Garlands of Sanctification and dripping with the oils of libations, poured over them during their magic transformation, so that their touch may become unreal and elusive, while the sanctuary, the space of the miraculation, was obscured and drowned in some musical sounds of the unearthly kind.

The practice of females giving themselves to strangers for religious purposes seems so foreign to our present civilization that this phenomenon deserves some consideration in trying to understand its mentality.

Before returning to the Indian ceremonial which was shrouded in the mysticism of the temple, it is important to note that the same general idea existed also in other lands, often performed openly with great and glittering pomp . . . all that against the spiritual background of ceremoniously sacrificing animals to please the invisible mights . . . which is equally out of tune with our contemporary sentiments.

In a comparison with an innocent present-day custom and its motivation, we may think of girls offering their car-wash to passing customers to donate the proceeds of their services to their church, without losing their dignity as individuals. This comparison may, of course, be only partly valid, and as long as we assume that the services of the temple-girls were nothing hidden, but a publicly accepted practice, at that time and place.

In this respect, a passage of Herodotus [I.199] is of interest:

"Every woman who is a native of the country (Assyria) must once in her life go and sit in the temple of Aphrodite and there give herself to a strange man. Many of the rich women, who are too proud to mix with the rest, drive to the temple in covered carriages with a whole host of servants following behind, and there wait; most, however, sit in the precinct of the temple with a band of plaited string round their heads – and a great crowd they are, with some sitting there, others arriving, others going away – and through them all gangways are marked off running in every direction for the men to pass along and make their choice. Once a woman has taken her seat she is not allowed to go home until a man has thrown a silver coin into her lap and taken her outside to lie with her. As he throws the coin, the man has to say, "In the name of the goddess Mylitta" – that being the Assyrian name for Aphrodite.

The value of the coin is of no consequence; once thrown it becomes sacred, and the law forbids that it should ever be refused. The woman has no privilege of choice – she must go with the first man who throws her the money. When she has lain with him, her duty to the goddess is discharged and she may go home, after which it will be impossible to seduce her by any offer, however large. Tall, handsome women soon manage to get home again, but the ugly ones stay a long time before they can fulfil the condition which the law demands, some of them, indeed, as much as three or four years. There is a custom similar to this in parts of Cyprus."

THE PRESENTERS

The Presenters were sometimes women and sometimes castrati. They were named according to their type and key of voice, and talked grammatically in the first person form. The happening was named "the connubium" or "the rite of incubation." The transformation from the simple mortal to the celestial semidivine was called in the script "the act of presumption" or "assumption." The presenters were sometimes called "Eulogist, or Lector," in the masculine term, so that we suppose a male voice, and were sometimes called "Redactrice" in the feminine gender, hinting at a female voice and were possibly suggesting that the text was even composed by a woman for added charm. The 'castrati' are called as such and judging by the style of their far-out, abstract and dreamy texts, we would match it to a virginal breaking voice of a child (supposedly coming from the painted lips of the nearby female) intermixed, as indicated by the 'stage-directions,' with the tender sound of cymbals. The castrati played an important part in later times, which are, by inference, applicable to the temple-presenters of that kind.

Lovely boys, – "the consecrated ones" – could be had in the temples too, representing some of the many androgynous divinities of India. Even Buddhist monks kept boys for the use of worshippers. Brahmins had love-boys in their temples and even the Tibetan Lamas believed in sanctified and glorified boy-love, which they practiced communally, as a purer way of life, freed of female encumberment.

Stranger still were the Ghulamiyeh, or 'She-boys' which were girls dressed as boys and loved as such. The reason for it was that many boys were so conditioned, since boyhood, to homosexuality, that they later used their wives in this manner, and because they were used to this type of sex with their wives, they also expected the same in the temples, and therefore the temples had to be stocked with Ghulamiyes, because in heaven, which they represented, boys were also promised "crowned by flowers, heavenly perfumed and rosy of cheeks."

THE TEMPLE SCULPTURES

HALF WAY TO HEAVEN

The presence and meaning of the tremendous mass of erotic statuary on the Indian temples still mystifies the experts.

It was suggested that the reason for this extraordinary display may be to protect the sanctuary from lightning and others thought that a form of "sex-education" might be intended, but the very same proponents of those ideas admitted at once that those motivations failed to be convincing.

In the following a new approach to explain this phenomenon is herewith submitted:

The temple was assumed to be the 'Half-way-Station' between heaven and earth, so that the way from earth to heaven led through the temple to the paradise. It was therefore understood that the temple facilitated the transportation towards heaven, and, in fact sold you the 'Ticket' into paradise, in the sense of a travel-agency, on a commercial basis, that is: in return for the donations given to the temple. Consequently, the Temple made propaganda of that location, to which it was in the business of selling the admission. In this sense the temple was giving information about the locality which is the destination of the impending voyage in lavishly picturing and praising that district.

The location to which the temple promised transportation, was the paradise of delights. Therefore the temples displayed on their outside, carved in stone, scenes of paradise, which were scenes of multiple lovemakings, as those lovemakings were to take place in paradise. The puzzling lovescenes decorating the outside of temples are therefore functionally the same as the 'shop-windows' of a Travel-Agency which displays scenes from the unknown land or destination, the sphere where, as the holy scripture says: "ALL DESIRES ARE FULFILLED, NONE WHOSE DESIRES ARE NOT FULFILLED."

The clergy, therefore, ordered artists to display on the sanctuary the most arresting and eyecatching display of the commodity obtainable through their agency, which were the paradisial limitless experiences of love. This display was arranged – if this down-to-earth comparison be permitted – like the oranges on an Italian fruit-stand, piled high, in a monumental arrangement for tectonic reasons in conical structures row after row, to achieve an overpowering effect. The directives to the artists were to put all their powers of invention to work to think up variations of 'Desires' and methods to 'Fulfill' them. When running out of inspirations, they fell into repetitions, which appear now as special "Rhythms" and "Heavenly Bands" suggesting the never-ending "Magnificat" of eternal bliss.

To make the vision of paradise still more attractive was to show the beautiful celestial brides in seductive poses or actually in pursuit of the male souls, which feature is then often repeated in Etruscan funeral art, although in the Mediterranean the male was shown as the aggressive partner in amorous scenes.

The great Indian sages of old wrote many ponderous volumes about the art of loving, elevating it to the importance of a general science, a technology of physics, mixed with psychology, to induce the most effective soul-experience.

As literary works were missing concerning the technology of inanimated matter – (like gravity, hydrodynamics, etc.) – it seems that this type of

5

body-technology took the place of what we today call the sciences of physics, mechanics etc. in general.

The temple-sculptures may therefore have kindled in the population a greater interest in the Paradise and thereby in the role the temple promised to play as mediator, because what appeared to some more primitive people as a simple body-function assumed now before their eyes the proportions of a tremendous field of possibilities, worthy of knowing, or at least worthy of learning about it from those who so obviously displayed their know-how in that matter.

In this way the temples not only called attention to the existence of the paradise as such, but also demonstrated visually that the pleasures therein might be greater and more varied than the multitude was able to imagine, and attracted thereby much of the population and some important donors to their establishment, who otherwise might have bypassed the whole idea of paradise as one of the many pretty fairytales without substance and reality, so that it was precisely the 'Reality' of the paradise which was convincingly established by the manifest size and splendor of its display. We therefore see that the motivation of the temple was less the 'sex-education' of the individual, as it was the 'visual persuasion' of the people to believe in the 'reality' of paradise, and the most manifest identification of the temple with that desirable sphere.

The bridge from the sensual to the religious was established by declaring the personages shown in those embraces, or smilingly presiding over them, to be divinities or heavenly apparitions who looked with great favor on amorous matters and who, in fact, had 'created' Love, so that any pursuit of it was received by them as a homage to their exalted persons and it was finally accepted, as a matter of faith, that all lovemaking was of divine origin and that any practice of it on earth was to follow its celestial paradigma.

In Bengal we have a great number of temple figures which are made with less virtuosity and artistic bravado, but instead express this idea with great simplicity and clarity. They show the divinities of Love in sublime beauty and grace with a lyric tenderness of soul, – and below them, smaller in size, some squatty earthly human beings, less beautiful, and rather coarse and even vulgar, now clumsily executing their divine precepts.

रसभोग और तृप्ती
ALL DESIRES FULFILLED

18

THE FORE-TASTE OF HEAVENLY BLISS

Like merchants handing out samples of their wares, so did the monks offer in the temples, 'samples' of the heavenly bliss which awaited the blessed in paradise – to which, as we have seen, the monks could arrange transportation – and which was the commodity they had to offer. Therefore the samples of heavenly bliss which were staged in the temples were also understood as a fore-taste of the permanent condition which awaited the mortals in the next world.

However, it was emphatically and repeatedly stated that the lusts provided by the girls in the temple, fall greatly short of the bliss experienced in the celestial Above. It is said with a certain precision that the voluptuousness of the Apsarases is ten-thousand times greater than provided by their earthly replicas, the consecrated girls of the sanctuaries. The situation was such, that one could well get a sample or 'fore-taste' of heavenly bliss through the courtesy of the temples, but it was not possible to experience paradisical delights in toto on earth and therefore one still had to make an effort to reach the celestial realms after death with the much needed help of the temples through one's very own earthly largesse. The real prizes of heaven were the Apsarases, images of beauty and youth-eternal, the daughters of Indra, King of the gods. However, their earthly replicas, the temple-girls, had a patroness-saint of their own, called Laksmi, who stood for the 'Felicity of Love.' The Indian temple-girls were her devotees and were believed to follow her command, and were serving, as it seems, as a model for the Hierodules (Holy Slaves) in the Aphrodite temple at Corinth, where those girls were considered to be 'priestesses' of the divinity of love, and as some reports say, "had almond-shaped eyes, golden skin and chatted with each other in a language nobody could understand and were skilled like monkeys." The possibility of that transfer from Indo-Asiatic temple-girls to the Hierodules, and thereby from Lakshmi to Aphrodite exists, because Lakshmi already appears in the Rig Veda, around 1000 B.C., while the Aphrodite cult at Corinth started around 600 B.C. when the big wave of Oriental-Asiatic traders arrived at that port, who wanted to find at the end of their arduous and perilous voyage, a place for the sensual worship to which they were accustomed. A hint at the Eastern influence on the figure of Aphrodite may be that her image or person was split, at that time, in different manifestations, which partly contradicted themselves or were the opposite of each other, as usual with the split and opposed 'Avatars' of Indian high-divinities. This particular branch of the Aphrodite figure was called "Aphrodite Hetaira" and was shown to "ride on the back of the lascivious ram." To ride on an animal was usual in India where the idea of the 'Vehicle' on which to ride denoted a sort of 'basis of operation' of a given divinity – (here the male lasciviousness) – while to ride on animals was not for the gods in Greco-Roman lands and appeared now as a novelty coming from Asia – (similar to the Bacchic Dionysos figure returning from Asia on top of a donkey with sensual characteristics, to hint in a simplified way at the Eastern teachings which he represents and brings along).

Another hint at the possible transfer of features of Lakshmi to Aphrodite might be the vision that both of them arose from the sea, whereby the story of Lakshmi is not only older, but also technically sounder, which therefore looks like the later projection of the Lakshmi story onto the quite awkward saga of the birth of Aphrodite. There were, of course, the fabulous Love-Goddesses in North-Africa, like Ishtar, etc. . . . but none of them was said to be born of the sea or riding "lasciviae dorso caprae" so that those two features point not to southern influences but to a direct Indo-Asiatic transfer to Corinth.

Lakshmi was also said to be the 'Genetrix' of all the living beings and we have to this effect a slightly spurious hymn, said to have been the guiding chant or creed of the Hierodules in India and then in Corinth:

"Lakshmi I am,
and have created to the Lust
the countless Selves of this earth
that are the living beings, . .
and all of them are Me.
Embrace therefore each-other
as you are all the children of My soul.
Love unrestrained for love is Me,
caress each-other as I am Felicity.
Worship me thus,
as this is all the tribute I want:
Take openarmedly of all delights
as I created your desires . . .
From joy springs all creation
by joy it is sustained,
towards joy it ever moves
to Beauty, Lust and Bliss."

This poem seems to present the speaker as being Lakshmi herself and it is said that those lines were spoken by the girl to introduce her person to the Asiatic stranger in the temple at Corinth, to make him feel at home, but also hinting at the magic transformation of the Ganika (hetaira-actress) into a heavenly apparition for the time of their maithuna.

As usual with lofty libido-centric Idols, so shifted the image of Lakshmi too, in later times towards a fertility-symbol, and as soon as the materialistic chain-reaction was discovered, leading from sensuality to fertility to prosperity, Lakshmi was fused with Sri, the protectress of the rice crop and became a divinity of Wealth and Fortune.

While Lakshmi was shown in older times with the 'Conch' in hand as the symbol for the female sex, the new 'Sri-Lakshmi' appeared now holding an ear of rice and later even the Horn-of-Plenty. To make the transition from heaven to earth more complete, she was said to be born of a furrow and was called "Daughter of the Earth." The Furrow had before the connotation with the female sex, but was then re-interpreted as the furrow of the field . . . and she became "the farmer's help." In remembrance of her more grandiose times, the peasants still put Betel Nuts, symbols of the sweet intimacy of physical love, on her little altars in the fields . . . which later changed to donations of matches, safety-pins and tiny coins, found in front of her images.

For divinities too; gaining down-to-earth respectability meant the loss of the miraculous and otherworldly status.

As to the question why Love-Divinites were created, to begin with:

The fact that for the average Indian of that time the escape from the cycles of re-birth to Nirvana was the ultimate wish, shows that he looked at life on earth as a thorny path through suffering, oppression, menaces, poverty, hunger and plagues.

Therefore, sex must have been for him a most surprisingly a-typical experience on earth. That the simple insertion into a "worthless" female should evoke highly euphoric sensations was an incomprehensible mystery in itself, but most of all: the sensations were in such a complete contrast to the miserable pattern of life on earth, that they had to be, by simple logic, a phenomenon and epiphany of non-earthly and therefore divine provenience.

REJUVENATION

We may ask why nature takes the trouble to change the human appearance in old age.

There are, of course, sound medical and strictly biological reasons for all those changes, but if one wants to believe in a metaphysical design of creation and a transcendental wisdom of Nature, one could speculate as follows:

As women are no longer fruit-bearing after a certain age, it may be in the 'Grand Design' of nature to reduce their attraction to the other sex by making them unsightly and thereby 'crossed out' from the list of individuals recommended for procreation. To this end, nature 'retouched' the non-desirables so as to signal to a male, from far away and on first sight, a fruitless and therefore useless receptacle of his genetic material.

Although that signalling to the outside of a lesser desirability applies also to a man, it is said that he is nevertheless able to father a child in advanced age, and nature, as it seems, endowed him therefore even then, with a certain desire to do so, and maybe even with an urgency, as he feels the end of his days approaching, the breaking of the biological chain which came from a nebulous past and should lead through him, the only operative link of that chain, into an equally mysterious infinity. There is also the tearful nostalgia back to the image of his own youth, which can be found now only as a faint echo in the youth of his partner, radiated back at him . . . and as many believed, infusable into his own body by the simple fact of proximity.

The same belief cropped up when ailing kings were on physician's orders to sleep while flanked by two very young and healthy girls, so that their emanation of youth and health should infuse the body of the exalted person. The same as an aura or magic fluidum of death was assumed, so was it thought that a seeping transference or osmosis takes place of invisible rays of youth. The basis of the belief in the contamination through death may have been observations concerning communicable diseases, while the basis of the idea of transferable youth might have been the observation that we act differently with very young people and assume their mode of expression, even their language, and while we may feel a careful distance to older people, we seem to open our souls without any care to the charm of youth and absorb with elation its emanation. The Indian texts pay hardly any attention to infants, but claim that the 'budding-power' of a sixteen year old girl far transcends the confines of her person and is radiating into all nature around her with a life-infusing charge.

With their great interest in physical love, it could not escape the attention of men that in aging their manliness may flag and fail. How much they were preoccupied by this problem shows in the enormous amount of thought and literature they devoted to aphrodisiacs . . . which are, as seen in the light of modern science, physically ineffective. However, they may have had a psychological and thereby psychosomatic effect on those who believed in them. Men probably found by experience a new love-partner to be the most effective stimulant. There was, therefore, a special clientele of aging gentlemen seeking the magic encounters in the temples to restore or rejuvenate their capacity for enjoyment, just by the fact that their mysterious partner was a very young creature, a spring incarnate. Some very old texts declare that females too can expect nymphic pleasures at random in paradise, as it was assumed to have been in the prehistoric herd, or the mythic world of the 'Golden Age' where to make love to whomsoever, was the blissful mode of existence. While the Apsarases are pictured as seductresses, the souls of the earthly females re-appearing in the next world are shown as tender adolescents of chaste manners, who are received by equally young but MALE Genii of Love - (maybe as an allusion to the former possibilities they could enjoy in paradise).

The question of rejuvenation of men in paradise is charged with much stronger emotions and a sense of urgency. Men in the Beyond are sometimes shown with magic fetishes infusing them with the vigor of Fauni by wearing their masks as shown on certain Etruscan monuments which are already tinged with Greco-Roman mythology. But the ever-presence of the thoughts and preoccupations with priapic felicity in the next world we can see in the everyday formula of 'thanks' used in India, for instance as pronounced by a street-beggar in response to an alm – (equivalent to our "God bless you"):

60

"May your manliness never flag in paradise"

as well as in the negative the curse, in case no donation was forthcoming:

"May thy pitzle get snarled in paradise!"

Gustave Flaubert, in his travel notes appears quite perplexed by a little boy who wishes him, in thanks for an alm, a long sex and lasting connubium in paradise.

The explorer, Sir Richard Burton, reports a long list of similar formulations concerning the central location of the paradisial thought within the every-day life in the districts between India and the Mediterranean . . . possibly aided by the five-times-a-day prayers which are greatly concerned with the ascent to paradise.

Burton also remarks that the tendency of men to day-dream of amoral erotic scenes, especially in lonely deserts and tropical forests, was cleverly diverted by religion into moral channels – by telling the Believers that if they properly behave here on earth, all those day-dreams will become reality in the Above.

SEMI-DIVINE MANNEQUINS

Not all the people could afford to make love to a semidivine. But they somehow vaguely heard that it is pleasing to the temple – and thereby pleasing to the gods – if one makes love in the temple to a female divinity or her stand-in or effigy. The simple people probably could not figure out exactly what it is that pleases the gods, and settled for the general idea, that if you 'give' yourself to the gods – (or their official effigy) – you 'communicate' with their aura. Maybe in a slight similarity to shaking the hand of a governor or touching the toe of a statuary. There were then many believers who wanted to give their persons to a divinity in the temple but could afford only a reduced price. The clergy understood those conditions and erected statues in the temple that could be embraced. They were sometimes quite beautiful, sometimes schematic like a totem – and sometimes highly realistic as far as the female anatomy is concerned. After the first astonishment, one could imagine on second thought that it could be a very lovely feeling for the true believer to melt this way, with pure heart into a divinity. Who that divinity was did not matter as long as she was obviously there to receive the souls as a representative of the divine graces. Those statues were sometimes of wood and impressively painted, but mostly of stone. The coolness of touch probably conveyed beautifully 'the majesty of the divine,' looking down on the faithful with pearls and smiles. But some of the public wished for more response and animation. For those, statues were made that were hollow inside, so that a little girl-servant could be hidden in them, who had to moan and pour sandle-oil on the part of the man, for a more naturalistic illusion. The monks were fond of ingenious contraptions, because the priestship was recruited from the most ingelligent specimens of the population and loved deus-ex-machina effects. They invented and operated the mechanism which, suggesting a holy emission from the divine, flooded the temple, to the delight of the pious believers, a signal to embrace each other to become one in spirit with the divinity and leave the temple in an alleviated state of mind and spiritual purification and nirvana-like wishlessness. The monks were masterful illusion-makers of extraordinary gifts, and as miracles were at all times the fabric of which piety was made, they elevated the minds of the people to the transcendental for which their emotions were thirsting.

It is for us to imagine that sometimes such a poor little girl, concealed within a statue as in a dark broom closet, might have fallen asleep and missed her appointed duty and that the true believer might have kicked the divine statue to wake her up in the way malfunctioning apparatus is kicked into action again.

Those statues were very popular and we have no record of any complaints – except by Buddha, who, in his earlier writings, explicitly forbade the "sexual intercourse with statues of gods and godesses in temples." About the mannequins of goddesses we have spoken. But in addition there were also male idol-statuary for the use of pious women. The phenomenon as such is not new, as such statues of male sex are known to us from the devotees of Kalee, who abandoned their persons to them, in the absence of living male victims, in a religious ritual which they practiced in caves smeared with cow-dung and blood under gruesome incantations. Sometimes they caught a living man, strapped him down and exhausted him, one after the other taking their turns. From such victims who were sometimes British colonial officers, we have several descriptions of those rituals. After they could get no more enjoyment out of the living man, those women gave themselves to some statuary with a lingam of polished stone over which they poured sanctified oil as a libation, with ceremonials and ecstatic incantations. Then, in view of all, woman after woman lifted herself onto that statue and twisted herself into union with its lingam while embracing the statuary closely and muttering adoration-prayers.

Of women in sexual union with religious idols or mannequins, we also have reports by Herodotus (5th Century B.C.). Those statements were then verified by hieroglphyic inscriptions, which were deciphered around the turn of the century and checked against Herodotus. At Mendes, in Egypt, a living ram was kept, representing the divinity Amun, in whose sanctuary women presented themselves in a ritual divested of all clothes and were publically enjoyed by that divine ram. Herodotus watched those rituals – as it seemed accessible to all – with a certain fascination and called it a "prodigy" – (meaning: extraordinary and monstrous). The original Egyptian papyri explain the ram to be the "representation" or the "incarnation" of the divine power of nature, whose blessing is received by the pious with reverence. This ceremony is listed in a rather monotonous way together with some other rituals of Amun, dealing with caresses of the statue of Amun (this time represented in human shape), by priestesses, placed on his lap. Amun also had a harem, whose members were officially called "Amun's concubines" and consisted of special priestesses who had to keep the divinity, or its different effigies in good spirits. It was very prestigious to belong to that group, because at times it was the daughter of the King who was their high-priestess. There is also the typical blend-over from the 'pleasure-principle' to the 'fertility aspect' in later readings of the Ram symbol. The same as we have a "semantic shift" in the language, we also have a 'symbol-shift' in mythology. That shift started out with the ram as representing the force of nature – (the same as a waterfall did represent the

4

25

forces of nature at places, to which women gave their persons in open ceremony). The power of creation was originally represented by the Ram in copulatory position, but was later represented in human form, at the time of the priest-Kings – as a blend of God and Man – and it was then that Amun too assumed human shape. The King assumed the earthly power of the State, and thereby Amun became the protector-symbol of the State.

(The divinity was called 'Amun' in Egypt and 'Amon' in Greek.)

The old and very strong identity between sensuality and religion is strange to us, because in our times sex almost stands in opposition to religion. This wedge between sex and religion was possibly started by Buddha. At least, his teachings worked in the direction of splitting the carnal from the spiritual. The reasons for that initially close union between sex and religion may have been that both were emotional experiences, both equally mysterious and unfathomable to primitive man – and therefore, seemingly related. As we see it today, sex is anchored in the deincephalon, and religion is anchored in the equally inborn drive to the transcendental. However, primitive man did not analyze it this way and assumed both manifestations originating outside of himself, namely – in demons or genii, or divinities. People were seeking actually for unifying symbols, like the Greek construction of 'Eros, God of Love,' melting 'Sex and God' into one unit. Or: Siva, the arch-divinity, in the form of the mysteriously rising phallus, or Amun, Lord of divine blessings in the form of the salacious Ram.

Communal worship and rituals show a preference over solitary prayer, possibly because they create an atmosphere, in which spiritual emotions of the individual are echoed and reinforced by a spiritual environment . . . like one's own voice is amplified in a choir. And more specifically, applied to the women with the male mannequin, the statuary or ram: Simple, primitive people were not geared to abstractions. "The divine spirit entering a being" is a lovely stanza in our parlance, as we have a purely spiritual vision of the phenomenon, – in India the same lovely infusion was acted-out by the woman, in which its actuality occurred and produced physical feelings that were 'real' and therefore, – for her way of factual experiencing – unquestionably 'true.' The fact alone that those copulations were performed openly and publicly must convince us that not only the feeling of purity was attached to them, but even an ethical value of communion with the divine powers of the Above.

In this way, at annual festivals of tremendous splendor, no lesser personality than the Queen of Egypt lowered herself upon the lap of the great divinity Amun to conceive from him, in this way, the new Pharaoh. This ceremony demonstrated to the population the most intimate union and thereby the absolute fusion between the divinity and the human recipient by entering her bodily.

As philosophical arguments and theosophical postulates were at those times only for the very limited class of sophistes, the real believers, the people, had to be convinced by visible facts . . . and as the Hierogamy, the union with the divine, was performed at the highest level, there could be no doubt in the people's mind about the propriety of the idea and procedure, which found its way down to the before mentioned Hierogamy with the Ram, as the embodiment of the divine, and the various mannequins as the stand-ins for the great genii of the Above, until the act of copulation as such, assumed the symbol-value of the union with the exalted being in general, to please the gods.

Those basic ideas, restrained otherwise by the dignity of a majestic and mysterious decorum, developed in India into a wild tropical growth, embracing and covering like a jungle the sanctuaries and population, with an organized supply-line of ever new and ever more acrobatic and less inhibited temple girls, whose arts were then artlessly imitated by the harlots of the streets, and what was to begin with a 'divine blessing' in the arms of a semi-divine during a magic union, degenerated to a casual 'good luck' token with the strumpets in the streets and doorways. The temples, too, taking the increased volume of venery as a triumph of religion, became more and more permissive, until their sacrosanct structure was totally overgrown by solicitous peddling of amorous specialties, defiled statuary, and mass-excesses, supposedly in imitation of the Beati in Excelsis and the premordial paradise.

> "It was the Egyptians who first made it an offense against piety to have intercourse with women in temples. Hardly any nation except the Egyptians and Greeks has any such scruple, but nearly all consider men and women to be, in this respect, no different from animals, which, whether they are beasts or birds, they constantly see coupling in temples and sacred places – and if the divinity concerned of those sanctuaries would have any objection to this, the divinity would not allow it to occur."
>
> [Herodotus II.64]
>
> "All of the Indian tribes I have mentioned copulate in the open like cattle; their skins are all of the same color, much like the Ethiopians . . ."
>
> [Herodotus III.101]

Against a background of what must have appeared to him as a thicket of lust and superstition, Buddha, in his early writings, forbade not only sexual intercourse with male and female images of divinities in temples, but later he even forbade lovemaking in temples by the public in general (as was usual during the great Siva-Parvati festivals).

Buddha declared about 500 B.C. that in heaven, the blessed do not have sexual intercourse in the earthly manner, which is called "the rural practice" – but sexual union in celestial spheres is enjoyed by 'smiling' at each-other, because this is the way the Beati in the Above beget their children there. It is interesting to note that in spite of all his courage for radical reforms, he still could not dare to go so far as to claim there was Not 'enjoyment' – Not 'sexual union' – and Not 'begetting of offspring' in heaven. Therefore, if one wishes to copy heavenly conditions in the temples, he said, from now on the way to do it, is only to smile at each-other. – (therefore the many smiling temple-statues of the Buddhist style – and possibly in imitation of those images the Asiatic habit of smiling after its original meaning was forgotten.)

In this roundabout way Buddha wanted to stop the love-bouts in the temples by still permitting the idea of imitating heavenly occurrences in the temples, but, on the other hand, by claiming that those occurrences in heaven had different procedures, namely: a transmission by magic, instead of the carnal embrace.

Buddha was also teaching that the beautiful females of heaven – (and again he did not dare to claim that they did Not exist) – were in reality, the personifications of one's own 'good deeds' on earth – and hoped thereby to destroy a great deal of the purely sensual zeal for those Nymphs. Because if they were the incarnations of good deeds, their sensual quality would be greatly reduced. As a consequence of that latest modification, not many donations to the temple were forthcoming, because nobody felt inclined to make a big investment here on earth towards finding female moralizers as lovepartners in the other world, who, devoid of the unrestrained carnal passions of the Apsarases, appeared instead bodyless in representing abstract notions, such as 'Good Deeds' – which deeds in themselves lost their attraction by being personified by those non-voluptuous creatures.

And so a new form of religious poverty came over the temples, which nobody liked or enjoyed – not the monks, not the people, and not the dance-girls who had to become heraldic images of good deeds.

All that lasted not too long, because it was too artificially devoid of human nature. Buddha died at a beautiful ripe age, highly honored and respected by all, and on his votive-monuments, the people pictured him in the heavenly paradise as a saint surrounded by damsels, because there just was no other way to signify heaven but by a multitude of Apsarases, as they were, spiritually and physically, the very substance of paradise, which would be, without them, un-imaginable and for the artists, an iconographic void.

The oldest conceptions of the heavens still remained, as expressed in the prayer to Soma, divinity of immortality:

SOMA

"Forsake me not, I need your drink.
Where the light of eternity shines,
Soma guide me there.
Where the glittering creatures appear,
where the beings float to one's eternal lust,
where all wish and desire is granted,
where all the pleasures are fulfilled,
in Joy without compare and felicity without end,
there make immortal me, Soma, merciful God."
[Rigveda IX, 113, 7]

EVERLASTING MANLINESS IN PARADISE

MORALIZERS IN HEAVEN

Concerning the deflating experience of meeting a Moralizer in heaven instead of a sensual Apsara, we have a report by a poet Viraf who, like Dante, claimed to have visited heaven and hell, as recounted in the Pahlavi books:

> "When the soul of Viraf went forth from its body, the first thing which it beheld was the Cinvat Bridge which all souls must cross before they pass to the future world. There he saw before him a damsel of beautiful appearance, full-bosomed, charming to the heart and soul; and when he asked her, 'Who art thou? and what person art thou? than whom, in the world of the living, any damsel more elegant, and of more beautiful body than thine, was never seen by me,' she replied that she was his own daena (religiosity) and his own good deeds – "it is on account of thy piousness and noble actions, that I am as great and good and sweet-scented and radiantly smiling, as I appear to thee."

A few more excerpts from the same narrative:

> "Before entering the Kingdome of the blest, he had to pass through Hamistakan, the resting-place of those whose good deeds and sins exactly counterbalance. There they wait for the renovation of the world.

> Then the steps lead to where the virtuous are, those who contracted next-of-Kin marriages, all of them brilliant and walk about in great pleasure and joy. Then the pilgrims came to a river – which came from the tears of men shed from their eyes in unlawful lamentation for the departed and those relatives who made an exaggerated and irreligious display of grief."

We see again that mysterious drift of ideas circling the globe, the pruning of emotions, the turning away from sensual percepts and the aiming instead at moral values, taking hold in India at the same time as the stoic philosophy overtook Greece, without that the Greek thinkers were known to Buddha, or Buddha to the Greeks.

SUB-CULTS

As there are 'Sub-Cultures' in our times in protest to official patterns – so were 'Sub-Cults' established in India, at that time of chastity, as not all the temples conformed at once to the teachings and requests of Buddha. Some of the temples, in fact, made an effort to compensate the people in their sanctuaries, for what they now missed in the austere Buddhistic shrines and were, so to speak – 'boot-legging' love-scenes and love-bouts in their establishments, as so often happens in times of prohibitions. As the liquor in the 'Speak easies' was less good and the excesses greater, so were the performances in the temples of the 'sub-cults.' They were almost 'protest-sessions' against the 'New Order' – in staging the most libertine and hedonistic notions of the Vedic paradises, according to the sanctified lines of the scriptures, as of the Mahabharata: "Originally all women had sexual intercourse with whomsoever they pleased, just as was the case with primitive men in the first Krtayuga and this state of things still prevails in Uttarakurus."

MAHABHARATA

Out of that mentality, that 'the old times are better times' – came the feeling that the pre-Buddhistic times were the better times. It was like a reunion of the alumni in a college, that people got together to think with nostalgia of happier past days. As the alumni celebrate this get-together with drink, merrymaking, and fraternizing, so did those sub-groups in temples, together with some equally nostalgic clergy and dance-girls. The orgies then and there were really much wilder than in pre-Buddhistic times – also because a spirit of doom prevailed as on a sinking ship – the ship of sweet religion and bleakness was to come thereafter, the bleakness of joyless religion. People took notice that the holy scripture of the Mahabharata – (which even Buddha did not dare to dispute) – clearly stated that according to the will of the divine and paradisacal creation, not only "women had sexual intercourse with whomsoever they pleased, just as was the case with primitive Men" – and that humanity shall return to this state of divine purity. This was then the justification for all, together with "have all wishes fulfilled, none whose wishes are not fulfilled." Men now brought their wives and concubines along, who in conjunction with the temple-belles had all the pleasures imaginable already here on earth and the sampling of 'bliss eternal' got larger and more sumptuous. Finally, as in the time of 'Prohibition,' people took to bouts in their own private houses. There were different types and degrees of those unions, like the Dakshnacharis where the wives and concubines of the partygoers represented temporarily the incarnations of goddesses, divinely ornate and enjoyed alternately by all in those rather intimate rituals. There were also the Vamacharis, whose members were less known to each other and which had a more mystic atmosphere, re-enacting the dawn of creation, involving also animals, staging the more grandiosely divine epoch of the still intermingled state of the earthly creatures, assuming this to be the truly paradisacal condition before things were rather pedantically sorted out, separated and alienated. Animal contacts are shown so frequently in India's religious art because they want to hint at the premordial aura of the creation, where the spark of love set the universe into motion. The sequence of evolution was assumed to start with the gods leading via the diverse demons to the animals and from there to the human race, so that the animals figured as an earlier state of creation and therefore closer still to the divine presence. Those re-actualizations of the twilight of creation were called Chakras, meaning 'circles' or 'cycles' in the sense of re-cycling the children of creation, and shown in religious art often as a gigantic wheel of time in whose spokes the creatures of the earth are interwoven.

Another sub-cult, moving the semi-religious manifestation away from the center of the temple, were the Lenasoghikas or 'Cave-Hetairai.' They were almost a counterpart to Hermits or Holymen in cave dwellings, who gained through deep meditation almost the rank of semi-divine creatures. But their way of life was to comfort with body and soul the distressed devotees of the Mahabharata, the holy scripture, promising voluptuous delights in the heavens whose replica one may taste on earth. The cave-Hetairai tried to mirror the bliss of paradise here on earth, for those who felt abandoned by the temple and its reformed doctrines. This done, for a medium-sized douceur, to the benefit of the distressed souls of others, the Lenasoghikas also worked on their own improvement in an attempt to become as close as possible to a replica of the divine Apsarases, the real prize of heaven. To that end they used the diverse customers as mannequins for their own training. In their attempts to emulate the eternally passionate Apsarases, they also prayed together with their male stand-ins for the souls to be rewarded in paradise. The Cave-Hetairai could also sing and play an instrument, so as to create a refined atmosphere in the cool shade of their caves, as a mixture of nature, love, religion and art, an experience which enchanted sophisticated and wealthy clients. Those semi-religious females were also actresses who re-enacted in the primeval setting of the caves the evolution of humanity, the slumbering earth slowly awakened by the spark of love, as well as the life-development of the individual female soul, from innocence to the first sweet stirrings of desires, through all voluptuous delights and excesses, to a final apotheosis in the heavenly spheres. We have many of those descriptions by enchanted poets who were great admirers of the Lenasoghikas and their tender charms. After the death of Buddha those sub-cults became more popular and degenerate, because they did not have the counterweight of the great personal authority of the holy man himself. Buddhist shrines increased in numbers, but their conviction diminished to a more formalistic bureaucracy. Buddha was shown in heaven with more and more preference and gusto in the process of being tempted by lascivious girls, – zestfully illustrating a legend in which the bad demon Mara tries to prevent Buddha from becoming a saint by sending him an assortment of terrestrial temptresses, which Buddha, of course, refuses. As Buddha did not want to be shown as a person, on monuments, out of noble modesty – on some visual presentations he is only indicated by an empty chair in the middle of each composition – surrounded by provocative women, so that the artist presented really only a multitude of gaudy, naked females to be admired by the spectator, instead of showing the holiness of Buddha. The post-Buddhist shrines sported, soon after his death, decorations consisting of complaisant nymphs dressed in jewelry only, offering all the old willingness of the flesh, but now, in addition, with a smile – of which the initiated knew the real meaning.

BUDDHA

THE TRADITIONAL BUDDHA

It is supposed that Buddha lived from 560 to 480 B.C. and that he died when he was 80 years old. He was from the noble house of the Shakyas and his father was said to have been a governor. In the traditions of reincarnation Buddha was, before his birth, in heaven, and chose, looking down from there, his mother-to-be. He elected Maya, the wife of a king (Shuddhodana) who made a vow of chastity and was never touched by her husband. After a pregnancy of ten months, Maya gave birth to Buddha, without having been fertilized by a human being. Seven days after the birth of Buddha, his mother, Maya, died, because the gods decided that the precious being that shrouded Buddha during his "world-becoming" should thereafter never serve wordly matters, that someone who gave birth to a Buddha should never again bear a child. The parallel to Christ is obvious, who also was born by a Virgin – (who was married). Similar to Zarathustra, (ca. 600 BC.) Horus, etc. We can assume that this was the expected 'life-style' of exalted beings, at that time underlining the cosmic involvement to show the importance of the event – maybe similar to the reports of Suetonius, that each time a Roman Emperor was born or died, some astonishing and marvelous occurrences took place in the heavens. There are reported some other features about the childhood of Buddha that were, about 500 years later, ascribed to the story of Christ . . . like special lights and radiances in the nightly sky, – the astonishment of the sages over the wisdom of the infant, etc.

Prince Siddhartha, as Buddha was called then, was educated and grew up under the guidance of a sister of his late mother, who was married too, to the same King Shaddhodana, in a palace of greatest splendor.

In a text [A3, 38] Buddha says of himself:

> "I was spoiled, very spoiled. I was anointed with nothing
> but Benares-Sandel (oil) and was dressed in Benares fabric.
> By day and night a white parasol was held over me. I had
> one palace for the winter, one for the summer and one for
> the Rain-Season. In the four months of the rain-season I
> never left that palace and was constantly surrounded by
> female musicians."

Guatama – (another name for Buddha – derived from the Vedic sage in his ancestry) was then married to a young lady of noble birth, Gopa by name, but still had, in addition, a harem of the most beautiful dance-girls.

At the age of twenty-nine years Buddha was told that his wife gave birth to a boy. On the very same night Buddha left his wife and newly born son, without awakening them to say farewell. Nor did he take leave from the many dance-girls of the harem who "enchanted" him before. After having crossed three provinces, he discarded his princely vestments and took the garments of the poor, which were handed to him by a divinity. He cut his fragrant hair, to renounce the glamor and the carnal pleasures of the earth and sent his servant home with his horse. The horse died, because it could not bear the separation from its master.

Here again we see that whatever happens in the life of an exalted person involves the miraculous. Many horses died, but the horse of Buddha died of a broken heart. A great number of women died in childbirth, but when the mother of Buddha died, this quite usual occurrence was miraculized as a very special provision of the gods to underline his importance.

Before Buddha became the solemn divinity, he was also called Bodhisattwa, which means "The Saviour" – similar to the Christian title of "Salvator mundi."

Buddha seems to have made some experiments in hallucinations, then purposely provoked by overexposure to the sun, and thirst and to hunger. This sheds an interesting light on the general practice by holy men of that era, who were using hallucinatory conditions to gain exalted inspirations by practically forcing their mind into leaving their body and thereby to purge their person of all existent associations. This abolishment of the mundane mental scenario was believed to create a void which by necessity could be filled instead only by extra-terrestrial emanations.

The saints in the time of Buddha used that method which was practiced until the Christian advent – especially frequent were walks into the desert, with extreme sun-exposure, hunger and thirst. At the time of Buddha the saints, in contemplation, also used drugs – (not Buddha) – and the great god Siva is often shown reeling in holy intoxication while his wife, Parvati, brews him another cup of hemp – which is obviously not his first.

Buddha said, after he went through a few of those experiences, that they are not necessarily the way to higher insights, because they weaken the body and mind. He confined himself from then on to the observation of suffering and meditation upon its alleviation.

After seven years of solitude, contemplations, and ascetic wanderings, Buddha got his divine enlightenment under a tree – (from then on called "The Tree of Enlightenment") which since then stands in the middle of the celestial paradise and is shown as such in Indian art. This "Tree of En-lightment" was later said to stand in the biblical paradise of Adam and Eve and to bear fruits which were forbidden, because they were identified with the 'teachings of foreign religions' and only later projected to carnal sin.

Buddha assembled apostles around him and preached his gospel of chastity and poverty. Some of the patrons supporting Buddha including a lady called Migaramata and a courtesan called Ambapali, who later changed her ways, reformed, and became a nun – (see Magdalena). There is even a Judas-like story of betrayal through one of his disciples who wanted the death of Buddha, but instead met death himself. Buddha died from something he ate and solemnly entered the Nirvana. Buddha was educated in the aristocratic tradition which he showed throughout his life in his noble bearing and actions. He had a natural grace in his appearance, a refined taste and exquisite manners in dealing with all persons, whether their station had been high or low.

It probably can be said that it was Buddha who for the first time separated religion from the dark premordial brew of sensual demonology and created a majestic edifice of morality – unknown before – which still had room for compassion. This Buddha-centric religion does not rely on a god above, who is supposed to guide and to right all wrongs, but instead charges humanity with all responsibility in conducting its affairs . . . remaining, however, compassionate and not vengeful.

APOTHEOSIS

THE SYMBOLS OF RESURRECTION

THE CHAIN OF DEVELOPMENTS

The monument of the Sivatic phallus seems to be the earliest image of Life-Eternal and the resurrection, imported from the East and thereupon found on European graves.

We see, however, that the Symbols of resurrection in the Etruscan and later Roman funeral art gradually changed from purely Indo-Asiatic manifestations, via several quite remarkable morphological shifts, to Greco-Roman figures, acting-out the originally Eastern visions of a joyous next world.

In the funeral art of India, this generative totem stood for the idea of "raising upward" and pointing to the Above, the paradise and everlasting creation. In a second connotation it was a symbol for "youth" as promised in the Holy Scriptures, to be the condition of re-birth and resurrection, and thirdly it was a symbol for "bliss" expected in the celestial realm and the "everlasting manliness" in the embrace of the amorous daughters of Indra, the courtesans of Heaven. Its upward sweep also hinted at the elevation and escape from this earth of toil and sorrow.

> "No doubt that the merit of each mortal by erecting a
> Siva-phallus is ten million times greater than donations of
> goldfilled soil, or ten thousand horses, or the disclosure of
> water in the desert, or consoling the sad and miserable ones
> of this earth."
>
> [Mahanirvanatantra XIV.6]

So it is that also today simple people of India paint erect stones, even mile-stones, with Minium red and pay homage to them, as the symbols of the Great Divinity of perpetual Creation.

6

37

To our great amazement we now find the very same phallic monuments of India, identical in size and configuration, on Etruscan graves, made of Italian stone, while in Italy of 600 B.C. Siva was not known. This seems to be a solid proof that the Etruscans either came from India, or that they imported Indian doctrines. Whatever happened, the transfusion, in any form, from India to the Etruscans living in Italy, seems documented by those phallic grave-monuments. Because the Mediterraneans believed that the dead go underground and remain there, this abrupt hint at Life-Eternal may be considered to be the first symbol of Resurrection in the Greco-Roman sphere.

7

It is true that some phallic monuments cause consternation in Western people and they, in some embarassment, wish they would be displayed, if at all, in a somewhat more discrete manner, but we also see the reverse of this East-West sensibility in groups of Eastern tourists taking snapshots of opulent nude female figures decorating the facades of our libraries and similar highly official buildings, while in our feelings those figures have a purely symbolic meaning and we disregard completely their anatomical details leading to sensual speculations, so that we are forced to admit that a similar symbol-abstraction may take place in the Indian mind concerning the symbol of Siva.

The degree to which the Sivatic monument lost its anatomic connotation is shown by the fact that the oldest Etruscan phallic gravestones were also set at the graves of women. ["Corpus Inscriptionum Etruscarum" No. 3326]: "To Hermi (the wife) of Capznei, Memorial to the daughter of Capznei" plus: "To the daughter of Atnei" – and No. 4544: "To Thania Leunei."

8

This, however, changed in later times when the Indo-Etruscans were adopting more and more of the local Italian sentiments. To this effect we see a skypos [Boston No. 97.372] which shows a man and a woman, as it seems parting from each other on the threshold of death, – depicting the male figure as standing in front of such a phallic gravestone, while the female is seen before her burial place to be, in the form of a Hut. As this presentation dates from a relatively later time, the fourth century B.C., when the purely Etruscan style was flooded by Italic influences, – we can assume that the Hut or house-shaped grave-monument relates to the vision of a 'home' for the soul, of the Villanovan tradition, later more amply involving Persephone as the 'hostess' of the dead, while the Sivatic emblem was still associated in Italy with the male sex. The Hut is therefore a hint at an uneasiness to see a female buried under the insignia of the erect phallus, – which shows that the conversion of this monument from the physical to the transcendental had not taken hold in the Italian feeling.

13

Similar to the idea of the Boston Skyphos 97.372, on the stelae of Athens [Reinach II.374] we see a cippus of rather masculine outlines as the monument for a man, while the stela for a female again resembles a hut or even a little memorial shrine.

Those memorials, sometimes in the shape of small huts, were carefully preserved as endearing objects and are displayed now in great numbers in museums – while most phallic emblems were destroyed by crusaders of various callings, who thought that anything looking sensual is a manifestation of evil spirits.

After the stark and direct object-transfer from India via the Etruscans wore off, the sentiments of the surrounding Greco-Roman sphere quite gradually infused a new symbolism into those foreign formations.

Consequently we see a re-modeling and re-interpretation of the clearly phallic embodiment in Italy by losing, at first very slowly, its anatomical identity towards a rather nondescript formation, but still suggesting the magically arising potential, the 'NUMEN' of ancient Roman belief.

In later times this same formation was successively transformed into a 're-sprouting staff' – first by delineating some leaf-like ornaments on that object, which later developed to a plant-like sprout coming out of the ground with a bud on top, – (a physical extension of the dead man's body as we see it on some Herms?) – still later altered into a veritable staff with rich leaves breaking out of it, and finally re-appearing as a re-foliating bough carried triumphantly in the Dionysian train by pubescent boys.

9 While stelae for women hardly hint at any relation to their Afterlife, the post-Etruscan grave monuments of males often make reference to "everlasting manliness" in the next world, [NM 806] as the hope and aim for a second existence in the Above, promised by the doctrines of the East. This is sometimes expressed by bounding rams, combined with the drink of Immortality symbolized by a cup, which is shown as such on many vase-paintings.

10 The hope of finding gentle Females in the Beyond is also often alluded to, whereby the formerly so frightening Harpias are blended over into the Sirens at first, and then from there into some seductive creatures with broad Oriental hips, smilingly awaiting the ascending soul. [NM 2546]

11 All those very direct hints at the promise of the Eastern paradise were later again gelled into a tradition reverting to Greco-Roman formalism, in using the local grave-monuments, merely embellished by elements of the Etrusco-Oriental symbol-language used as ornaments whose original meaning was by now forgotten. [NM 1028]

12 All this concerns the upper part of those symbols of resurrection in funeral art, but also the base of those phallic grave-stones sometimes make reference to the "everlasting manliness" of the departed, by using the image of the Bull as symbol, not only concerning the possibility of enjoying the celestial maidens, but also to indicate the latent force of the soul to break out of its earthly confinement, in glorious defiance of Death and the local doctrine of Hades.

14 Still connected to the phallic symbolisms, in its aspects of Rebirth and Joy, we see on the covers of Etruscan ash-urns [Villa Giulia] as well as on sarcophagi [Naples] the image of the soul of the deceased as being welcomed or guided by two emissaries or genii of the next world, both of them with erect phalli, as their identification with the spirit of the sphere to which they belong and which they represent — reminiscent of today's doormen wearing the insignia of the establishment they serve, which is, in the case of those emissaries, the realm of pleasures. This same fundamental insignia and most archaic totem of generation being also the counter-aspect of destruction, and thereby of life protracted beyond death. To denote those emissaries also as agents of transition, they wear torches to guide the soul from the subterranean darkness to the spheres of eternal light. The torches, by themselves, are symbols of the transition from the manifest substance — (the body) — that perishes like the substance of the torch, to be transformed into light, symbolic for the de-materialized and liberated soul.

RECEPTION IN THE BEYOND

Those guides from the next world may also serve as 'Guardians of the Gates' – so extensively mentioned in the oldest Sumerian and Egyptian texts, relating to the world of the dead. Also in the Egyptian 'Books of the Dead' it becomes evident that the soul of the departed has to know the names of all gate-keepers of the realm of the dead and has to justify to them its passage, so that we understand that the gate-keepers had a very prestigious position and the power to reject the soul, or else to welcome the dead with joy and honors, as seen on those sarcophagi. The hope for a "reception with outstretched arms" – as we see it in the eloquent and touching death-prayers of Egypt – is the most intense desire of the departing soul.

In some cases we see a Faunian figure actually lifting the dead from the ground and in many other instances the dead appears as just awakening in a trance-like condition, still weak on his legs and steadied by Satyrs and wine-crested and sensuously tender young men – maybe as a hint that the doctrine of a resurrection to felicity originally came via those Dionysian emissaries, or devotees, triumphantly from India to the Mediterranean lands.

15

The re-awakening of the dead to a joyous Thereafter, and his loving reception there, is staged on many sarcophagi, ash-urns, stelae and mirrors, by showing the soul of the departed, mostly in an Apollonic epiphany, as received, guided and embraced by symbol-figures of that next world, appearing as Fauni, the images of lust and perpetual Priapic vitality – and Dionysian ephebes as being the embodiments of the state of intoxication, assumed as being the atmosphere into which the soul is now about to enter. Although we see in some cases also a Female awaiting the hardly awakened dead with embraces.

16

17

18

The possibility that those figures of reception may sometimes be male Hierodules in the great "Celestial Sanctuary of Love" seems not out of the question, because such "servants" to divinities of love existed plentifully in oldest times in the great Asiatic temples dedicated to those Queens of Love. They left their traces in the texts of the earliest Church-Fathers who fiercely condemned the semi-religious practices of those earthly embodiments of heavenly joys.

But we even find reflections of those half-spiritual personages in classical Greek mythology:

> "Eos bore Kephalos a son, Phaethon, who was carried away
> in his young manhood by Aphrodite; who made him a
> servant in her holy temples by night, a divine daimon."
> [Hesiod, Theogony 986]

41

"Divine daimon" possibly meaning: a spiritual being dedicated to the divinity. This can be understood as a euphemism for a boy who fell under the spell of love (Aphrodite) and became a male Hierodule or servant in her sanctuaries, but it seems rather to be a periphrasis for the sudden early death of a youth . . . as other Greek legends speak of somebody being "carried off" . . . to the Island of the Blessed . . . or a certain Amphiaraos, "carried off" by the loving girl Eos . . . and, of course, the story of Hylas, carried away by Water-Nymphs, – all being pleasing euphemisms to explain mysterious deaths or disappearances.

19

To be taken away from this earth by spirits of love, to a realm of eternal endearments seems to be the substance of all those sagas, which conform in this respect to the Indo-Asiatic picture of Afterlife, and which thereby formed a bridge or liaison between the Mediterranean and the Indic visions of death, and as we see it staged on those urns and sarcophagi, to be received in the next world which is represented by spirits of love. Those spirits are in the Greek mythos shown as uncertain figures of diverse names, . . . and appear consolidated in the Indian vision to one definite outline which is represented by the Apsarases.

20

On some ash-urns or sarcophagi or even on vase-paintings of later times, we see beautiful Nymphs abducting souls of men. The images of those females fluctuate between visions of the Greek Harpies, the "soul-snatchers" with wings and claws, who mellowed to beautiful creatures of compassion, to the angelic Lasae, the Etruscan genii of Fate and Transition, and finally to the Apsarases with their typical hairdo and frank intimacy with their male partners.

In later times came the still exotic resurrection symbols of the pineapple and the pomegranate, seemingly bursting with seminal power, and clearly pointing back to the tropical foreign lands from where those new doctrines were coming – as neither pineapples nor pomegranates grew in Italy at that time.

But closer then to the Mediterranean appeared the pine-cone as seminal symbol related to resurrection or life after death. The pine-cone was understood to be the seed of the evergreen tree, which was a symbol for Attis, who was in turn the main symbol for resurrection as the image of the nonwilting vegetation and its rebirth after its wintery death-sleep. Attis of the biblical lands is shown as a charming youth, very obviously disrobing his emblem of generation, not only as a symbol of re-sprouting, but also as bringer of felicity.

Still later (and now strictly Mediterranean) funeral monuments show as male symbols for re-birth the cock, in earlier version in its generative function with a hen – (in an unmistakable parallelism also used as a sign for public houses, even in conjunction with the Three Graces) — but later in a more exalted and spiritual allegory the cock on graves is shown as crowing, as if awakening the slumbering soul of the dead to the rising dawn, the ascending light of Mithras.

Oriental or later even Greco-Roman women on couches festively inviting the soul, flanked at times by servants, but mainly by the usual torch-bearing angels of Death on sarcophagi. Oriental women with the "corona immortalis" in hand — (derived from the Indo-Etruscan garland of immortality) — inviting the tired soul to a sweet repose on their richly draped couch [Museo Etrusco, Volterra.]

In a next step of development there are countless females of the Beyond on vase-paintings blending-over into Ephebes, still with the full and heavy Oriental body, but sprouting a male sex, despite the elaborate coiffure and prominent jewelry, often criss-crossing the body in Indian fashion. Those vases are from a time when the soul was assumed to be hermaphroditic in character . . . possibly influenced by Asiatic divinities of that kind [Vienna].

In later, and now totally confused versions, we see on sarcophagi the Indian idea of liberated joy in the next world, projected onto the Bacchic cult — (which was a strictly terrestrial affair). Homa, the sublime elixir of everlasting life, was replaced by secular wine and its rustic festivals. The heavenly females "of wonderful beauty" were re-interpreted as love-intoxicated Maenades and Bacchantes in the Dionysian train, later converted into healthy peasant-girls harvesting grapes, to have the "fabulous" ending in the "reasonable."

21

SELENE AND DEATH

22

Selene impersonated the Moon, reigning over the Night, which was understood in funeral art as Night-Eternal, that is, Death. The connection between Moon and Death is very old and widespread.

In the Rig-Veda we find the following passage:

> "The planets send ethereal beams to the earth. Man is born
> through the influences of Sun and dies under the influence
> of the Moon. Death comes from the Moon. The Moon gives
> coldness and when a man becomes cold, he dies."

In the Rig Veda are also hints at a union of the Moon with Soma, spoken of, as Soma in the "lap" of the Moon. Soma is the drink of immortality which was elevated to be a divinity. Thereby we have a very early connection of the Moon to immortality, which may have influenced the role of Selene, the Moon-Maiden, in her relation to the soul after death, as seen on sarcophagi. It seems that the symbol-speculation was then, that in the lap of the Moon you find immortality, Soma, or: If the Moon loves you (that is Selene) you will find in her embrace, that is in her lap, immortality. The sarcophagi therefore show Selene as being ready to embrace the deceased – (in the features of Endymion) – whereby he will be admitted to immortality in her lap.

The Vedas further state that the "Fathers" (in this Indian concept) reside in the Moon. Those "Fathers" are not the Mediterranean "Manes" but seem comparable to our apostles and are powerful saints and protector-figures, who were elevated to immortality, which is said to be in the lap of the Moon.

The expression to be in the "lap" of a divinity intends to say that they are now the Beati – as one would say "she holds him in her heart" – (as the Heart is the love-symbol of today, while in archaic times it was the lap) – but still using the old inference that bliss is identical with the love in the lap of heavenly females.

24

The most interesting part, however, is the possibility that the "Father Figures" seen on the Endymion sarcophagi, may represent those immortal "Fathers" awaiting the deceased, who is shown as Endymion. Those "Father Figures" would represent an amalgam of the Vedic mythology with the Mediterranean Selene myth, which seems quite possible as we see the Vedic Water-Nymphs staged on the same sarcophagus with Selene.

A further connection between the Moon and Death is Kalee, the terrible image of death, pictured as receiving the "Soul-Substance" of the corpse and triumphing over the act of creation. Kalee, the death-symbol, is shown with the necklace of Skulls and as "moon-crested" and so are her attendants, all wearing the moon on their foreheads.

We see a parallel to this thought in the function of Tefnut, receiving the soul in love, and passing it into the realm of the Blessed between the stars.

The Veda says that the Sun (a female) is married to Immortality (who is Soma, being a male). But it is also said that Soma resides in the lap of the Moon. According to the harem structure it was, of course, most usual that a male Lord had several women, but it seems more appropriate in this case to think that we deal here with symbolisms which indicate that the Sun, as well as the Moon, are immortal – or expressed in sensual terms, so well liked in India, that both have an affair with Lord Soma, who rests in their laps. If we now translate the (Indian) Moon into the (Mediterranean) Selene, . . . it would mean that those who enter her lap will partake of eternal life . . . and therefore she is shown ready to embrace Endymion, representing the deceased. This is a hint that the deceased will not only have eternal life in the next world, but also that he will enjoy this eternity with a celestial and amorous female . . . thereby conforming exactly to the Indo-Oriental vision of paradise . . . the oddity being, that all of it is represented on a Roman sarcophagus.

Later, the Upanishads – ("Secret Teachings") – around 800 B.C. established a clearer relation between the souls of the dead and the Moon, and it is suggested that the waning and rebirth of the Moon was considered a symbol, or celestial paradigma, for the death and re-birth of the soul.

The magic identification between Moon and Death existed also in Eygpt.

> "If you wish to make him die you use this magic: Paint your eye with green eye-paint" – (establishing correspondence with the greenish face of the moon) – "you now address the full moon and speak: you so-and-so, give all his names exact, you be now the moon" – (identification of the living with the death-symbol) – "he perishes excellent for sure."
>
> [Lyden Papyrus, Col. XXIII]

(The Egyptians liked salesman-like language for emphasis.)

Hesiod, around 700 B.C., in naming some personifications of abstractions, says that Night bore Fate and Doom, Moros and Ker, who later developed into the figure of a Death-Demon or Death-Angel. As Night is equated with the moon-crested Selene, we again see a fixed relation between Selene and Death.

To place the figure of Selene in the chain of developments in funeral art, we may have to look at the very consequently 'ascending' transition leading from the still SUBTERRANEAN and strictly Greco-Roman Persephone via the Waternymphs of already Eastern provenience, to the euphoric females of TERRESTRIAL Bacchic tribes, later rarified to become the Graces and still later the muses of a somehow ELEVATED sphere, to finally lead to the clearly CELESTIAL Selene between the stars.

From this later epoch, around the second century A.D., we have a great number of so-called 'Endymion Sarcophagi' which show, however, Selene as the central figure and as the stand-in for the Eastern 'Amorous Females after Death' joining her beloved Endymion in the heavenly Night.

23   The story of Endymion and Selene in short:

Kalyke and Aethlios had a son Endymion, a most beautiful man, and shown in funeral art with Apollonic features, who was cast into perpetual sleep – (as an euphemism for Death) – and was loved by Selene, the personification of Night, thought of in sepulchral images as Night-Eternal, that is Death. So that on sarcophagi we have scenes showing a beautiful youth in eternal sleep, representing the deceased, who is received in love by a female in the celestial spheres. – (the end of the story depicting by coincidence or transmission the Oriental promise of
26   Afterlife).

The genealogy of Selene is vague and various, as she, being the Moon, is at times understood as a 'Heavenly Body' . . . (in both meanings of the word) . . . and as such the daughter of Zeus and in other versions his beloved. Another story makes Selene the daughter of Hyperion, which, according to Homer, is an old name for the Sun, Helios, who is her brother. All of which makes us believe that we deal here not with a person, but with a semi-astronomical allegory. According to some indications it seems to be safest to think of Selene as 'Queen of the Night' and as the Moon reigns over the night she became its impersonation. As 'Queen of the Night' she then relates easily to 'sleep,' to its bigger brother, which is Death, and to the 'Night Eternal' on sarcophagi.

25   The reasons given for the eternal sleep of Endymion are so divergent in different authors, from Hesoid to the Alexandrians, that we may well suspect the inflow and overlay of a foreign world of visions over a shadowy Mediterranean saga, and the already shaky genealogy surrounding the person of Endymion, is lending itself to embrace exotic elements as an echo from foreign lands.

The similarity to the Indo-Oriental pattern is obvious, as the Female awaiting the dead is of semi-divine rank and cast in the active role.

The motives of eternal youth, attributed to Endymion, are certainly reminiscent of the promise of the Oriental paradise. No reason is ever given why eternal youth is granted to Endymion, so that a transplant of that feature from the East becomes more probable where eternal youth – ("everlasting manliness") – is promised in the Thereafter of carnal pleasures.

SUMMARY OF SELENE

Selene, although moon-crested and Queen of the Night, never represented Death in Greco-Roman mythology, because the "Moon-to-Death" connection was Indian and Egyptian and about 1,000 years before the prominence of Selene in funeral art – where she 'counteracted' Death, as she inherited from the Eastern beliefs the aura of bestowing immortality, and combined it with the Mediterranean figure of love, but this time "in the Indo-Oriental lap" of the Moon-Goddess and fusing thereby that Mediterranean and romantic vision of the Moon, back into the Eastern ideas of sensual felicity with the celestial females after death.

We see then that there is a gradual mixture of ideologies and a shift in the value of symbol-figures in funeral art, which could not be explained with the help of only one mythological basis, and we may come to the conclusion that Death has a mythology by itself, using the figures of many other mythologies as actors or marionettes around this great Mystery-play of fears and hopes.

THE PERSISTENT WATER NYMPHS

In several instances that connection to the original Apsara vision is made especially clear: The Metropolitan Museum of New York has a beautiful 'Endymion' sarcophagus [No. 24.97.13] showing Selene, one breast exposed but with a mournful facial expression, being guided by an Amorette towards the sleeping Endymion. However, this Endymion seems to have a dream-vision of his own which is shown floating above him, in the person of a WATER-NYMPH – (we remember that "Apsara" means "those of the waters" and that they are shown as Water-Nymphs in Greco-Roman art). This reference to the original promise of a celestial female of the Eastern

24

type seems to be the center of the death-thought especially as another Amorette is shown to lift the death-shroud off Endymion to reawaken him to that dream-vision of the Oriental coinage, while he pays no attention to the approaching Selene. It seems then that this fundamental and central dream-vision is flanked by quasi intruding and later Greco-Roman elements – one of them being Selene and the other an 'Ancestor,' looking down from the Above, symbolizing the idea of the Manes, to whom the dead is now returning. This ancestral father-figure with beard has the square 'Butterfly Wings' to indicate that he is the Spirit of a dead person. While in the instance of this sarcophagus [No. 24.97.13] the Apsara-Waternymph connection in the Above is especially clear. We have many instances where Water-Nymphs appear in the Above on sarcophagi, in a central position as the supreme promise of Afterlife. Some of them are shown in the waters of the celestial spheres – even in little boats or riding animals of the sea – but more often just with a water-pitcher in hand as their insignia and joined by celestial figures of the next world. One of those Water Nymphs emitting a veritable cascade of water from her pitcher, appears on the rarely noticed rear side of the sarcophagus [No. 47.100.4] of the third century A.D. in the Metropolitan Museum of New York. Another sarcophagus [38.793] at the Casino Rospigliosi in Rome, shows the sleeping Endymion leaning on the winged ancestor-figure while a Water-Nymph, in a much smaller scale, . . . meaning: at a far distance, . . . seems to float above him like a dream. That Water-Nymph looks down on him with parted legs, while emitting water from her pitcher. We see again the moon-crested Selene approaching with a mournful face and guided to Endymion by several Amorini . . . to no avail as it seems, as Endymion dreams of the Water-Nymph in paradise.

25

As to the chain of developments in the figure of the 'Female after Death' leading from the subterranean Persephone via the still Greco-Roman girls of more heavenly graces to the Orientalized Waternymphs and from there to Selene, we see that in some remarkable cases all the Nymphic derivates – (like the 3 Graces, the Maenades etc.) – were skipped, and that the transition proceeded directly from the Water-Nymphs to Selene, overlapping both visions in co-existence on several monuments. The progress of time and the change of ideas from the earlier Water-Nymphs to the later Selene, is shown by the fact that the Waternymph appears like a dream of the past on a smaller scale in the background floating on a cloud, while the figure of Selene is shown as a reality in the foregound, descending from a naturalistic chariot.

The strange fact that both Selene and the Waternymphs appear in the same picture . . . although on different levels, could simply mean that the artist did not want to give up completely the exotic and by then time-honored tradition of "Those of the Waters" as the ultimate dream-destination . . . while he had to modernize the scenario using Endymion and Selene as main actors. It also could be thought that the encounter with Selene was a 'first stage' of the other-worldly adventures, while the nirvana-like state involving the Waternymph awaited the alter-ego of the dead, which is shown as Endymion, at a later time and place.

The dramatics of the Moongoddess and the dead in a rarified sphere of an almost-touch . . . but never shown in embrace . . . may reflect the contemporary Mithraic visions of purity identifying the Moon as "The Light shining in the Darkness" which gained great strength in the last centuries of the pre-Christian era. The Mithraic dogma postulated, that the dead is but asleep and will be awakened to see the light . . . so that the vague possibility exists that Selene is merely the awakening-agent while the luxury of the dream awaits the soul of the dead at a later stage.

24

THE NEMEAN LION AND HERACLES

It is said that Selene between the stars, gave birth to the Nemean Lion. Because of the technical-gynocological difficulty of that vision, we must assume that we deal here with a symbolism – similar, maybe, to the wondrous pronouncement of Aristophanes that Night and Chaos gave birth to Love. In our case the idea seems to be that Selene, Goddess of the Night, also understood to be the Night-Eternal, that is Death, created as a 'Symbol-figure' the all-devouring monster-Lion, who is shown on many sarcophagi as eating up a variety of living beings, like lambs, antelopes, horses etc. – in short: the terrible Night of Death, represented as a majestic Lion, persistently depicted in 'larger than life' proportions compared to all other figures shown on those sarcophagi – is merciless devouring all living creatures. True to his role as Death himself, it is also said that the Nemean Lion was invincible, that is, that nobody can overcome Death. The fact that the Lion is persistently shown to be much larger than any other figure on the sarcophagi means to express the idea that Death is larger than Life, hinting thereby at the "tremendous majesty" of Death . . . "Rex tremendae majestatis."

27

However another mythological saga tells us that Herakles, as one of his marvelous deeds, killed the Nemean Lion with his club, skinned that formidable beast, and from that day on wore its hide as his proudest

49

insignia. Therefore Herakles became the symbol-figure of overcoming Death-eternal and as the liberator from Hades, and is often seen on Etruscan mirrors and later sarcophagi as the Hero of the Apotheosis and Resurrection. One of them shows Herakles, with club in hand, and clothed in the skin of the Nemean Lion, actually opening the door of death to free some souls from the subterranean spheres. To make absolutely sure that we deal here with Herakles and his marvelous deeds, we see in an ornamental and retrospective fashion, flanking the central stage of action, the same Herakles-figure killing the multiheaded Hydra (often mixed up with Kerberos) and some other of his feats. As a further verification of the process, we see the figure of Hermes-Psychopompos, the guide of the souls through their extra-terrestial adventures and dramatic re-appearances, awaiting the just liberated souls to conduct them to the upper spheres – and, as shown on many sarcophagi, to unite them with celestial beings.

31

It is also mentioned that King Eurystheus was so afraid of the Nemean Lion that he was hiding in a pot buried in the earth at his approach, which really means that the king was afraid of death, which in fact was envisioned at that time as the terrible Lion of Nemea. The trick to 'play dead' to be overlooked by the Killer was much used at that time, as well as the burial of bones or ashes in a pot, which was an early Etruscan tradition of 800 to 700 B.C.

The same Nemean Lion, still over-dimensional, as befitting the idea of the superior power of the all-devouring Death, was later shown in the role of a guardian of the four corners of the sarcophagi – (similar in its protection to the powers of Sphynxes or Gorgons) – to scare away evil influences from the entombed. The head of the lion on the Doors of Death were placed there maybe as a warning in the form of a picture-graphic name-plate on the door, that here starts the domain of that awesome Lion of Death. His still ferocious features with dangerously bared teeth changed later into a more benevolent and faithful guardian of the tomb and the soul of the dead. In this function we see the head of the lion as a protective spell on doors . . . originally on the doors to the netherworld on sarcophagi, but later on doors in general, and even today on many of the Italian doors, from the portals of palazzi on to the modest little doors of peaceloving citizens.

In early Christian times, the Lion is sometimes shown on tombs to be tamed by an apostolic figure [Torlonia 31.957] as an allusion to a paradise where the Lion was thought to co-exist peacefully with the gazelle, lamb or ibex. This type of paradise turned 'full circle' away from the 'pagan' Greco-Roman celestial figures and back to the visions of the Mahabharata, where the premordial status of the world is equated with the post-mortem paradise of the blessed, where all will live in mutual love, as they did in the

Prehistoric Herd at the dawn of time. But Love that was to begin with a pre-condition to Creation, was to become under the guidance of the apostolic figure a renunciation and reconciliation after death.

LIONS IN TOMBS

The lions attacking gazelles, a scene so often shown on Etruscan grave frescoes, may well be derivates of the Nemean Lion, because their attitude is not, as usual with other lions, to defend the tomb or soul of the deceased against Demons, but instead to overtake and to attack, the gazelles being their helpless prey.

This new role of the lion is so surprising because gazelles never symbolized Demons or Monsters but were chosen to represent the charm and agility of Life itself . . . which then seems here tracked down by the all-devouring Death.

It is possible that the identification of Death with an attacking Lion is very old, and that the story that Selene, being the Night-Eternal, produced as an offspring the Lion-of-Death, was a clever combination of later mythographers. Guarding and Killing is not a direct contradiction. The archaic Lion-guardian had, of course, the power to Kill, so that the guarding and killing had an intimate relation, as the Lion was chosen to be the best guardian because he was also the most powerful Killer.

The later symbol-combination confronting us on sarcophagi and grave-murals seems to assume Selene as the moon-crested Queen of the Night-Eternal in a rather timeless state between the stars, while her Lion is functioning as the earthly 'executive' force to do the actual Kill, and is understood as a subordinate offspring from that 'cosmic' cycle of becoming and waning.

The fact that we sometimes see lionesses painted in tombs may be derived from the older idea of the Lioness as the defender of the tomb and soul of the deceased based on the figure of Durga, wife of Siva, the many-armed defendress against Demons, shown in the image of a lioness and sometimes riding on a lion as her "Vehicle." In the still fluid state of mythology at that time, the painters may not have been sure to what symbolism they should incline, may it be Death in the form of the Greco-Roman Lion of Nemea, or the Asiatic lioness as the protectress of souls, as both symbols were equally valid and appropriate in grave-chambers. This

29

51

overlapping of forms and symbolisms may have its analogy in the many vaccillations between Egyptian and Roman figures, produced by Italian artists or the Apollo-Buddha amalgams found on the borders of Asia.

The images of the lionesses may also be the result of the very persistent, new, but vague rumors of a Female element in the Thereafter, projected now onto the vision of the Lion of Death. The artists at that time had no intention of creating "documents" exactly illustrating precise thoughts, but rather equalled their contemporaries in floating through a haze of tentative imagery, freely connecting sagas, and animals with human shapes, streaming to them from many lands, as exotic, beautifully tempting possibilities of never-ending symbol-connections.

One painter may have copied the designs from other tombs, but, following the new vogue, may have felt more up-to-date in replacing the old Mediterranean Nemean Lion with the Asiatic Durga-symbol. The repetition of the general composition, on one hand, but on the other hand the obvious over-emphasis laid on the breasts of the Lioness to underline the femininity, would suggest this possibility.

The Lionesses could also be a reminiscence of the pre-Vedic Durga because before they were consecrated by Hinduism, Kali and Durga were thought to be formidable monsters of destruction . . . so that her image on the walls of burial places appears well justified, and would, as far as the aspect of doom and death is concerned, parallel or duplicate the meaning of the Nemean Lion, and thereby confirm the assumption that the Lions as well as the Lionesses are thought to be images or symbols of death . . . (We have to think of a time where no other pictorial death-symbols existed.)

The post-Vedic Durga was, however, representing, on a higher and sanctified level, nature's cycle of birth and death so that this image and meaning of hers would also justify very well her presence on those tomb-frescoes, in their upper registers, traditionally showing the realm of divinities. In the 'Tomb of the Lionesses' for instance, the very prominently shown and supernaturally big breasts, in combination with their ferociously opened mouths, full of sharp and bared teeth and their paws ready to strike, would hint at this typical Durga-symbolism of Becoming and Perishing.

THE DOUBLE-LIONS AND THE LIONESSES

In Egypt of old, the Lions were believed to see by day as well as by night. They were thought to watch over the sinking of the sun in the West and over its re-awakening and ascent in the East as they had the title of the "Guardians of the Two Horizons" and therefore became the symbols of the cycle of Day and Night, the eternal coming and going of time, the cosmic perpetuancy and as such the re-emerging after death. They were shown on the head-rests of the living and the dead as guardians of the sleeping and the promise of dawn, and in funeral art as the symbols of re-birth, as the sun was thought to die and to descend to the subterranean realm of the Dead, to be reborn in the East, ascending from 'the grip of the earth' to renewed splendor. On the head-rests Sleep was equated with Death, and the Awakening with Resurrection. The idea of the apotheosis is often associated with the Double-Lions and inscribed on head-rests:

> "They lift up thy head to the Horizon
> thou art raised up
> thou art Horus, the son of Hathor"
> [Chapter XLVI, Book of the Dead]

(In this case the dead appears re-born by Hathor, which presupposes that he gave his Soul-Substance to Hathor – in similarity to the Pharaoh who wants to become the lover of Hathor – while the older belief assumed the rebirth through Tefnut.)

The head-rests were often made in the form of the crescent Moon hinting at the chain of associations leading from Sleep to Death to Night, over which the moon was reigning and where the Blessed would rest "in the lap of the moon" after their earthly departure.

53

On grave-inscriptions and funeral-papyri the reborn soul is pictured to rise, sunlike, over the Double-Lions, representing the horizons of the East and West. In some cases [Papyrus of Heruben, XXI Dyn.] the newborn soul is shown with the 'Lock of Youth' falling, as usual, on its right shoulder, to indicate its rejuvenation, and floating within the arising sundisk, which is surrounded with the serpent of Eternity. The Double-Lions also symbolized Yesterday and Tomorrow, looking in both directions, the Past and the Future, and upholding the image of the infinite chain of days, the cosmic time.

The Lionesses were images of 'Defenders' – (possibly because they were known to fiercely defend their cubs and being more powerful than any aggressor). It was also said that they lent their skin to the supreme god Re to defeat his enemies – (the Pharaoh is still clad on solemn occasions in a lion-skin to commemorate that myth and to identify himself with Re). – In their defensive role, the lionesses are found on the four corners of temple-roofs, as rain-spouts or gargoyles, to actually "spit out" the emission of Seth, the evil storm-god, when a rainstorm beat down on the sanctuary. The Lioness, in short, was thought of as the powerful Defender and understood in funeral art as keeping the specters menacing the soul of the dead away from the sepulchre. Because hordes of strange creatures were believed to still exist in the lawless voids "outside the creation" – as it was called – who lurked and held their sway in macabre darkness, before the gods, who descended from the sun, put light and order in the world's chaos. It is possible that those visions of this premordial state were inspired by the not yet cultivated jungles of the mountain-regions, populated by nameless creatures of menacing nature – in contrast to the irrigated fields, as order, canalization, sluices and dams were ascribed to the doings of the gods. The at first nameless specters were later condensed to more specific creatures of evil intent, sometimes listed to be 4000 . . . all of which were held at bay by the lionesses defending the sanctified realm of the dead.

It seems strange that the Egyptians, giving so much thought to death and creating the most tremendous grave-monuments, had no specific Death-God. They had symbols for the protection of the dead and his resurrection, but no personification of Death itself – (this in similarity to the Greco-Roman mythology, where we have figures surrounding the circumstances of death, like Hekate, Selene, Persephone, Hades, Charon, etc. which are really only post-mortem personalities, but also no Death-God). It is still stranger – and points to a very obvious gap in its mythological representation – that Death, while never shown iconographically, is still addressed in Egyptian inscriptions, – (his actual name being again omitted) – as follows:

"Vanish O thou who comest from the shadows
who enterest secretly and hast come
to cast the spell of death on this child . . ."

Maybe it was thought that only this which had been created by the gods,
has a manifestation and a face, and that death is 'Non-creation' and therefore has no image, no personality, and, as it seems, not even a name.

This absence of the 'Person' of Death existed also in Italy. Even our now
conventional symbols of death were not yet established, like the Skeleton,
the Skull with crossed bones, the Hour-glass, or the Sickle as the active
instrument of Death, and not even the benediction of the Cross "after the
fact" with its protective function. Because death was assumed to be final, in
Greco-Roman lands, there was no arsenal of revival-symbols available to
the artists. At the same time, however, India and Egypt were practically
overflowing with such symbols, and also were reputed to have the highest
developed mythical technology of reviving the souls towards another life,
and of knowing all secrets and most elaborate spells, and all the figures,
necessary for that mysterious conversion-procedure, as the resurrection
was there the central idea of the burial and the actual aim of the deceased.

This then explains why the Etruscans employed such outlandish symbols in their grave-chambers, probably imported from India and Egypt,
simply because local Italian symbols were not in stock, and non-existent to
express those doctrines which were not known before on Italian soil. In the
Etruscan twilight of beliefs, and their transitions, the grave was thought to
be the residence of the soul, in need for protection, which was at first
attempted by helmets and urns at the Villanova time and little huts for the
remains and the excorporate spirits of the deceased, later being reinforced
by the defending lions. Due to the ever stronger influences from the Orient,
the idea of protection entered a second, totally Eastern phase: the ascent of
the soul towards its re-birth, which used then the symbol of the Double-
Lions – (still called "The Guardians") – but this time of the arising sun on
the Eastern horizon – after its demise into the earth in the West – as a very
plausible parallel or paradigma to the death of the individual descending
into the earth to be reborn to the heavens . . . after having, like the sun,
wandered through the nightly spheres of the dead. This shift from the idea
of the Guardian to the revolutionary and totally foreign doctrine of Resurrection must have been a tremendous step at that time in Italy, but was
facilitated by the most welcome Double-Lions, being at the same time the
symbol for the guardian as well as the symbol for re-birth, due to their title
of "Guardians of the Two Horizons."

SUMMARY OF LIONS

In conclusion it can be assumed that the tomb-painters had the following elements at their disposition:

We skip here the Lion as seen on the oldest seals and the Assyrian types as expression of power, the ferocious, the invincible etc., and confine our review to images of Lions which are suitable for grave-chambers, again slipping for a moment into the position of the painter.

There is the Lion as archaic guardian but his function of defending is rather taken over by the "Horror-Faces" on the gables of the tomb, which, in the Asiatic tradition, scare away evil specters.

A more suitable emblem seems to be the Nemean Lion, the symbol of death, befalling all creatures, even the most endearing ones, shown as gazelles. All that according to a divine cosmic law of the Eternal Night, shown as Selene, which might be a comfort to the survivors to see the departed received in Love by that queen of the eternal spaces, as shown on the "Endymion" sarcophagi. All that according to Mediterranean mythology, whereby Selene seems to be the latest version of the "Female in the Beyond" – after which only "inexplicable voluptuousness" – "inexplicabili voluptate" [Apuleius, Met. XI.6] – was awaiting the soul in the Beyond, without, however, explaining the reason for it, in using the postulate of 'voluptuousness in paradise' which was built upon the hearsay that amorous girls would populate those spheres.

Now turning to the inflow from Asia: There is the Lioness as image of Durga, as the defender of tomb and soul against all evil Demons and Specters. However, her attack on the gazelle is out of character and makes us guess that we deal here either with a simple feminization of the Nemean Lion, somehow superimposing the 'Female after Death' over the traditionally accepted Nemean symbol of death, or else we deal here with another type of Durga.

The archaic Durga was the symbol for 'Becoming' and 'Death' – so often found in Asiatic divinities – and would lend itself thereby very well to symbolize the tragedy of death, including the hope of rebirth. On the actual paintings the supernaturally accentuated breasts of the Lionesses may indicate the aspect of 'Becoming' and the ravenous teeth and claws may indicate the aspect of 'Destruction' – the gazelle representing life itself – as also seen in this sense on sarcophagi in connection with the Nemean Lion. Due to this analogy the Lion as image of death attacking the living seems to be a fixed symbol in funeral painting and plastic arts, while the female version of it appears as a variant of it, connected to the Vedic Durga with her tantric associations to Kalee, the black 'Mother' image, who is also the 'Destroyer.'

Why in Asia a female figure was chosen to represent Death and Destruction is a greatly debated question.

The answer might be that a DUALITY seems to be the pre-requisite of each Asiatic high-divinity. The state of affairs where one divinity holds the Beginning and another would hold the End of the thread of life in its hand would indicate the incompetence of each of them – or their limitations – which is a contradition to the terms of a supreme ruler. Therefore the duality of Life and Death has to rest in one and the same emanation. As the life-giving is obviously a feminine function, it becomes necessary to appoint the same power also reigning over Death, which brings us, by the necessity of logic, to the 'Mothers' of Horrors and Death.

The quasi psychoanalytic approach suspecting a split-personality in the universe, one representing the Good – (Ormazd) – and the other the Evil – (Ahriman) – belongs to a later, more sophisticated era of 'specialists' – so typical for the administration of a vast empire, like the Persian, to subdivide and delegate authority over districts and specific competences.

DEATH HAS NO IMAGE

Hesiod, in his effort to bring order in the "Chaos of the Invisible" was cataloguing several personifications of abstractions. Between them Thanatos as the demon of Death, who, interestingly enough, does not appear later in any myth or cult and left no image in art. This seems all the more remarkable as Death must have been at any time a most dramatic event, but had again, as in other lands, achieved no 'personality.'

The reason for this phenomenon seems to be that in the haze of pre-history there was but a vague brewing amalgamation of demonic forces, suspected to inhabit all of nature, but only later some of them advanced to the rank and image of divinities.

The criterion of that 'promotion' to the status of the divine seems to have been the possibility to visualize some of them on human terms, in human-like form and character. But in a defensive impulse and an instinctive fear, as it seems, humanity had shied away at all times from infusing this specter of Death with the breath of an autonome personality, to Golem-like stalk the living. Therefore an image of Death as such, was never created. – Otherwise it can be said that it was art, literary or visual, which lifted the image of other totems out of the realm of demonology to specific personalities and to Olympian majesty.

This was the glorious destiny of some, but many of the vague and powerful specters of earliest times were never promoted to gods and remained in their premordial infancy outside the pantheon of light, as, for instance, the Gorgons and Harpies, the Erinyes and many more. Others, like Sphynxes and Centaurs, were re-infused in later times with new and sometimes foreign mythical powers.

Their destiny was like that of the rain-drops on a window: sometimes the most powerful remain where they are, while others, maybe quite secondary and obscure droplets, fuse with other drops and develop to swift streams overtaking all the others and gaining spectacular prominence. This same fusion with other divinities and foreign meanings we can observe in mythology, so that we often see visions of tremendous importance, like Death, left far behind, while some little figures fuse with other streams of thought to be re-infused by their vitality and magic. In this sense it may be the fact that nothing fuses with Death that made him remain arrested in his initial place, the realm of the Invisible . . . with allegiance to none and as the enemy of all.

ARIADNE
(an intermediate symbol-figure)

32

Another figure symbolizing the idea of resurrection was Ariadne which created the vogue or tradition of the many and magnificent 'Ariadne Sarcophagi.' Ariadne was abandoned by her beloved Theseus at Naxos, where she fell exhaustedly asleep, but in some versions she even dies, representing thereby the loss of the sweet things of life blending over into the stupor of death, according to the Greco-Roman assumptions.

However, and here comes the Eastern wellspring of thoughts: She is reawakened to a new life of sensual pleasures by Dionysos and his ever lusty entourage of Fauni and Satyrs to a love-oriented next world.

33

Although the saga illustrates the Orientalized adventure of a female after death – (and the 'Ariadne Sarcophagi' were possibly used as resting-places for women) – the main action on those sarcophagi shows the alter-ego of man in his wonderful surprise to find a female, (Ariadne) after death – and there is left no doubt that this slumbering apparition is meant to be his, as he is guided by Amorettes and genii of love, and pulled by Dionsian Fauni and Priapic spirits towards her, while those genii of pleasures lift the shrouds from her body to expose to him the seductiveness of her figure – to which he reacts at times in an unmistakable manner.

GRAPES AS SYMBOLS OF RESURRECTION

Many funeral chambers of Egypt were decorated with images of grapes and wines.

In the tomb of Sennefer in Thebes, for instance, the whole interior is covered with painted grapes and wines, coming out of one single stem and root behind the image of Osiris, the god of Death and Resurrection. As wine was associated with the idea of joyousness, this symbolism seems to hint at a revival from Death to Joy.

Supporting this notion would be the fact that Hathor, symbol of youth-eternal, love and joy was the patroness of wine, so that it is probable that we deal here with the idea of Resurrection from Death (represented by Osiris) – towards youth, love and pleasures, (Hathor) – which is the Indo-Asiatic vision of Afterlife.

To this it has to be said that Osiris, although resurrected after gruesome adventures, remained still the more tragic aspect of death, – while Hathor, replacing him later, as the image of youth-eternal and pleasures in the form of a Female in the Beyond, was obviously an effect of Asiatic influences, because neither Egypt nor her neighbors thought of a joyous condition after death, except the Asiatics.

The question remains: How did those Asiatic thoughts get into Egypt? The parable goes: "If a snake eats a rabbit, the result is a Snake-plus-Rabbit" – but who was the snake and who was the rabbit? The answer is: First the Asiatics invaded Egypt, and then Egypt swallowed a good piece of Asia, so that a mutual infusion of ideas was taking place.

Said tomb of Sennefer in Thebes was made at the time of Amenhotep II (1450 to 1425 B.C.) who tried to defend the Asiatic Empire which his father Tutmosis (Tuthmosis) III had conquered, by sending wave upon wave of Egyptian soldiers and administrative personnel to infiltrate the Asiatic provinces and to fraternize with the local population. We therefore see at that time an overlapping and intermixture of Asiatic-Egyptian influences which infused many aspects with Asiatic ideas, also concerning the visions of Afterlife, which could account for the shift towards the new protectress of the dead in the person of Hathor.

But we must also go back to the invasion of Egypt by the Asiatic Hyksos who dominated Egypt during the 18th to the 16th century B.C. – to see that there was ample occasion, during those years, for Egypt to absorb Asiatic ideas.

More than that, there was at that time even a transmission from INDIA, via the so-called "Indo-Iranian Unity" which was established around the same time, and can be traced due to identical divinities as well as the famous "Cinvat" Bridge, leading to Paradise, which are appearing in the Indian Rigveda as well as in the Iranian Avesta. The names of the divinities Mitra, Varuna, Indra and the two Nasatyas, for instance, who appear in the Rigveda, reappear in a treaty between the Hittite King and the prince of the Hurrian Kingdom in Mesopotamia, to show that confluency on an intellectual-mythological level – connected too, by the character of those divinities to the ideas of Afterlife.

There is no agreement amongst the experts concerning the exact time of the "Indo-Iranian Unity" and the intrusion of the Asiatics into Egypt, but there is agreement by all, that both events occurred approximately at the same time, or that the "Indo-Iranian Unity" shortly preceded the establishment of the regime by the Hyksos.

The highly spiritual Mithraic visions of Persia are outside that stream and are of a later date.

Now coming back to the question of wine and Afterlife, it seems interesting that wine had, next to Hathor, another patron-saint, in the person of SETH, the god of storm and battle. Characteristically, the HYKSOS worshipped only Seth as their protector, and actually claimed the region of their invasion as the "Territory of Seth," consecrated to be his vinyard, so that we could say, in a sort of symbol-shorthand, the wine invaded the Mediterranean from Asia. This is supported by the story that Dionysos, the god of wine, came from the Asian lands. The actual story goes that Dionysos came from India to the Mediterranean, but, as we know from the representations on sarcophagi, Dionysos became the symbol-figure for the IDEA of joy in Afterlife, and is shown as such, with a train of his votaries, who are the believers in that idea, invading, that is: victoriously converting the Western lands to the Indo-Oriental doctrines of a happy Thereafter. As mentioned before: the fact that Dionysos is shown as a miniature on sarcophagi, means to show that we deal here not with the person of Dionysos, but with an IDEA which guides that train of converts, shown as frolicking Fauni and Maenads . . . into which the souls of the dead are transformed after arriving in the blessed spheres of the Above.

We now have two leads, connecting the Wine with the Thereafter:

One via HATHOR, patroness of wine, and patroness at the same time of the souls in the Thereafter, being the image and symbol of the promise of youth-eternal and joy in excelsis – (replacing the somber Osiris).

The other via SETH, also patron of the wine, but in the image of the Asiatic invaders, the Hyksos, bringing the wine to Egypt (as shown there in the grave-chambers) symbolically indicating the atmosphere of the Indo-Oriental Thereafter through the allegiance to Seth, the wine-god – (as counterpart of Dionysos) – bringing with him the Eastern doctrine of the re-birth to a sweet Beyond.

In both cases the symbols – (Hathor and Seth) – are hinting at the acceptance in Egypt of the Eastern vision of the Thereafter . . . and both of them utilizing Wine as its visual medium, to express this totally novel and foreign complex of ideas. Wine was the common denominator, while Hathor expressed FELICITY, it was Seth who was the "determinative" for ASIATIC – together, in the usual way of hieroglyphic expression: ASIATIC FELICITY was painted as a promise in grave chambers of Egypt, as the new environment awaiting the soul.

Because not the Egyptian, but the Greco-Roman funeral monuments are our main concern, we repeat in short the reasons why we see on Italian-made sarcophagi so many scenes depicting grapes:

The older tradition, to show the train of Dionysos on sarcophagi, symbolizing the idea of the joyous Thereafter invading the Mediterranean lands believing in the dreary Below, became so naughty that it seemed no longer compatible with the later more moralizing sentiments – (under Augustus). Therefore, the figure of Dionysos was more and more replaced by grapes, either in a heraldic-ornamental manner, or manipulated, in a more naturalistic style by some earthly harvesters, or gay Putti who were now replacing the Dionysian revellers.

The notion that the grapes represent the body of the deceased, which has to be crushed to re-emerge as wine, in the sense of "Spirit" – can not be supported by evidences in funeral art, and might be a backward-projection of a later Christian symbol-chain where wine, replacing the drink of Soma, symbolized the sacrament of immortality. The way in which the grapes are treated on those earlier sarcophagi, would clearly exclude the notion that they represent the bodies of the deceased – in the manner in which they are gayly crushed and eaten – this gayety, however, can well be traced, step by step, to the images of the old Dionysian train, where many figures are shown eating grapes or squeezing them directly into their mouths.

34

THE CARINTHIAN STELA

The vines and grapes at times fill, as a decoration, whole funeral-chambers, ["Tomb of the Axe"] so that it may be that the dead was thought to be now physically in the realm and abode of Dionysos, equivalent to the sphere of happiness. This type of decoration, however, is late and Roman, which suggests the vague possibility that the vines and grapes were symbolic for "entering a new land" – because whenever the Romans entered a new land the first thing they did, was to plant wine there. This possibility

35

seems less far-fetched when we see on a Roman funeral monument in Carinthia not only the Oriental dance-girl, promised in the next world, but also a young boy – (the soul?) – as "wanders-man," traditionally shown with a bundle on a stick over his shoulder, so depicted on secular reliefs as "Wander-Bursche" seeking his luck in another land . . . very similar to the little American boy shown on folksy pictures, who is leaving home. On this Roman grave-stone in Carinthia it might also be significant that this soul-as-a-boy is wandering towards that Oriental dance-girl and that he brings with him a little basket with fruit and flowers, most probably as a present for the celestial damsel, to win her favors – as explained in the chapter "The Gifts of the Dead." This little figure may therefore permit us to see that there was a tie-in with the Roman soldiers wandering into a foreign land, as the monument was, no doubt, set on the grave of one of the many Roman legionaries.

There were, however, like subterranean rivers, vague associations of Dionysos with Egyptian divinities related to death and the blessed Beyond. Especially in the time of Alexander the Great arose a growing trend to show divinities with the attributes of several others, to create a sophisticated atmosphere of "free thinkers" so typical for the Alexandrian time of great embracement of all people, to create an all-including religious commune. But in spite of that new infusion of death-symbolism into the figure of Dionysos, he remained that subordinate vision on sarcophagi.

THE MINIATURIZED DIONYSOS

This chain of shifts in the visual arts may have gone through its historic development, independently from the ideological stratum, in which Dionysos became the symbol-figure for the joyful Thereafter, because he was said to have come from India to the Mediterranean – (meaning really that the Doctrine had come from India to the Mediterranean).

In this allegory, or religious ideal-symbolism the train of Dionysos was then identified with the train of Votaries which followed the teaching of the Sweet Beyond, from the East through the many lands, like a "Crusade" of actual people, (embraced by some, and by some resented as noisy demonstrators for "Free Love") . . . but then idealized as the 'Train of Dionysos' . . . Dionysos being their 'ideal-symbol' – (not a real person) – expressed in visual arts as his being in the 'background' of their thoughts, shown on the reliefs as the 'second plane' – or being miniaturized as the symbol of an idea . . . as it was customary to show abstractions and ideas as miniature-figures.

We thereby see that the original Indian free-for-all lovebouts in the next world were made acceptable by their projection onto the Dionysian tradition, which became an image of carefree merrymaking like a carnival pageantry.

What really happened was a mixup and amalgamation between the native Dionysos, the old and bearded god of wine, who was round-bellied and who had his own seasonal festivals, – with a figure of a very different stature and meaning: the sensual ephebean image of a young man with a mysterious Asiatic smile, coming, as the legend says, from India, as the missionary of sweet embraces in extraterrestrial spheres after death.

Based on those intertwining notions, – Mediterranean enough to be acceptable, mysteriously half-transparent enough to puzzle the imagination, and sensuous enough to please the eye – a rash of stereotyped Dionysian sarcophagi developed, which are now the most numerous of all such monuments.

PILGRIMAGES AND SANCTUARIES

In earliest times, when man was imploring the Invisible Mights, who were mostly Daimons, he was seeking the company of his fellow-man, maybe in fear of being alone while being faced with those awesome specters, maybe because his invocations and petitions seemed more powerful and urgent when supported by the many.

Out of this tendency developed the communal prayer, the temples to shield them, and finally the "state-religions" where the mass of the people invoked the gods to protect the masses, the land and their communal endeavors.

Yet there remained a longing for a personal religious experience which could not be derived from public cults, a reaching out of the single creature for divine blessings. The compromise between those two tendencies was the pilgrimages of men to great sanctuaries. Those sanctuaries then replaced the god-images by their sacrality, and the arduous voyages, the 'reaching-out' of man. The union with the divine was there symbolized by initiatory procedures which gave the individual the solemn feeling of having been admitted to celestial graces which would strengthen and purify his existence. It was the function of the big sanctuaries and the so-called Mysteries to stage the magic rebirth of the Soul and thereby the new allegiance of the individual to the Invisible spheres of the Above.

TEFNUT AND ELEUSIS

ACTUALIZATION OF ADMITTANCE

Some contemporaries thought that the Mysteries of the Orphics were kept so secret because of the indecency of their rituals which, in fact, culminated mostly in the physical union of the Novice with the representatives of the divine spheres. Symbolically or otherwise, the priestess, as a gate-figure, received the Novice – to symbolize and solemnize the fact that he has given his Soul-Substance to her and was admitted and consequently reborn by her into the elevated confraternity of the Neophetes.

This mode of expression is, however, a hint at the great antiquity of the ceremony, when the semen was believed to be the "Soul-Substance." This belief was not only very old, but also astonishingly widespread over regions and cultures which were not necessarily connected with each other, including the Javanese of Indonesia, the Bengals, the Babylonians and the Egyptians. The Egyptian texts are most eloquent and clearly readable to us and are of attested antiquity. There we see Isis as traditionally shown in resuscitating in this manner the "Soul-Substance" of Osiris, painted as a beautiful physical actuality while those illustrations are paralleled by explanatory texts, leaving no doubt as to the procedure.

Also in most solemn religious papyri, pronounced in the face of death and addressing the supreme divinities – [Papyrus of Ani, PT.SI second Arit, line 3] the Soul-Substance is spelled out hieroglyphically in the picture of seminal fluid emitted from the phallus with the devout reference to the sanctified Ani himself and addressed as: "Hail, Eater of Shades!" – offering his soul in this most explicit manner.

SOUL-SUBSTANCE

This method of giving one's soul by means of the "Soul-Substance" is especially remarkable, as the Egyptians had a very strong ideal of purity and chastity. We find in their texts expressions like: "purify myself of passions, the excreta in the heart" . . . or, in the Negative Confessions: ". . . I have not fornicated in holy places . . ." and the perpetually reoccurring epithet "the Pure." On sarcophagi it is written: "Save me! Keep me beside you, for my breath is pure, my heart is pure, my hands are pure . . . I appear before you after full purification, embalmed, pomaded with magic oils to favor the unfolding." — But despite all earthly ideals of chastity, the exchange of seminal fluid within religious presentations was devoutly glorified as a sacral act, because of its significance as the solemn giving of the soul, by means of the "Soul-Substance."

This may be similar to the kiss of a priest to a sacerdotal object, a book, a band, a ring, in contrast to a kiss of carnal union. The Kiss, by the way, was evaluated less as an opening of one body towards another body, than the confluency of the own life, symbolized by the breath, with the other person's life. Similar in its non-carnal character also to the ceremonial kiss of Knightship in the "Legion of Honor" ritual, which symbolizes the acceptance into the confraternity of the elevated.

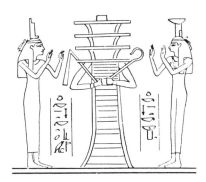

The Soul-Substance of Osiris was a spiritual matter, represented on his monumental posts, the djed-pillars, where he is shown with the horns, the symbol of the sensual Ram-god Amun on his head and the two Uraeuses, symbols, as the inscription says, of "the vital fluid in the spine, the serpents of fire to rewarm the heat of Isis." — Of this union, as we know, Horus was born, representing the earth, which elevates the act of the soul-infusion to a divine sphere of cosmic significance.

In the "Pyramid Text" [632.1635] Isis prays to Osiris: "Thy sister Isis draws near Thee, joyous of Thy love, place her that thy xemet enter her . . ." Xemet is the Soul-Substance written in the hieroglyph of sperm issuing from the phallus. The same hieroglyph with different "determinants" also means "emission of soul."

It becomes thereby evident that it was fully accepted as a valid symbolism to give one's Soul-Substance, that is one's Soul, to the divine spheres, represented by the high priestess of that realm, and by her receiving the soul in this manner. With the gesture of love in conjugal embrace the acceptance of the soul into those spheres was actualized and sealed.

DOCUMENTATION OF REBIRTH THROUGH TEFNUT

Attached to the act of soul-giving was the idea and promise of birth-giving, as its consequence. The female recipient of the soul-substance was thought to be impregnated in this way – (in a highly spiritual speculation) – and to be able to re-issue the soul by its re-birth through her into the celestial spheres of eternity.

On an exalted level it is Isis who receives the soul-substance from the dead Osiris, to give birth to Horus. On the secular level it is Tefnut who receives the soul-substance of the mortals, to re-issue them in the Above. This system of Re-birth becomes obvious by the following fragments of death prayers:

> "Osiris. I rise towards you. my purification done. I have
> entered the goddess and the goddess has taken me, I am
> now son of the priestess, priest of this realm. The Knot is
> unloosened. Oh, powerful Osiris! I am just born! Look at
> me, I am just born!"

> ". . . given to the realm, taken by the realm, re-born by the
> realm, purified on the day of birth, first day of true life
> eternal, of millions of years."

It can be assumed that "Goddess" and "Priestess" are synonymous, as the priestess represents the goddess, and that the "Goddess-Priestess" then represents the entire "Realm" of eternity.

The expression "Son of the Priestess" seems to suggest that the soul was first conceived and as a result of that conception then re-born anew through the priestess to the realm, after the soul has entered her – in the form of the Soul-Substance.

In the statement "I am now Priest of the Realm" – the expression "Priest" means by definition, to be a consecrated member of a spiritual community, in this case – of the Beati in the Above.

"Given to the Realm" makes reference to his soul, spelled as Soul-Substance, which he has given to the priestess representing the Above.

"Taken by the Realm" means that the realm of Eternity, represented by the priestess, has received his soul in this manner.

"Reborn by the Realm" suggests that after the priestess has conceived from him, he was reborn by her.

"Purified on the Day of Birth" indicates the purification his soul has experienced by this highly religious birth-procedure . . . whereby he re-appears as his own son, otherwise called his "Alter-Ego."

Fragments of Inscriptions:

> "Isis, sister, wife of Osiris, reviving in adoration djed, otherwise called dad pillar, the spinal column of Osiris with the magic fluid of potency, vital fire of which Osiris inseminates, impregnates"

> "Isis, sister-beloved worshipping djed, the spinal column of Osiris, source of Fire of Life supporting crux ansata of life and vigor, heat for Isis, sister-beloved (partner) of impregnation"

> "Tefnut, Mother of Souls who Conceiveth each Dead in Osiris" (Osiris means here 'realm of the dead' or 'realm of the Blessed') "The Soul will become Emission issued from Tefnut"

> [Translation: A. Champdor, Anhai and Hunefer Papyri.]

This last inscription is entirely self-explanatory and needs no further comment.

THE GATE-FIGURE

The goddess in question here is Tefnut, as mentioned in other parts of those papyri, and the priestess seems to be representing Tefnut, and in this sense to be identical with her as the recipient of the soul, and re-issuing the soul as her "son" and thereby making him a priest-consecrated to the "Temple" or realm of eternity.

The personality of Tefnut thereby becomes of interest and we find the following: Tefnut is not a person but a conception of the heavens. She and her brother Shu hold up the sky and slip between the lovers Earth (Geb) and Sky (Nut). Tefnut is therefore something between heaven and earth, not a liaison, but rather that which separates the earthly from the heavenly, the mortal from the immortal, which makes her signification to be the "Gate-Figure" in the passage of the soul to eternity . . . so that one could almost say that the dead has to pass "through" her to be re-issued into the realm of eternity.

Tefnut is also identified with the re-emerging of the sun, rising in the morning over the horizon, expressed as "freeing the sun from the grip of the earth" . . . and in this sense a symbolic allusion to the soul's rising from the earth and ascending to the Above.

It is interesting that this "Gate-Figure" Tefnut is a female and the possibility suggests itself that it had to be a female, to first technically receive the Soul-Substance and then to give birth, ideologically, to the new soul in the celestial realms.

It is possible that in greatest antiquity a woman stand-in received the soul-substance as we have it in the most primitive rituals, and that this female was later given the rank and significance of a priestess and still later the title of a representative of a goddess who is the Gate-Figure between earth and heaven, or death and eternal life. In a still later epoch her standing was further elevated by declaring that the goddess herself took the guise of her own priestess. In this chain of events we see the promotion of the originally random female to receive the soul, elevated successively to the prestige of the divinity.

The Indian counterparts to those female "Gate-Figures" were the heavenly Apsarases, who received the souls of the Blessed in physical union. They are, however, not priestesses representing divinities, but they are semi-divinities as such, daughters of Indra, princesses of heaven and lovers-extraordinary in one. The difference from the Egyptian vision seems to be the much simpler and more physical approach of India and insofar the more compact idea as it tells exactly what the souls do after they entered the Beyond – while the Egyptian theory falters from the moment on, when the soul is finally admitted to the realm of eternity – or, to be more exact, the theories split and fizzle in several directions which can not be reconciled with each other. It is an open question whether or not the Egyptian vision influenced the Indian vision, or vice-versa. A possibility for such an exchange would have been the "Indo-Iranian-Unity" which is a time when Egypt's eschatology was long established; however, as the more primitive-physical versions of an idea are mostly older than the complex intellectualized abstractions, the Indian version would rank as older. But if we assume no connection between the two similar theories it would just indicate the fact that the Indian people were more physically minded, while the Egyptians were more sophisticated – as shown in their elaborate science of astronomy, in contrast to the Märchen-type conceptions the Indians had concerning the heavens.

The possibility finally exists that two almost identical ideas sprang up in different lands without mutual influences, and without any connection . . .

It was only a very small segment or late period of the Egyptian eschatology which envisioned a happy celestial Thereafter, which is mentioned here only for reasons of comparison with the Indian and Greco-Roman conceptions. The existence of Egypt's dead in their tombs was mostly thought to be more than dreary, so that one may suspect those euphoric visions of Afterlife to be a consequence of Eastern influences.

The Egyptians generally believed in a sub-existence of the dead in the grave that should be nourished by food. To ease the burden of the relatives in feeding the specter, the food was painted on the walls to become actualized by invocation. But over the centuries the tombs were more and more neglected, so that the dead resorted to emploring – (by inscriptions) – passers-by to revitalize the painted victualia for the dead's consumption, and later begged in humiliating persuasion that in the interval of many days just a bit of water might be poured out for them instead of food. In still later times, abandoning all hope and trust in their own families, the dead implored miserably of passers-by to just pronounce his name, to give the lonesome sadness of his spectral being some moments of shadowy presence.

The ideas regarding the Egyptian dead went through many different phases, which were so intertwined and overlapping that no clear ideological development can be plotted. The reason for it might be that the various great religious centers of old Egypt were fiercely competing with each-other, praising their particular brand of doctrines and divinities, – (sometimes pirating from each-other a divinity which became more popular than their own) – and had not the slightest interest in the unification of doctrines, which left us, as we look back on all the variations now, with a maze of contradictions and confusions. A "successful" divinity of one temple-district was quickly amalgamated with a less popular or powerful of the other, which resulted in double-names and hyphenated triple-names and overlapping competences and visual representations, the snatching of Syrian and other high-divinities to show them as supporting too the locally accredited gods.

THE GIFT-WRAPPED GODS

Adding to the general mixup was the custom of sending to an ailing king divinities from other lands to help him. They came "gift-wrapped" from other monarchs dispatched in forced marches through terrible deserts in which many of the accompanying priests perished. Arriving at the sick king, those foreign divinities were destroyed – (that is: pulverized, mixed with excrement and burned) – in case they did not help, . . . but when the king recovered upon their presence, they were installed with all honors in the local sanctuary, but under another name and with another ritual, concocted by the local clergy, so that we have the desperate situation of the same divinity, appearing throughout the lands, under completely different names and rituals and competences.

THE SOUL OF THE DEAD AND THE SOUL OF THE LIVING

If we understand Apotheosis as the transference from the earthly status into a spiritual sphere, we also have to think of Tefnut, the gate-figure of Egypt, who receives the Soul-Substance of the dead to give, so impregnated by him, birth to his Alter-Ego, as his own offspring, but transferred thereby into the celestial realm.

Related to that process seem to have been the diverse Mysteries where, however, the soul of the still living initiate was thought to die to the profane world a "voluntary death" (voluntariae mortis) to have his soul mystically re-born (natale sacrum) within him during his lifetime, as well as into a blessed future after death.

The mental technology in both cases is so similar that we may speculate that its idea was transplanted from the older Egyptian thoughts to the mystery-cults which sprang up in the Eastern Mediterranean.

The difference between the two happenings seems to be, that the Tefnut-procedure took place between the soul and the divinity in the purely imaginary spheres of the Above – while the "sacred marriage" at Eleusis was performed here on earth, – symbolically or otherwise – between a living initiate and the earthly priestess of the divinity – (Demeter).

On the outer reaches of the idea of the apotheosis we could think of the Temple Girls of India, who too, represented a figure of the celestial pantheon, to elevate the devotee to their status, within a "sacred marriage" – (however, only on a temporary basis).

THE SACRED MARRIAGE

The rebirth through Tefnut is almost gynecologically simple and well documented. The thought behind the physical union with the priestess at Eleusis is not explained, as all ceremonies of those Mysteries were for centuries shrouded in greatest secrecy and are still a puzzle. However, as Demeter was representing the earth, we could suppose that the idea was that the body unites with the earth, or enters earth when dying, to be re-born by her into a spiritual sphere, after death.

The amazing similarity between the role of the priestess in both cases, and the reference to "re-birth" of the soul into a blessed eternity may provide for the first time a most valuable key to decode the few fragments we have, regarding the elusive Mysteries of Eleusis. Accepting a basic parallelism between Tefnut and the Eleusian Demeter as "Gate-Figures" between earth and the re-birth into a spiritual existence, all the mysterious hints we have about Eleusis would easily fall into place and suddenly make sense if we understand them as a variant of the pattern set by Tefnut.

Hippolytus (and a very few who were initiated at Eleusis, but later turned away from the "pagan ways") reported that at the high point in the Eleusian procedure the Hierophant – (the male high-priest) – announced:

> "SHE WHO IS MAGNIFICENT
> HAS GIVEN BIRTH TO A
> SACRED CHILD, BRIMO,
> HAS ENGENDERED BRIMOS"

If we assume that the mysterious BRIMO is meant to be the new-born Soul, we see the exact parallel not only in Tefnut but also as being illustrated on the "Sea-Sarcophagi" where the new-born soul appears as a CHILD.

The expression: the SACRED child is paralleled in the Tefnut texts, where the new-born is said to be "now a PRIEST of the realm" which means that he is now a member of a fraternity or congregation of the sanctified – equating "Priest" with "sacred" to mean in both cases the purified and elevated ones.

". . . has ENGENDERED Brimos" meaning: that the priestess has begotten, procreated and cause to exist Brimo, the Soul-Child . . . which falls again into the idea and process suggested in the Tefnut-texts where Tefnut is thought to get impregnated with the soul-substance and thereupon gives birth to the spiritual child. However, the plural used in this last sentence seems to hint that she went through that act many times before, which may indicate that she has proven to be the right person to do it, as past experience shows – or to say: "You have come to the great expert to perform that miracle."

"She who is MAGNIFICENT . . ." could mean: the 'real' divinity, as the earthly priestess seems to conceive, while being the epiphany or earthly guise of the goddess. NOT to call the name (Tefnut or Demeter) of an exalted divinity was a very usual sign of great respect – like in "Adonoi" (our god) for Jehovah especially in Semitic lands, or "The Lord" in Christian usage.

As to the three intertwining ideas of 'Death,' (in the case of Tefnut) – 'Initiation,' (in the case of Eleusis) – and 'Sacred Marriage,' (in the case of the priestesses) it may be significant that in Greek "marriage" was called TELOS which is "consecration" and that the initiation-rituals had a marked similarity with death-rituals (to die to the profane world to become a member of an exalted community). It seems that we have here the three elements united to one single complex out of which sprang the vision of Tefnut and the ideas of Eleusis. The fact that we have very eloquent Tefnut-texts may therefore shed most valuable lights on the Mysteries at Eleusis, which for centuries escaped any understanding.

THE ENACTMENT

As to the much disputed question of how realistic those "sacred marriages" were performed, it would seem that the Tefnut-procedure was purely a fiction or imagination insofar as it was thought that she received the soul-substance from the dead, because the person to be elevated was dead at the time of such an actual transfer. But this fact seems to have never disturbed the Egyptian thinking because we have many illustrations and papyri indicating that a divinity gets pregnant by a mummy – for instance no lesser divinity than Isis is shown re-animating the phallus of her dead brother-husband Osiris – which is specifically called "re-animating the spinal fluid" – meaning: the "soul-substance" – (as depicted in the Papyrus of Ani) – so that we can think that to conceive from the soul-substance of the dead may have been an accepted religious fantasy. However, an earthly priestess of Tefnut must have existed because great trouble is taken to repeatedly explain that the priestess actually is Tefnut in her earthly guise. Whether she had a living counterpart representing the dead, is an open question. A certain text about a bald-headed priest, impersonating the dead husband, makes such a hint – which might be a blasphemous joke – (however rather rare in Egypt).

At Eleusis, on the other hand, the initiates were, no doubt, living beings and the priestess of Demeter was an actual person too, but the "sacred marriage" and the giving of the soul may have been acted-out by symbols which were ceremoniously united. We have a rather vague hint [Clement of Alexandria, Proterpticus II.21] that something was given into a box and then taken out of the box. According to another text the box was symbolic of the female, the lap (of Demeter---?) and that a grain was produced out of that box – (which may have been symbolic for the birth of "Brimo," the esoteric alter-ego of the initiated?) Because Demeter was a "Grain-Goddess," grain was logically her child, and thereby symbolic for the new-born soul-child of hers, – this in similarity to the so-called "Corn-Osiris" out of whose body corn was shown as sprouting. We see here again how easily and logically all enigmatic hints we have would conform to the pattern and idea of Tefnut.

The same text also says: "I took out of the chest (box), having done the act I put again into the basket, and from the basket again into the chest" – this is the most explicit text we have concerning the procedure!! Although the word "act" is associated today often with sexual matters, at the time of the writer it was not necessarily understood in this sense, however the meaning of the word "act" remains open to speculation.

In other texts, so often re-copied that its origin can not be traced, it is said that a model of the female "Lap" – (of Demeter?) – was one of the cult-objects found in the temple consecrated to Demeter.

If we would suppose that this holy unmentionable "Something" would be the symbol-object for the Priestess-goddess of Demeter, this ceremony would easily conform to the description we have, but also to the ideology of the Tefnut-Demeter procedure, as a symbol-pantomime . . . and would also explain the reluctant expression of the "Act" as well as the rumored accusation of said "cult-object" and the aura of indecency surrounding the Mysteries in the eyes of the outsiders.

While we may tentatively try to understand the meaning of the symbolism in general, the giving of the "Self" to the Gate-Figure of the above, we fail to see what the priestess is doing while the ceremony is in progress, to justify the description of a "sacred marriage" or otherwise more guardedly called a "close relation in which the initiated were brought with the priestess – which made for happiness in the next world," – which would rather point to a more or less realistic procedure, sometimes called "impure rites" and sometimes regarded as unjust accusations.

The re-birth, the "natale sacrum" as Apuleius calls it, of the consecrated is obviously an exalted religious fiction, which was thought to take place in excelsis, so that an actual staging of this event would never have been attempted here on earth, in a realistic temple-procedure.

Based on the similarity with other rituals and their performances, we may finally assume that in the great sanctuaries the symbolisms were acted out on a high spiritual level, while in smaller temples, which had to compete with the popularity of the famous places "to make a living" – rather burlesque versions of the same ideas were offered – the smaller they were, the more daring their performances 'to attract customers' to sort of 'side-shows.' We have clear evidences of such competitions between famous and wealthy shrines and poor but fiercely ambitious temples in Egypt and the sanctuaries in Asia-Minor, written by contemporaries.

The same as in show-business star-performers are a powerful magnet, so were great divinities from foreign lands high in demand for the success of a religious enterprise. The image of Demeter was to various degrees blended-over into the great and locally accredited goddess Anahita, also representing the Earth, the grain, and the abundance springing from nature, and was shown, Demeter-like, with grain as her attribute, but also fondling animals to incite them to procreation, but basically she was the protectress of the harvest and the land, so that whole districts proudly called themselves "Lands of Anahit" – the golden mother of corn. In her temples, she also "took into her" devotees to promise them a magnificent Thereafter, in Mysteries which were performed in a great many of her sanctuaries. From their description we have the impression that they too varied greatly in the realism of the performances. So do we have in descriptions from early Christian writers, who eagerly found faults with pagan sanctuaries, no hint as to "impure rites" connected with the cults of Demeter-Anahit in Armenia. The same opinion we have from Agathangelos, another early Christian.

However, Strabo, the great geographer [63 B.C. to 25 A.D.], writes that her great sanctuary at Erez (Erech) in Akilisene was a center of obscene forms of worship and swarmed with Hierodules of both sexes. There too the daughters of noble families acted as priestesses in giving themselves for money to strangers with the promise of a sweet thereafter. Strabo also remarks that those priestesses were, after their considerable time of temple-services, nevertheless eagerly sought in marriage. Faustus of Byzantium, as late as the fifth century A.D., writes that outwardly Christianized Armenians continued – "in secret the worship of the old deities in the form of fornication" – . Even medieval authors call the same conditions "the shame of Sidonians" and describe similar rituals in the many smaller sanctuaries of the Chaldeans, Syrians, and Mesopotamians. We therefore can assume that not only the fight for survival and competition with the great Mysteries forced the smaller sanctuaries to offer more and more realistic 'sacred marriages' and hierogamies with their priestesses, but that this form of naturalism also increased with the more Easterly geographic locations of the lands, to culminate in the Indian temple-practice where the intercourse with the semidivines was considered no longer a promise of beatitude after death, but rather as a terrestrial sample of the bliss in paradise. Or, more exactly, the pattern shows that the Indo-Asiatic practices, infiltrating the Mediterranean, assumed on their way to the West a more and more spiritual and symbolizing tinge, as the very roots of the Eleusian Mysteries are not of Greek origin and can be traced to very early Asiatic patterns and visions.

From the "Homeric Hymn" we may learn that the Eleusian cult existed already in the seventh century B.C. but it may be of interest to our study that the "Secret Cults" and "Mysteries" came from the East to Greece mainly around 600 B.C. when the power and influences of the Etruscans were strongest. The ritual in those secret shrines were called "Orgia" the later meaning of this word – (really derived from "ergon" = the work) – is a hint that the outsiders thought those cults to include the sensual participation of their votaries.

The fact that the secret of the Mysteries were kept so well can be explained in the following manner:

In contrast to the great official State-ceremonies, invoking publicly the blessing of the commune and the land and keeping the divinities satisfied by sacrifices on their terms – the Mysteries were dealing with the elevation of the individual and the salvation of its soul from death eternal. About the idea of this personal salvation "out of the myriads" of ordinary mortals, we can read in a fragment of the "Liturgy of Mithra":

> "Today, having been born again by thee, out
> of so many myriads, I have been rendered
> immortal . . ."

As this special status was conferred upon him on terms set by the Mysteries, part of those terms being the Secrecy, the individual would, of course, not wreck the foundation of the structure upon which his special status was built, and wipe out his personal advantage by breaking those terms. Besides: the sharing of the secrets would serve no purpose, because the "mantle of protection" put around his soul would never include those who are not initiated, even if the procedure would be known to them.

PLAYS FOR AUDIENCES

Also the procedures of the Mystery-pantomimes, often accompanied by choral singing, were as such not new, because in earliest primitive temple-presentations appeared already miraculized in so-called "sacred plays" in glorification, the creation, birth and nuptials of divinities ad abstractum. Those enactments appeared only then as wanton, after the Epos presented the gods as totally human, "all too human" beings, in the Homeric tradition – (which was resented by many as anti-religious and disgraceful). But pursuing that "modernism of 700 B.C.," this new-found irreverent naturalism came hard to the borders of the seemly, and over-stepped, at times, those borders, to become a lubricious and orgiastic farce or burlesque to the amusement of the public. However, the temples competed for their audiences which were their material support and did not mind being spoken of. On the borders of Greek culture there were barbarians and semi-nomads, but also inside Hellas were slaves and loose folks who heard about such sensational performances and the charlatan-priests and imposters of any kind, who shamelessly exploited that trend. – In the words of Lucian, [Alex. 37.38:]

"In peasant-shoes
reeking of garlic,
came they to watch
the scoundrel-priest
at the end of the ceremony,
he himself as Endymion
in concubitus with a Selene."

Reflecting now back at the "Sacred Marriage" and the "Enactment" it seems that in those semi-literate times the people wanted to "see" mythology instead of reading about it, so that a strange twilight-mixture of theatricalized religious mythology arose, as a divine puppetry, to keep those audiences spellbound.

Not always was there the burlesque type of performance, in the sense of a derisive persiflage of mythological stories and visions, but there was a lot of religious showmanship involved to attract the interest of the rural population.

Here follows a description based on Lucian [Lucius, 53ff.] and Apulieus [Metamorphoses, VIII 24ff.]. The descriptions of those authors has been confirmed by an inscription recently discovered at Kefr-Hauar in Syria, which says that a servant (female) "sent by her mistress, the goddess of Syria, has brought back seven sacks of coins to the sanctuary." The coins were collected by giving her person to the more affluent of the spectators. There is another memorial inscription which says that the mother of a certain "servant of the goddess" had dedicated her life as the daughters did, to collecting coins for the sanctuary of the divinity. [Fossey, Bull. Hell. XXI, 1897, P. 6a.]

"Led by an old eunuch of dubious habits, a crowd of painted young men marched along the highways with an ass that bore an elaborately adorned image of the goddess. Whenever they passed through a village or by some rich villa, they went through their sacred exercises. To the shrill accompaniment of their Syrian flutes they turned round and round, and with their heads thrown back fluttered about and gave vent to hoarse clamors until vertigo seized them and insensibility was complete. They then flagellated themselves wildly, struck themselves with swords and shed their blood in front of a rustic crowd which pressed closely about them, and finally they took up a profitable collection from the wondering spectators. They received jars of milk and wine, cheeses, flour, bronze coins of small denominations and even some silver pieces, all of which disappeared in the folds of their capacious robes. If opportunity presented they knew how to increase their profits by means of clever thefts or by making commonplace predictions for a moderate consideration."

EGYPT

THE ASIATIC INFLUX INTO EGYPT

THE "INDO-IRANIAN UNITY" AND THE HYKSOS

It seems probable that the "Indo-Iranian Unity" and the appearance of the Hyksos in Egypt are connected.

The so-called "Indo-Iranian Unity" may have come about by the presence of the great masses of Asiatic people migrating towards the Mediterranean, via the Middle-East along the old route of Iran, Sumer, Akkad, Syria and Mesopotamia. The "spearhead" of that same movement, formed by the more aggressive elements, may have penetrated further ahead into Egypt, there to become the Hyksos – "the Foreign Princes," – (or "Chieftains of Foreign Lands").

A hint at such a development would be the fact that both events took place at the same time (ca. 1650 B.C.), and that the Hyksos – coming from the Middle-East – occupied at first the Eastern side of the Nile-Delta. Also, that after 100 years, when the power of the Hyksos was broken, no diplomatic correspondence was found anymore to attest to the importance of those Indo-Asiatic tribes in the Middle-Eastern lands. The rise and fall of the Hyksos seem therefore parallel in time and politically interwoven with the "Indo-Iranian Unity." For our purposes, the main interest in this connection would be the fact that the Hyksos were linked via Iran to India and could have imported notions of the female-oriented Thereafter into Egypt – one of its manifestations being the switch from Osiris to Hathor, which was not a gradual shift, but an obviously foreign doctrine superimposed in its completeness over the Osiris-oriented eschatology of Egypt and replacing the regency of Osiris over the Thereafter in favor of a female.

The Background:

Signs of the "Indo-Iranian Unity" appear from 1800 B.C. on and seem to disappear after 1600 B.C. and are marked by documents using divinities as witnesses to treaties who are prominent in the Indian Rigveda as well as in the Iranian Avesta – (Mitra, Varuna Indra and the two Nasatyas).

Our main interest here is the possibility of an influx of ideas from India into Egypt, by means of the mass of Asiatic peoples, reaching back to India and flowing via their Iranian connection into Egypt. That we deal here with Asiatics is attested by the "Ka-mose stela" discovered at Karnak in 1954, dealing with the expulsion of those invaders which are persistently called the "Asiatics" and very definitely are the Hyksos.

Concerning the transfer from India via the "Indo-Iranian-Unity" to Egypt, we have to go by "circumstantial evidence." The circumstances in this case are the invasions from Asia, reaching back to India – and the evidences are the changes being thereupon noticeable in Egypt's eschatological visions.

As to the invasion of the Asiatics into Egypt and their expulsion, we have between others the following document:

Excerpts from the letter-stela of Kamose to the Hyksos ruler Apophis:

"Your back has been seen, O wretch! I am victorious! My army is after you! Your country is mine. So your wish has failed, wicked and miserable Asiatic! I will drink of the wine of your vineyards, the Asiatics which I captured from you will press it for me. I did not leave a thing in your dwelling, the town of Avaris now it is empty, the Asiatics have vanished. Miserable Asiatic, wicked of heart who had been saying: 'I am the lord without peer as far as Hermopolis and the House of Hat-Hor.' I shall burn their cities, make into red mounds them forever, because of the damage they had done in this part of Egypt, they who gave themselves over to serving the Asiatics, when they invaded Egypt, and had abandoned Egypt, their mistress . . ."

As to the connection of the Asiatic Hyksos reaching back to India – (via the Indo-Iranian Unity) – we have some linguistic as well as archeological evidences, for instance concerning the horse.

Linguistic:

A remarkable number of Iranian words and expressions dealing with horses are actually Indian, showing the influx of Asia, reaching back to India, so that the transmission of other ideas, including eschatological visions, seems probable. – For instance, the Turn or Lap in horseracing in India called "Wartana" reappears in the Hittite "Vart" – or the Indian word for "Horse-groom" being "asva-sama" reappears in the Hittite "assusanni" designating the same profession . . . etc., while on the mythological level we have the Indian "Mithra" corresponding to the Iranian "Mithra" and the Indian "Soma" equal to the Iranian "Haoma" . . . etc. which shows that not only the horse was swept in from the Indo-Asiatic sphere, but also spiritual material, reaching back to India, was part of the big Asiatic wave transporting the Hyksos into Egypt. However, around 1600 B.C. the Egyptian word for "Horses" was "Susim" and for "Chariot" was "Merkabot" which were taken from Egypt's eastern Semitic-speaking neighbors, hinting that the Egyptians were not on speaking-terms with the invaders.

But as linguistic is here not our main concern, we rather revert to archeological evidences.

Archeology:

From South-West Russia reaching into Egypt proper, we find horses in many graves, indicating that this animal was probably introduced into Egypt from the East around 1600 B.C. – that is, during the reign of the Hyksos, and it is claimed that it was due to the fast moving Asiatics on horses and horse-drawn chariots that they succeed in overrunning Egypt. – The horse-drawn Asiatic chariots with spoked wheels, were found in Egyptian graves, dating exactly from the invasion of the Hyksos, and were still considered to be a great curiosity in Egyptian lands. However, later, from the time of Tuthmosis on – (about 1530 B.C.) – a special unit called the "chariotry" fought in all the royal battles. The chariot of the Pharaoh was regarded as a deified object with hymns dedicated to it, while the horses participated to some extent in its exalted aura. The royal pairs of horses had grandiose names, like "Victories at Thebes" or "May Mut be satisfied" – which served Ramses (Ramesses) at Quadesh. Still later, in the New Kingdom, herds of horses were raised at the edge of the Delta, especially at Pithom, partly being presents from Asiatic Kings, together with the warrior-goddess Astarte, brought to Egypt from Canaan as "Mistress of the Mares."

We find the most interesting documentations inscribed on the walls and corridors of the chambers in the Pyramid tombs of Unas, a king of the V th Dynasty, and of Teta, a king of the VI th Dynasty, the sum of those inscriptions being called the "Pyramid Texts."

The "Pyramid Texts" date from around 2600 B.C. before the Indo-Iranian episode and rather at the time when Indo-Asiatic tribes invaded Persia under the Hittite-King Hattusilis, so that it is assumed that we deal in the "Pyramid Texts" with an earlier inflow of Eastern ideas, probably of a time between 3000 and 2500 B.C. when Susa and the Dynasty of Ur – (Sumer) – became prosperous and powerful and when Egypt imported all its timber from those districts (now called Lebanon) . . . together, as it seems, with some ideologies of Afterlife, especially dealing with the ascent to the Above, which was then a new and revolutionary conception.

> "There is strife in heaven, the primordial gods
> see a new thing arise, the dead King.
> The Ennead of Horus is dazzled,
> the Lords of Forms are in terror of him.
> He (the King) seizeth the sky,
> he cleaveth its metal,
> He setteth alive in the West,
> The dwellers of the Nether-World
> follow him, as he raiseth
> renewed in the East.
>
> [Pyramid Text: Utterance 257]

"He cleaveth its metal" makes reference to the Egyptian idea that the firmament is a plate of metal, above which the heavens are located. Generally it is assumed that the Blessed climb on top of this plate of metal by means of a ladder, but to "cleave" the metal is a special, most extraordinary feat of power and violence.

That he "setteth alive in the West" means to say that he reaches the world of the West – (that is the realm of the dead) – alive! More than this, he seems thereby to start a revolution of the dead in the Nether-World, who follow him to the East – (which is the realm of Resurrection) . . . derived from the fact that the sun rises in the East.

81

The same exalted mood of violence, bordering on the horrendous, is expressed in the canibalistic visions of the Unas-Text, lines 512 to 514.

[512.] "Unas eateth their magical powers, and he swalloweth their Spirit-souls; the great ones among them serve for his meal at daybreak, the lesser serve for his meal at eventide, and the least among them serve for his meal in the night. [513.] The old gods and the old goddesses become fuel for his furnace. The mighty ones in heaven light the fire under the caldrons where are heaped up the thighs of the firstborn; and he that maketh those who live [514.] in heaven to go about for Unas lighteth the fire under the caldrons with the thighs of their women; he goeth about the two Heavens in their entirety, and he goeth round about the two banks of the Celestial Nile. Unas is the Great Power, the Power of Powers."

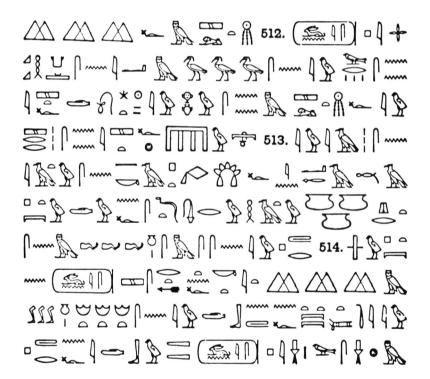

The notion that by eating another being its spiritual powers are absorbed, appears among primitive peoples in many forms and was practiced by some wild races and savage tribes still around the time of Muhammad.

THE PHARAOH BECOMES THE LOVER OF HATHOR

HAY-TAU was originally an Asiatic divinity, slightly akin to Attis, in representing the re-sprouting of the vegetation, and in this sense, symbolic for the resurrection, the eternal vigor of life. He entered the Mediterranean sphere via the Assyro-Babylonians. Due to the general drift from Asia to Egypt and the resulting amalgamation of divinities, HAY-TAU came by the way of Byblos to Egypt and was now written there with the Hieroglyph of "Bull-Husband" – (great lover) – as epithet, and was given as such to Hathor as "cult-partner" or paramour . . . (as all Asiatic divinities had a female love-partner) . . . called in the Middle-East a "Ba-alat," as the female form of a Baal "The puissant" written with the phallic signet of potency, as another sub-title of Hay-Tau.

In the new partnership of HAY-TAU with Hathor, the original spouse or Ba-alat of HAY-TAU must have felt left out or jealous, therefore we see from now on – (on cylinder-seals) – "The Lady of Byblos" – (the official title of the Ba-alat) – assuming the Horns and Sundisk of Hathor as her own crown. It actually was, of course, the priestship of "The Lady of Byblos" who did not want to be deprived of their divinity and the contributions of her devotees, and therefore made their abandoned "Lady of Byblos" slip into the personality of the now reigning Hathor.

The main constellation in Egypt was now HAY-TAU as symbol of resurrection, but also of potency and lust, connected as lover or husband to the sensual Hathor, the image of eternal youth and joy in the Thereafter.

Consequently we see princes of the Mid-East calling themselves (on stelae and seals) "Beloved by Hathor" or "Lover of Hathor" as shown in the hieroglyph of mutual fusion or conjugal union.

On another relief, the "Lady of Byblos" crowned with the insignia of Hathor, is depicted as embracing the Pharaoh himself – while the Uraeus-snake on her crown is shown as touching mouth-to-mouth the sanctified Uraeus on the Pharaoh's forehead in a kiss of stunning intimacy hinting at a bodily union or mutual life-giving.

We finally find in the "Pyramid Texts" the wish of the Pharaoh – (three times repeated for emphasis) – that he may re-appear in the next world NOT in the features of Osiris, but in the person of HAY-TAU, the lover of Hathor.

The implication being that the Pharaoh – (and probably other mortals too) – wished at that time, not to be absorbed anymore by the tragic Death-God of old, – and also that they were not content with the (admittedly vague) "divine protection" of Hathor – but that they wanted instead,

37

according to the Asiatic pattern, the divine Hathor as actual LOVE-PARTNER, while they themselves should re-appear as HAY-TAU, her divine paramour, – her Baal under the sign of the "Bull of Power & Passion."

The physical union is clearly implied in the hieroglyphic expression of the Soul-Substance emitted in the signet of "delight."

There it has to be said that the "Pyramid Texts" are of an earlier date than the invasion of the Hyksos and even earlier than the great rise of the Osiris cult – and that they contain numerous references to Hathor, who was, however, considered an Underworld deity, as "Queen of the West" – the "land of the dead" . . . and only on another level of understanding, and divested from the odium of death, she remained the goddess of joy and love in the Above . . . in which capacity she only later joined those elevated to the heavens, at first as a majestic figure, changing later to the image of compassion, still later blending over to a comforting attitude, to finally become the embraceable "Female in the Beyond" of the Eastern visions.

SETH AND THE ASIATIC INVASION

The images of the divinity SETH resemble an Afghan dog, the wild and ferocious animal which accompanied the Asiatic invaders. Plutarch saw in Seth the personification of evil. In Egyptian mythology he developed out of a storm-god and stood now for violence and destruction and was said to have killed Osiris (representing the old order) and as being the enemy of Horus (representing life on earth). The Hyksos, identifying Seth with their own divinity Ba-al, were considered by Egyptians to be cruel Barbarians, demolishing temples, plundering and burning villages. "For what cause I know not, a blast of the gods has smote us" – are the words which begin the Egyptian account of the Asiatic invaders overrunning their land.

As soon as the Hyksos were expelled by Amosis, [XVIII Dyn. 1567 B.C.] the image of Seth was degraded and hymns were praising the defeat of Seth by Osiris and Horus and celebrated the fact that Seth was castrated by Horus – (his power was taken away) – and that he was flayed and finally burned at the stake.

> "throwing excrement in his face,
> Horus carried off the testicles of Seth
> doing this with his fingers (3) himself"
> [Papyrus Ani, P. 36 Line 68]

His statues and great reliefs were mutilated and destroyed (sometimes altered to represent other divinities).

But some fear-inducing glory remained attached to the powerful image of the divinity as such – (similar perhaps to Napoleon even after his defeat) – so that the Kings Sety I and Sety II were proud to assume his name, about 200 years after the expulsion of the Hyksos and the downfall of Seth. His image shifted towards the symbol of "Victory in battle" – "The Powerful" – "The Invincible" so that we have from that period images of Seth as "Defenders" standing in the prow of the bargue of Re and killing the evil monster Apopis. The kings of that later Dynasty were called "The Great Seth of Battle" as an epithet.

THE QUEEN AND HAY-TAU

As soon as HAY-TAU was firmly established in the Beyond, now eclipsing Osiris and having Hathor as his spouse, a very strange thing happened to a dead female: She is shown to be guided by Hathor into the next world . . . and we wonder what might be her situation and destiny there.

Does she become a concubine of HAY-TAU, the former Asiatic Baal, who is now the Lord over the Egyptian Afterlife and the lover of Hathor? The status of the concubine would have its parallel in the Ram-god Amun – (also a symbol of reproductive powers) – who was surrounded by numerous females with the official title of "Concubines of Amun" – being the priestesses in his sanctuary here on earth and ready to please him with caresses or otherwise.

As the wife of the Pharaoh was generally considered to be his sister, and the Pharaoh assumes the form of HAY-TAU, it would appear that the dead queen is then sisterly united with her husband – (A): either in competition with Hathor, as one of his concubines, – or (B): actually assuming the personality of Hathor, as the beloved of the Pharaoh, who is now reappearing as HAY-TAU "The Puissant."

(A):   The idea of the dead queen becoming the concubine of the Pharaoh in the next world would have – (besides the "Concubines of Amun") – another parallel, as the Pharaoh in his earthly life had, next to his sisterly spouse, also a harem of concubines.

Officially and for the dynastic records, the Pharaoh was married to his sister. However, we have a relief – ["Collars Stela" XIXth Dynasty, Louvre] – showing the Pharaoh as giving to his "CHIEF OF THE ROYAL HAREM" the grand collar of gold "for his good and loyal services rendered." This meant that the Pharaoh had, next to his dynastic wife, also other females for his pleasures, and maybe deeper affections . . . which makes the situation thinkable that he, as a "divinity" in the Beyond, had his wife as well as Hathor as his beloveds.

As the Pharaoh states that he, as HAY-TAU, wants to be the husband of Hathor, it would make the queen his concubine, which may not mean a demotion of the queen because, according to earthly life, the concubines may receive the deeper affections, while the official spouses – in this case Hathor – are only for the record and to propagate the royal line. But for the sake of prestige, he liked to be seen in public as the beloved of a divinity. Therefore the divinized Pharaohs had to be shown on monuments hand in hand with high divinities, and on inscriptions to be called their "Beloved" . . . just as citizens of today like to be photographed while shaking hands with a high dignitary.

(B):   The other possibility seems to be that the dead queen actually slips into the personality-appearance of Hathor and thereby becomes the beloved of her husband – now being HAY-TAU.

We have, in fact, a tomb-painting where the Pharaoh is shown to be welcomed in the next world by a figure which bears the features of his queen and those of Hathor at the same time. – [Tomb of Ramses (Ramesses) III of the XXth Dynasty, in the "Valley of the Queens" at Thebes] – that is several hundred years after Egypt was exposed to the Asiatic influence by the Hyksos.

There a female figure is greeting the Pharaoh who is now shown without the crowns of earthly regentship, but with the grand collar and royal tunic and the white sandals of the wandering soul, and on his forehead the Uraeus of protection, scaring away his enemies, who are now the specters of the deep.

The surprising head-gear of the female, however, consists of the "Vulture-Cap" normally worn by the queen, but surmounted by the two horns framing the Sundisk, worn by Hathor. This rare combination of the two emblems seems thereby to merge Hathor and the queen into one and the same person. That female then clasps with one hand the hand of the Pharaoh while her other hand is lifted in the salute of welcome, which is responded to by the Pharaoh with the same gesture.

As in older days the Pharaoh reappeared in the features of the subterranean Osiris, it seems that now the queen may reappear in the features of the heavenly Hathor, the new protectress and beloved in the Above, to be re-united as such, with her husband.

In conclusion it can be said that in the Egyptian heaven there were in fact females – but they were not the type of the Indian Apsarases or the Oriental

"Hur al-uyun" the pleasure-girls of luxuriant sensuality, but rather spiritual apparitions, similar to the very numerous female divinities populating the Greco-Roman Above.

It therefore seems that a dead woman could not look forward to personal enjoyments in the Indo-Oriental fashion: "having intercourse with whomsoever she pleaseth . . ." [Mahabaharata VI.7]. There are, however, hints that lovemaking in heaven is not totally excluded. In the "Pyramid Texts" of the Kings Unas and Teta, (also spelled Tety) at Sakkara, [line 268], it is said that King Unas (his celestial double) became the husband in physical union with a goddess Mauit (also spelled Mut or Mouet) . . . and that another goddess united with King Teta and had conceived from him. These remarks may shed a light on the possible relation of HAY-TAU to Hathor . . . especially because King Unas was visualized in his Apotheosis, to be of tremendous and divine powers, like HAY-TAU.

Sample of the text:

> "The sky poureth down rain, the stars tremble,
> the bowbearers run about with hasty steps
> the bones of Aker tremble
> and those who are ministrants to them
> betake themselves to flight
> when they see UNAS rising in the heavens
> like a God . . . ."

According to those Pyramid Texts, it seems therefore that an apotheosed king could have a physical union with a goddess which was later denoted by clasping her hand; however, no such freedom was accorded to the spiritual double of the queen . . . except, maybe, if she appears in the guise of Hathor, who received the dead in some manner.

Concerning the question of the dead queen sharing her husband as a concubine with Hathor, and maybe with other females, we have another text from the pyramid of King Teta (sometimes spelled Tery) where he resembles HAY-TAU in being called the "fecundator" and his name is written, identical with HAY-TAU, with the epithet of the Bull of power and passion. This personality is then projected onto the dead king in heaven where his alter-ego is pictured as resembling an Asiatic Baal, or Lord over a harem and he is described as:

> "Lord of heaven and all the beings therein
> and as such Lord of all the females therein"

written again as their "fecundator" in phallic hieroglyphs three times.

THE CHANGES IN THE ABOVE

In Egypt's funeral texts we have the most confusing contradictions concerning females in the next world. When taken together, as one complex, the inscriptions are so divergent that it becomes impossible to reconstruct a system according to which earthly females are admitted in heaven – so that the best experts gave up on that question in puzzlement and dismay.

The solution of that riddle seems to be that we deal here with several different versions, separated from each other by time, and representing a chronological development, which even shows a very definite pattern and direction:

In the older and original Egyptian version there were female divinities permanently stationed in heaven, similar, as we said, to the Greco-Roman pantheon, and no earthly women were elevated to the Above – (an exception was the wife of the Pharaoh, already of semi-divine status on earth, and deified like him, who joined as such the "Brethren of the Gods" in glorious reception).

The later texts were, as it seems, the results of Eastern visions of a sensuous paradise which infiltrated the Mediterranean and thereby also Egypt. According to those Oriental-Asiatic concepts which pictured a female element in the next world, the Beyond of Egypt shifted gradually towards some amorous relations between the male and female divinities and souls in heaven. It is significant for the direction of this development that we see a drift from the originally divine population of the Above to the admission of mortals of less exalted status.

Historically we see three significant steps in this development towards the Eastern visions:

1.) The sombre and male Death-God Osiris is eclipsed by Hathor, divinity of love and joy.

2.) The Pharaoh wishes to reappear in the next world in the image of an ASIATIC lovemaking divinity – (Hay-Tau) – to become the love partner of Hathor.

3.) Ordinary men wish for lovemaking in the next world, a wish which is apparently granted by the custodians of the official faith, the priests, who wrote the "Books of the Dead" in which lovemaking in the next world is stated as one of the legitimate wishes of the deceased and its fulfillment is promised.

ENIGMAS OF THE PYRAMID TEXTS

In the "Pyramid Texts" of King Unas there are two very perplexing lines: I.181, which, so far, have eluded our understanding. They say that King Unas, in the process of his apotheosis, made love to a goddess, as well as to a girl who offered him the bread.

Because we deal here with a rather majestic inscription displayed in a formal and elaborate sepulchre describing the proper elevation and sanctification ritual of a glorious personage on the threshold to Eternity, it cannot be assumed that this reference is made to a frivolous or unseemly act of the Pharaoh.

This statement is so short that it seems to make reference to a well known procedure or an appropriate ritual, known to all at the time, despite the fact that it seems most extraordinary to us today to make such a suggestion regarding any dead person, let alone the sanctified monarch.

We can, however, understand that the eminent scholars of the Victorian Age – (Wallis Budge of the British Museum, etc.) – who made the transliteration of the hieroglyphic inscriptions, found it not proper to make any guesses as to that seemingly scandalous matter, or even to speculate on such things, so that we stand now before a blank and a puzzling enigma.

Although there are more modern transliterations, the archaic wording of Budge is said to ring more truly Egyptian in character.

PYRAMID TEXT, LINE ONE
(The Heavenly Embraces)

In those early times of the Pyramid Texts of the 5th to the 6th Dynasty (around 2600 B.C.) the hieroglyphs changed from the "visual" or pictographic expression to the "phonetic" system based on the sound of syllables or letters, and it is therefore that some of the more hidden double-meanings – (connecting Mauit with the Soul-Substance) – were clarified only later.

The actual inscription says:

UNAS UNITED (phallic sign) WITH THE GODDESS
MAUIT, AND ALSO UNITED (phallic sign) WITH THE
YOUNG FEMALE WHO BROUGHT (offered) TO HIM THE
BREAD

Unás, l. 181.

This text, as it stands, is a great mystery, but with the connection of two names, all would easily fall into place and would make those lines conform to a well established ceremonial thought and system, known to us from several later texts, and would even find its parallel in some other cultures.

THE TEFNUT-MAUIT AMALGAM

If we assume that the goddess MAUIT had at that time the function of Tefnut as the "Gate Figure" between heaven and earth, and if we remember that it was standard procedure to give to that "Gate Figure" the "Soul-Substance" upon entering the next world, to be re-born by her into the spheres of eternity – (see chapters "Soul-Substance" and "Tefnut and Eleusis") – the first statement (line ONE) would be at variance with the normal procedure only insofar as MAUIT is named instead of TEFNUT which could be explained by the fact that we deal here with a very early period where procedures and personalities were not yet exactly standardized as to the divinities involved who were invoked almost at random and intermixed with local favorites of temporary prominence, and also because we deal here with the personality of a great King – instead of an ordinary mortal – which warrants special treatment. If we would compare the position of Tefnut to St. Peter, as "Gate Figure" to the heavens, as far as ordinary mortals are concerned, we could likewise imagine that to receive an a priori holy figure, a great divinity of heaven would be dispatched to welcome this exalted person.

The identity of Tefnut with Mauit is especially reasonable because both of those celestial females stood for "Moisture" or "Liquid" – which could be understood in the meteorological sense as Dew or Rain, but also as the "Soul-Liquids" which included the Tears of emotion, the Sweat of fear, but above all the seminal fluid, believed to be the most direct emission of the soul, – which to receive seems to have been within the competence of both divinities of the "Moisture," Tefnut as well as Mauit.

According to latest research it even appears that Mauit is the ancient Egyptian word for "Semen" so that her symbol-identity with the function of Tefnut seems practically assured.

Besides Mauit, there were many of those "Gate-Figures" between Heaven and Earth which the soul has to pass, and whose almost endless lists of variable names are recited in the Book of the Dead. But as Mauit is especially mentioned in the oldest texts and Tefnut in later fragments, functionally in the same position, we may assume an evolutionary connection between both figures, which makes the appearance of Mauit and her relation to the soul of the Pharaoh less enigmatic.

It also shows in other texts that a king does not divest himself of his soul, like a garment or coat given to a checkroom girl upon entering a locale, and also that a king is not re-born by the gate-figure into heaven, because he keeps his "Royal Ka" in eternity, while he may, however, transmit the mortal or earthly part of his soul upon arriving in the upper spheres to a divinity in bodily uniting with her, a ceremony described in line ONE.

PARENTHESIS

Maybe it should be mentioned that what we call the "Soul" was believed in Egypt to consist of many aspects or elements of which the KA is the most indestructible aura, while the AKH is, as the inscription says ". . . just as the body belongs to earth, so does the AKH belong to heaven . . ." (the root of the word AKH means: "to shine") or what we may call the transcendental medium. The BA might be called the Alter-ego, capable of travelling around and taking action on its own, even taking possession of persons or gods or animals in whose physical shape the BA reappears. Finally there was the SHADOW as well as the NAME which all together belonged to the specific personality of a being. A transmutation from one aura or etherial soul-fluidum into another status is sometimes hinted at, so that a conversion of the semi-corporal BA into the sublime AKH seems possible in our present case, while the "Royal Ka" remains untouched throughout any such magic reappearances, floating, as we may imagine, like a halo over whatever stages the other-worldly manifestations of the King may traverse.

92

The formidable guardian-Figures and hostile specters of the Deep were later changed into "Reception-Figures," as soon as the Thereafter assumed a friendlier atmosphere and were made specifically female – possibly due to Eastern influences where females were said to receive the departed in love and bodily union, for which the malevolent specters could not qualify. Those friendly "Reception-Figures" seem to have invaded the Mediterranean thinking on a broad scale, especially seen in the Etruscan funeral art, showing genii gently cradling the dead person in their arms – (reminiscent of the soul re-born as an infant?) – but later changing into priapic Fauni guiding the Apollo-like alter-ego of the deceased, shown to be still protected by an earthly charm-amulet, into the new realm of sensual pleasures. (Ashurn Villa Giulia, sarcophagus of Naples etc.). As Apollo, the god, does not wear a charm amulet on a string around his neck, this identification of the dead person (who could not be left without the magic protection of amulets) with Apollo is very touching and significant.

All the female figures we see in funeral art of that earlier period of transition, never represent earthly females elevated to heaven, as the ideas concerning the possible apotheosis of men excluded equal rights for women. There were female figures in Egypt's heaven, but they were not earthly women elevated to heaven, but only goddesses, born as such by gods. But even those goddesses had no such possibilities as the male deified kings who could conjure up to them from earth any female they would desire, even "out of the arms of her husband." Such privileges were denied to apotheosed females after their earthly departure, concerning the conjuring up to them any earthly males of their liking, – (although there were some elegant women in Babylon etc. who had a male harem, so that the idea must have presented itself). Not even the born goddesses of Heaven could call up men from earth for their pleasures, as the merely deified Pharaoh could, but it seems that they had their compensations by the male souls, admitted to heaven, who ritually were to embrace them, as well as in their liaisons within the celestial clan of gods.

PYRAMID TEXT, LINE TWO
(The Acceptance of Offering)

The second statement (line TWO) easily makes reference to the ceremony of Reception and the gesture on the part of the Pharaoh to accept the offering of the symbols of welcome and hospitality – (this acting-out of the gesture was in later texts called the "Embracement" of Welcome) – But we must remember that a "young female" was included and part of the offering in oldest times, and connected to a whole chain of symbol-associations – so that accepting the bread only, would leave the "young female" unaccepted, which would amount to an unheard-of refusal of hospitality by ancient standards, where even the refusal of a lamb caused a political crisis – as being too inferior, while a girl was expected, who seems to have been the proper and usual gift of welcome, as we can learn from various old texts, between them the Hittite clay-tablets of the 14th and 13th centuries B.C. and documents of the biblical lands bordering on Egypt. This was done less for the amusement of the guest – (as we learn from speeches written for such occasions) – because the females represented the land, and the sovereign – (as such a guest was treated) – was thought to be the possessor of all the females of the realm, – the giving graciously of his vital force – hieroglyphically called "the Fluid of Potency" – to the representative of the land was considered to be a rather solemn gesture expected on the part of the arriving dignitary.

It would appear more logical – and this is an important argument – that the "pater familias" or the mother, representing the house, should offer the bread of welcome, which obviously would exclude the component of intercourse with the pater familias or his wife. The fact that the representatives of the house do not perform this ceremony – (even symbolically) – makes us believe that the girl is thought to be the specific 'soul-receiver' representing not the house but the realm, in our case the realm of Eternity. It therefore seems possible that on the secular level a desirable (young) female is sent to the threshold not mainly to be 'taken' by the guest as a present, but rather to entice the guest to 'give' himself to the new precinct, which is, on the spiritual level, as in our case, the Beyond and the celestial sphere of Eternity.

THE TRANSFER OF PRESTIGE

Our abstract notion of 'Prestige' was in archaic thinking expressed as 'Power' by the phallic "Bull or Husband" hieroglyph, as a physical allegory, and united as such with the girl. We notice that on the earthly level we do not deal with "Soul-giving" but rather with a transfer of 'Power' to the domain the guest is entering. During all that the girl plays the passive part like the land and soil to be fertilized and blessed, and by no means the role of Tefnut, the exalted figure by whose graces the arriving 'guest' is physically reborn into paradise, after she received him or his soul in bodily embrace.

BREAD AS THE SYMBOL OF THE BODY

The symbol-connection between giving the "Self" with giving the bread is hinted at in many instances of old and magical ceremonies, from the North African and Sicilian custom of baking bread in human forms, eaten then as fertility stimulants, to breads in the shape of the female sex which was broken open in a suggestive manner and offered to men, as a rather crude identification between body and bread, the very offer hinted at in the Unas text, – which was later more and more refined and was finally leading to the very sublimated religious Christian symbolism of body and bread in biblical times, at the "Last Supper" – up to the now barely recognizable hostia-allegory of our days.

It may be significant to note that the offering to a guest of a "young female" is amazingly widely practiced, including the Eskimos and Middle-African tribes – (as reported, for instance, by Sir Richard Burton who, at his welcome to an African realm he was entering, received a young female of noble birth, representing the precinct, to unite with her his being and presumably in a metaphysical sense, his soul.) A female, representing the land, to be physically united with a person appears in many ceremonies evoking the blessing of prosperity, is found in many ancient and primitive cultures, reaching from Central Africa to the Arctic and is even practiced in some jungle enclaves along the Amazon River – without any connection to Egypt's eschatology – which seems to give to that embracement-ceremony a very deep magico-spiritual importance, performed, to begin with, on the earthly level for the good and sound magical purposes of increasing the fecundity of the land. The ideological background seems in those cases to be the draining away of any malevolent spirits or demons in the newcomer, and to convert them through the act of communion – (as by a communal meal or pipe-smoking) – into the receiving the Soul or the infusion of the magic spirit, the vital forces and potential of the newcomer. Those widespread earthly considerations may have become so firmly established that a similar procedure was supposed to take place when the Soul appears as a 'newcomer' at the gates of heaven, which seems to be hinted at in the Pyramid Texts, to be later perfected to the esoteric transaction between the dead person and Tefnut, where the soul in the role of the newcomer gives over his being to that divinity. We also notice that the idea of fertilizing the realm has now changed into fertilizing the divinity of that realm, for the highly sophisticated purpose of the soul's own rebirth into Eternity.

THE HATHOR-TEFNUT AMALGAM

Hathor, the girl of joy, was frequently fused with Tefnut, the Gate-Figure to the heavens . . . this 'Hathor-Tefnut' figure was then called "Guardian of the Mountain of the Dead" – (Hathor of female pleasures, replacing the tragic death-god Osiris due to the Eastern doctrines of Afterlife which gradually invaded also the Egyptian eschatology) – Those "welcome-to-pleasure" symbol-figures of 'Hathor-Tefnut' were extraordinarily popular and widespread and were found in sometimes touchingly primitive sanctuaries in Thebes and Memphis, but, also in Byblos, the terrible copper mines of Sinai, where misery and death were daily companions of the slaves, and even at far-off Punt, deep down to the South-East of Egypt. She became a saviour-figure, a promise of sweetness after death.

The combination of Hathor with Tefnut clearly shows the Oriental hope for a sensual next world.

The Tefnut-component represents now the figure to make love to, upon entering the celestial spheres, as mentioned in the Unas text – in which, however, it is not said what happened AFTER the soul had passed the gate to the realm of the Blessed. – (The Pepi II texts make us in fact believe that the reward of heaven consists merely in being admitted to the divine company.)

The amalgamation of this "first stage" Tefnut, with the "second stage" Hathor, the divinity of eternal beauty and merriment, is used to characterize the joyful environment into which the soul is now entering, after it has passed the gate of heaven – or had been reborn into heaven by Tefnut or

MAUIT, her equivalent. We also have the deep involvement of Hathor in the rushes with the offering of bread, so that we can see in the "young female" as mentioned in the Unas text, a Hathor-equivalent of former times.

This Hathor-Tefnut amalgam actually brings together the two figures of the famous Unas text, mentioned there separately, hinting thereby at their distinct functions, which were later united to that most interesting "Hathor-Tefnut" fusion – to prove in retrospect their earliest relations. They were "in tandem" so to say, in time and name, before keeping the MAUIT-figure as the first encounter, while the pleasure-component comes later, inside of heaven, represented by the girl with the bread.

The "tandem"-situation results in:

> Mauit changing into Tefnut, the gate-figure,
> receiving the Soul,
>
> While the Girl with the Bread changes into Hathor,
> the image of Joy and Pleasures.

THE ANONYMOUS FEMALES IN HEAVEN

As to the question of women in Egypt's heaven, we read in the "Book of the Dead" [Chapter CX], given to the mummy of a prosperous man, however not belonging to the high aristocracy:

> "May I become a KHU (spirit) in SEKHET-HETEP
> (celestial paradise), may I drink therein, may I eat therein,
> may I make love therein, may I never be in the state of
> servitude therein, may my words be mighty therein . . ."

Then, as usual, the accomplished fact is projected ahead of events, so as to guide destiny by magic in the right direction:

> "O, UAKH (realm of the Blessed) I have entered into thee,
> I have eaten the bread, I have seen Osiris, my father, and
> I have gazed upon my mother, and I have made love." –
> (end of text)
> [Wallis Budge I.168, 169]

The fact that the man sees his mother in heaven would indicate that earthly females too seem to ascend to the realm of the Blessed.

That he made love, presupposes that some other females, besides his mother, must be there, but it is astonishing that his wife or wives are not mentioned in this connection. It is also interesting that in the Pyramid Text of King Unas homage is given to his mother, but no mention is made of his wives, who probably were his sister, half-sister and cousins, according to the custom of the time . . . We, however, remember that he is said to "carry off women from their husbands wheresoever he pleaseth, whensoever he pleaseth" [lines 628, 629]. All that may suggest an inflow of earthly women into heaven – or their spiritual doubles, who are enjoyed by the spirits of men.

This existence of consenting females in Egypt's heaven is new and surprising.

The prominence of lovemaking within the death-prayer may be a hint at the novelty of that paradisial feature.

We also notice the Oriental inequality in the treatment of men and women, which is expressed in the idea that men are provided in the Above with a multitude of nondescript females – (maybe of the Huri type?) – while, in reverse, no male companions of pleasure are ever mentioned to await earthly ladies in heaven.

All that would point to an Oriental-Asiatic inflow of ideas, probably dating from the reign of the Asiatic princes, the Hyksos, in Egypt and the direct inflow of Indian ideas facilitated by the "Indo-Iranian Unity." This infusion from India took place about 1000 years after the Unas and Teta texts, which conformed to a different vision in which all privileges were given to the apotheosed king and none to less exalted mortals, who could only beg the gods to grant them after death a semi-earthly existence by tending the fields, permitting them to eat and to have the benefit of cool breezes and water, while no females are mentioned, and no love, at those early times.

This lovemaking in the Thereafter, however, appears abruptly as a "foreign matter" or later overlay over the Egyptian concept because it is stated bluntly and disconnectedly as an annex to the usual text, without a hint as to the personality or partners involved with the deceased, – while in the Indo-Asiatic doctrines, of which that notion is derived, we have a tremendous build-up of those lovepartners encountered in heaven, in the persons of the Apsarases, daughters of the main-god Indra, and thereby no less than royal princesses of celestial rank, whose supernatural sensuality and beauty is extravagantly praised. Innumerable sculptures make the public well acquainted with their personifications, down to their costumes, hairdos, jewelry, smiles and gestures – while the replicas of those Eastern paramours of heaven remain nameless, anonymous, and without any visual manifestation in Egypt. It thereby becomes evident that we deal in Egypt only with a vague hearsay, coming from a region where those celestial beauties were thought to be an actuality.

Another reason why the Egyptian texts treat the lovemaking of mortals in heaven as "foreign matter" may be that in Egypt sexual intercourse by mortals was considered not compatible with religious matters, and as Herodotus reports, forbidden in temples, and mentioned repeatedly in the "Negative Confessions" as "not have I fornicated in holy places, my heart is clean, my soul is pure . . ." – all that in stark contrast to the temples of India and the Hierodules in the sanctuaries of the East. Sexual matters concerning divinities were, however, treated in the texts in the most explicit manner . . . see the Birth of Tefnut . . . etc.

The strongest hint at a transplant of that foreign idea remains the fact that the lovepartners in heaven appear nowhere in Egypt's mythology or iconography or texts, funeral or otherwise – while we have in the East, from where the idea of those celestial lovers came, rich and exuberant texts and visual presentations of those celestial brides, even down to their noble ancestry and their lofty and ribald psychological makeup.

Returning to the question of the mother:

As to the encounter with the mother and in view of the fact that lovemaking is done in the Beyond but no other female is mentioned there:

It could be speculated whether or not the lovemaking is related to the mother and if we deal here with the "Return of the Mother-complex," not only in the Freudian sense, but as the legitimate expression of a generative cycle closed: the return to where you came from, or to return the Soul-Substance to her who gave you your soul to begin with. To return the Soul-Substance in the transition from death to rebirth into Eternity is often mentioned, whereby Tefnut, the gate-figure on the threshold to heaven, plays the part of the Mother-Beloved, receiving the soul of the dead in loving embrace and giving birth to him in a motherly fashion into the realm of Eternity, whereby the dead calls himself the SON of his Mother-Beloved.

The magic drift towards the mother-figure may equate her with "Mother Nature," that is: Nature itself, or the "Pool of Nature" out of which all creation arose, and to which all creatures return.

We have in earliest times the great Amun in the "Pyramid Texts" at Thebes equated with the ithyphallic "Min of Coptos" as "Kamuthis" – "The Bull of his Mother" – as well as the relatively late documents of 1564 A.D., where Renato de Laudomière reports from his voyage to Florida, that the native Indian King Athore – ("a handsome, wise and honorable man") – was proud to have married his mother and joyfully showed to the explorers the children he had with her. – ("After he married his mother, his father ceased to live with her") . . . down to reports from our time, that some criminals at their execution and soldiers on the battlefield, in the face of death, or on the threshold to eternity exclaim "Mother!"

While to unite with the mother in a metaphysical sense, or otherwise, is not out of the question, it seems more probable that the Mother-figure which the apotheosed spirit sees in heaven, would rather belong to the type of the MANES or beatified ancestral figures, so well known in Mediterranean lands – and that the wish to make love and its fulfillment were stated by the clergy in the "Book of the Dead" as an abrupt and disconnected annex, without any relation to the foregoing, and without even vaguely understanding the scenario of those encounters which were so well known in the East, due to their re-enactment, daily performed by the Temple-Girls.

100

SUMMARY OF CHANGES

We may repeat in a short review the general development.

At first no mortal woman would enter, heaven, except the deified queen. No amorous encounters are mentioned as taking place in the Above.

The sombre death-god Osiris is eclipsed by Hathor, divinity of love and joy, as "protectress" of the dead, at first.

Next, the Pharaoh wishes to reappear in the Beyond as an Asiatic puissant love-god, to unite with Hathor as her lover.

Later is is said that the Pharaoh makes love to several other divinities in the Above, who are now his equal.

Then it is mentioned that the Pharaoh makes love to a mysterious girl with the bread, not identified until now, but a Non-Goddess.

To illustrate the sovereign power of the deified Pharaoh it is said that he can call up to him any earthly woman, even out of the arms of her husband. It seems that thereby the heavenly realm is for the first time open to earthly females, (although only by appointment).

Thereupon a mother-figure of a plain citizen appears in heaven, while to her son is granted the privilege too, of lovemaking in heaven, but it is not known who his partner is . . . so far it seems like a privilege ad abstractum, with no specific female in mind, as a sign that lovemaking in heaven, following the Eastern visions, is now accepted in Egypt as the legitimate wish of each mortal.

Although lovemaking has become a major concern in Egypt's heaven, the professional lovemakers, the Apsarases and Houries of the East, are missing. It is, however, implied that such creatures are in heaven, as the good citizen is permitted to make love there and as his partner seems not to be his legal spouse. It appears that Egypt's clergy shied away from the last step of Orientalizing their heaven, by permitting a swarm of "bad girls" to have their sway in the pure Above.

Finally it must be said that, while there is a definite sequence and clear direction in the changes of Egypt's heaven, it is not possible to establish dates of that development, because of the rather autonome temples of Egypt and their clergy who yielded at different places at different times and degrees to the Eastern influences. We also deal often with interwoven beliefs, where the most advanced views concerning lovemaking appears as a modernistic afterthought and appendix, while the main text is still clinging to Osiris, the most archaic ruler of the Beyond.

101

FEMALES IN THE BEYOND

While the Afterlife of men is fairly well described, the destiny of women of different lands in the next world was, as it seems, never traced in a single outline, and shall be the subject of the following study . . . The clues to those mysterious visions often had to be drawn from obscure hints in forgotten texts and strange details, to give us a composite picture of the other-worldly adventures awaiting the earthly ladies.

FEMALES IN THE EGYPTIAN BEYOND

We talk here about the earlier times in which the Pyramid Texts were written, while later, after the contact with the East, by means of the Hyksos, – (in the "Third Intermediate Period" ca. 1080 to 745 B.C.) – women had a status similar to men.

It seems that at those earlier dates and in continuation of the earthly rights of the victorious, where the King could choose for himself any female, also the apotheosed Pharaoh could elevate some females from the earth to become his concubines in the Above . . . according to the following inscription:

> "He carries off the women from their husbands
> to whatsoever place he pleaseth
> whensoever he pleaseth . . ."
> [Pyramid text Unas and Teta, line 629:]

The foregoing makes reference to the idea that an earthly woman may, after her death, be elevated to become the concubine in the celestial harem of a divinity of extraordinary male powers and passions. (HAY TAU or Unas or Teta, in the case of HAY TAU related to Attis and Adonis, the images of the eternal re-birth of youth and beauty.) This vision may therefore have been a great comfort for a lady departing from this world, to be

102

taken away and elevated by a divinity to the Above and there to be beatified – at least at times, as usual for a concubine in the hierarchy of a harem.

The idea of becoming a concubine had no degrading connotation. As shortly mentioned before, the concubines of the Ram-headed god Amun were earthly females thought to be the beloveds of a powerfully masculine divinity – to whom, according to archaic thinking, "all" women belonged – so that the actual concubines were the "specially chosen" out of the multitude of earthly females.

It may be significant that this cult of the "Concubines of Amun" was especially highly developed after the notion of Females in the celestial spheres was absorbed from the East.

To form an idea of the celestial vision of earthly women as concubines of a divinity – (which was, no doubt, patterned after the earthly lifestyle of the so chosen) – it may be mentioned that the earthly domain of Amun – (according to the "Inventory of Ramses III." ca. 1170 B.C.) – included in addition to tremendous treasures and tracts of land, 81.322 slaves and 421,362 heads of cattle . . . etc., so that we can assume that a replica in heaven of that luxurious earthly estate was imagined to be the new domain of the elevated female . . . and the same as the "Concubines of Amun" pleased him in his earthly sanctuary, it could be assumed that the females around the deified Pharaoh had the same pleasureable duties and occasional affectionate responses in an atmosphere of "Power & Passion" surrounding the magnificence of the celestial Pharaoh, so far removed from the daily chores of their earthly existence.

THE DIFFERENCE BETWEEN MALE AND FEMALE ELEVATION

It seems that in oldest times the apotheosis in the sense of a 'deification,' was reserved for the Pharaoh only, and was extended in a limited way to mortals of lesser rank, consisting in a mere 'elevation' of the deceased to the Above.

This form of "Elevation" was thought to be the destiny of the females too, after their earthly departure. There was no glorification of a female after death, no transformation into another being, but she seemed instead to remain somehow her self, and being welcomed as such in the heavenly spheres, without change of rank or outer appearance. Even a queen is shown to re-appear in the Above in her earthly features.

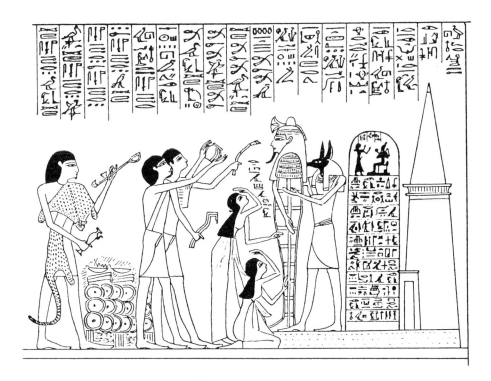

This in contrast to the fate of men, who – (at least according to some beliefs) – were actually re-born into the realm of the Blessed as "Sons" of a divinity – (Tefnut) – in a purified state, consecrated to the heavenly realm, or pictured as the classical Egyptian mummy with beard, sometimes shown with its soul escaping, or cared for by divinities or lamented in funeral rituals, while no dead female is ever seen in any of those situations.

The Egyptian females were recommended in death-prayers for the "Adoption" by female divinities of the Above, to be – (not by birth) – but only in title their children.

Another difference between the male and female elevation is that the divinity receiving a male in the Above is mostly Tefnut, while the protectress of the females is Hathor . . . and never Tefnut as the receiver of the Soul-Substance. Hathor, however, as the image of Love and Joy appears also as the protectress of men, which makes her the great Protection-Figure in general for the souls of males and females alike, be it in the Below of earlier times, or in the Above after the Asiatic influx.

THE PROTECTORATES OF HATHOR

The connotations concerning the male and female with the image of Hathor seem different, insofar as for the males she symbolizes in later times – (when "Love in the Above" became a fashionable speculation) – aspects related to lovemaking – while for the females she seems to have absorbed the more feminine aspects of Hathor, related to eternal beauty and happiness . . . and in the case of a queen a formalistic but smiling encounter with her, as a divinity of high rank.

Hathor is one of the divinities of Egypt known from the early part of the archaic, or late Predynastic period – (A most venerable image of her from this time is in the British Museum No. 32, 124). To begin with, she had many cosmic aspects, the one of the cow being the most persistent. The image of a Cow is difficult to reconcile with "Wine-drinking, Music and Dance" – and her connection to those mundane patterns is therefore bewildering and often questioned.

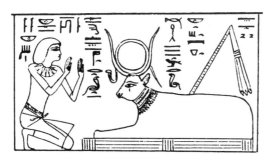

The answer seems to be that to begin with the Bull was the archaic image of 'Creative Power' or the 'Power of Creation' in a cosmogonic sense, and as in oldest times all male divinities had 'Cult-Partners,' the 'Cow' appeared as the most obvious female counterpart of the "Bull" – and it seems possible that out of that partnership with the Bull developed the image of "Hathor the Cow" as the "Supreme Female" with her patronates not only over the cosmogonic districts of Life and Death but also later, and being a female, over the female districts of beauty, dance, love, and music, the carmina of bewitchment – but also over the motherly aspects as a formidable image of protection, the most powerful instinct observed in the females of the animal world, protecting their young, applied then to the protection of the souls. – We see on many divinities or specters of Protection the wings, not to permit them to fly, but rather as a means or symbol of protection – for instance the Vulture-Cap of the queen, clasping her head, wings down, is not only protecting her, but making her the symbol-figure of protection.

105

Hathor was in oldest times an 'Underworld' divinity, but her domain shifted later to the Above, without giving any reason for that change, which must be regarded as 'foreign matter' in the general structure of Egypt's death-cult.

Several inscriptions beg that the soul of the dead should be admitted to Hathor instead of to Osiris.

"Through the eternal night between the stars
not to Osiris guide me but to gentle Hathor
divine princess of joy, to Feast of Hathor,
patroness of Love in the Fields of Satisfaction . ."

The "Fields of Satisfaction" also called "the Fields of Yslu" or "Fields of the Rushes" originated in the idea of a heavenly lake, vaguely similar to the Elysium, with the rushes sacred to Hathor, out of which she is shown to appear at sunset in an eerie manner – (sometimes seducing mortals by offering them wine and bread, as a sign of welcome – if the wanderer accepts, he is never seen again). While "Satisfaction" could be understood, because of its hieroglyphic expression, as being akin to amorous felicity – (Xemet, or Khemet, as the delight of the soul, or "the desire of the heart," but written with the phallic hieroglyph).

In some other versions the border of the desert is made synonymous with the 'Gates of the Nether World' and it is said that at times one can see a dead person welcomed there by Hathor – emerging from a tree and offering him bread and water – and if he eats and drinks from those symbols of reception he is considered a 'Friend of the Gods' and as being accepted in their sphere and will never return – (probably meaning that his ghost will not haunt the living).

Many of those often repeated stories, striking in people the cord of the "true" – as somehow, somewhere seen before but long forgotten, may have had originally an earthly provenience, to be elevated only later to a semi-divine happening, like this eerie story of "Hathor in the Rushes" – using as 'mythological raw material' the girls of pleasures on the outskirts of settlements, who offered their persons after sunset to the passer-by . . . out of which may have developed the vision of lustful Hathor, offering her body, symbolized by the bread, while the setting of the 'Evening' was foreboding the impending 'Death' of the person whose mistress she is to become in the other world. All that appears as an admirable intermixture of the local earthly scenario with the far-off Indo-Asiatic teachings of the Thereafter and its female embraces.

HATHOR AND THE FEMALES

As to the change in the role of Hathor from the 'Underworld' to the 'Above' and finally the idea of adoption of the dead female by Hathor as her 'daughter,' we have the following fragments:

"In earlier times (before 1400 B.C.) Hathor was called
'Queen of the West' – (west is the realm of the dead) – and
'Protectress of the Theban Necropolis.' She is also called
'Lady of the Below.'
(IN THE BELOW)

"She shall make thy legs to walk with ease in the
Underworld"
(STILL IN THE BELOW)

"Around 600 B.C. she is thought to elevate the souls from
the Below to the Above."
(THE ELEVATION)

"She (i.e. Hathor) shall make thy face perfect among the
Gods, she shall make thy thighs large among the
Goddesses"
(NOW IN THE ABOVE)

"Thou (i.e. the deceased female) O daughter of Hathor, art
made to triumph, thy head shall never be taken away from
thee, and thou shalt be made to rise up in peace"
(ADOPTION BY HATHOR)

"In the latest epoch – (after 300 B.C.) – a dead person was
no longer called "in Osiris" but "in Hathor."
(RESIDING WITH HATHOR)

"In the dynastic period the personality of the deceased was
merged in that of Osiris, just as during the Ptolemaic period
it was merged with Hathor."
(MELTING INTO HATHOR)

To sum up the situation it could be thought that in earlier times Hathor was the Protectress of all souls in general, and that she in later times represented rather the joy and love in the Beyond, the female element, the Beloved, so greatly desired by the male souls – while for the souls of the females, she remained in her archaic role, the stately and majestic mother-figure of Protection.

THE RE-APPEARANCE OF FEMALES

The main differences between the re-appearance of males and females seem to be that – (around 1350 B.C., the time of Tutankhamun, of which we have very ample funeral texts) – it was believed that the soul of a male re-appears in the next world as newly born, divested of its past form, created by the embracement of his departed soul with a divinity, normally Tefnut – but in the case of a Pharaoh, the "grand goddess of the KA-royal." This 'shadow' of the dead appears then in the eternal night as black – (meaning as NOT-person) – shown as a figurine painted black, but with the "Lock of Youth" – indicating that he is a child, which later appears in a mask of gold, being the body and skin of the gods, whose company he finally joins as their equal (to describe this most complicated conversion here in the shortest terms).

In contrast to it, there seems no re-birth or fundamental conversion of a female to take place after her earthly departure, judging from pictorial presentations, where the full-grown queen is shown to be welcomed by diverse divinities in the next world. The very meagre references we have in the pyramid texts of Teta and Unas would indicate too, that those kingly and now divine spirits take grownup (married) females up to their spheres, right out of the arms of their husbands – but it is stated also that "all the females" are theirs, as those divinities represent the male and fecundating element ad abstractum . . . sometimes said to be responsible for the fertilizing innundations of the Nile, at their command, "the Word of Power."

One of the most detailed descriptions we have of what happened to a non-royal female after her death is contained in "The Book of the Dead" given to Anhai, who was a priestess of Amun at Thebes during the XXth Dynasty.

But while this beautiful papyrus describes and illustrates abundantly her travels through the dark spaces before she is permitted to enter the realms of Eternity, it fails to tell us what happens to her as a woman, after she

109

reaches the heavenly spheres. We see her passage between the well-known semi-divine figures of the Inbetween. We see her plowing the heavenly fields as if imitating a man's occupation, because it is not the lifestyle of a Lady of rank to plow. A remarkable feature is – (never associated with an elevated male!) – that she is shown with a Sistrum in hand which is the insignia of Hathor, possibly hinting that she is now "adopted" by Hathor, – as sometimes expressed in funeral texts. Remarkable also is the fact that she does not appear – as men do – in the form of a mummy but in a white transparent dress, . . . and that we do not see her going through the procedure of the "Opening of the Mouth" which is equivalent to being able to speak "The Word of Power" in the Beyond, that is, to be in a commanding position, in contrast to serfdom.

The question has been raised why a woman is never shown in the Beyond as a mummy, but instead in light and half transparent gowns, open in front, and fragrant with flowers.

However, if we remember from the Pyramid-Texts, that the deified Pharaoh calls up to him from the earth any woman he pleases, we can assume that he wishes her not to appear before him as a tightly sealed mummy – (which he would have laboriously to unwrap, or as a soul-baby) – but instead in the most readily accessible and enticing form.

WHY WOMEN ARE NOT RE-BORN IN THE ABOVE

The reason for the fact that women are not re-born into the realm of eternity, might be purely technical: A male is thought to give his "Soul-Substance" in the form of his spermatic fluid to a female divinity (Tefnut), who thereupon gives birth to him in the heavenly spheres. We can see that this system becomes inoperative in the case of a woman, because a woman can NOT emit a spermatic fluid, and therefore Tefnut can NOT become pregnant by a female and therefore can NOT give birth to a soul-baby representing the deceased lady.

In the strange twilight of Egyptian mythology, fluctuating between the most extravagant miracles and the most down-to-earth logic, such a purely technical consideration might have swayed the theory of the female Apotheosis to the effect that a "re-birth" of her own soul in the Beyond, via Tefnut, is not feasible, and that she can be only "adopted" as a grown-up person by some figure of the Above . . . be it by Hathor or by a deified Pharaoh into his celestial harem.

FEMALES IN THE GRECO-ROMAN BEYOND

In comparing the Egyptian vision with the Mediterranean mythos where earthly male persons are said to be carried away by loving nymphs – (Hylas, etc.) – as an euphemistic interpretation of death, – (maybe influenced by the Eastern idea of the dead, embraced by nymphic females) – we may see in the Egyptian idea a reversal of personages, as it is said that a MALE divine lover (similar, maybe, to the story of Ganymed) "takes the wife from her husband whensoever he pleaseth" to an enigmatic destiny.

We can, however, discern on later Roman sarcophagi, that the soul of a matron re-appears as a rejuvenated little girl – (with identical hair-do) – in the next world to be embraced and kissed there by a winged genius of love. If we assume that she will be transformed thereafter into a Maenad, she is in for some adventures with the male element, represented by love-oriented Dionysian Fauni. This transformation is sometimes hinted at, where a Roman lady is pictured on her death-bed, the corona immortalis on her head, and with the Maenadic Thyrsos in hand and even the torn lamb of the Bacchi ["Tomba del Triclinio" from Tarquinia, now British Museum]. We also see this same transformation of a dead male person into a member of the Bacchic train . . . so that the Dionysian costume of the dead lady may be taken as a hint that this transformation into a Maenad is possible also concerning the soul or alter-ego of a female after her death – at least sometimes, may be in the case of an actress who was celebrated during her lifetime because of her uninhibited ways, – as such monuments are very rare.

39

We, however, see a representation of the Empress Faustina the Younger as Venus, united with Mars, who was not her husband, but according to mythology the beloved of Venus. This monument seems to be based on the idea of a glorification of a person into the image of a divine or mythological figure, as far as Faustina is concerned.

62

Beyond that, we may discern the Eastern influx of visions, according to which a love-oriented encounter in Excelsis is assumed after death, in contrast to the doctrine of Hades, the same elevation of a female to the Above is also shown on the great relief in the Conservatori palace in Rome, where Emperor Hadrian watches the ascend of his wife Sabina to an uncertain Above.

While the Eastern doctrines assumed that amorous encounters awaited men in the Thereafter, it was the Romans who extended similar privileges to females too, after Hadrian, – (Emperor 117 - 138 A.D.) – who was keenly interested in Oriental doctrines and promoted the acceptance of foreign religions – (of which the Pantheon erected by him, bears witness).

This background may have had a bearing on that monument of Faustina the Younger, as she was the wife of Emperor Marcus Aurelius (161 - 180 A.D.) and the daughter of Faustina the Elder, wife of Emperor Antonius Pius (138 - 161 A.D.) who was an intimate friend of Emperor Hadrian – (who, by the way, also erected monuments – even in Egypt – to his Antinous, in the image of a divinity).

Another hint at the Oriental influence may be the active gesture of Faustina-as-Venus, compared to the passive attitude of Mars, who, according to the position of his legs, rather draws away from the advance of Venus – which is reminiscent of the representations in Eastern art, where the active role is given to the loving females in the Beyond.

It is true that in earlier times of the Hades-visions, Death was connected to grave visions only, but due to the infusion of the East, artists felt free, at times maybe all too free, to picture the amorous delights of females in the Thereafter, in comparing them to Ariadne, awakened from her Death-Sleep by Priapic figures, also shown in the extreme on some of the Etruscan Mirrors. The austere calm and noble resignation of earlier monuments was in those later times eclipsed by joyously overstating the new promises of Afterlife projected onto Greco-Roman imagery in the form of turbulent Dionysian trains embracing Nymphic creatures, willing or otherwise, amplified by scenes of abductions, still later elevated to all sorts of glorious "Divine Marriages."

On later Roman sarcophagi of stone the reappearing soul of the dead person, be it male or female, is characterized by "Butterfly-Wings" looking rather like little paddles, – while the loving genii of the next world are shown with larger "Birds-Wings" with feathers. We thereby can clearly differentiate the attitudes taken by the soul, from those of the celestial apparitions.

40

It is repeated on so many sarcophagi, that it may have some meaning, that the otherworldly genii are shown kissing the arriving soul, while the soul is depicted as touching the belly of the celestial being – even if the soul appears as a rejuvenated matron, that is now as a young girl, touching, as it seems, calm and confidently the lower part of the body of a male and winged emissary of the Beyond, suggesting maybe a future tender relation of a certain innocence, as both of them appear as if on the threshold of adolescence and although her celestial male partner is nude, the reappearing female soul is clad in a chaste robe, which might be her death-gown. Those encounters are surrounded by an intensely sweet and lyrical atmosphere, in a pose which is repeated by the famous "Amor and Psyche" of the Capitoline Museum. It may not occur to many visitors that the "Psyche" originally represents the soul of a dead female, while Amor represents the result of an "Equal Rights Movement" of late, permitting females the same amorous enjoyments in the Thereafter, as were granted to men.

The rejuvenation in the next world is shown on many Roman sarcophagi. But as youth would serve no purpose in Hades, rejuvenation there is never mentioned in Greco-Roman doctrines. Rejuvenation is, however, part of the Indian promises of Afterlife since oldest times, so that the later re-appearance of that same idea on Roman sarcophagi must be considered to be a clear sign of the inflow of the Eastern dogma into the Mediterranean sphere.

The following text was probably spoken by a priest at a cremation:

"To the 'Ender' to Death be reverence!
This man shall be sharing in the world
of immortality, amrita . . .
Thou shalt ascend and not descend!
Let not the flesh-devouring fire
menace thee, move afar from the
funeral pyre!
Heaven shall guard thee,
the moon shall guard thee.
Darkness shall not come upon thee,
nor the demon that tears out the tongue!
Soma (the drink of immortality) delivered
thee from death-eternal.
I have snatched thee from death
I have obtained thee;
thou hast returned with renewed YOUTH!"

[Atharvaveda, Book VIII.1] – a collection of magic spells.

The reference to the "Moon" relates to the idea that the moon is a female and that the Blessed have the pleasure of lovingly resting in her lap . . . the Moon being symbolic more for a Nirvana-like fulfillment than a Desire, was taking its place as a "general" Female in the Beyond of a cooler and more spiritual type than the restless Apsarases.

The modification of the Eastern dogma, made in Mediterranean lands, consists of the assumption that Females too, are permitted to reappear as rejuvenated in the next world – not merely as "Soul-Babies" but at the heighth of their nubile charms and shown as giving their persons over to genii of love.

The Fauni and Satyrs have goat-feet and the horns of rams and are thought to be half human and part animalic. As the old sculptors were impressed by the fact that male animals approach the females from the back, it is curious to see that the Satyrs too admire mostly the backside of the Maenads – to which those females often react by lifting there the drapes of their garments.

Parallel to the sarcophagi where the portrait of the female appears in the center-medallion, to be seen later as being received in rejuvenated condition by celestial genii – we have the portrait of a soldier, probably at the time of his death, while the rejuvenated epiphany of his soul appears traditionally as Apollo with Lyra in hand, his tutelary figure being however Chiron, the teacher of young Achilles, as it seems appropriate to show a military man associated with that Hero-figure. The same re-appearance of the soul in the image of Achilles is very frequently seen on funerary mirrors, found in North-Italian grave sites.

But a considerable number of Roman sarcophagi show the wife, in the company of her husband, on her voyage into the next world, often in a cart drawn by horses and watched over by genii of the Above. The sphere to which they travel is at times suggested by clouds and stars, so that we see a clear break with the original and official idea of Hades, and notice the adoption into Roman thinking of the Eastern visions in the elevation to the Above, and the company of a female – (never seem to have existed in Hades) – even if the female is only his own legal spouse. (except in fanciful Sagas).

There are some rather enigmatic plaques and fragments which may suggest that females are re-awakened from death to a sensual surrounding in the Ariadne tradition, or showing the naked soul of a female lifted from the ground by celestial apparitions, some of them in the rather Maenadic fashion with one bare breast and the hair in disarray, while others may resemble classic Greek divinities and the background suggests the Elysium. The awakened female looks aghast, the eyes wide open as if confronted with an incredible vision. We finally have a funeral postament (Campo Santo, Pisa) where a female who has not the appearance of a Maenad, but rather of an earthly woman in excelsis, willingly opens her drapes to admit a priapic Faun, the symbol of lust, so that it seems that in later Roman times females too were thought to be admitted to pleasures in the Beyond.

41

42

43

FEMALES IN THE ETRUSCAN BEYOND
(The Scarves)

Possibly related to the symbols of the Apotheosis is the question of the most mysterious large fringed scarfs, shown on the Etruscan tomb paintings. Those scarfs were never explained, but they are such unusual, constantly repeated and prominently displayed fixtures of those wall paintings, that we must suspect them to have a specific meaning, especially because, in their discarded condition, they are seen only on scenes suggesting the spheres of the Beyond, and not on vistas representing earthly life, as on the paintings depicting fishermen, hunters, riders, acrobats, wrestlers, charioteers, etc., where they are shown as being knotted around the waists of men.

The scarfs worn by the Etruscans were not the type of loincloth used by anybody in the Mediterranean region, certainly not in Italy. The most similar to them would be the Egyptian Kilts, but they are cut semi-circular and have no fringes or patterns. They were uniformly white, of linen and not of wool, and remained the same from 3000 B.C. to the Roman period. The Egyptian dress was so uniform that a prince could hardly be distinguished from a workman and the queen from her maid. The Ethiopians, Syrians and Phoenicians, Medes and Persians too had an unmistakably different cut of dress – (although some Persians appear on Etruscan frescoes, but they are clearly marked as such, and not in a very flattering manner either).

The only people wearing those long and fringed scarfs were the Indians, as seen especially on the earlier temple-sculptures of India and identically on the tomb-paintings of the Etruscans, as in the "Tomb of the Bulls" and on both men in the "Tomb of the Bacchantes" etc.

It is about a one-foot wide and four-feet long scarf, wrapped from the back to the front and knotted there, exactly in the Indian fashion, as shown on the temple-sculptures of Konarak and many others.

The cut and color of the Etruscan fringed scarfs, worn as a loincloth, becomes very clear because we often see them discarded and hanging unfolded on tree-bushes – (probably what Athenaeus calls "lattice-wands") or the tree-bushes of the "Garden Eden" (Garden of Delights) in the next world. Some painters put the scarfs on the wall or ceiling of the tomb itself, but on the Etruscan Death-Mirrors they again appear hanging on shrubs, in conjunction with definitely Oriental-Asiatic females of the next world, sometimes invitingly standing before elaborate beds, so that the symbol-connection between those very specific Scarves, the Beyond, the Females and Lovemaking becomes most obvious. On the Mirrors as

92

93

well as the tomb-paintings (both of them being Etruscan and made in Italy!) those scarves have very characteristic fringes with knotted tassels, again hinting at the Oriental import, as tassels are never seen in Greco-Roman art.

For the reason why they are thrown away we have no other hint than the description of the Etruscans by Athenaeus XII.517:

> "They indulge in love affairs and carry
> on these unions sometimes in full view
> of one another, but in most cases with
> screens of latticed wands, over which
> clothes are thrown."

Those discarded scarfs seem therefore not so much the "abandoning of the earthly hull" when entering the next world, as some may think, but rather the getting ready for the enjoyment of the celestial damsels.

47
This hint at the impending tender unions, as given by the discarded clothing, is somehow in its principal meaning akin to the hint expressed by the offering of the Betel Nut, and it could be thought that one symbol fortifies or verifies the other symbol's meaning.

To show that the quote by Athenaeus is not a random remark but part of a whole picture of the Etruscan lifestyle, which was then projected onto the Thereafter, here follows the whole paragraph, devoted by Athenaeus to the Etruscans, which is, by the way, the most detailed and authentic information we have, regarding those mysterious people. Athenaeus proved conscientious and exact whenever he could be checked against other texts and documentation. In his enormous work DEIPNOSOPHISTAE (The Philosopher's Symposium), he quotes about 1,500 other authors.

The translation is made verbatim from the original Greek text.

> "Among the Etruscans, who had become extravagantly
> luxurious, Timaeus records in his first book that the slave
> girls wait on the men naked. And Theopempus in the
> forty-third book of his "Histories" says that it is customary
> with the Etruscans to share their women in common; the
> women bestow great care on their bodies and often exercise
> even with men, sometimes also with one another; for it is
> no disgrace for women to show themselves naked. Further,
> they dine, not with their own husbands, but with any men
> who happen to be present, and they pledge with wine any
> whom they wish. They are also terribly bibulous, and are

very good-looking. The Etruscans rear all the babies that are born, not knowing who is the father in any single case. These in turn pursue the same mode of life as those who have given them nurture, having drinking parties often and consorting with all the women. It is no disgrace to be seen doing anything in the open, or even having anything done to them; for this also is a custom of their country. And so far are they from regarding it as a disgrace that they actually say, when the master of the house is indulging in a love affair, and someone inquires for him, that is undergoing so-and-so, openly calling the act by its indecent name. When they get together for companionship or in family parties they do as follows: first of all, after they have stopped drinking and are ready to go to bed, the servants bring in to them, the lamps being still lighted, sometimes female prostitutes, sometimes very beautiful boys, sometimes also their wives; and when they have enjoyed these, the servants then introduce lusty young men, who in their turn consort with them. They indulge in love affairs and carry on these unions sometimes in full view of one another, but in most cases with screens set up round the beds; the screens are made of latticed wands, over which clothes are thrown. Now they consort very eagerly, to be sure, with women; much more, however, do they enjoy consorting with boys and striplings. For in their country these latter are very good-looking, because they live in luxury and keep their bodies smooth. In fact all the barbarians who live in the west remove the hair of their bodies by means of pitch-plasters and by shaving with razors. Also, among the Etruscans at least, many shops are set up and artisans arise for this business, corresponding to barbers among us. When they enter these shops, they offer themselves unreservedly, having no modesty whatever before spectators or the passers-by. This custom is also in use among many of the Greeks who live in Italy; they learned it from the Samnites and Messapians. In their luxury, the Etruscans, as Alcinus records, knead bread, practise boxing, and do their flogging to the accompaniment of the flute."

[Athenaeus, Deipnosophistae, XII.518-519]

[Transl. C.B. Gulick, Harvard University Press]

THE GARLANDS

The garlands worn around the neck are typical for the Etruscan funeral art and have their counterpart in Indian iconography, while they are entirely foreign to the Mediterranean tradition.

In Indian art they seem to be a symbol for elevation and spiritualization of those who wear them.

In some cases we even see a river sanctified by such a garland, held over it by two heavenly beings, – the river which Buddha had crossed on his wanderings. This river is thereby blessed for all times. [Reliefs from the northern torana, Stupa I. Sanchi.]

Quite similarly we see heavenly beings holding or just depositing such garlands on the now empty chair on which Buddha sat. The chair is glorified and miraculized into a magnificent throne. The heavenly genii, while lowering the garland to the throne, hold, surprisingly enough, a spare-garland in the other hand, as if there would be a plentiful supply of prefabricated garlands available somewhere, to be handed out on occasions.

But just this rather curious Indian situation is reflected again in the Etruscan tomb frescoes, where a good supply of exactly those garlands is seen stored and dangling on the ceiling . . . obviously in the Beyond. More than this, we even see a person in modest dress, manufacturing such a garland, and hanging up the finished garlands in front of her. This person has the tight elbow-length sleeves with the very pointed ends, which is typically Indian, – ["Tomb of the Hunt and Fishing" – Tarquinia,] – the upper register, as usual, indicating the Above.

The same technique of hanging up garlands on the ceiling is also seen on the reliefs of some of the Etruscan sarcophagi, depicting scenes in the life of the souls after death. It therefore seems probable that the stored garlands are ready for newly arrived souls which was obviously the thinking of the painter who suggested that the garlands are manufactured in the upper sphere.

60

However some sculptors show on stone-sarcophagi a great many garlands of that kind hanging like sausages on the ceiling, while some personages are in amorous pursuits of the most obvious kind, giving the impression that those sanctifying garlands might be in their way, physically . . . or mentally? This last thought seems too naive if there were not a medieval painting which shows holy men taking a bath in a river, while they hang up their Halos in the meantime on the sky above them, as it seems, exactly for the before-mentioned reasons, that the Halos are physically in their way, or that the taking of a bath is too profane an action to wear the Halo, the crown

48

of heaven, during that procedure.

There is a scene in heaven [second century B.C., Barhut, Bihar, – Indian Museum, Calcutta], but NOT connected to death, which deals with the birth of Buddha, where he is shown to be spiritually conceived by diverse Genii. On this relief the same garlands are hanging on "Wish-granting" trees, while others descend from heaven, so that we may think of them as "Blessings granted" when they fall down from those trees onto a mortal.

On the many terracotta figures, showing the deceased reclining on the cover of their sarcophagi, we see those very same garlands, so that the "falling from heaven" as well as their manufacture in the Above, may teach us that they are the insigniae of divine blessings, now distinguishing their wearers as belonging to those to be elevated . . . and even more: that their wishes will be granted in Paradise.

44

45

46

In some cases we see a worldly and still living hero rewarded in this fashion; in other cases a mythological person who just killed a dragon or monster. On those occasions the garland is either lowered upon him by genii or is falling miraculously from heaven, but we see again the strange sight of a multitude of prefabricated garlands which possibly means that the heavens are full of graces . . . the same as it is stated in the scriptures that "there are MILLIONS of Apsarases," that they are superhumanly passionate and grant MILLIONS of orgasms to emphasize the miraculous by the multiplicity of appearance, not running down the single phenomenon by repetition but overwhelmingly orchestrating it into a "Magnificat" not in size, but as to repetition . . . as we see it also in India's ornaments on temples, fabrics and jewelry, all of it basking in pluralities and the prayer-mills, with the same tiny sentence, repeated a million times. This principle of pluralism seems even extended to the many-armed divinities and the many women in the harems, on earth and in the heavens.

Between the worldly heroes who are crowned with a garland by a heavenly apparition, we see a very interesting case where Siva himself puts a garland on the head of a deserving man, who is "King Cola who took the Ganges" as the inscription tells us. [Relief from the Brihadisvara Temple, as late as ca. 1000 A.D.] The unusual feature is that such a high divinity puts the garland carefully with both hands on the head of the king, who is bowing before Siva in the gesture of prayer, which leaves no doubt about the sacrality of the garland and the act itself. The relief shows clearly how the garland is bound, which corresponds exactly to the garlands seen in the Etruscan beyond. As to the feature of "Wealth in Excelsis" it is amusing to see that Siva has on each finger a ring and is also otherwise loaded with jewelry. The so elevated King is, according to Indian iconographic tradition, represented much smaller in size than the divinity.

A remarkable hint as to the significance of the garland in India are images of the monkey general Hanuman who was a heroic ally of Rama in his fight to victory over the evil demons, the Rakshas. As a thanks for his services he was rewarded immortality, which is denoted by one of those soft garlands around the neck on the statues of this general, who is depicted as an otherwise naked monkey. The fact that the garland is used as the symbol for immortality . . . meaning the immortality of his soul after death . . . gives an important hint as to the possible meaning of those same garlands shown on the tomb-paintings and funerary sculpture of the Etruscans.

Other examples of the significance of this specific type of garland in Indian iconography, are found in the great many illustrations which show in a sequence the very popular life-story of the beloved and revered Krishna, the poor cow-herd who developed into a saint and is finally shown as being elevated, that is – richly covered with jewels in excelsis. Those sequences show Krishna, the boy, as a little prankster in the beginning, stealing butter, etc. and later, as a young man enchanting the gopis, the milk-maids. But later he is performing miraculous deeds, and as he is developing into a more and more spiritual being, he is successively shown to appear with one of those long and soft garlands around his neck, the very same which we see again on the Etruscan grave monuments adorning the departed, who are shown either reclining on the covers of their sarcophagi, or painted on the walls of the tombs.

There was a trend in Indian mythology, or was it a hope, that an originally human being can attain supreme elevation to immortality by good or noble deeds on earth – (this in contrast to the Greco-Roman tradition in mythology to humanize gods downwardly). Following this idea, we have many representations of the great religious sage and teacher Mahavira of the seventh century B.C. – (that is before Buddha) – who is shown to be handed that specific garland by the divinity Sakra as a sign of his "consecration" – (sacrality?) – and "elevation of his soul to eternal life."

Considering all evidences, it seems that on the Etruscan funeral monuments, too, the garland is a symbol for elevation, spiritualization, blessing and consecration to the gods.

We see in much later Roman art also a sacrificial animal brought to its death with a garland around its neck, and the significance seems to be that this creature was thought to be elevated and sanctified – vaguely equivalent to the inscriptions "Dis Manibus" or "Dis Manibus Sacrum" with the name of the deceased on gravestones, as it was customary from the Augustan age on.

There is a beautiful sarcophagus in the Bardo Museum of Tunis, which shows the most astonishing fusion of Eastern and Mediterranean symbols, united in tender harmony. It presents, framed in orientalizing filigree work, carved in stone, the "Three Graces" as the traditional stand-ins for the celestial Nymphs of the East. But the great surprise is, that they hold in their hands the "Garlands of Sanctification" as if they would be ready to bestow them, upon the souls of the departed. Those garlands might be symbolic for their favors and equivalent to the Blessings of Paradise. We see here the absorbtion of the typically Indian symbol for "Wish-granting" and "Elevation" into Greco-Roman iconography, to illustrate the Eastern dogma of the Thereafter.

49

FEMALES IN THE INDIAN BEYOND

Concerning the adventures of earthly women in India's Afterlife, we have no information. The idea appears here and there that women, like animals or plants, have no eternal soul. This is astonishing in a people so totally committed to the idea of the transmigration of souls and their re-incarnation, that the soul of a woman should not be thought to come from somewhere and to go somewhere after her death, and that she should be the only creature to be excluded from the eternal cycle, which makes provisions for the re-appearance of the most humble beings, be it even in the form of a worm or an ant. Even exalted women, like the mother of Buddha, simply die and are never heard of again and have no place in heaven among the saints. There seems to be no upward-traffic from earth to heaven for women – although we have many representations in visual arts of male personages being sanctified and elevated to the divine spheres, such images are totally missing for females.

Women, according to Indian literature, are comparable to sweet fruits which are here to be enjoyed because of their beauty and pleasures in consuming them, as long as they are fresh and juicy, but which are totally discarded thereafter. The word "Widow" is a curse in India and a woman was expected to join her husband after his death, not to be united with him in the next world, but rather to remove her person, considered now to be a burdensome nuisance.

However, it was recognized that women, in some mysterious way, hold the greatest secret of all: the phenomenon of fecundity, the miracle of creation, and they become, as such, akin to supernatural beings, divinities and patron-saints of many of nature's inexplicable manifestations, of "production" like trees, fruits, wells etc. Those celestial female symbol-figures were never thought to be transformations of earthly beings but originated as embodiments of abstractions in a spiritual sphere, similar to the female figures of the Greco-Roman pantheon, but without the loveplay of the Mediterranean figures of the Above.

While no ascent of earthly females to the Above is known, celestial princesses are, in a reversed process, often represented by earthly standins ... on a temporary basis, during many ceremonies. At the Siva-Parvati-Festival, for instance, where any of the female visitors of the temple take over the function of Parvati as the lovepartner of Siva, or in the Tantras where the female cult-partner assumes the personality of Lalita during intercourse, or the Cave-Hetairai, a sort of female Hermit, who enacts with her visitor the role of some premordial queens of nature ... down to the most usual Devadasi, swarming through the temples, ready to impersonate various heavenly females for a moderate fee. Even the images of female donors in the sanctuaries are not pictured as now being elevated to a celestial environment, due to their pious actions, but are shown, strewn with jewelry, in their earthly existence as temptresses displaying their negotiable assets as concubines of the rich and mighty, in the act of being blessed by the genii of the Above who descend upon them, but with no attempts on the part of those earthly ladies to go up to the higher spheres for their sanctification.

Those donor-statues in the temples were then understood to be Lalita, the goddess of Beauty, Wealth and Happiness in her earthly Avatar or manifestation, again in the sense that the goddess descended on earth and not in the sense that the great courtesan was elevated or apotheosed. Some inscriptions explicitly state that the earthly being is not transformed into the goddess, but that the goddess appears on earth in the form of her earthly replica or impersonatrice ... again denying even those pious females, despite the great donations, their final apotheosis.

Although it is said that the earthly person was created in the image of the divinity, the reverse may be true, namely that the divinity Lakshmi was created in the image of the earthly courtesan, because the sequence of the divine attributes fairly well describes the mundane progression from Beauty to Wealth to Happiness – ("The Rake's Progress") – and also the fact that Lakshmi being the casual consort of Siva, who was represented by the phallus, may have been an euphemism for the 'powerful lover' of the courtesan, and thereby the celestial paradigma of the eternally earthly constellation of the virile potentate, bringing a beautiful female to wealth and glory ... a dream so often dreamed by men and females alike in romanticized guises endlessly running through fairy tales ... to be finally elevated to Mythology.

RADHA, THE CELESTIAL CONSORT

The only description of a female elevated to heaven concerns Radha. On first sight the apotheosis of Radha, the beloved of Krishna, seems to be an exception, but we deal here with several versions of the Krishna story: Some are pre-Christian modifications and a number of them very different post-Christian additions, which only then include her apotheosis. Krishna appears first in the Mahabharata, about 600 B.C., as a lovelorn cowherd who dreams, understandably, of being surrounded by amorous girls, which story was around 400 B.C. – (still in the Mahabharata) – expanded to the more glorifying notion of Krishna becoming a soldier and charioteer. In a later text, the Bhagavata Purana of 200 B.C. to 200 A.D., the original saga is greatly expanded and altered and presented in the form of romantic poetry. The new features are that Krishna was made a divinity, and that it was said that his cow-girls were married, but left their husbands for Krishna.

Samples from the Bhagavata Purana (the Song of God):

> (the girls, including Radha, say to Krishna:) "Those stupid Brahmans, our husbands, mistook you for a mere man. But you are God . . . We came to you despite our families. They tried to stop us but we ignored them. If they do not take us back, where shall we go? . . ."

As to the romantic quality of the same poem:

> "The cowgirls joined hands and Krishna was in their midst like a lovely cloud surrounded by lightning. Singing, dancing, uniting with him they passed the time in extreme bliss. They took off their clothes, their ornaments and jewels and offered them to Krishna. The gods in heaven gazed at the scene and all the goddesses longed to join. The singing mounted in the night air. The winds were stilled and the streams ceased to flow. The stars were entranced and the water of life – (probably Soma, the fluid of Eternity, said to be in the 'lap' of the Moon, where the Beati rest in a timeless state of bliss) – poured down from the great moon. So the night went timelessly on for six months when the dancers end their joy . . ."

123

Then Krishna takes the girls to the Jumma River to bathe them "and then after once again gratifying their passions, bids them go home."

In this second version of the Krishna-story – (which is not mythological, but the fantasy of a poet) – Krishna was changed from a Hero to a Divinity, strongly patterned after Christ, with halo etc. . . . and was also elevated to heaven, and Radha, as a mere annex to Krishna, was shown as being attached to him – still conforming to the old Eastern vision of bliss in the Beyond, represented by the company of a loving female, being the very definition of the heavenly scenario . . . and forced into the story in this way only as an ornamentation to the apotheosis of Krishna . . . All this after the story of Christ and his apotheosis was well known and had greatly impressed the East – (also evident in the Koran, conceived at about the same time, where Mohammed makes many references to Jesus).

The sudden introduction of Krishna as a god had so greatly perplexed the writers of the later parts of the Mahabharata, that an appendix was added, the Harivanasa, explaining the new personality of Krishna, still further developed and embellished in the Bhagavata Purana [10 & 11] in the ninth and tenth century A.D. which became only then the present rendering of the Krishna story . . . including Radha and her apotheosis as permanent and celestial consort of Krishna.

Returning for a moment to the just mentioned Mohammed and the general prohibition of earthly women in heaven, but realizing that we deal here not with India proper and the much later epoch of about 620 A.D., we may quote from the Koran, Chapter 43:

> "When the birth of a daughter is announced to one of them
> (the believers) his face darkens and he is filled with gloom.
> Would they ascribe to Allah (in heaven) females who adorn
> themselves with trinkets and are powerless in
> disputation?"

But Mohammed, on the other hand, promises to the true believers females in heaven, who are, however not the daughters of Allah, but "dark-eyed Houries, arrayed in rich silks and fine brocade" – [Koran, Chapter 44]. This is a deviation from the Indian dogma, according to which the Apsarases are the daughters of the supreme deity Indra – (who is the equivalent to the Mohammedan Allah).

THE GLORIFIED ADULTRESS

A much later poem, the Gita Govinda (the song of the cowherd) – written in Sanskrit by the most famous Bengali poet Jayadeva, around the twelfth century A.D. – pictures Radha still as adultress, however glorified and almost un-earthly – (which we may consider as the first step towards her apotheosis).

In Cambodia and some other places Radha was thought to be an avatar, or earthly epiphany of Lakshmi, the goddess of Beauty, Youth and Joy and as such the sakti or divine paramour of Vishnu, who was identified with Krishna, so that Radha, in this roundabout way belonged a priori to the celestial company, without the need of an apotheosis – an idea which inspired later poets.

Eventually, in the fourteenth century A.D. the Brahma Vaivarta Purana was composed in an effort to re-define the status of Radha as Krishna's "Eternal Consort" – (as the basis of her apotheosis) – and it was claimed that Radha was to begin with of celestial descent and was only due to a curse, temporarily changed into the human shape of a cowgirl – and further on, that Radha's husband was never married to her person, but only to her shadow — and finally, that Krishna had secretly married Radha at Brinda-ban . . . and that her passion for Krishna was therefore not adulterous but conformed to the requirements of morality. This last version of the story never became popular and is hardly ever heard of in later times. The reason for it may be that adultery was felt to be the spice of romance, as seen at the same time in the romantic literature of Europe in the Middle Ages, as well as in the Orient and even in China . . . again suggesting a time-spirit circling the globe. Everywhere, at that time, marriage was seen as the gray background which some destiny had ordained, and against which the "Great Passion" stood out, heroically overcoming or sometimes being crushed by the powers of fate . . . the glorification of the heroine being often her reward.

It could be thought that the elevation of Radha had a "social" significance too, because until then only princes claimed to be the kinfolk of divinities — (see Buddha) — while now, like Christ who was of humble birth, Krishna the cowherd was elevated to the divine status and with him in this new social trend, was Radha, the cowherd's girl, resplendent with jewels, admitted to the Above. The "equal rights" of the humble, the un-wed and the women, was part of a new social consciousness "bobbing up" and was even extending to the right of their apotheosis.

". . . lawgivers in their desires to reduce the human race to one level and bar citizens from luxury, have caused a class of things called justice to bob up. Since the lawgivers were carrying on their fight against the unfair advantages of the few, the praise of justice began to be exalted by the many . . ."

[Athenaeus, Deipnosophistae, XII:546:]

RADHA AND KRISHNA

GIFTS OF THE DEAD

THE PROBLEM

There are objects found in graves and shown in funeral art, on sarcophagi and grave stelae, which are of earthly use, but often seem to have no relationship whatsoever to the deceased person, like arms in the graves of children, saddles and daggers in graves of females, while some graves of men show trivial household objects like cooking and spinning utensils, ornate hand-mirrors and cistae with toiletry articles and female trinkets.

There is considerable controversy about the meaning of those objects. Opinions were advanced that those earthly and profane items might be:

A.) Possessions of the deceased, forming part of their immediate personality – (difficult to maintain regarding the arms in children's graves).

B.) A nostalgia assumed in the dead towards the abandoned life so that the items in the graves should be a souvenir, a memento, given by the living to be taken along into the next world as a keepsake by those departing.

C.) That those objects might be mysteriously transformed by magic in the next world to some usefulness in the sublime after-sphere of the spirits – (this in similarity to the idea which existed in Egypt, concerning the "Grave-Concubines" for the amorous needs of the dead, and the little figurines of workmen, the Ushabti, who were thought to assume their respective functions when magically revived in the next world.

D.) There was finally the assumption that we deal here with a purposeful Non-Logic, an attempt to fuse, in the face of death, the earthly past with the esoteric state of the Thereafter, thereby dissolving the boundaries between the past and the future existence, the intention to bridge the frightening abyss between the manifest and the non-corporal, a liaison spilling over between the two spheres, to make the transition more smooth and less abrupt.

127

Faced with the great difficulty of substantiating any of those theories, we may advance the following hypothesis, subdivided in several steps, according to their historic development, a hypothesis which accommodates with ease the diverse enigmatic items:

MALE SUBTERRANEAN JUDGES

1.) In oldest times even kings were thought to come, after death, before some subterranean judges. In a rather touching replica of earthly frailty, the first step of the deceased was to bribe the judges. To be able to give gifts, the dead persons had to have gifts on hand, and therefore such gifts were given to them in their graves. In confirmation of this theory we have several texts to that effect and we also see that in districts where seven judges of the dead were assumed, there were seven precious gifts found in the graves, while in districts where three subterranean judges were assumed, there were three precious gifts in the graves. A further confirmation comes from the fact that the Gift-Objects in the graves were exactly those items which were traditionally used to influence the benevolence of powerful personalities in earthly commerce. This we can ascertain by comparing those items with lists of presents, enumerating the gifts received by monarchs and duly recorded by their treasury personnel. – See Letters of Mursilis II and Muwattallis – 14th to 13th century B.C. of the Hittite sphere, mentioning such practice and Hattusilis inventory of gifts received, like draperies, copper objects, arms, jewelry . . . some listed to be from Ahhijawa, some to be simply from Assuwa, Hittite for Asia, etc. and we have several hints in letters that great importance was ascribed to such gifts in the districts ranging from South-West Russia to the Middle East where exactly such gift items were found in the graves. In the Greco-Roman sphere there were Oriental metal-helmets found in graves from a time where metal-helmets were not actually worn in the Mediterranean and being clearly gifts from far away satrapies, but now, together with pleas for mercy, obviously intended in the graves as gifts for the subterranean judges.

As to the scenario of the Netherworld, we have some descriptions which convey an atmosphere of great realism in resembling the world of the living – however, tinged with an eerie melancholy. So we see, for instance, that all the former kings and the great of the lands, rise to greet the King of Babylon upon his arrival, in a gesture of earthly formality, while their speeches are of gruesome resignation. It has to be mentioned that "Sheol" is the word for "Nether-world" in Hebrew.

> Sheol beneath is stirred up
> to meet you when you come,
> it rouses the shades to greet you,
> all who were leaders of the earth;
> it raises from their thrones
> all who were kings of the nations.
>
> [Isaiah 14.9]

Another glimpse of the great Below we get from Sumerian tablets, describing the arrival of the great King Ur-Nammu in the Netherworld. In substance, the tablets say that the king distributes gifts to the seven judges and then brings gifts to two high dignitaries of the Below, one of them being "The Scribe of the Proceedings" – "to make sure of their support" – (is he expected to tamper with the records? we wonder) –. Thereupon Gilgamesh, the hero, who has become one of the "Judges of the Netherworld" shows the king his habitation where he has to await trial, and instructs him about the rules and regulations within the realm of the dead.

From another Sumerian tablet [K.198] we learn some of those rules – which at times escape our understanding – but generally conjure up the uneasy atmosphere of a cave of bats or the grand and dreamy dungeons of the "Carceri" by Piranesi.

Between other things he is told to walk in the realm of the dead without sandals and make no outcry, otherwise the shades would pounce upon him, and not to awaken the great woman, naked of breast and body . . . etc. Mentioned also is Namtar, the daimon of Fate and Death, as well as Nergal "The Ambusher" – (of Death) – being the Vezirs of Ereshkigal, queen of the Netherworld . . . and the seven dreadful Judges.

All the judges of the Netherworld were assumed to be males, which would explain the masculine type and character of the items found in graves of infants and women as perfectly proper and fitting, when understood in their function as "Gifts to the Judges."

On the other hand it would exclude the theory that those gifts are "Objects of Nostalgia" or "Personal Possessions" or that they may in a magical way or otherwise serve the deceased person in a next existence.

MALE SUBTERRANEAN DIVINITIES

2.) In older and more savage times those "Gifts" were bribes to the JUDGES, but in a later and more mellow mentality they were thought to induce the benevolence of the DIVINITIES of the Deep, who were still assumed to be patently male personalities – however no longer in the character of wild chieftains, fond of hunting, fighting, and riding – but more of the religious-mythological tinge, as evidenced by the more and more sacrodotal character of the gift-items. The type of those gifts shown changes later to sacrifices given in pious devotion, or gifts to the gods as endearment, like the Egyptians bringing perfumes in little flasks to gods, so fond of fragrances.

According to that idea we now see on many presentations on funeral monuments and paraphernalia, the dead person extending his hands holding holy oils and sacrificial libations, to chthonian divinities in a ceremonious manner, to honor them and to be graciously received in their sombre abode underground, which assumes a new aura of ritualistic pomp. The persons are shown on those monuments and paintings with the palms of the hands down, to address the divinities of the Deep, (while the palms-up position indicates the approach to the divinities of the Above).

The subterranean divinities are still shown to be male and bearded and in majestic draperies – and, in some cases appear to be crowned as if to hint at their past development leading back to the rather terrestrial gift-giving tradition between monarchs, – and in some cases melting into the vision of "Priest-Kings" of old, or may represent more probably Minos, who was King and Chief-Judge of the dead in one person. Those rather sumptuous figures are sometimes reminiscent of the High Priest in the Orphic mystic, where an elaborate ritual, involving highly smybolic objects, was staged to assure the passage of the so-ordained into a better spiritual world.

DIVINITIES, MALE OR FEMALE

No inscriptions identify those exalted personages as either Priests, or Kings or Gods. This omission is so universal that it might point to the fear of mis-naming and thereby offending a divinity in the Above or the Below. This in conformity with the careful, almost lawyer-like approach to divinities, intent on closing all "loopholes" of possible offense legally, as to read: SI DEUS SI DEA.

"TO THE DIVINITY, MALE OR FEMALE, IN THE ABOVE AND / OR BELOW . . ."

130

3.) Coming now to the most puzzling trivial household items found in the graves and shown on grave monuments, we notice that at this very time in the historical development, PERSEPHONE, wife of Hades, suddenly appears as the Hostess of the dead, presiding over animated banquets of the departed — however, still under ground.

It seems logical therefore, within the framework of that rather home-like atmosphere of hospitality, that the guests bring some "Guest-Gifts" of domestic sort to their Hostess, befitting the idea of a female househould-establishment. We even have textual evidences attesting to that notion on grave-inscriptions:

" . . . BLESSED TRAVEL TO THE PALACE OF PERSEPHONE"

or:

"HERE IN THE ABODE OF PERSEPHONE RESIDES
. . . .
(name of deceased)
AFTER EARTHLY LIFE"

Those epigraphs are so numerous and uniform that they mark a well established tradition of a certain time, where also the writers and poets omitted the word "Hades" and made reference instead to the "Realm of Persephone."

Also from the same period are many sarcophagi picturing the world of the dead as a House and elaborate much on the big door of that rather palatial Residence into which the dead seems to wander and which closes after him with a heavy finality.

Following the same trend of thought we also see ash-urns of stone in the shape of a House, no doubt the domain of Persephone, into which the dead had disappeared, and where, as far as it contains his ashes, he is "residing" there now.

This remarkable mythological shift from the severe MALE Judge and Lord of the subterranean world of the Shades to the amiable FEMALE figure of a Hostess, may well have been influenced by the new hear-say now coming from the East to the Mediterranean, that there is a "female element" of some sort, most kindly awaiting and attending the souls of the departed. The idea of banquetting was probably imported by the Etruscans, as shown on their grave-paintings. As Persephone was the only prominent Female known to the Mediterranean mythos, residing in the regions of the dead, the vague rumor of the "Females in the Beyond" was therefore projected onto her figure – in combination with the Etruscan banquetting. The Eastern version of the paradisial Brides was thereby translated into the attitude of a generous Hostess "attending" the souls of the departed and in a stretchable double-meaning of "pleasing" them physically. The fact that Persephone had a well known case-history of having been raped several times by various persons, made her transition from the beloved to her present Hausfrauish role a bit easier – as a great many of the famous hostesses of the day had a similar background. The rape of Persephone was so present in the mind of the people that it became a frequent subject on sarcophagi and a favorite in theatrical plays. The flash-back to her past is sometimes hinted at by the most generous decolletage and sliding drapes, in which that "Mistress" of the Deep is now depicted as a sensual figure, (Palermo, death-cups) conforming to the faint echo from the East, of the Celestial Brides, now imported by the Etruscans.

While none of the banquetting souls would dare to suggest any intimacy with Persephone, she still projects great female charms within that rather sumptuous scenario.

Of course we have, to the south of Sicily, Hathor, the divinity of love and Joy in Egypt, receiving the dead in the Above, but any link is missing between her and Persephone of the Greco-Roman lands and the speculation drifts rather to the possibility that Hathor and Persephone were both side-effects from the infiltration of the Eastern dogma of female company in the Thereafter.

During that phase in the development, Persephone, in Etruscan funeral art, is often fused with Alpan – (Alpanu or Alpnu) – as a charmer in the Underworld, akin to the Roman "Libitina" apostrophed as "libens dedit." She is shown on mirrors wearing magnificent jewelry and a grand cape which is opened to show that she is otherwise elegantly naked. Some give her the title of "the otherworldly libido" – but it is safer to consider her the first image of the 'Female in the Beyond,' however still placed in the Below.

Persephone received her sensual hue in a passive manner (her rapes, first by Hades and then by Peirithous) and is, in spite of all, a regal figure like Aphrodite who lost none of her dignity in her adventures – while Hathor is, according to many stories, of a naughtier disposition and at times an active seductress in the spooky marshes of the Nile.

GUEST GIFTS TO PERSEPHONE

Whatever her background, Persephone is now understood as Hostess of the dead and receives "Guest-Gifts" from those who are entering her residence and marbled abode as her House-guests. This makes the household gifts found in graves, of males and females alike, entirely plausible and compatible with the mundane tradition of that time and region. In literary sources we again find the guest-gifts of the day to be identical with those articles as they were found in graves or as they were shown in funeral art, like casettes for jewelry, some made of ivory, some containing still precious objects, some golden earrings (Met. Mus. N.Y.) making specifically reference to death and the survival of the soul. But there are also some more modest trinkets and pins for women – flower vases, and even domestic spinning utensils – (so difficult otherwise to relate to male inhabitants of the grave). There are further Alabastrons for perfume, and especially little hand-mirrors, which were the most usual bring-along gifts for hostesses in earthly life, but now engraved with scenes related to the Beyond . . . which will be described here later. In a more modest or homemaker approach, flasks with oil or wine appear, as a small symbolic contribution to a household, as this was customary too, in the world of the living, to bring to a Hostess. In some cases the deceased is shown bringing only flowers or fruits or a chicken or bird, plucked or living, as it was usual at rural parties in Italy – (and still is today). Those fruits later appeared more and more lavishly in quantity and arrangement on sarcophagi, until they became avalanches from a "Horn of Plenty" – (in a strange similarity to the picturesque cascades of foods displayed at restaurants today in Italy). It seems possible that the otherwise quite enigmatic garlands of fruits and flowers decorating funeral monuments, originated in those earlier gifts to Persephone, as hostess of the dead – as well as the birds and rabbits appearing frequently together with those donations. – (The heaps of food in Egypt's sepulcheral art were meant to nourish the alter-ego of the deceased and were not a gift to any heavenly personages.)

133

MIRRORS

MIRRORS USED IN THE BEYOND

Now returning to the hand-mirrors so frequently found in graves, even of men, to discredit the ideas of personal belongings of the dead, their nostalgia towards their earthly past, or their re-use, however transformed, in their future semi-existence. To be sure of their use and the addressees intended for, we see those hand-mirrors on ash-urns (Karlsruhe) actually held and used by their recipients in the Beyond, be that Persephone, the very mistress of the realm, or by some Nymphic creatures in orientalized veils flouncing their charms, or of the Maenadic type, blending-over at times into the image of Aphrodite, or indiscriminately into figures of her entourage, her Attendants, the three Horai as the celestial dancers, or simply the "Three Graces" – known from many sarcophagi to represent the sultry females of the next world. The fact that ash-urns (Karlsruhe and Villa Giulia) clearly depict those other-worldly Nymphs as holding and using this very same type of grave mirror means that the idea of the "Females in the Beyond" was at the time of the "Mirror-Gifts" well established in the Mediterranean – however, the exact personalities of the recipients were still vague and the artists were uncertain how to translate those celestial Odalisques into creatures of the Greco-Roman mythos.

The Mirrors are of enormous importance to us because they verify the assumptions made rather vaguely, based on the representations on sarcophagi and stelae, concerning the scenes of the Thereafter taking place in the celestial waters – (forming the basis of the Sea-Sarcophagi) – and many other hints which are suggested less clearly in funeral art. Due to the fact that the mirrors, in a sort of "short-hand-description," pictorially show the main elements of the transition into the next world and due to the inscriptions they so generously display, they make us sure of the interpretation of the enigmatic but silent funeral monuments created at the same time.

In general it should be said that the designs on those mirrors seem to be etched rather than engraved. It appears quite possible that the Etruscans actually invented what we call today "the Etching" – which consists in covering the surface of the metal with a layer of asphalt – (well known to them) – and then drawing the design on this surface with a stilo, so as to lay bare the metal along the path of the line. After that, the mirror, otherwise protected by asphalt, is immersed into an acid – (possibly vinegar) – which eats out and thereby deepens the bare lines to a uniform degree, so typical for the mirror-designs. This is in contrast to an "engraving" which is much more laborious to produce and which creates lines of varying depth and width and by which technique the slightly trembling lines are almost impossible to create, which are, however, frequently seen on the drawings of the mirrors. In some cases an expert can tell that a tracing has slipped, which would have been corrected at once by an engraver.

The great ease and speed in which patterns and designs can be copied and transferred onto the asphalt and then just be "drawn" through the layer of asphalt on the copper, could explain the exuberant joy of discovery, the almost talkative facility of expression we feel in those mirror-designs, which left us those valuable documents of Etruscan thinking, while the many inscriptions of identifying names made us acquainted with much of their mythological visions.

THE OUTER ORNAMENTATION

The fact that, so far, about 1,500 engraved mirrors were found in Etruscan graves or around their tombs, deserves our special attention because they date from the sixth century B.C. onward, which was just the time when the Eastern influences most strongly infused the Mediterranean thoughts of the Thereafter. Those mirrors thereby become a veritable guide through the different stages of that development, whereby we can plot, step by step, the chronological rapproachment leading from the Hades-doctrine up to the Oriental-Asiatic visions of a plurality of willing beauties, to choose from, awaiting the re-born soul of the dead in the Above.

The great quantity of mirrors invites us to organize them into groups.

First, we may divide them into those which were presents between the living, or objects of actual use . . . and those which more probably were mirrors given to the dead and found in graves and assumed to be bring-along gifts of the dead to the otherworldly personages as an endearment.

Our main interest in this study belongs to the latter type, because they tend to reveal to us something about those figures of the Beyond, and the general beliefs concerning Afterlife and Resurrection.

HARPIES

Equally important as the engravings on the mirrors to show that we deal here with "Death-Mirrors" is their outer ornamentation and their stands, handles and postaments. They very often show Harpies, the "Soul-Snatchers" as governing the scene. Here we note at once that the very "personality" of the Harpies underwent a most remarkable change, which runs parallel with the general shift from the grim and sombre Below of Hades towards the sensual paradise of the East, the feast of desires fulfilled in the Thereafter by a swarm of Celestial Brides.

While the original Harpies of the Mediterranean were described as hide-ous filthy monsters with dishevelled hair, living on decomposed bodies, we see a gradual change of those creatures into mellow females, at first **50** motherly, cradling the soul of the dead in her arms, blending over later into frankly sensual and truly beautiful naked charmers with soft bodies and smiles, at times even shown in a love-bout with a stretched-out man, who seems to be rather sleeping than dead, following the novel doctrine that death is but a sleep — (his arms shown as lifted over his head is the pose of a sleeping person, and not of a dead one). There the Harpy, characterized as such by her bird's foot, descends on him as a physical lover, thereby **51** conforming to the Indo-Oriental vision of such union of the departed with an otherworldly enchantress. We may see here an interesting amalgama-tion between the Mediterranean idea of the Harpies carrying away the soul, and the Eastern-Egyptian thought of a female, bodily receiving the "Soul-Substance" of the dead in love. There might be a vague hint that the dead, in this seemingly passive position, assumes the features of Pan, to sym-bolize his joyful response, as we see in other representations [Louvre] that men in the next world re-appear with the emblems of Pan when in intimate contact with the females of the Beyond, the same as we see females with Thyrsos, transposed into Maenades, when reappearing in the Above. The prominently shown "Staff of the Wanderer" next to the male figure, may be the usual hint, so often seen as the symbol of the "Journey's End" when depicting the deceased at his final repose.

THE WINGED CREATURES OF THE BEYOND

In old Greece the girls of easy virtues were called "Pornai" – which may be connected to the idea in the Odyssey, that the Sirens turned the men who listened to them into pigs. The Near-East was well known to the Greeks, as some of the Eastern Hierodules started to ply their trade in the sanctuary of Aphrodite at Corinth. We have some very old texts condemning their rites even in their homelands to the East and South, calling Erech "the city of Hierodules, courtesans and sacred prostitutes to whom Ishtar was mistress" – (Ishtar, the Near-Eastern goddess of Love).

It is possible that the Sirens had very different roots and connotations, some related to the realm of the dead, some celestial and some terrestrial.

It is sometimes assumed that the idea of the Harpies originated in the "Soul-Birds" – as the souls of the dead, but with the often suspected dangerous power of the dead to draw others to them, however still bearing the odium of the enchantresses, due to their song or otherwise, which may be related to the vague visions of the sweet death-related female seductresses from the East. These are cases where we see them in a receptive mood, but slightly menacing. There are many such "Soul-Birds" in the museum of Naples suspended on threads, hanging in the vitrines. They are beautiful, as the souls of loved people are thought to be charming too. This may be the ancestry of the "beautiful" Harpies who regained more and more human features in their anatomy as well as in their sentiments, like those of protection and mourning.

We thereby see two connections of the Harpies: One via the Sirens to the Pornai, possibly derived from the earthly females of seduction and downfall, projected onto the spheres of the supernatural and the sensual females of the Eastern Beyond.

52

53

54

137

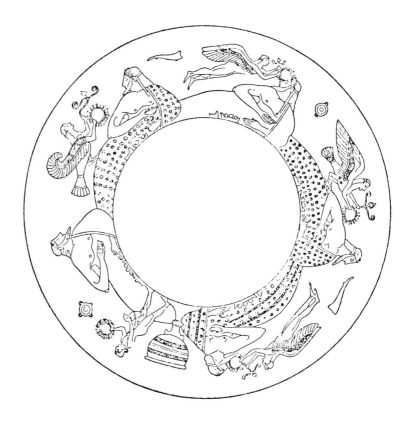

In this connection it may be remarkable that some Sirens on early pictures show Asiatic features and hairdoes and at time are blended over into winged "Erotes," – [Louvre] – handing some garlands of sanctification and the drink of eternal life to the souls in the Beyond, wearing Etrusco-Assyrian beards, while on a Corinthian container of ointments, from the earlier sixth century B.C., we see such a mysterious creature of mixed morphology of far off lands, inscribed as servant to Venus. – It certainly seems that their bewitching songs enchanted more than frightened the men in the Odyssey. It is possible that a later version or branch of the Sirens and Harpies developed into the Etruscan Lasae, the winged creatures carrying off the souls, yet being of female charms, who are said to be at times involved in amorous adventures.

The other: Associating the singing of the Sirens with Song-Birds, or the more otherworldly Soul-Birds representing the magic chant and lure by the souls of the dead, attracting the living to their realm.

Despite their physical charms, the Harpies sometimes interfere with destiny, stopping a youth who is chasing after a rabbit, the very symbol of life, maybe so that they themselves can embrace his soul, which now appears in the image of a winged Eros. This idea is indicated by her gesture of reception. The bird-like body of the Harpies and Sirens may have led to the idea of their songs, dramatized later into the deadly calls of temptation in the Odyssey.

We finally see the Harpies on mirrors as faithfully guarding the souls of the dead, the same as we see them in often angelic dignity watching over the dead on stele and sarcophagi. Sometimes also on the rims of the mirrors, and in a philosophical allegory, there are shown symbols of Life, in the form of cocks, and multiplying rabbits and love-driven dogs – the most often observed exponents of joy and life – all chasing each other along the rim of the mirror, while their paths lead and end up at a Harpie, presiding in noble calm over all pursuits of life and happiness as the final figure who awaits all the living, not cruel, as it seems, but divinely pre-ordained and almost comforting.

55

*

There is still another version or branch of the Sirens and Harpies combined, which developed into the Etruscan Lasae, the winged creatures carrying off the souls, yet being of female charms and almost blending into the "Females of the Beyond" – (as off-spring naughtily conceived between the Below and the Above) – but rather understood to be figures of the gentle transition of the soul from the Below to the spheres of Love.

A picture of a Pontina Amphora of the seventh century B.C. shows a man and a woman – (possibly Koronis and her lover Tityos) – being carried off by two winged Lasae, one of them, in a familiar gesture, is running forward, while looking backwards, and pulling the supposed Koronis along by her garment.

The interesting part is, that each person seems to have its "personal" Lasa, meaning, that two persons require two Lasae, who seem to be of different sex according to their different vestments, which would admit the possibility of male and female Lasae, or at least that some specialize in carrying off men and others to take away the souls of women.

Another feature of interest is that those archaic Lasae have three pairs of wings: one pair on the shoulders, another on the hips and the third pair on their calves, which is an Eastern pattern, often seen on Assyrian genii – which would be a hint that the Lasae developed out of Eastern apparitions.

THE BETEL NUT

Other figures on the stands of mirrors are Etruscan Nymphs of the Beyond, now frankly patterned after their Indo-Oriental model, in their typical turbans and big circular earrings, one of them – (in the Cleveland Museum of Art) – is striding in one direction but oddly turning her head backwards as if inducing somebody – (no doubt the soul of the dead) – to follow her, holding out, as a reward and enticement, a Betel-Nut, the Indian symbol for "Loving Intimacy" – (see pictures of Krishna and Radha where he puts a Betel-Nut between her lips, the labial penetration by this acorn-like object being an allusion to love-making). To make it clear what the strange gesture of striding forward but looking backwards means, we have a wall-painting in the "Tomb of the Bacchants" at Tarquinia, where an identical girl is shown in the same position, definitely pulling a suntanned bearded man – (no doubt the deceased) – with her into paradise. She has exactly the same strapped turbanette or "Tutulus," the same big and round earrings and Oriental dress with pointed ends as the Cleveland girl, and does, on the painting in conjunction with a man, motivate clearly her otherwise astonishing gesture by facing her companion. The Cleveland figurine has her left foot on a tortoise, symbolizing Music – [Homeric Hymm IV. 23-59] – and the same reference to Music is made again on the painting of Tarquinia, showing a musician playing a string-instrument, fabricated from a tortoise-shell, like the original Hermes did. To dispell any doubt of what the girl with the Betel-Nut is up to, we have the relief of the Louvre where several girls with exactly the same hairdo or banded tur-banettes and exactly the same earrings, make love to men. That this scene takes place in the Etruscan Beyond is indicated by the fact that the "sanctification" or "Death-garlands" hang from the ceiling. Concerning the importance of the Betel-Nut we have another Etruscan figurine – [No. 491 of the British Museum] – which is winged, to hint at her heavenly provenience, and is also therefore shown without boots, but again holding high in her right hand, a Betel-Nut as a temptation or price to be gained, while looking downward to somebody to follow her, which might be accentuated by her left hand lifting her skirt, while her lips are parted as if she would call out to somebody to come with her to the paradisial Above, and there to win her graces. The Betel-Nut symbolism is important because the Betel-Nut was not known in Italy, and it therefore shows, – so to say as a "tracer" – how a purely and exclusively Indian symbolism infiltrated – via the Etruscans – Italic lands. It cannot be assumed that the bronze-casters multiplied figurines whose meaning was NOT understood by anybody. Therefore, as this rather unseemly symbolism became known in Italy, it

56

58

59

60

57

141

must be assumed that quite a stream of other information may have infiltrated from India into Italy, most probably also concerning the Eastern Paradise.

Still belonging to the idea of Frames are the engraved ornamentation we see surrounding the central scenes on the mirrors.

IVY, WINES AND GRAPES

The Ivy remains green also in winter, when all the other vegetation seems to die, and in this respect fell into the class of evergreen trees, which were, as in the Attis and Adonis allegory, symbolic for Resurrection or the non-perishing soul. Ivy is therefore used as an ornament surrounding many mirrors, so to say as a "Frame of Mind" within which the scenes are supposed to be understood.

Another plant which often surrounds the main image are wines and grapes. They are the symbols of Dionysos, who, in turn, is a symbol-figure, coming from the East, for the Eastern doctrine of felicity in the Thereafter translated into Mediterranean terms, represented by the ever lustful Fauni and their playmates, the Maenads.

THE SHIFT TOWARDS HEDONISM

After this short excursion into the symbolism shown on the rim and the stands of the Death-Mirrors, we now turn to the stories told by the engravings of the mirrors proper. Here we discover again a very significant thematic shift and development towards the paradisial vision of the East, using in a logical way and definite progression different figures of the Mediterranean mythos to illustrate the increasingly clearer demands of showing in funeral art the joys of a hedonistic next world. Those demands were made by the customers or patrons of the mirror-makers, who were only partly, but to an increasing extent, informed about the new, tempting but secret doctrines coming from the East.

That the mirror-gifts of the dead was an Etruscan matter is established by the fact that the inscriptions of the Death-Mirrors are written exclusively in the Etruscan lettering, and that they call all personages shown by their Etruscan names.

142

THE FLOWER OF SENSUALITY

There are also blossoms sometimes appearing on frames showing very prominently their organs of propagation, which are then understood as images of sensuality. Those blossoms are seen at times, in super-natural size, forming part of the central composition. The fact that the "Flower of Sensuality" is so frequently seen on frames and connected to vistas of the Beyond, to otherworldly genii and apparitions of Fate, being involved or actually running towards that flower – (which, at times, blends into the Snake of Sensuality) – seem to be foretelling the destiny of the soul in the next world. This is one more hint that in the mind of the people Sensuality and the Thereafter became synonymous. The flower as the symbol for physical union gives to those visions of the next world the connotations of beauty, purity and fragrance.

We have to appreciate the inventiveness of the artists, faced with the problem of showing symbolically "Physical Union" and may admire their simple and tasteful expediency of using the "Flower of Sensuality" – and must admit that we have, even today, no valid symbol for such a hint.

More than the opposed organs of generation in the blossom, the plant itself suggests the re-sprouting of the soul towards the light, which is here understood as the light of Eternity, and also reveals pictorially the transition from the budding of the flowers, as the dawn of the soul, and its longing, to the final opening to its tender unification.

On the left upper corner of a sarcophagus there appear for instance two "Flowers of Sensuality," a plant otherwise not known in the Mediterranean, and never used in any other connection – and it seems that the Water-Nymph, unfolding in promising readiness, is looking at them to call our attention to this symbolism.

91

69

97

98

FEMALE FIGURES ON MIRRORS

THE SEQUENCE

The gradual shift from the Mediterranean idea of the BELOW in Hades, towards the Eastern vision of the multiple females in the ABOVE shows the following progression.

THE CAST OF ACTORS:

I.) Female in the BELOW .... Persephone

II.) The dead from the BELOW to EARTH LEVEL ... Aphrodite

III.) From EARTH LEVEL to the ABOVE .... Ariadne

IV.) Female from the BELOW to the ABOVE .... Semele

V.) Single lover in the ABOVE .... Selene

VI.) Choice of females in the ABOVE .... Three Graces

VII.) The spiritual females in the ABOVE .... The Muses

No exact date can be assigned to each of those chronological phases, because the Eastern thoughts – (like later Christianity) – penetrated the land at different times in various degrees of completeness.

This sequence and typological system is shown here to begin with, so that we remain focused on the main symbol-features and do not get lost in the details of the following stories.

I.) PERSEPHONE: (The Female in the BELOW)

The case of that mistress of the BELOW was described before. In short it could be said that she was the first attempt to find a Mediterranean equivalent to illustrate the purely Eastern idea of a "Female after Death." We must not underestimate the predicament and final inventiveness of the Italian sculptors, because the idea that the dead man in the coffin should want to tangle with a female after his death, stunned and repulsed the Roman artists, before they could think of Persephone, although being a majestic figure for the Greeks and Romans, as an elegant solution of that eerie problem. – (Of course, they did not know, at that time, that the soul or alter-ego of the deceased was supposed to go through a phase of re-birth and rejuvenation before embracing the celestial creatures of love.)

II.) APHRODITE: (from the BELOW to the EARTH LEVEL)

A later wave of information told the artists that the idea of Hades has to be abandoned, and that there was a perfectly new idea of a re-birth of the souls, for which a symbol-figure has to be found. The sculptors, thereupon, used the story of Aphrodite and her beloved son Adonis, who died every year – but was re-born every spring, with the renewed vegetation – (according to the Attis cult). The scenario changed thereby from the subterranean realm of the dead to the EARTH LEVEL, to which the soul seemed to be re-born, in the shape of little flowers, as well as the earthly re-appearance of the youthful Attis, proudly displaying his male sex, as the promise of earthly fertility now entering the lands . . . his earthly procession was received with the jubilation of the women on a purely, almost utilitarian level, signifying abundance. We see Aphrodite therefore as the female agent bringing the dead (Adonis) up from the realm of the subterranean shades to the surface of the earth.

III.) ARIADNE: (from EARTH LEVEL to the ABOVE)

Ariadne, abandoned at Naxos, is said to have fallen in a trance-like sleep, in other versions to have died there. She was, however, awakened by Dionysos, who "married" her, surrounded by his jubilant Priapic train. On sarcophagi Ariadne became the symbol-figure for the reawakening after death, to the semi-divine spheres of sensual joy which was allegorically presented by Dionysos and his love-intoxicated votaries of Fauni and Maenads.

145

IV.) SEMELE: (from the BELOW to the ABOVE)

Further information coming from the East indicated that the dead not only will be rescued from the dreary BELOW, but that he will be elevated to the ABOVE. The artists thereupon chose as the symbol-figure for this apotheosis, Semele, the paramour of Zeus, who died a sweet death by the blaze of his divine splendor, having received from him the child Dionysos, who, after he grew up, went to fetch his mother Semele from the regions of the BELOW and elevated her to the cosmic sphere of the ABOVE, "between the stars" – that is not yet the Olympian region of the gods. This became one of the most popular scenes repeatedly shown on death-mirrors, the implication was still a purely filial relation between a good child and his mother.

V.) SELENE: (the single lover in the ABOVE)

Now came from the East the hear-say that a sensual relation will exist between the soul of the deceased and some celestial female. Groping and searching for a new symbol-figure within the Greco-Roman mythology, the artists chose Selene, queen of the night, (here relation to Death was explained in the chapter concerning "Apotheosis") – who was in love with the beautiful youth Endymion, who fell in an eternal sleep – now equated with death and the very person of the deceased. – (This identification of the dead with the figure of Endymion was made very obvious, as we have several "Endymion-Sarcophagi" – where the face of the gracefully sleeping Endymion is the only thing not finished on the otherwise finely executed pre-fabricated sarcophagus, just waiting to portray the facial features of the deceased onto the body of Endymion.) We see on those "Endymion-Sarcophagi" the moon-crested Selene rushing tenderly towards her lover and have thereby the first enactment of a love-relation, by figures of the Mediterranean mythos, conforming to the Eastern vision of a celestial female lover after death in the ABOVE, and the same hint that death is only a sleep, from which there might be a sweet awakening in the arms of that loving female.

VI.) THE THREE GRACES: (the choice between females)

There came, however, a new and still more specific information from the East, that there will be SEVERAL female beauties to choose from in the next world, whereupon the sculptors represented the 3 Graces as symbol-figures for this new requirement, posing now for the first time in the nude, or in

Oriental type veils, as the promise of a sensual paradise awaiting the dead in excelsis, with a choice of female love-partners.

VII.) THE MUSES: (the spiritual multitude)

Responding now to an even newer wave of information coming from the Asiatic Orient, requesting the presentation of a great MULTITUDE of females in the ABOVE – (meaning the Indian Apsarases and Oriental Houries) – the Mediterranean sculptors, in obvious despair, and in collision with the local precepts of decency, – (especially now in the era of the spiritual and celibate Mithras and the dawn of Christianity) – reverted to the Muses as the newly spiritualized image of the females of the Above, but less as the paramours of the deceased, and instead, as it seems, rather praising his virtues in a post mortem eulogy, directed at the passer-by.

APOLLO IN FUNERAL ART

In the foregoing typology we talked about the FEMALES appearing on the mirrors.

Among the MALE figures of the next world, the most frequently appearing image is that of Apollo which therefore attracts our first attention.

THE APOLLONIC EPIPHANY

(The avatar of the Dead)

The question whether Apollo is meant as a Guardian over the grave, or if the dead person actually assumes the personality of a mythological figure, is answered by the "Endymion Sarcophagi." We illustrate here only the example of Endymion, but there are many other sarcophagi which are obviously prefabricated workshop pieces kept in stock and waiting for customers. Those sarcophagi are finished, except for the faces which are merely blocked-out, to later bear the features of its future occupant, so that those very popular pieces clearly show that the deceased or his effigy — was actually equated with the protagonist in a mythological scene or

147

allegory. We also see the portrait of the deceased, reappearing in the seashell of the re-birth out of the sea, and the dead warrior, with his monogram inscribed on his person, in the arms of a celestial female, so that there seems to be no doubt that also on the plaques the dead person, or his alter ego, is identified with the Apollonic epiphany to a greater or lesser degree. We see the same phenomenon also in the identification of a human being with the avatar of a divinity, not so much in the classical world proper as in those regions lying just east of it. Also from there came the very early belief (around the seventh century B.C.) – that a worthy worshiper of Dionysos could gain, under certain conditions, such identifications with the divinity as to appear on inscriptions by his characteristic epithet of "Bakchos" – in conjunction with his name as a donor.

In India too existed the idea that some deserving person would be accepted in the company of the gods and that his spirit would thereby become "God-like" (devatma), a divinized epiphany.

Beyond that spiritual elevation, it is suggested that the deceased would re-appear with an alter-body. Buddha said:

"... out of his mortal body arises another body of spiritual sort – (rupim manomayam), complete in all its limbs and members and of transcendental substance – (abhinindriyam)."
[Majjhima-Nikaya, II, 17]

"The deceased ancestors – (pitris) – are made divine beings, and in the company of the Gods lead a life of eternal felicity"
[Rigveda X, 15, 16]

"He (Vamadeva) soared from this world, and having obtained all his desires in the yonder heavenly world, became immortal – yea, became alike the Gods. Therefore He, his Supreme Self, is called Indandra."
[Aitareya Upanishad I. iii, 13-14]

Further, following the same idea, we have the "Funeral-Apollos" as a Greco-Roman tradition, where the soul of the dead is commemorated in the image of Apollo. This very same idea of assuming a divine or mythological epiphany after death, we know from Egypt, where the deceased not only assumes certain exterior features and attributes of Osiris, but is also addressed officially as "Osiris so-and-so."

Against the idea of considering the objects on which Apollo appears as being nothing more than donations to the God Apollo, speaks the fact that we repeatedly see the Apollonic figure on the mirrors as being elevated with the help of genii related to death and resurrection. Apollo the god obviously does not need an elevation with the help of genii of secondary status. We will see later that it is another conception of Apollo which may have intruded with the Etruscans into the funeral art of Italy, based on meanings which this divinity had in Eastern lands.

As to the question of whether or not it is within the Greco-Roman thinking that the soul of a dead person can re-appear in the outline of a divinity, we have the example of Augustus, who permitted the erection of statues of divinities bearing his facial features. Admittedly, it was only in the Eastern provinces where divinities with the features of Augustus were created, but just this fact is a hint that those ideas dwelled there, or came from there, to intrude, via the Etruscans, into the funeral art of the Mediterranean.

It is true that the deification was originally reserved for reigning personalities only, but the idea as such was thereby established in the minds of people. Later we see a very general trend of extending privileges of the exalted persons to the lower echelons of the population, paving the way for the common belief in the possibilities of the transfiguration and the epiphany of ordinary mortals.

Mythology is said to be the mirror of the mind of a people. Accordingly we see the Greco-Roman mythology swarming with the metamorphosis and elevation of mortals, becoming almost a routine operation at the end of stories, to spare some deserving or heroic figures the descent to dreary Hades. This was understood as an act of clemency on the part of divine graces which was hoped for also to apply to the departed.

SENECA AND PLINIUS

(The split between philosophy and funeral art)

At a later time of doubts in this hoped for "Happy Ending" – by means of a transformation of the soul into the image of an exalted being, Lucius Annaeus Seneca (ca. 4 B.C. to 65 A.D.) in his "Apocolocyntosis" (a persiflage of the word "Apotheosis") dealing with death and Afterlife, severely condemned the prevailing idea of the deification of mortals, or as he suggested, the elevation of a pumpkin to the image of a divinity.

Plinius the elder, [23 to 79 A.D.] ascribes those visions to Vanity. But in disparaging it, he clearly describes the prevailing ideas of transformations which we see manifested in funeral art.

"THE HUMAN VANITY EXTENDS LIFE INTO THE
FUTURE AND IN SELF-DECEPTION LIES TO ITSELF
ABOUT LIFE BEYOND DEATH, IN ASSUMING THE
IMMORTALITY OF THE SOUL; AT TIMES ITS
TRANSFIGURATION, AT OTHER TIMES ASCRIBING
LIFE TO THE VENERATED MANES IN THE BELOW,
AND IN MAKING OF HIM WHO CEASED TO EXIST
EVEN AS A HUMAN BEING, A DIVINE APPARITION."

[Plinius, Naturalis Historia, VII.56.188]

With respect to the Apollonic epiphany, the original wording: ". . . alias immortalitatem, alias transfigurationem. . ." makes it especially clear that there was the belief that the soul may re-appear in a "transfiguration," meaning not a purely spiritual glorification but defacto taking the shape of an otherworldly "figure" – while the word "apparition" makes reference to an actual "appearing" in contrast to a mere fiction – so that we have beyond the many visual manifestations in funeral art of that time, here also a textual evidence of this belief, written by an eminent "eye-witness" well acquainted with the customs of that very age.

While Plinius considers such a transfiguration of the dead person into a divinity as an aberration – (meaning: unacceptable according to classical Greco-Roman thinking) – he never-the-less documents for us that such ideas existed de facto on a broad basis, at his time.

62

61

We have a group in the Museo Nazionale Romano in Rome, showing the Empress Faustina the Younger, glorified to appear as Venus, together with her lover Mars, or the representation of Emperor Comodus in the guise of Heracles in the Capitoline Museum . . . which again hints at the idea of a "transfiguration" of a person into a divine or mythological apparition, which was fashionable at that time, despite the fierce protest by old classical philosophers.

This development may have started with the archaic "Grave Apollos," whether as a portrait or as a symbol-figure to remember the departed. We then see the vague mask of Apollo on early sarcophagi and the figure of the dead reclining on the cover of the sarcophagus, at times with a hairdo patterned after the Apollonic mask, maybe as an attempt to become similar to him, in the next world. The public, now conditioned to the thought of a deified epiphany by the glorification of emperors and generals, simply demanded from the sculptors more and more identity of the dead with Apollo following the example set by that type of glorification accorded to exalted personages. The artists complied, of course, with the wishes of their patrons because they wanted to sell their ware . . . and it is probably there, that the great split occurred between Funeral Art and the classical Greco-Roman thoughts, which was so severely condemned by Plinius.

The inscription under one of the Funeral Appollos [National Museum, Athens, NM 385] of about 500 B.C. says:

> "Stop, traveller and lament
> by the grave of the dead Kroisos
> whom raging Ares killed
> while he was fighting among the first"

Some of the Kuroi [NM 20] are inscribed as "argyrotoxos" – (the silver-bowed) – meaning Apollo, some [NM 30] as being "set up by his father at his son's grave."

So that the Funeral Apollos and Kuroi seem to be very closely related and the glorification of the dead into a semi-divine or mythologized apparition seems to be a latent thought, vaguely surrounding those monuments between the seventh and fifth century B.C.

After a votive or dedicatory statue or plaque had been made, the proper place to deposit it was thought to be the sacrality of the sanctuary of Apollo, the patron and protector of young men . . . comparable maybe, in Christian times, to the funeral plaques and monuments in churches, also hinting at the idea of dedication as well as of the individual's elevation by his presence in the sanctified realm. As a possible parallel we also may think of the canonization, elevating mortals after death to a semidivine rank, which is accepted, without exact definition, by most people as a tradition, graced by its transcendental purity. This could have been the attitude, in old times, also concerning the Funeral Apollos and Kuroi.

ORIGIN OF APOLLO

(The Asiatic connection)

While there is an apparent split between the classical Greco-Roman conception of Apollo and his image in funeral art, which relates him to death and resurrection, we find his components outside the Mediterranean mythology, which have their roots in Eastern lands: The origin of Apollo is non-hellenic. He is supposed to have come from the interior of Asia-Minor – (together with his sister, Artemis of Ephesus) – and also seems derived from the Hittite god Apulunas, the divinity of the gate to the above – (therefore his Etruscan name of Apulu) – He has his title of "Agyieus" as the guardian of the gate, together with his other epithet of "Apollo Catharsius" as the ritual purifier, not only concerning the odium of death surrounding the grave, but also protecting the living from the magic attraction and dark powers of the departed souls. Apollo thereby assumes not only his position between the realm of the living and the dead, but also acts as a link between the Hellenic mythos and the more archaic chthonian gods. It is assumed that the Etruscans, coming from the East, brought Apollo to Italy as a funerary deity.

The religious meaning of the "Funeral Apollos" is still doubtful, but we may also expect that a split between the religious and the tradition, according to which the maker of those stelae followed an established custom, disregarding any exact religio-magic symbolism.

We might have here a situation comparable to the cross on graves in our days, where we can not establish the exact relation between the deceased and the actual formation of the cross, because there is a whole chain of associations and legends attached to the visible symbol — which might also be the case concerning the Apollonic epiphany.

In naming Artemis the "Twin-sister" of Apollo, we may discern the tendency in Asiatic divinities of opposite avatars, as Destruction and Creation – (the Siva-Vishnu principle). – In his oldest Eastern form Apollo was thought to be the Death-god of men, – while his "Twin" or counterpart was the many-breasted and pre-hellenic Artemis of Ephesus, who stood for nourishing and sustaining life, the multiformed creation symbolized by all sorts of wildlife depicted on her statues.

But beyond that contrapost of Male to Female, and Life to Death, we see even within each of those symbol-figures the Asiatic system of opposite avatars, as Artemis is not only the protectress of life, but also wields the power to destroy it, . . . be it as the huntress of animals, or as the one who said to gave death to women in childbirth – the same as Apollo was the protector of young men, as well as the one who brought them down with his bow and arrow.

The Romans, making their first contact with Apollo partly through the Etruscans and partly by way of the Greek states of southern Italy, erected the first temple of Apollo when the "Funeral Apollos" were already a time-honored tradition.

BIRTH OF THE HELLENIC APOLLO

(out of the dark waters)

> There are two legends. One is based on the "Homeric Hymn" – but as this poem was written for the festival of Apollo, it is an exuberant glorification and therefore less reliable as to its contents. The other seems to be the better story which goes as follows: The Titaness Leto was loved by Zeus and conceived from him the twins Apollo and Artemis, but no land would receive her when the time of birth drew near, because the whole earth feared the anger of Hera, when receiving her rival. Hera, in fact, decreed that Leto shall not bring forth her children in any place where the sun was shining. Leto fled to the little island of Delos, where Poseidon evaded the decree of Hera, by submerging that island, so that the sun could not shine on it, and there the divine twins were born.

This version seems to be the common ground on which the representations are based, so repeatedly seen on Mirrors, Plaques and Sarcophagi alike, as all of them show the rebirth out of the dark waters, as being symbolic for the idea of Resurrection from the dark and deep to the light in the Above – so that we can assume that this story must have had a broad base in the belief of the people in the last pre-christian centuries – disregarding the fact that it was contrary to the classical dogma.

In conclusion it could be assumed that this radical departure may be ascribed to the tremendous impact of the Eastern visions, according to which the funeral art represented more and more the idea of the Resurrection after death, which totally contradicted all classic concepts and the official dogma of Hades, and according to this new vision also the Apollonic epiphany may have changed from representing a thought, to representing a figure . . . a figure which was later even set in relation to other symbolic apparitions.

APOLLO AND THE MUSES ON SARCOPHAGI

Before we talk about the sarcophagi where Apollo is shown with the Muses, we may call attention to some sarcophagi – (connecting his image actually to a dead person) – where Apollo with Lyra is shown as the central ornament – quite similar in its composition to the Three Graces, appearing in this central position, obviously as a promise of paradise, awaiting the soul of the dead. (see Title-page).

124 In the specific case of this sarcophagus [Porto Terres, Basilica San Gavino] we may see the parents standing left and right, looking at the image of their departed son in the allegory of Apollo, while his meeting with the Nymphs, as shown on the plaques and mirrors, appears as the continuation of his adventures in the Beyond.

With Apollo or Apollini directly on a sarcophagus, his relation to death in funeral art is thereby established beyond any doubt.

123 We see in later times Apollo the GOD, now bridging over into his Greco-Roman status as Lord of the Muses, originally a device to show him with a multitude of females, as suggested by the Eastern paradisial vision. This new constellation of Apollo and the Muses was now symbolized in funeral art by Masks and Instruments, as Apollo was shown consistently with his Lyra in hand, and the emblem of the Muses were the theatrical masks. The stage of action and scenario was now definitely set in the Above and the trend was towards spiritualization. Neither arms nor precious saddles, nor gifts of food and drink were now appropriate to bring to those exalted spectral bodies in their rarified spheres. The masks and instruments were not thought to be gifts of the dead for their actual and physical use, but more as a dedicatory symbolism to put at the feet of those spirits upon entering their region.

Because Apollo was a symbol-figure for the deceased, the alter-ego of the dead was now pictured as "With the Muses" in the Above and no longer "With the Manes" the shades of the dead undergound. The Masks and Music-instruments, which are so puzzling on funeral monuments, appear now as appropriate gifts for the Muses, who were thought of no longer as Hostesses, but the "Companions" of the dead – (who was from now on appearing as their playmate or even Lord, in the features of Apollo). To underline this state of companionship, the dead appeared on later sarcophagi adorned with the insigniae of the Muses, as if belonging to their clan.

The transition from the "Three Graces" to the Muses can be understood in the following manner:

After Apollo was firmly established as the central figure on stelae and sarcophagi there came the request from the clients, the patrons of art, to the artists, who made the sarcophagi, to see that Soul-Apollini joined with the "Female Element" according to the Eastern vision of the Thereafter. But in a more intellectual trend, leaning away from the Asiatic sensuality, that "Female Element" – shown before as the Three Graces, – should no longer be the promise of lust, but some females – (still females were requested!) – should hint, in the sense of a eulogy, at the spiritual importance of the dead.

It seemed therefore logical to pair off the dead who gradually slipped from the corporal Apollini into the image of the highly spiritual and glorious god Apollo with the Muses, because according to Greco-Roman mythos, the Muses were the females surrounding Apollo in a subordinate position, quasi as satrapies reigning over the specific provinces of his domain, like acting, singing, dancing . . . etc.

Out of this constellation developed an opulent trend, showing Apollo in the center, surrounded by all the Muses as a magnificent pageantry, filling the broad side of the sarcophagi. No interaction between Apollo and the Muses is suggested and it seems questionable, at times, that the sculptors still remembered that the image of Apollo should represent the transfiguration of the dead, as those reliefs may remind us of the line-up of all the actors for a "grand finale" seen in theatrical performances.

At other times Hermes Psychopompos is seen behind the Apollo-figure, suggesting that Apollo is representing the dead person, who was brought up from the regions of the shades by this faithful guide of souls. In some cases the Muses are shown with their lips parted, as if they were about to sing or as if they would form a speaking-chorus, as was usual on solemn occasions in the theaters of that time. A hint at singing is made in their competition with the Harpies – understood this time perhaps as the Sirens with their eery songs seducing the living to come with them into their realm of the dead, and where the Muses are shown too, with open mouths and facing the onlooker, as on a stage, their music being of the mysterious spheres of immortality. The change from the macabre Harpies to the semi-divine Muses, illuminates well the general trend from the dark and murky to the light and sparkling visions, concerning the Thereafter. We also have hints that the new ideas were thought to be "victorious" over the older and more dreary dogma. We even notice a joyous exuberance in the newly won break-through from the "body-snatchers" and the shades of Hades, to the doctrine promising the elevation of the dead to the spiritual sphere of the Muses, suggesting that it is their noble and exalted company which the dead may now enjoy. To this effect we have, for example, a very amusing sarcophagus in the Metropolitan Museum of New York showing a contest between those two types of celestial females, in which the Muses appear to be victorious over the tribe of the Harpies. Illustrating this idea, we see at the right-hand corner – (meaning: as the end-result of this contest) – one of the vanquished Harpies fallen to the ground while one of the victorious Muses lustily plucks some feathers out of her wings.

ETRUSCAN ALPHABET

We deal in the following with Etruscan inscriptions and names. The Etruscan alphabet of ca. 700 B.C. is engraved on an ivory tablet measuring 2 inches by 3½ inches and was found at Marsigliana near Albegna. Here are some later variations of the earliest Etruscan alphabet.

ARCHAIC ALPHABET 700 TO 500 B.C.

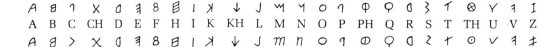

| A | B | C | CH | D | E | F | H | I | K | KH | L | M | N | O | P | PH | Q | R | S | T | TH | U | V | Z |

LETTERS ON LATER INSCRIPTIONS

Here also are the names of some personalities frequently engraved on the mirrors. They must be read from right to left, while the sequence on pictures goes from down to up . . . (the way in which plants and people develop.)

ETRUSCAN NAMES

ꟼAꟻJA , ꟻAꟻJA	..ALPAN	Female in the Below
VJVꟻA , VJꟻA	..APLU – APULU ...	Apollo
ƎꟿVTꟼA , ƎꟿVTꟿƎ	..ARTUME	Artemis
ꟅIꟿVTA , ꟅIꟿVTꟅ	..ATUNIS	Adonis
ꟼOVꟼꟛ , Oꟼꟛ	..CATH	Sungod
ꟅꟿVJ8V8 , ꟅꟿVJ8V8	..FUFLUNS	Dionysos
ꟛJꟛ꟠꟠Ꮎ , ꟛJ꟠꟠ꟼJƎ	..HERCLE	Heracles
AꟅAJ	..LASA	Female Genii
ꟼAƎꟿ , ꟿAƎꟿ	..MEAN	Nike, Victoria
ꟅꟿVOꟛꟿ , ꟅꟿVꟘꟛꟿ	..NETHUNS	Neptun
AITOVꟼ , ITOVꟿ	..NORTIA	Fortuna
AJꟿƎꟅ , AJꟿƎꟅ	..SEMLA	Semele
ꟼAꟅƎO , ꟿAꟅƎꟘ	..THESAN	Aurora, Rebirth
AꟿJAO , AꟿJAꟘ	..THALNA	Iuventas, Hebe
꟠ꟼAO , ꟠ꟿAꟘ	..THANR	Death & Rebirth
AIꟿIT , ꟿIT	..TIN, TINIA	Zeus
ꟼA꟠VT , ꟿA꟠VT	..TURAN	Aphrodite
Ʂꟿ꟠VT , Ʂꟿ꟠VT	..TURMS	Hermes
IꟿV , IꟿV	..UNI	Juno
JƎ꟠VA , JIꟅV	..USIL, AUREL	Auroral Apollo
ꟘꟿA꟞ , OꟿA꟞	..VANTH	Death & Destiny

157

In the following we go quickly through the illustrations shown in the back of the book.

Those pictures are provided with short captions, but in many cases more has to be said about them. The main text should provide this opportunity. It will by necessity repeat things which are said in the captions, as well as features which are mentioned before, explaining the background and development of certain appearances and their constellations.

This seems desirable because some appearances can best be demonstrated by pictures of the objects in question, while their development must be explained by showing their historic background.

It is interesting that no mirror or cista shows the tragic ending of a soul being refused the Above or of being consigned to the dreary Below. This seems to be one more hint that those engravings were thought to have the magic effect of directing the destiny of the soul in the right direction, namely: to a happy ending in the Above . . . besides, of course, the function of warding off evil influences, by the "shielding" effect, ascribed to symbols of the "good" . . . as in our times the sign of the cross, or in the case of the Mirrors and Cistae the loving reception in the Above, staged by Nymphs or exalted figures.

This in contrast to the Skyphos 97.372 of Boston, where Charun, the merciless demon of death, assigns to the parting man and woman the abode underground. This Skyphos was however, NOT found in a grave, meaning that it was not meant to be a Gift of the Dead, directing in this way the destiny of the souls . . . similar to a great number of funeral monuments not given into the graves but remaining above ground, depicting the tragedy of death, without the intention of influencing, by pictorial presentations, the future path of the soul.

13

THE SOUL CARRIED OFF (EOS)

Eos is the goddess of Dawn, the Latin Aurora, the sister of Selene, goddess of the Night and sister or daughter of Helios, god of the Sun. She is thereby a transition-figure between Night – (that is, Death) – and the eternal Light, which makes her a symbol-figure of Resurrection. As such she is shown "dawning" or ascending in a chariot drawn by horses and surrounded by radiance above some scenes related to Death, which are depicted on Etruscan mirrors.

67

In a second connotation she is shown as "carrying off" male figures whom she loves. In mythology there are special names for those males and love-stories invented, but in sum it can be said that she was not choosey concerning her victims, including giants, heroes, pretty boys and so forth, – so that an allegory becomes apparent, which visualizes the victim of Death as being "carried off" by a loving female – (similar to the Hylas vision) – but also being a reasonably good facsimile of the Eastern ideas of equating Death with a love-relation to at least one celestial female.

63

In practical terms we see that the stories of Eos fit very well cases which deal with the death of a soldier, who is then shown as being carried off, in full battle-gear by that loving and celestial female, whereby the figure of

64

159

Eos melts at times into the personality of a Lasa, the Etruscan Death-Angel with wings, who is also shown carrying off and comforting members of the human race.

There is a rather bizarre story connecting Eos to Immortality which may contain an allegoric meaning: Eos asked the gods to confer Immortality upon one of her men – (Tithonos) – but forgot to ask that he might be ageless too, so that he shrivelled away to an unsightly thing which had to be hidden and begged for his death. The "moral" of that story could be of a comforting kind for the bereaved: that an extended life brings about the plagues of old age, which are spared those who are carried off in a still lovable condition.

Possibly related to the story of Tithonos we sometimes see on mirrors a baldheaded and extremely emaciated man carried away by a celestial female, but this may as well make reference to a person who was sick and suffered long, and for whom the travel to the next world is a blessing. (According to Herodot III.99. there was a belief that sick people rapidly lose weight, which might be of interest as this idea is ascribed to Indian tribes and thereby possibly to the Etruscans.) Common to all three mirrors shown here is the fact that they are surrounded by Ivy, the evergreen plant, symbolic for the undying soul. Also common to those mirrors is the feature that the Eos-like Lasa is heavily dressed . . . in contrast to the pleasure-girls whom the soul is supposed to meet later.

THE FATE OF THE SOUL DECIDED

There are mirrors which make reference to FATE, of which Death is, of course, the most dramatic and noticeable manifestation.

To this group also belong mirrors showing the practice of Haruspex – (Hepatoskopia) which was then the method of predicting Fate by examining the liver of some sacrificial animal.

It is remarkable that the Etruscans have no personality in judgement of the dead, and it is therefore quite possible that the haruspiciae, shown on the Death-Mirrors, assumed that function . . . because it is not obvious that every single person would enter the paradise of delights, especially as they had the ugly and menacing specter of death in the person of CHARU as opposed by the mild and beautiful death-angels in the form of the LASAE (derived from the Greek Lares, naughtily begotten by Hermes Psychopompos on his way to Hades by raping Lala) and as the Etruscans had a very highly developed technique of cursing the dead, manifested in many tablets of lead, stuck into graves.

With those multiple choices between the possibilities of being cruelly hit with the hammer by the fiendish Charu, — or gently cradled and comforted by a charming Lasa — or being enmeshed in a horrible curse after death, — somebody has to make a decision on a higher level of what it is going to be. At least we can understand the anxiety to find out, to divine, what it is going to be — which might be the subject shown on the 'Fate' or 'Haruspex' mirrors.

A mirror dealing with the examining of the liver to foretell the fate, is from Vulcenti and now in the Vatican, Museo Gregoriano No. 1807, and shows a bearded man inscribed as Calchas, the master of the divination of historic fame, who is pictured as being winged, which may suggest that he is meant here ad abstractum as the 'spirit' of divination in general, like looking into the "Book of Fatum" — of Destiny and Fate, — or similar to the "Weighing of the Heart" in the death-mythology of Egypt, where the future of the soul is determined in this manner. But why is this engraved on a mirror? The suspicion arises that it was thought that there will be a sort of decision made, or fate of the dead foretold after death, and the person eminently qualified to make such a fateful pronouncement would be of the Calchas-type — and therefore it would be useful to flatter the ego and vanity of this decision-maker, to sway his judgement towards mildness. If you can not directly bribe a judge, the next best thing to gain his benevolence is to glorify his importance, — a technique known from the earliest prayers is the devout submission to a judge whose image is exalted, to gain his favors. Therefore, to appear before the judge with his picture in hand, beautifully framed, would be about equivalent to the student appearing for his examination with the picture of the professor, beautifully framed, in hand — which sounds too naive, but some traces of the same psychological attitude can be discerned in many dealings with superior mights, religious or otherwise. Therefore, this picture of the decision-maker is conceivably a flattering bring-along gift of the dead, to him who will pronounce the destiny of his soul.

66

The Tarchon mirror, shows a group of figures deliberating the destiny of the soul. The winged apparition on the handle, lifting as it seems, the whole scene to a higher level, indicates that all we see takes place in the Above. The central group consists of an Haruspex with a friendly facial expression — (a promising omen!) — examining the liver and being watched by Tarchon, the "Heros eponymos" of Tarquinia. The female between them, looking with great interest at the proceedings is one of the uncertain figures of destiny. At left, seemingly entering the scene, is an Apollonic

67

young man with foliated branch in hand, who wears an open cloak over his naked body. The imposing person at right with spear in hand is, according to inscription, "Velthune" head of the federation of the twelve gods and "Lord over the sacred Grove" – (sometimes associated with the realm of the chosen) – here possibly as guardian of this sphere, and waiting to see if the soul is admitted or rejected. In the background we see, as a good omen, the rising sun, foretelling the final outcome of the deliberation. All that is crowned on a still higher level by the quadriga of "Thesan" the glorious goddess of Resurrection.

The interpretation of this mirror hinges mostly on the Apollonic figure at left with the name "Rathlth" which is not known to us, but suggests the following hypothesis.:

Another mirror [G.K. LXXXII] shows the same Apollonic figure in the same location on the left rim of the mirror, as if entering the scene, also with the foliated branch in hand, as the insignia of resurrection, and the identical position of his legs and also naked under the retracted drapes ... but this time clearly inscribed as "Apulu" (Apollo) – to suggest the identity of the "Rathlth" figure with Apollo.

It seems therefore quite probable that we see on the Tarchon mirror the most usual epiphany of the dead in the features of Apollo.

This would mean that the mysterious "Rathlth" – (never heard of as a mythological figure) – could be the personal name of the deceased, who appears now in the image of Apollo – and watches modestly as the destiny of his wandering soul is foretold by the haruspex.

That high above, unseen by him, the quadriga of Thesan tells of his impending resurrection to the Light Eternal, may express the wish of those who gave this mirror as a parting gift into his grave as a protective amulet, with the usual intent to magically foretell the destiny of the soul. Just as today we also have funeral medallions and gravestones depicting the merciful reception of the soul – so did those mirrors, in a comforting way, predict the glorious elevation of the departed.

The re-appearance of the dead in the image of Apollo is the most usual of his otherworldly epiphanies starting from the primitive sea sarcophagi, continued on the plaques of Naples, to the Apollo-mirrors and attested by Plinius who confirms that such "transfigurations" of the dead into the images of divinities and mythological figures were usual in his time.

The personal identification of the dead individual with a mythological figure is not new or uncommon even within the modest volume of material presented here. To that effect we have the monogram of the deceased on his soul carried away by Eos, or the figure of Endymion, representing the dead, on some prefabricated sarcophagi, which are finished to the last detail,

64

except the face of Endymion which is left in the raw, to be carved later to the likeness of the deceased. So that the personal name of "Rathlth" inscribed over an Apollonic epiphany seems not out of the question on this Tarchon mirror.

The Etruscans had a special goddess of fate, called ATHRPA, derived from the Greek "Atropos," the inexorable, who appears frequently on Death-Mirrors. We see her, for instance, on the so-called "Athrpa-mirror" of Berlin, together with Aphrodite – (inscribed as Turan) – who lost her beloved son Adonis – (inscribed as Atune) – killed by the wild boar, which is also shown on the upper right of the mirror. All that being an allegory that FATE brings Death, but also that there is a rebirth to youth and splendor, and as in the Attis and Adonis ritual of those times, a jubilant reception by all females, greeting the bringer of love . . . and in this sense a Mediterranean re-staging of the paradisial visions of the East's reception of the revenant dead by the Celestial Brides.

68

We see that such a mirror, however sweet his allusion to Death may be, could hardly be an object of an earthly donation – (as some other mirrors were) – and was in fact, one of the many Death-mirrors found in Etruscan graves.

The mirror-makers probably had first to flatter the customer to make a sale, by showing the soul in an enviable position, in comparing the deceased to Adonis the Beloved, and Attis the Resurrected, although the mirrors ultimately served as a present of the deceased to the other-worldly Nymphs and also to guide the direction of Fate through picture-magic to a happy ending, which could be the reason why we so often see the divinity of Fate – (writing-equipment in hand) – with the "Flower of Sensuality" in her path, almost forcing destiny to lead to the symbol of sweet embraces.

In assuming that the divinity of Fate would not in retrospect signify the fate which brought the person to his death, but rather presided over, or decided on the fate his soul should suffer or enjoy after his earthly departure, we may again see here the half cunning and half naive speculation that picturing the figures involved in this last judgement, by glorifying them and their importance on the mirrors, could favorably influence their decision . . . as we saw it in earliest times concerning the gifts to the judges . . . and the supplicant attitudes before mighty divinities in Sumerian, Hittite and Egyptian prayers.

69

It seems possible that the reflective property of the mirrors became in time a secondary feature and that they remained mainly a gift-item, in which case it would have been proper to have mirrors addressing the divine and winged Haruspex experts, (who were males and no mirror-users in the usual sense) instead, with images of their glorification and importance – (as we donate an image of Christ to Christ, in a church) – in contrast to donating the mirrors to the Nymphic tribe, in the hope for their more romantic favors, who used the reflecting side of the mirrors in a feminine fashion, as shown engraved on many mirrors and cistae.

MIRRORS AS GIFTS TO THE FEMALES

On the mirror [GE.V.14] a small male person, totally naked and presumably the soul, brings a mirror and what appears to be an apple on a stick, in Greek called "Hedone" – (symbolic for the idea of Hedonism) – as an

70 endearment to a "beautifully" dressed female who makes the "soul" sniff a blossom. This action may make reference to the idea of the "Divine Fragrance" emitted by the female, and related to the "Recognition by Smell" – in short: to attract the soul and let it know that she is of celestial provenience. The dog we see is quite generally a symbol for sex-drive, and is shown to come from the female and approaches the little male with closed mouth – meaning: in friendship or asking for attention. On the lower register there is a big cock pursuing a small creature of a different species, which may represent a paraphase of the above situation. As the cock is a symbol for lovemaking, it may point to the incongruity between the "poor naked soul" – (Hadrian) – and the sumptuous Female of the Beyond. The fact that the cock is the bigger creature and lined up beneath the female, and the smaller animal is drawn under the soul-image, could mean that in this parable the female is the aggressor, according to the Eastern pattern, also shown on the Sea-Sarcophagi. In this connection it may be significant that the female wears an Asiatic turban, has round Oriental earrings and a cloak with the ornamented borders and the typical Eastern pointed ends with the non-Mediterranean tassels, so as to represent an embodiment of that outlandish creed.

As a variant to the Venus emerging from a shell, the allegory of Rebirth out of a flower is frequently used, inspired maybe by the idea of the

71 Anthesteria, the upcoming of the souls out of the ground in the form of flowers, re-awakening in spring, symbolic for the re-awakening of the soul after death. There might also be a kinship of those flowers to the Eastern vision of the "Lotus-born."

Winged figures mostly indicate a Lasa as the recipient of gift-mirrors and as much depends on the kindness of those spirits, they are mostly shown in flattering beauty. But it is Persephone who is the arch-figure of the Hostess, the great Lady in the realm of the dead, and therefore she is often shown as receiving the mirrors as bring-along-gifts. In return she is expected to give the souls a pleasant stay. This scenario conforms fairly well to the Mediterranean vision of the souls in the Below. However, we see the inflow of Eastern ideas by the fact that the soul is met there by Females in an amorous mood, sometimes described as "Servants of Aphrodite" – which, by the way, was the official title of the Hierodules in the Eastern sanctuaries of the various Love-queens. **72**

Sometimes the soul on its eerie voyage through the cold spaces of the In-between is shown with the traveler's cap or cape or boots, changing later in a more Apollonic appearance, while his "pleasurable stay" is then expanded to a frankly amorous reception, where Persephone appears **73** rather as a bystander, or mistress of a realm now in the Asiatic Above, being populated by girls of pleasure, to whom she seems to have handed the bring-along mirror, as it is now up to them to charm the arriving souls. (There was never a hint of making love directly to Persephone.) Persephone, however, holds at times an egg, the symbol of Rebirth, to denote the sphere after death and sometimes a pigeon, the insignia of Aphrodite, to give us a hint at the general mood in her realm of celestial embraces.

THE RECEPTION IN THE BEYOND

Some mirrors show in an almost schematic manner the most fundamental constellation surrounding the dead when appearing in the Above, involving a winged Lasa as his guide, and at least one celestial **74** female as his tender companion or seductress. The winged Lasa clearly denotes the setting of the Beyond. In some cases the soul appears as hardly metamorphosed, wearing a beard of the same shape as we see them on the Etruscan tomb-paintings. We see again that those mirrors, with their references to Death and the next world, were certainly not suitable for gifts among the living or for the toilet-table of a lady, showing a dead man – (her man?) – in the company of other females. On the other hand, such a mirror seems acceptable as a "bon voyage" gift to the deceased, or to recommend his soul to a friendly reception by "directional magic."

The so-called Dorow Mirror of the fourth century B.C., now at Berlin, depicting, at this relatively late date, the already completely Asiatic con- **75** ception of the Thereafter. There the soul or alter-ego of the deceased is

shown in its blissful reunion with a loving celestial female, translated into
a Maenad, characterized by her Tyrsos, while the soul re-appears reborn as
a youth with the "Corona Immortalis" on his head and caressing the face of
his newly found playmate with the left hand, while he holds in the right his
"Bowl of Sanctification" to show that he was duly buried with the proper
rites and blessings . . . as we see the same bowl in the right hand of the
deceased on Etruscan grave monuments, – (which bowl seems derived
originally from the "Begging-Bowl" – the insignia of Buddha after his
apotheosis, and considered thereafter a sacral object, like our crucifix in the
hand of the dying.) – In the middle of this mirror design we see a foliating
branch, indicating the re-sprouting life, so often seen as the re-foliating
staff of Psychopompos. – On this mirror we have on the earth-level two
snakes entwined, almost like emanating out of the body of the male and
female, and interlocked while facing each other, as a symbol of the sensual
union of the couple above. The snakes were used as a symbol for sensuality
as their embrace signified lust and not procreation. (The snakes are said, by
Aristotle, to be the animal remaining longest in copulation, hinting here at
India's ideal of prolonged intercourse.) The atmosphere of this joyful
encounter is also indicated by showing both as running vividly towards
each other with fluttering garments, while the designer is making sure to
clearly show the sex of the youth pointing gaily at the girl. However, the
most interesting part of this mirror, and surrounding the couple, are several
fish shown in dotted lines to indicate that they are under water – suggesting
by this means that the scene takes place within the waters, making reference thereby to the "Celestial Ocean" – so amply shown on the "Sea-Sarcophagi" as the realm of the paradise, the sphere of felicity after death,
according to the Indian scriptures, with the celestial maidens, the Apsarases, meaning: "those of the waters" – then re-cast as the enigmatic
Water-Nymphs on grave monuments, but here taking the shape of a
Maenadic love-partner, however still shown in the Waters of the Indian
scenario, while wearing the paraphernalia of the Mediterranean girls of
exuberant non-restraint, as the closest equivalent to the Eastern pleasure-
girls, the artists could think of.

A mirror showing Semele with her son Dionysos, uses Semele as the
symbol-figure for the elevation from the Below to the Above. But as it was
Dionysos who caused this elevation, we may encounter here another alle-
gory, based on the fact that it was the Eastern doctrine, – represented by
Dionysos, – which permitted the souls to be elevated from Hades to the
blissful Above. As Semele, who was condemned to the Below, "embraces"
Dionysos, the picture may contain the hint that the souls "embracing" the
Eastern dogma, are thereby lifted from the Below to the Above. In this sense

76

it seems permissible to call the re-appearing soul traditionally "Apollo" – if "Semele and Son" are understood to merely perform, in a secondary role in staging, the "pantomime" of resurrection.

RECEPTION AS HERO

Many mirrors depict the deceased as Hero. The beginning of this tradition may have been the fact that a soldier had lost his life in battle, and the thought may have been that he should be buried with a mirror as a gift to the otherwordly specters and genii of the Beyond, to endear himself to them, who were said to be female, connected to the Waters of Eternity.

A second idea may have been that the deceased used the mirror as a sort of 'calling-card' to present his person to the apparitions of the next world and be thereby introduced as worthy to be honored and rewarded by the females.

77

A third idea could have had the rather magical intention of guiding an event by projecting it forward in a picture, as the contrary of sticking pins in a picture. Following this thought, the image on the mirror may then give the female of the Beyond the idea or instruction to caress the arriving Hero in the realm of the Blessed.

If there was no direct reference to a soldierly death as a Hero, the mirrors often make vague reference to mystic figures of high prestige, letting the deceased appear in the aura of greatness in a rather abstract setting of pomp and pageantry, but mostly including the image of a beautiful woman and if we think of a mirror as a bring-along-gift to the otherwordly Nymphs, the flattery could be helpful to the donor when comparing her to the most beautiful female of all, may that be Helen of Troy or Aphrodite. It also may be advisable to depict the other females of the Above – (and there was a gossip reaching the Mediterranean that there are many of them) – not as Houries, the professional lovers, but rather as the noble 'entourage' of a great lady.

78

At a later stage the deceased was frankly depicted in the image of a great Hero, probably as a wish-dream of the bereaved for an apotheosis of the departed. They may have cherished the vision of seeing him received in love by a winged Lasa who herself would put the mantle of glory around him in the nebulous spheres out of which may appear to him his earthly companions, while still nameless beauties, the servants of Aphrodite in her

79

celestial sanctuary may slowly shed their hulls.

This rather earthly reappearance of the beloved was either considered a more convincing portrait of the deceased, or did the people in northern Italy, where the mirrors were made, not yet dare to transform their loved one into a divinity, as did the inhabitants of the South, who had a more flamboyant phantasy and believed in a greater nearness between the divine and the human condition.

The radiantly arising out of the deep of the premordial sea to the eternal light is often shown on mirrors, as the great hope and promise of Afterlife, whereby the manusculinity of that "Pool of Nature" is symbolized by the Beards of the serpents, their sharp beaks indicating their appetite for devouring all living eventually streaming into the Ocean. There is also the hint that the person actually developed or is reborn out of the morphology of the sea-creatures.

The premordial waters are indicated here by a line of waves which looks quite ornamental, suggesting thereby the possibility that the same ornamentation, seen on many other objects of antiquity, may in fact also make reference to the mythical waters of rebirth, and consequently would give a significance – (maybe overlooked before) – to the scenes above those lines of waves, – which are sometimes modified to appear as meanders.

In cases where we see, quite inexplicably, fish floating through scenes which obviously are taking place in the Above, those lines of waves would indicate the scenario of the Celestial Ocean.

Not only the transhuman creatures were thought to have arisen of the waters, but even on the religious level it is said that the dark waters preceded the emerging of the world itself: (Genesis, 1, 2) "Darkness was upon the face of the deep. And the Spirit of God moved upon the face of the Waters."

But it seems possible that the Etruscan thinking had been influenced by the much earlier Indian ideas of the rebirth out of the waters.

> "As the flowing rivers, bound for the ocean, disappear into
> the ocean after having reached it, their names and forms
> being dissolved, and are simply called ocean – even so, he
> whose goal is the Purusha, disappears into the Purusha and
> so his name and form is dissolved and he becomes free and
> renewed in parts and immortal."

[Prasna Upanishad VI.5]

RECEPTION AS APOLLO

Another mirror – [G.-K.76-PF.245] – also makes reference to the Sea and, as it seems, to the resurrection of the soul out of the Eternal Waters, the great "Pool of Nature" to which all eventually return and out of which all is re-born . . . (in a strange similarity with the Darwinian Theory).

On the mirror we see Neptune, (NETHUNS) who seems to hand over the newly arisen Soul, (USIL) to the goddess of Dawn (THESAN).

80

As the only attribute to identify himself, USIL holds in his right hand a very elaborate but symbolically small Bow-Insignia, which makes it possible to understand him as Apollo-like apparition, the usual glorification of the soul. The name USIL seems to mean "the Radiant one" – (similar maybe to the Epoptes, those who see the Light after their initiation in the Hellenic Mysteries) – on the linguistic detour which made from Aurum, gold, – Aurora, really "the golden one" – but meaning the Sunrise-personification. So we see "Him of the Light" actually encircled by a disk which might be a halo-like emanation of light around his head. Another hint at his rebirth seems to be a freshly sprouting plant on the ground between his legs, which bears the blossom of a lily – known to have very prominently showing organs of male and female sort, the female parts crowding with impunity around the arrogantly protruding male center piece, and having been symbolic, therefore, for male-female relations, – so much so, that those organs of the plant were cut out by especially conscientious clergy, when brought into a sanctified place . . . In our case this strategically growing lily may, or may not, be a hint at the impending encounter the soul would have with the Celestial Brides, promised by the Eastern Scriptures . . . similar, maybe, to the "Snake of Sensuality" shown on funeral monuments, rearing its head between the legs of Fauni, to denote the hedonistic atmosphere of the next world.

Another reason for the plant beneath the apotheosed soul might be a reference to the vision of the beatified Buddha, who is said and shown to be "Lotus-Born" – which idea is then so clearly depicted on the Sea-Sarcophagi where the souls of the reborn to the next world are seen as Soul-Babies sprouting out of flowers and plants. Noteworthy in this connection is the fact that the apotheosed Buddha also is shown to reappear in the Above with a disc of light, or halo, around his head and is eulogized as "The Enlightened." The sum of all those associations may then be projected onto the central figure of this mirror.

Usil, the soul, wears sandals, the usual hint at a wandering soul, coming from somewhere. Beyond that he is naked, except for a piece of drapery hiding his loin only, and greatly reminiscent of the death-shroud the revived souls have about them, when emerging from the grave, as seen on sarcophagi of that time.

The gestures of hand, so important with the Italians, seem to be as follows: Usil points with the hand in which he holds the Bow-Insignia at himself, as if to say thereby who he is, the radiant Apollini, shown on funeral plaques. Nethuns of the sea looks and points at Thesan, the Dawn, as if talking to her, to which she responds by putting her hand on the shoulder of Usil, with a pretty sure grip and pointing with her index finger right at his face, as if to indicate that the conversation concerns the soul, which seems to be delivered here from the sea to the spheres of the eternal light.

But the most interesting figure is below the arisen Usil, towards the handle of the mirror. It is a winged creature of the sea and all efforts are made by the designer to show that he, as the symbol of the eternal waters, is the male element of the creative force, the spermatic fluidum of cosmic dimension. Accordingly, he shows a male sex, flanked on his hips by fins – (this already being a poignant symbolism by itself, as the insignia of generation, combined with the attributes of the sea, to represent the eternally generative Ocean). His legs then develop into sea-snakes, and to further show the permeating maleness, those snakes have quite impressive beards, not enough with that, they also have the crests of cocks . . . all that, to show that not a specific animal was meant, but the 'element' of masculinity as such . . . and so that nobody misses the point, this personification of the sea holds a dolphin in each of his hands.

The re-appearance of the dead in the image of Apollo, hardly perceptible on sarcophagi, was clarified on the plaques of Naples without strictly stating that "Apollini" was related to Death, so that it was only due to the inscription on the mirrors that this relation is documented beyond any doubt.

On a certain mirror we see the Apollonic epiphany in the company of three females, who, according to the inscriptions over their figures, clearly illustrate the sequence from Death to Rebirth. This progression is symbolized by "Muira" (goddess of Fate and Doom) – followed by "Letun" (symbol figure for emerging from the dark waters) – followed by "Thalna" (goddess of Rebirth) –. We thereby see the story of his Resurrection developed in its proper sequence from left to right, and arranged around the figure of Apollo, as the glorification of the deceased.

81

(Concerning the figure of "Letun" see the paragraph "Birth of the Hellenic Apollo").

At other times Apollo is playfully shown with his sister Artemis, dressed as the great Asiatic divinity, probably hinting at the intimacy of the soul with the Eastern dogma, the belonging together, the familiarity understood as family-relation. The location of that charming encounter is, however, the Beyond as a Death-Garland hangs above them.

82

We finally see Apollo on a mirror in the role of Dionysos who awakened Ariadne. This permits two interpretations; either that the dead is united with a "Divine Female" in the classical sense of a Hierogamy, – or else that in a reversal of the usual situation, we deal here with the soul of a departed female, to which an Apollonic bridegroom is promised, who, in the role of Dionysos would re-awaken her to a new life of sensual pleasures, of which she is told by a Faunian youth.

83

THE SNAKE SYMBOLISM

There is a little grave-stone in the corridor of the Museo Vaticano – [inventory No. 2755] – showing two snakes eating fruits out of a bowl. The snakes being symbols of the Earth, eating up Life, symbolized by Fruits,

171

meaning that the dead person is thought of as the "Fruit of Life" which is now swallowed up by Death, personified by those creatures of the Earth. There are two more little snakes coming up from the ground and lusting at the bowl, suggesting that the Earth is actually greedy and waiting to absorb the Fruits of Life. In the middle of the bowl of fruit is a big pine cone or pineapple, the symbol of generative force, related thereby to the "Fruits of Life" – all that to verify the meaning of the two snakes on the mirror and their reference to the all devouring Ocean and its ultimate function of re-birth – designating thereby the whole object as a Death-Mirror.

We thereby see several symbolisms of the snakes: One is the snake of sensuality, this meaning possibly started by Aristotle (ca. 400 B.C.), as quoted by Athenaeus VIII.352. The other symbolism making reference to those silently approaching creatures of the Ocean or the Earth in their function of swallowing up all living. The third would be the snake of Eternity, forming a circle, and thereby slightly related to the two former thoughts in the aspect of eternal re-birth, while the shedding of their skin was symbolic for re-incarnation.

HERACLES AND DEATH

Generally, and in its main outline, we see a shift from the heroic to the visions of amorous pleasures. The reason for it is, that Death was a dramatic event as long as it was thought to be connected with the dreadful subterranean Hades. Matching this sense of drama and the miraculous was the figure of the Hero, overcoming the seemingly impossible obstacles and the horrid dangers. Having conquered the eternal death, shows the soul of the deceased quite fittingly reappearing in the image of the Hero. But later a new symbol-figure arose, replacing the soul of the dead, with the person of Heracles, who overcame the Nemean Lion, the very incarnation of Death. Consequently we see Heracles with his club very often on Death-Mirrors, freeing the souls from the Below, or being at the very beginning of an episode, which ends up with the liberation of the soul in the Above, surrounded by the radiance of Dawn, the personification of the glorious arising, all of it still in a highly dramatic mood, of pitting the Hero of Heroes against the most dreadful of all cosmic monsters, the image of Death itself, the invincible law of nature, larger than all the laws of creation. At the time, when the deceased was no longer identified with Heracles, the killer of Death was accorded his own veneration and glorification and was shown as bearded and forbiddingly strong. This atmosphere of Dramatics and Heroism was well founded, but as we will see, belonged to an epoch, which was overtaken by a new atmosphere, drifting into the visions of sweetness and love in the company of celestial Females. We may therefore call Heracles the last of the Hero-figures on the Mirrors, before they shifted to amorous hedonism.

85

87

As a liaison from one mood to the next, we have a mirror suddenly showing Heracles rejuvenated, melting over into the image of the "Darling" of the celestial Females, a stripling ready to be seduced by the quite knowing charmers of the heavens and paradise. It could be suspected that the idea of rejuvenation coming from the East, crept into this presentation, but it is more likely that the mood of dramatics was swept away by the new dream of amorous relations and dalliance in Paradise.

86

PARIS AND THE THREE GRACES

At a later time the problems of elevation of the soul from the Below to the Above seem to have vanished, as well as the terrible anxiety about the destiny of the soul after its earthly departure. The dramatics of its ascent, as well as the heroics for having accomplished that feat were no longer the subjects shown on the mirrors.

Instead of all that, we see scenes where the soul is shown in the role of "Paris" (the royal prince and "the most handsome of men") with the celestial females (impersonated here by Hera, Athena and Aphrodite), or the "Three Graces" (the servants of the goddess of Love) as a promise of the next world, awaiting the deceased.

88

The spaces of the Above are often suggested by outlines of clouds and the atmosphere of Love is conveyed by symbols and attributes of the lovegoddess Aphrodite, in the form of a pigeon or the Flower of Sensuality. Those flowers are mostly enlarged to assume symbolic proportions, with their generative parts shown with great botanical knowledge, isolating the male and female elements within the blossom, suggesting their impending union, as an allegorical parallel to the scenes of the "Judgement of Paris" or the "Three Graces" in the main picture above. This "allegorical parallel" is a very frequently used technique on the Etruscan mirrors to clarify, on a lower register, the deeper meaning of the scenes, staged by the main actors, in a pantomime of Greco-Roman mythology.

89

The females are mostly disrobed but richly decorated with jewelry, which conforms to the Indo-Oriental idea of "Wealth in Excelsis" according to which figures of the Above are strewn with jewelry, as a hint that we deal here with the Eastern females of Paradise, while the Greco-Roman divine and semidivine personages appear without jewelry at all. Jewels, according to Eastern thinking, are expressions of honor and elevation, as we see the female chosen between the others, often as crowned and the higher honored figures more richly decorated with "Bullae" of magic powers. So that we have here a perfect example of the typical mixture of the originally Eastern figures, still wearing the jewelry of their homeland, but translated into personages of the Mediterranean mythology, now protected by the magic amulets of the Etruscans.

90

THE EASTERN BRIDES

In some cases we see a Lasa assuming the role of the Eastern lovemakers of paradise. Although their function is akin to death-angels, but following the idea that all in the Above is given to love, it seems that even a Lasa can not escape the general mood of that sphere.

91

Reference may be made on those pictures to the story by Ovid about the Lares, – (assumed to be the pattern for the Etruscan Lasae) – that Lala (chatter) was sent to the Netherworld by Zeus, because of her indiscrete gossip about Iuturna, one of his loves, and Hermes Psychopompos, who was ordered to escort her to the Below, seduced her at that occasion, so that she became the mother of the Lares.

This link, connecting the realm of the dead with the idea of lovemaking, seems to have qualified the Lasae, combined with Hermes – (Psychopompos) – to pose as lovers on Death-Mirrors.

After this liaison-figure leading over from the Greco-Roman visions of a Love-and-Death-combination staged by Lasae, we then see truly Eastern Brides of Heaven greeting the arriving soul with the Oriental gesture of "Salam." They wear Indo-Oriental costumes of transparent and finely patterned robes, not usual in the Mediterranean.

92

Most interesting are the fringed scarves hanging discarded on walls and plants. They are well known from the Etruscan grave paintings, depicting the Above, where they indicate the mood of lovemaking, according to Athenaeus, who says that the Etruscans have the habit of throwing their loinclothes – (the scarves) – over "lattice wands" – (the shrubs) – when they settle down to lovebouts.

Some of the mirrors are even more explicit: They show at the lower register the eternal waters of Death and Rebirth, indicating that the above scene takes place in the celestial spheres.

There appear then Eastern Brides with makeup kits, to tell us that the girls had beautified themselves for the arriving soul. To make their expectations clear, they stand before an opened bed – in similarity to the Three Graces as seen on sarcophagi.

93

The reason why such a mirror is given to the deceased in his grave, might be primarily to have the object itself serving him as a gift to the other-worldly females. But the scene shown on the mirror might be understood in the sense of a grave-stela, imagining the dead person now in the company of celestial beings, as a last wish of the survivors to the departing, in telling him, pictorially: "Be happy in the Beyond!" – or imagining him as being received in this manner.

THE NUPTIAL WASHING

Another rumor coming from the East hinted that the spirit of the dead person would enter a nuptial relation with those Nymphs of the Waters – (meaning the Apsarases). The "Nuptial Washing" or "Lustral Bath" was firmly connected to the idea of a marital union, so much so, as to make reference to the marital status of a female – (who was not married) – by showing a lustral pitcher on her gravestone, suggesting maybe, that a felicity denied to her on earth, should be hers in the next world – in a

94

Hierogamy – (the wedding to the divine) – or due to her transformation into a celestial Maenad in the train of Dionysos, frolicking with the Fauni in excelsis, as shown on many funeral monuments... This situation might also be the answer to the frequent question concerning the destiny of females after death. This question is treated separately under "Reception of Earthly Women" admitting the possibility that, – (according them "equal rights" with the males) – joy and priapic bliss should be theirs in the Thereafter.

In special cases the artist wanted to combine the idea of a "Nuptial" with the element of the "Water" and therefore introduced the figure of Thetis, the beautiful Nereid, loved by Zeus and Poseidon, – who, however, got married to Peleus, a mortal. We can see the parallel of the deceased, obviously a mortal, loved and united with "One of the Waters" in a nuptial, attended and blessed by the divine clan, as a magnificent apotheosis of the dead person here in question.

95
The Nuptial Washing is an archaic ceremony found from the Himalayas to the Mediterranean, often attended by bridesmaids, as shown on funeral urns and plaques. Especially in arid countries, water has the symbol-value of purity and is supposed to wash away all sins and acts impure the bride may have committed before her nuptials. – (See also the purification in the Ganges.) Beyond the idea of purification the relation to future love-encounters is often hinted at by a pigeon, the emblem of Aphrodite, by Fauni, or by figures of priapic felicity.

105
The nuptial washing, as seen on Mirrors, the Cistae and on the Plaques of Naples, also denotes that the body of the otherwise chastely shrouded bride, is now handed over without restraint to her mate, meaning that not the "Persona" (the masked appearance), but that the "Ego" of the bride (her absolute Self), is the object of the transfer. At this moment of truth the bride therefore appears naked or dropping her shrouds, surrounded by brides-maids or servants – a theme very popular in India's iconography – and repeated here as related to Death and Resurrection, to signify "The great Encounter" of the soul in the Beyond, the environment of which is indicated at times by clouds and sometimes by waters.

Besides the magical ideas of purification connected to the "Nuptial Washing" there appears to be, in archaic times, a more realistic purpose in this procedure, of showing the bride nakedly to the prospective groom, to attract him to her.

In the mythological tablets [K.97.] of about 1750 B.C. of Sumer and Akkad, dealing with the affair of Ninlil, the celestial maiden, and Enlil, the bright-eyed god, her mother Nunbarshegunu, instructs her daughter as follows:

"In the pure stream, woman, bathe
in the holy waters do bathe.
Ninlil will walk along the stream
the bright-eyed lord will see you
the bright-eyed will see you,
will forthwith embrace you, kiss you.

                . . . .

In the pure stream the girl bathes
Ninlil walks along the stream
the bright-eyed saw her
the lord speaks to her of intercourse. . ."

The idea of tempting the prospective suitor by unveiling before him the bodily charms of the "Bride" re-appears in many versions on mirrors and plaques.

While assuming that the Etruscans had their background in India, as far as their ceremonial roots are concerned, a report from India is of special interest, which shows the connection between washing and a nuptial union.

The Oranons of Bengal worship the Earth as a goddess, and annually celebrate her marriage to the Sun-god Dharme. The ceremony proceeds as follows:

> All bathe, then the men go to a sacred grove (sarna), while the women assemble at the house of the village priest. After sacrificing some fowls to the Sun-god and the spirits of the grove, the priest is carried back to the village. Near the village the women meet the men and again go through a ritual of ceremonial washing. With beating of drums and dancing, all now walk to the house of the priest. Then the marriage is performed between the priest and his wife, symbolizing the union between Sun and Earth. After the ceremony all drink and dance and sing obscene songs and finally indulge in orgies without restraint. The Sacred Marriage of the Sun and Earth is impersonated by the priest and his wife to move the earth, by following their example, to become fruitful, and for the same purpose, on the principle of homeopathic magic, the population indulges in the licentious orgy to charm the ground into fertility.

177

However, the real interest for us is the Indian ritual of washing, as the preparation for a nuptial embrace, so frequently shown on plaques and mirrors, involving the soul of the dead and the celestial brides.

Before turning to another matter we may look at two features on the Mirror below: There we see the male obviously in the role of Paris (with Venus, Juno and Minerva, inscribed as such in Etruscan lettering). But the male is called "Elachsntre." As there is no "Alexander" in mythology to justify this constellation, we may have here another of the many cases where the dead person re-appears in the flattering image of a mythological figure. The departed are often inscribed by name on allegorical pictures, like "Velia" in the "Tomb of Orcus" at Tarquinia, or "Rathlth" on the Mirror, Illustration 67.

The other feature of interest is that the artists developed a curious and ingenious way to indicate that a garment is falling, that is, in a downward motion, in contrast to a drape which is either just incompletely covering a figure or being pulled upwards. A technique which is also shown frequently on Etruscan mirrors.

90

94

This technique consists in showing a garment retained high between the legs, while the rest of the drapery is shown as fallen down, suggesting the idea of disrobing by assuming that at first all the drapery was in a higher position. Retaining the drapes by the chaste gesture of closing the thighs, before letting the last shroud fall to the ground also indicates a coy hesitancy in the act of divestment.

THE MYSTERIOUS STRIGILIS

On several mirrors we see a youthful masculine apparition – supposedly being the alter-ego of the dead – with a "Strigilis" – (a body-scraper) – in hand. This seems to indicate that this figure, too, is cleansing himself, as the male counterpart to the female nuptial washing.

While it could be assumed, until now, that we deal with simple scenes of female toiletry, the fact that the male figure is present and at the same time going through this same cleansing-procedure, suggests an impending interaction between the male and female personages, which leaves little doubt that a mutual bodily contact is contemplated.

As the scenario is set in the Above, which is indicated by the mythological status, ascribed to the females, we see, in short, that the soul of the dead, reappearing in excelsis, is preparing itself for a physical encounter with celestial females who likewise, in ceremonial washings, get ready for this event.

Assuming now that those mirrors found in graves are "Bring-along-Gifts" from the dead to the specters of the Beyond, the engravings on those mirrors may have the purpose of suggesting – (by magic or visual persuasion) – to the paradisial apparitions that the dead, now re-born to similar celestial status, is ready, or has purified himself, for the nuptial adventure with those heavenly females, who are supposed to receive him in love – in accordance with the doctrines of the East.

Whether or not the "strigilis" in itself assumes a phallic symbolism on those engravings is open to speculation – as this instrument is usually a simple slightly curved scraper to remove oil and dust from the skin of athletes – but appears here transformed to such a degree as to hint at another meaning. This astonishing type of strigilis also resembles at times very much the "Snake of Sensuality" with a head and sinuous body. In this connection it may be significant that the male person is never shown as actually "using" the strigilis as a cleansing-instrument, but instead holds it more like a "bring-along-gift" to the females ... or as an insignia to legitimize his person, or to identify himself or his future function with that symbol.

All that would justify why the dead would like to have such a mirror at hand when entering the next world as a credential to introduce his presence to those marvelous but totally unknown spheres where he himself is a stranger to the company he is about to join and on whose good will he now depends, so that on his bring-along-gift, the actual mirror, the engraver has shown him in his desired situation – (maybe as an instruction to the dead or his encouragement?) – of being received on quasi equal terms by the

96

97

98

99

celestial company, at first in a dreamlike stillness – while his later intimacies with those figures are foreshadowed by their fallen drapes. A further hint at the impending atmosphere are the pigeons, who are, because of their forever displayed lovegames, the symbol for the amorous and thereby an Aphrodisian insignia, appearing also on sarcophagi to denote the sweet Above. We see at times the swan, due to its myth representing the desire for beautiful women and their silent consent – and often too those big and magic blossoms, insolently presenting their organs of procreation. The entire scenery, be it the clouds of the Above or a hint at the Ocean of Eternity, appears then enclosed by ivy, the Dionysian symbol, indicating – (also in India!) – bodily entwinement, the tight embracement of lovers and intoxication, religious or sensual.

RECEPTION OF EARTHLY WOMEN

There are some mirrors which suggest that the soul of a deceased woman may find some happiness with males in the next world.

We see on Roman sarcophagi a rejuvenated matron greeted by a male emissary of the next world, as a very tender hint at such a possibility.

100   On an Etruscan mirror we see a young or rejuvenated female greeted in the next world by an especially good looking boy in a romantic mood of mutual touching. There is a death-wreath which the ephebean youth may have taken off the girl, to tell her that she is not dead anymore in his company, while the girl arranges her hair to please him, or prepares herself for the ceremony of the Nuptial Washing.

Another mirror goes much further in depicting a male world of eroticism to which an earthly woman seems to awake. This woman wears the Corona Immortalis, and is not dressed but surrounded by an ample drapery associated with her death-shroud, which she seems to open voluntarily towards the company of Bacchian males who show intense pleasure at her presence.

The scene and circumstances are reminiscent of Ariadne, who was awakened at Naxos from her sleep, often associated with her death, by Dionysos to a new life of love in the company of Priapic spirits.

102   The male figures have the ears of Pan, but not his goat-feet. The apparition at right seems to be only "costumed" as Pan, which is reminiscent of the sarcophagus at the Louvre, showing men with masks of Pan, as it is said

180

that wearing the costumes of Pan and imitating his dances would infuse men with the virility of those spirits of nature. We see that fur-clad figure with human feet dressed in slippers, bringing an Amphora, probably with wine, and bearing in his right hand a torch, – known to us from funeral monuments as the insignia of an otherworldly creature. A little table has goat-feet, to indicate the locality as the realm of the amorous virility to which the female may have been awakened.

There are quite a number of mirrors dealing with the apotheosis of a Female and the promise that in the Beyond she will find a beautiful lover, like Adonis – (Adonis and Attis were also symbol-figures, especially in the Near-East, for the re-awakening of Life sprouting out of the dead earth in spring) – and here this allegory may be the guiding thought, hinting at the Resurrection.

In the specific case of mirror (G.K.V.25) the speculation that we deal here with the elevation of a Female is based on the fact that the winged apparition bestows the Corona Immortalis on the Female – (not, as usual, on the male). This apparition is inscribed as "Thalna" – one of the double-sexed genii representing the amorous complex between the male and female, and we may therefore guess that this figure blesses the deceased female with a love-oriented future in the Beyond. Thalna is also called "divinitá genitale" and is related to "Iuventas" and "Blossoming" or "Rebirth."

Another point is that an apparition of Fate, – Athrpa – seems to bring Adonis to the main female figure. We know this personality with writing equipment in hand from other mirrors, where she is often connected with a destiny promising sensuality. It would then be possible to interpolate that she gives the beautiful Adonis as a present or playmate to the central figure.

It is interesting that this central female has no name inscribed, which may remind us of the many sarcophagi where all figures are finished, except the identity of the deceased, because we deal there with a prefabricated funeral-object, waiting to be identified with the deceased. It is possible that we have here a similar situation, in which the mirror intends to be applicable to "any" female, and that therefore she is the only one whose name is omitted.

A further hint or promise of an impending amorous encounter is the opened bed – (Kline) – in the background, richly furnished with pillows which are still un-used.

It also seems that the female figure displays a stronger elan by opening her garment with her left hand towards Adonis, and encircling him with her right arm, while Adonis, although gently touching her "heart" shows no ardent emotion – (which is so clearly expressed on other mirrors) – and rather looks like a charming toy or present for the quite matronly looking

101

lady in the Beyond.

We finally see on the lower register – (which mostly indicates the "gist" or allegory of the main design) – a panther, being the insignia of the Maenads, who are representing the love-oriented existence of Females in the Above.

Here it must be repeated that for the traditional Mediterranean feeling, Death was still a fearsome, grave, and majestic complex, approached with shudders . . . and that it was, at that time, an utterly foreign and extremely daring thought of the Etruscans to have a female after Death given to euphoric pleasures.

The fact that we have no textual evidences concerning females awakening to love – (except of Ariadne) – may point to the great novelty of that notion, which seemed too daring and uncertain to be put into words – while the sculptors, – (again in a split between the official idea and funeral art) – delighted in showing rejuvenated females in the Above, affectionately touching and kissing genii of love, who are responding with gentle embraces, while Amorini fill the atmosphere.

It seems possible that textual expressions were thought to belong to the more exact science of the thinkers, who shyed away from pronouncements, while visual arts were accorded more poetic license in their silent gestures. We must not forget that all were tampering there with so-called "foreign superstitions" condemned by the conservative clan.

MIRRORS OF THE LIVING

Contemporary with the mirrors given to the dead, to be used by him as "Bring-along-Gifts" to the Brides of the next world or to the more somber personalities of Fate and Decisions, we have very similar mirrors, in earthly commerce, equally used as gifts of endearment, given from men to females between the living, in the hope of gaining their favors, or as thanks for favors granted.

Those "earthly" mirrors were, however, mostly engraved with scenes of Greco-Roman mythology, commemorating marvelous happenings, while any reference to death was, of course, strictly avoided.

The scenes of mythology were probably chosen to suggest that the receiving person was considered cultured and educated enough to know those "high placed personages" – as divinities were considered the "Ruling Class" and the gossip concerning their legitimate and illegitimate affairs should hint that the receiving person is well informed about the little scandals of that "Power-Elite" shaping the destiny of the world, and their dramatic moments, and were similarly prestigious as our present-day knowledge of history, which was, before written records existed, a sphere of colorful hear-say the same as mythology.

Another flattery expressed by the gift-mirrors of the living were the many inscriptions they bear, in Etruscan lettering, as a hint that the receiving lady was able to read, which, at that time, was quite an accomplishment and therefore a compliment, as lists of students in writing-schools show that almost exclusively the offspring of governors or high officials destined to rule, were the pupils.

As a consequence of the confined knowledge of writing, the inscriptions made by artists are not in all cases reliable, so that the identity of Hermes and Apollo, for instance, is at times questionable, as their roles were often exchanged. However, it has to be remembered that in oldest times "Apollo of the Roads" – called "Agyieus" – was equated with Hermes, the patron and protector of the wayfarers and the wandering souls. Their statuettes were affixed over many doors of houses, so as to wish to those who pass, a 'bon voyage' – applied later to the departing souls.

But we have to admit, on the other hand, that we can not know, today, all mythological stories which were in vogue at those early days and never came down to us through all the centuries of random destruction of documentations.

So we see, for instance, a most elaborate bronze mirror, of the British Museum [No. 542], its design not being engraved but cast in relief obviously in mass-production, a hint of being most popular at the time – and still, it shows Heracles abducting a female who is identified as Mlacuch by inscription, a name unknown to us and never found again in any record. It could be Peleus wrestling with the Nereid Thetis – (one of the waters!) – before making love to her ... as a Mediterranean translation of the embracement with the Apsarases, also being "those of the waters" – or it could even be Peirithous, the friend of Theseus, who raped Persephone, – (the female after death) – as that mysterious Mlacuch is regally dressed, however with the typical Etrusco-Asiatic slotted and Orientally bordered sleeves – which, by some stretch of imagination could make her one of those Oriental Brides of Heaven which, this time, is shown to be picked up by force by the soul of the departed, which re-appears, not surprisingly, in the image of a hero, as Heracles, who overcame Death.

THE PARALLEL ON CISTAE AND PLAQUES

In general the cistae repeat the images we know from stelae and mirrors, but the use and meaning of those quite elaborate containers remained an open question, because at times they contain toiletry for ladies, but they must still be regarded as funeral-objects because they are found in graves and their designs make reference to the idea of resurrection – (but, strangely enough, never to death) –. Because of the little huts, containing the ashes of Etruscan females, it was assumed that they too were containers for the ashes of departed ladies. With great uncertainty it finally was assumed that they had a twofold use: as "make-up-kits" for the living, as well as containers for their ashes – but why were they found in graves? The most disturbing was the fact that those make-up cistae were found in graves of men.

According to the "Gifts of the Dead" hypothesis all would, of course, fall easily into place: The cistae could be understood as "Bring-along-Gifts" to Persephone or her otherworldly derivatives like the Horai, the Three Graces, the Waternymphs – etc. and there it would make no difference if those cistae were found in the graves of men or women; and would amply justify such gifts in the graves of men, as they had more reasons to endear themselves to the otherworldly females and, in fact, it is quite possible that the majority of cistae came from the tombs of men.

That the cistae were used as containers for toiletry is shown on the mirrors (D.G. 18) where we see one of the many scenes, assumed to be a "nuptial washing" and where just such a cista is prominently shown, together with a waternymph and a water-basin.

The suggestion that we deal here not with an earthly "genre-scene," nor with a mythological happening is based on the following factors: The image is framed by laurel, used in the "coronae immortalis" – even with the little flowers in the middle, indicating the exalted sphere of the dead. There are shown 3 naked females, or nearly so, in the act of disrobing, the standard scenario on the mirrors depicting the Three Graces, as the "Females of the Beyond." Those females wear jewelry which is not usual for Greco-Roman divinities, but a requirement for Oriental females, especially of the semidivine type, according to the Indo-Asiatic idea of "Wealth in Excelsis." The arm-rings, worn by all of them, are typically Oriental-outlandish and so are the criss-crossing bands or strings of pearls over the breasts of each of them. In this respect all three of them are dressed alike, which would hint at their equal rank. The diadem of the central figure may designate them as elevated creatures, while the bodily familiarity in which she is held by her sister-figure would discourage the thought that she

103

184

should represent a high-divinity like Persephone or Aphrodite with her attendants, the Horai or Three Graces, of which the usual triad would be shown in addition to her or next to her, so that we would rather classify the three females depicted here as the famous triad in itself, devoted to the goddess of Love.

Now, after having placed the scenario with all probability in the Orientalized Above, and the persons designated to the type of the Three Graces, as stand-ins for the "Females in the Beyond" – this mirror-engraving seems to demonstrate that those celestial and otherworldly beings, in fact, accept and use such a cista, possibly given to them by the deceased as a "Bring-along-Gift" – because we have truthfully to admit that the cista shown on this mirror, is out of proportion in size, and treated with more elaboration than anything else, as to form the center of interest.

From the standpoint of composition it is of importance too, that the cista is, quite improbably, hanging on a branch, artificially brought by this means on the level between the faces, that is: the sphere of greatest attention . . and while the bodies of the females are mercilessly over-cut, intersected, interrupted and partly hidden by arms and drapes, nothing seems to dare to interfere with the full display of the cista, which seems to be treated as a highly valued gift on the part of the females as well as on the part of the donor . . . the wandering soul, which hopes for a friendly reception.

While this specific mirror – (D.G. 18) – has the merit of showing a cista "in use" by the "Females of the Beyond" as its recipients, there is no doubt that the cistae in general make reference to Resurrection and the next world, by the scenes engraved on them, showing Fauni and Maenades, and above all Hermes Psychopompos, the guide of the arriving soul introducing the dead in his epiphany to the Celestial Brides.

But before leaving this special mirror-design, it may be interesting to note that this very cista shown here seems to convey the idea of the Italian artist that the otherworldly Females are of "Olympian" status, as the vision of the Oriental Beyond was not known to him. This notion is expressed by the Greek ornament on the cista shown, which is most unusual on Etruscan objects, but here the artist naively translates those Eastern apparitions of otherworldly embraces into figures located in the Greek Olymp . . . but still costumed in a non-Greek fashion.

If nothing else would convince us that the cistae found in graves make reference to the Etruscan understanding of the Indo-Oriental Beyond, we would be forced to that conclusion by the sculptures on the legs and on the covers of the Cistae, because they show, beyond any doubt, the souls as being carried away by winged apparitions and as being uplifted, revived and received by embodiments of the realms of joy.

In some cases [Rhode Island No. 06.014] we have on the cover of the cista the premordial creatures of the sea, the Indo-Oriental "Celestial Ocean" to which the dead return and out of which they are reborn. We also see on its engraving the old and balding man on the end of his earthly path, tired, with the staff of the wanderer in hand, resting finally on a barren rock, flanked by two columns, presumably in the "Palace of Persephone" – and looking imploringly at Hermes Psychopompos, who proudly presents the old man's rejuvenated soul, re-appearing nakedly, but with the cap and calmys, typical for the traveller who came from afar, to the otherworldly nymphs, shown at their nuptial washing, one of them holding the Thyrsos of the Maenades, to indicate their mood towards the impending encounter with the revenant soul.

104   The famous Cista of Karlsruhe [F 1859] could be interpreted in different ways, while there is agreement as to its sepulcheral classification, the features of greatest interest to us is the washing of the hair at a fountain, which most surprisingly duplicates the same scene shown on a plaque of Naples. This points to a very widely spread belief, expressed by this symbol-gesture, as most of these cistae seem to be made in the North of Italy and the plaques of Naples come from its extreme south, while the same scene is also repeatedly shown on mirrors which were produced throughout the land.

Of the astonishing re-appearance of this scene we will talk in the paragraph "Hairwash on Plaques, Cistae and Mirrors."

We see on that cista the usual nuptial washing by an assembly of nymphic creatures while the entourage of Dionysian and Faunian apparitions suggests that we deal here not with a genre scene, but with the scenario of the sensual Beyond.

Of special interest to us is the figure on the left, who actually uses such a mirror, assumed to be a bring-along-gift. We see engraved on that mirror the image of a winged soul, presumably being the donor himself. In addition to the mirror "in use" we also notice a cista at the foot of that nymph, and an instrument in her hand which is believed to be used for parting the hair. Such instruments too were often found in graves and were classified as toiletry. For whom that beautifying and cleansing effort is made is not clarified on this cista, but we have so many mirrors showing those females set in relation to an arriving soul, that we may safely assume that all toiletry efforts and manipulations with the hair are also made in expectation of a similar encounter.

It may strike us as odd that the furnishings of those sumptuous upper spheres are so meager, and we realise that those otherworldly females have in their celestial establishment nothing else but what the souls brought to them as a gift – (except for the fountain). We notice that the toilet-cistae, the mirrors and the combing-stick those Nymphs seem to depend on, are the donations from arriving souls –. It might be a comforting thought for the mortals that their gifts will be greatly appreciated by the celestial females, but we may discern a possible sales-effort on the part of the artisans who fabricated those gift-items, to show to the customer how greatly those gifts would be appreciated in the celestial realm, so devoid of similar goods.

The mirrors and cistae really conclude the chapter of "The Gifts of the Dead" because they could be considered as Bring-along-Gifts of the dead to the otherworldly apparitions.

But we see the mirrors leading over to cistae, still showing their use by the females of the Beyond – and then we see to our surprise some of the motives and personages re-appearing on plaques, so that we must consider the plaques as belonging to the same complex of thoughts and beliefs.

Although the plaques are possibly only Ex Voti – and donations to some spiritual beings – those very same beings appear plentifully on sarcophagi and gift-mirrors, so that their re-appearance on plaques may shed some light on the whole system of ideas.

SUMMARY

THE GIFTS OF THE DEAD

The objects found in early graves were to be handed over to the subterranean Judges of the dead, as captatio benevolentiae, upon arrival of the departed in their sphere of power – (therefore the arms etc. as those Judges were assumed to be male).

In a shift from the idea of the Judges, patterned after worldly luxury-loving Lords and Chieftains, fond of precious arms and saddles, the personalities reigning the subterranean world of the dead assumed a rather abstract and religious tinge, to be approached in reverence and with sacrifices, so that the objects found of that second phase fall in the class of sacradotal paraphernalia, often shown in the hands of the deceased extended towards majestic divinities, not in armor but in priestly robes.

In later times – after 600 B.C. when the notion of "Females in the Beyond" started to infiltrate the Mediterranean from the Orient, a FEMALE, Persephone, the only Female the sculptors could think of as related to death, was elected to represent the subterranean realm and was cast in the role of a Hostess, graciously inviting the dead to a banquet in her home – converting the amorous mission of the otherworldly females thereby into a still receptive, but Hausfrauly attitude. The dead were thought to be her "House-Guests" and following earthly traditions, brought "Guest-Gifts" along. The items found in graves of that period are meant to be received by a Female and therefore have the startling homemaker and trivial character and also explain the female trinkets, mirrors, toiletry boxes and perfume bottles in graves of men.

The transformation from the "Subterranean Female" – Persephone, to the "Females in Excelsis" was leading over the "Water-Nymphs" – in translation of the original Apsarases, meaning: "those of the Waters" as the charmers of the other world, and described to be in the "Celestial Ocean," the Paradise. Those Eastern visions were further translated into the MUSES, logically combined with their master Apollo, especially meaningful as Apollo was a symbol-figure for the deceased, so that the alter-ego of the dead was now pictured as "With the Muses" in the Above, and no longer "With the Manes" the shades of the dead under ground. The Masks and Music-instruments appear now as appropriate gifts for the Muses, who were no longer thought to be hostesses, but the "Companions" of the dead – who was appearing as their playmate in the features of Apollo. To underline this state of companionship, the dead appeared adorned with the insignia of the Muses, as if belonging to their clan.

In a general review of this subject, it seems that without the separation into different trends and beliefs, the "Gifts of the Dead," when taken as a single complex, form an impenetrable jungle of contradictions:

As Masks and Music-instruments can not be reconciled with Judges, nor household items with Muses, Persephone not with arms and warriors not with female trinkets, and the forever repeated three girls washing themselves have no echo in either mythology, the least in the very country where their images were created on funerary objects, and where their connection to death does not exist on a Greco-Roman ideological basis.

As an epilogue to that development, it could be said that when it transpired in later times that the main aura of that blissful Thereafter was LOVE, a whole new tradition was springing up, showing Eros as representing the realm of the dead, especially on countless vase-paintings.

Those vases were placed on house-altars at the anniversary of the death of the beloved and filled with flowers at the Anthesteria or similar days of remembrance.

QUALIFICATIONS AND LIMITATIONS

To qualify the foregoing to a limited range, it has to be said that not all objects found in graves were "Gifts of the Dead." There were, for instance, shoes and boats to facilitate the voyage of the deceased to the next world – probably to cross over the waters to the Elysian fields and to promenade there in comfort and style, – or else they were thought to be emblems of symbolic value and not for practical use by the dead.

In some graves we find little dogs and toys being the favorite playthings of children buried there, or we see on covers of sarcophagi the child as if asleep, but still clutching those items . . . which would, indeed, fall into the class of "Personal Belongings" embraced by the Ego of the dead and thereby forming an integral part of his being. The same classification also is applicable to arms found in graves of men and trinkets in the graves of women.

Coins found in the mouth of skeletons were thought to be an obulus for Caron, the ferry-man bringing the dead over the river Styx to the abode of the Shades. Similar rituals and manifestations belong to a more complex group of visions "in the twilight of reason," the "poetic license" of treating the dead at times as living, – (like pouring honey into his sarcophagus, etc.)

– comparable to the ambivalence in which people would say today that a certain beloved of theirs is buried on a hillside graveyard, so that he can see from there the lake which he loved so much during his lifetime, while it is obvious that the buried person cannot see, nor enjoy the honey. The Egyptians designated a special part of the soul as BA – (represented as a bird with a human head) – which can remain with the dead, but more often prefers to visit places which were close to the heart of the deceased during his lifetime. This interesting sub-division within the soul after death facilitated greatly the semi-logical arrangement of contradictory fears and hopes concerning the destiny of the deceased, but such a split of the soul-components was not known in Greco-Roman lands, where a fearful mystery shrouded the Thereafter of a soul, a fear that longed to be calmed by the serene grave-monuments of the classical period, which co-existed with – (but was at times invaded by) – the turbulent post-mortem scenarios of the Etrusco-Oriental phantasies.

Another exception to the idea of the "Gifts of the Dead" seems to be that we sometimes find in sarcophagi what appears to be a painstaking assembly of minute belongings of the dead, like little pins and even threads, which seem too inferior to be given to the great specters of the Beyond.

We could think that they were given to the dead in fear of robbing him in any way, or to arrogate any of his possessions.

Maybe the deceased was thought of as a guest in the house of the living, who had to depart, and as you would return to a houseguest anything he had forgotten in your abode, and as a sign that you did not profit from his departure, you return to him, symbolically the tiniest objects he has left, which were assembled meticulously – ("metus" meaning fear), to demonstrate your absence of greed.

We know of instances in mythology where the living were eager and impatient to lay their hands on objects of a dying person – implying a death-wish intermixed with greed – but in all those stories the guilty was punished by fate or the gods in a terrible way. This means that those tendencies were prevalent in real life in such intensity that they had to be counteracted or blocked by the most powerful and horrid punishments – revenge and torture – like the gruesome story of the Sumerian Dumuzi (ca. 1750 B.C.), the stunning incidence where a god turns pale and weeps and begs for mercy after he lusted to absorb the power and possession of a dying person – and was, arms and hands turned into snakes, nevertheless carried off by the cruel demons of subterranean punishments "cold of heart."

There also might have been the frightening thought that the dead may return to look for an ever so minute item of his possession taken from him on the sly. A revengeful soul is a formidable adversary, seeping through cracks and walking through walls and bolted doors, or even worse: appearing out of the dark with revengeful address, to retrieve what was withheld from him, to right any wrong, done to him in his hour of death. Of those circumstances, too, we have examples in classic literature but also in later works to show that this fear and vision was ever present and might have been calmed or counteracted by that painstaking return of the tiniest objects to the dead, as a demonstrative ritual . . . comparable to washing the hands of any guilt.

There may further be a reason for those quasi worthless items in the graves, in the fear that those possessions might be contaminated by death, or infiltrated by the demons or specters of the dark realms, or simply transmit the odium or aura of the moribund to the survivors.

At certain times diverse divinities or semi-divinities were thought to be involved in the process of death, with whom one could make some deals, like compensatory exchanges in sacrificing several persons in replacement for his own life – leading to the mass-slaughter of individuals to compensate for the extended survival of an important person, a King or even a powerful lady who had years added to her own life by sacrificing to the death-gods a number of persons each year on her birthday as a present to the lusting demons.

Following the same train of thought, garments of a woman who died in childbirth were given to a certain divinity in homage to show that the company of the living does not begrudge her for having taken her due, and therefore being satisfied, at least temporarily, would spare the living. In those cases we see Death respected as a special personality who had to be satisfied to gain him as a friend, or at least as a "Party in a deal" – by not treating him as an irrational enemy.

There are many objects and rituals which were arranged to satisfy the dead, to glorify him, to calm his possible impulses of revenge and envy – where NO gifts were involved.

There are some others, having mainly the survivors in mind, to disinvolve them from the fact of death, to absolve them from the possibility of having caused it or hastened it by wish or deed or magic.

There are procedures directed at the odium of death emanating from the very presence of the dead person, his escaping soul, erring around and not yet pacified.

There are further purely defensive objects, like amulets, or Sphynxes as guardians of the dead, or the heads of Medusa to scare away all evil spirits. All those talismans are no "gifts" to anybody and deal neither with the dead nor with the survivors and are not even addressed to the great figures of the Beyond – but instead to uncertain specters, the Larvae and Lemures in the realm of demonology, personifications of curses etc.

There are even gifts-TO-the Dead rituals dealing with the ambivalence in which the departed is considered at times as dead, and at times as alive, as wandering, appreciative, or otherwise – of our interactions with him (see Anthesteria), to maintain a bond of friendship with him, as long as he does not reach out for you.

We finally see some sharply aggressive safeguards taken by the living towards the dead: From the late Neolithic Period, the earliest time of which we have evidence, it appears that the Egyptians believed in an existence beyond the grave, which seemed insofar of material character as they placed food and offerings in the tombs of the dead, probably to pacify and to honor him, but possibly also to contain them there, because in an effort to prevent their return to this world and lay claim on food and possessions, the heads of the departed were often severed from their bodies and their legs cut off. – This in similarity to the so-called "Grave-Concubines" the little female and sensual clay-figurines which were astonishingly broad-hipped in contrast to the otherwise slender statues of Egypt, and given to the dead for his possible enjoyment, when revived by him through magic, – as those figurines, too, had broken off legs to prevent them from philander-ing to other graves or even to the living. That their legs were not broken off by accident is proven by the fact that the glaze of those figurines extends around the stumps of their legs, showing that they were fabricated to begin with, including this gruesome safety-feature, applied also to the human corpses in more savage times. This mutilation of the dead was done defen-sively to make the living sure of the undisturbed possession of their worldly goods including the undisturbed enjoyment of their spouses, because already long before the Dynastic Period, the idea prevailed that the dead still longed for an extended and pleasureable existence, possibly including some sensual desires for the living.

To some milder and more persuasive efforts by the living belong the "Letters to the Dead," sometimes picking an argument with the ghost of the departed, sometimes requesting him in stern language to desist from re-appearing in dreams and sometimes threatening him with actions against him. Those letters to the dead were written on pottery bowls which were put in the tomb with food for the dead person. The idea was that the ghost would surely find those inscriptions when he comes for his food and would have time to read them, while he was munching his rice, or whatever there was. There are many of those food-bowls preserved, the letters to the dead inscribed on some read as follows:

"To the excellent spirit Ankhiry . . .
You have raised your hand against me . . .
What have I done to you? . .
But you have acted that I must bring
Complaint against you, before the
Divine Ennead in the other world
And a decision will be made between
You and this letter-accusation . . ."

A woman complains to the ghost-image of her first husband that he reappears to her to disturb her during the happy moments she has with her second husband, and she too threatens action against him by the authorities of the other world . . .

PANEL OF AN ETRUSCAN FUNERARY URN

As a postscriptum it might be said, that the erotic objects found in Etruscan graves could, despite greatest efforts, not be explained, according to Mediterranean thinking.

They do, however, conform perfectly well to the scenario which was promised to the souls of the departed in the scriptures of the East.

مبنت میں لا فانی عمیسی

ETERNAL LOVE IN PARADISE

193

PLAQUES

THE PLAQUES OF NAPLES

THE WATER NYMPHS

110

The stone-carvers had basically the same problem as the metal-workers who engraved the mirrors: With their information based on vague hear-say, they had to find figures of the Greco-Roman mythology to represent and to act out the foreign ideas of the Thereafter.

The parallel developments we saw in the mirrors, we now find in a number of rather mysterious plaques. Especially interesting, at first, is a set of them in the Museum of Naples.

There we see two elements:

The Water Nymphs – (sometimes spelled "Lymphae," being the old form for Water-Nymphs) – and Apollo, called "Apollini" according to the inscriptions carved in the stones.

The Apsarases of India re-appear in the Mediterranean, transposed into Water-Nymphs. The basis of this conversion is the fact that "Apsara" means "Those of the Waters" – ("Apsa" in Sanscrit being cognate with the Latin "aqua"). – The Apsarases, as we saw, are the maidens promised in the Eastern heavenly Paradise, and as the Above is assumed to be the Celestial Ocean, those females were – (in their oldest form) – thought to float in the waters, this description of them was then translated in the Mediterranean into "Water-Nymphs."

But what their actions were in this other world, was not yet transmitted to the Mediterranean – or seemed maybe too improbable, or too indecent to be shown on a funeral stela – because for the Romanized Etruscans, Death was still related to a somber sanctification, shown by the grave expression and attitude of the dead, resting on the covers of their sarcophagi – while for India the ascent to Paradise was boundless jubilation. However, some rumor of a "nuptial relation" must have been hinted at, which was then translated in a "nuptial washing" as a combination of the elements of "Water" with "Nuptial."

SEA AND LAND NYMPHS

Here we should remember that the Greek word NYMPHE actually means "Bride" or "young nubile female" and thereby bears the connotation of the amorous and embraceable, fitting in this manner the idea of their Eastern model, the Apsarases, so that we see on those plaques the Waternymphs as stand-ins, equated with the Oriental Celestial Brides. To identify them as Water-Nymphs, on some of those funeral plaques we have those females manipulating water in some manner, pouring it out of pitchers or vases or sea-shells. Generally we have Waternymphs understood as Well-Nymphs **108** personifying wells and springs of the land; this means Sweet-Water-Nymphs, but here they appear more often with Sea-Shells, which suggests that the maidens to be presented are NOT ordinary Well-Nymphs, but are related somehow to the Ocean – (meaning the Celestial Ocean) – unknown to the Italian sculptors. This relation is hinted at on one of the plaques, by showing beneath those Nymphs bearing Sea-Shells, the Lord of the Seas, **109** Neptunus or Oceanos of the Deep, as if those maidens would have arisen from him, or would be his emissaries to the spheres of the Above. The vagueness of their identity is admitted by the fact that they are not the usual Nereids, immersed in the waters, but rather some mysterious beings, never heard of before, not Well-Nymphs, not daughters of the Ocean, but some-things newly connected to Death and Afterlife.

DIVINE MARRIAGES IN THE SEA

At that time those nymphic creatures got into near-collision with the females on the "Sea-Sarcophagi" who had, however, a totally different ideological background – but there are, nevertheless, some sarcophagi showing marriages in the sea of the Thetis type, with jubilant Nereids in an atmosphere filled with fluttering Amorettes and jumping dolphins. But all that left out the personality or alter-ego of the man in the coffin, because he could not be associated with the happy bridegroom, the bearded Lord of the Sea, shown by the sculptor, and the fashion of the aquatic weddings ebbed away.

HAIRWASH ON PLAQUES, CISTAE AND MIRRORS

This vision was replaced by a trend which showed the dead person, or his alter-ego on land, but in the company of Water-Nymphs who were characterized as such by bearing water-pitchers emitting water, or sea-shells from which they poured water. Some more enterprising artists solved the problem of combining Water with Females by having some maidens scooping water from a fountain, or washing their persons or even washing their hair, which could be taken as a preparation for a nuptial encounter with the deceased, who re-appears now with the features of Apollo.

104

A partly broken plaque of Naples shows one of the maidens washing her hair, which gesture and procedure is repeated, as we said, on a cista or ash-urn, now in the museum of Karlsruhe. It is most remarkable that the washing of hair – (so seldom seen in art) – is repeated on a cinerary urn and at a stela too, involving in both cases three nude Nymphs of the "Three Graces" type, in front of the soul-image of the dead, and it therefore seems that we deal here with an important symbolism – which would be quite inexplicable if we would not have the engravings on the mirrors to tell us that the "Three Graces," confronting the soul in the Beyond, belong to a definite phase in the development of the paradisial visions, imported from the East. The nuptial washing in conjunction with the "Three Graces" also clarifies without any further doubt the meaning of the "Three Graces" seen as a promise to the soul of the deceased to be his partners in a quasi nuptial relation in the Thereafter. Because although Apollini is shown on the plaques simply confronting the Three Females, it is their washing – (so often repeated on grave-mirrors) – which hints at their getting ready for his impending relation to "Those of the Waters." This hint is then verified on the mirrors where "Apulu" is named by inscription and the Females as personages of the Above.

105

PLAQUES AND APOLLINI

106

Some of the Plaques of Naples are dedicated to Apollo and some to the Nymphs.

We may understand this in the following manner:

The dead person is glorified in the image of Apollo and the plaques, dedicated to Apollini are "Memorial Plaques" commemorating the dead.

The plaques dedicated to the Nymphs are emploring those other-worldly

196

spirits to kindly receive the deceased, and those plaques are therefore addressed or dedicated to them and deposited in their sanctuary.

This is confirmed by other plaques which equally emplore and thank the Water-Nymphs in districts where they were understood as protector-figures of the seafarers.

On the votive or funeral plaques of Naples we see now this Apollini confronted with the Water-Nymphs, as a static constellation without any mutual rapport, as if simply listing the elements, the Waternymphs and Apollini, as actors in the next world, and without hinting by any pantomime their relation, so that their attitude in the next phase of this encounter could be questioned, as we do not see a Waternymph ready to receive him, or to seduce him.

107

111

This breathless "Still" of the situation as seen on the funeral plaques seems, however, suddenly broken by a figurine discovered on the cover of a cinerary container, also by chance in the museum of Naples – (or maybe found nearby) – where a Water-Nymph, characterized as such by a water-pitcher on which she leans, and which emits water, – is shown spreading out on the ground in a most seductive mood, with her drapes pushed down, in the languid pose of giving herself. This ash-urn of marble explains then very clearly the role the Water-Nymphs, in general, are supposed to play, in continuation of the dream-like still seen on the plaques and also on the late sarcophagi where the dead person, in the role of Endymion in eternal sleep, although visited by Selene who longs for him, nevertheless seems to dream of the far away image of a Water-Nymph, floating on a cloud over him, as the true and persistent promise of otherworldly felicity in the Above, – (as mentioned later in the paragraph "The persistent waternymphs").

112

After some time the tradition of the plaques became monotonous, so that some artists, fond of innovations, showed the still enigmatic celestial females as dance-girls in swirling robes, floating towards Apollini, who was then understood in his role as the genius of music, with Lyra in hand, while the maidens blended over into the image of the Horai, accentuating perhaps the component of sensuous joy in the Thereafter, because during that epoch the Horai were portrayed as the followers of Pan or dancing to the tune of Priapus.

113

Other artists understood the celestial maidens simply as the scenario or stage-setting of the next world, awaiting the soul of the departed. Those plaques became grave and ceremonious and especially devoid of any interaction.

In a further step towards a formalistic approach, the Brides of the Beyond were reduced to emblematic symbol-figures in a paradisial landscape, solemnly holding their sea-shells, as if offering the refreshment of their

114

waters to the soul, maybe understood here as the drink of immortality. But now it was mainly the broad and grandiosely ornamented frame of the plaques which called attention to the importance of the departed or the donor, who is often portrayed or mentioned by name.

115

Finally we see the three Water-Nymphs on later Roman sarcophagi in a rather inferior position, probably misunderstood as being the Moirai, the sombre figures of Fate, related to the "Daughters of Evening" as Night bore Fate and Doom. The word Moirai actually means "the Allotters" and they are those who visit a newborn child and decide the course of its life, and in this capacity were the objects of many cults and inscriptions on monuments. They often appear on Etruscan Death-Mirrors under the name of Athrpa, from Atropos "the Inflexible." They are mostly shown as triad, measuring in some way the span of life, sometimes by filling containers – (bringing about the connection to Water-nymphs) – or they appear singly with writing equipment – (as seen on Etruscan Death-Mirrors) – writing in the Book of Fate.

116

APOLLO ON PLAQUES AND MIRRORS, CONCLUSION

Before leaving this difficult subject in this sphere between Archaeology and Funeral-Mythology, we may, in the sense of a summary, repeat the following:

We could consider the possibility that those plaques do not represent the alter ego of the dead in the image of Apollini, but that they are votive-plaques, in the sense of "ex voti" dedicated to the divinity of Apollo, who may have had a sanctuary there and a local cult.

We would be helpless to explain the Water-Nymphs on the plaques if we did not have the Mirrors, where the element of the Water is repeatedly shown as the basis of Rebirth, and where, in fact, the soul of the dead is pictured as emerging from the Waters and as being given over by Neptun, as shown here, to the goddess of Dawn, who is symbolic for the Apotheosis of the soul, now being pictured with a halo, in the so called auroral moment of his epiphany.

80

On a mirror we also see the Apollonic apparition, with bow in hand, as a naked soul. The three females (in sequence from left to right) are inscribed as "Muira" the spirit of Fate and Doom –, further, "Lethun," who gave birth to him in the darkness of the waters, symbolic for his arising from the

Darkness of Death and the Oceanic Pool of Nature, – and finally, "Thalna," the divinity of Rebirth with the blossoming staff . . . clearly showing the progression of this Soul-Apollo from Death to Rebirth and to renewed life in the Above.

81

In conclusion it could therefore be said, that we have the information about Apollo, in relation to the Water-Nymphs from the Plaques, while we have his involvement with Death, the Sea and his Rebirth from the Mirrors and Sarcophagi.

THE PLAQUES OF ATHENS

THE GROTTO NYMPHS

We saw that the Plaques of Naples represent the Apollonic apparition in a static relation to Water-Nymphs.

The Plaques of Athens show again three Nymphs with an Apollonic figure, but added to those principal elements is now the person of Hermes Psychopompos, sometimes called "Nymphagogos" meaning in Greek to be the one who brings the bride (nymphé) to her groom.

This very name and the function it implies, verify the assumption that the soul, after death, appears as the "Groom" and the Nymphs as his "Celestial Brides" – thereby fulfilling the promise of the Eastern scriptures – which is so amply illustrated in the funeral art of the Mediterranean lands.

Another new figure, persistently appearing on the Plaques of Athens, is Pan, indicating the amorous atmosphere of the scenario, to underline that nuptial relation.

Viewing now all elements on the Plaques of Athens in combination, we have the glorified image of the dead (as Apollo) – introduced as "Groom" to the Celestial "Brides" (by Hermes Nymphagogos) – while the figure of Pan accentuates the nuptial atmosphere, by equating the Nymphs with the heavenly Horai, the servants of Aphrodite, and setting them in relation to the Apollonic epiphany.

More specifically we see in the National Museum of Athens a plaque [NM 4466] of about 400 B.C. and found in the "Cave of the Nymphs" at Mount Pentelicon, showing Hermes, connected in this composition to a triad of Nymphs, – facing an old man who is entering the stage, while an ephebean youth pours him a drink, which is on several other images characterized as the Drink of Immortality, given ceremoniously to the souls of the chosen when entering the Beyond. The connecting link between the Nymphs and the old man is Pan, which quite clearly hints at an amorous relation between the now sanctified man and the celestial females. The bearded man is inscribed as donor, but it is obvious that the donor may, at times, also be the supliant who appears on the plaque, because the reason for donating the plaque might be that he wishes to reappear after his death in the situation which is pictured on the plaque, that is: to be given the drink of immortality and to be thereupon received by the otherworldly Nymphs.

A votive-offering at Pompeii, donated by a suppliant, shows an elderly and bearded Dionysos who is about to enter an amorous encounter, while he is reached by one of his votaries the same type of cup as seen on this plaque of Athens, only this time it is said to contain a "Satyrion" which is a lovepotion. Combining now the drink of immortality with the idea of a lovepotion brings us back to the so often mentioned notion of "Everlasting Manliness in Paradise."

The bearded man on the plaque of Athens seems to hold in his left hand some grapes, which might be a hint at the Dionysian scenario he wishes to enter. The grapes could also be a present to the three Nymphs, who are thought to belong, in spirit, to the train of Dionysos . . . as we see them sometimes connected to Pan or Priapus, all of them related to the concept of hedonism. If the grapes are thought to be a "bring-along-gift" to the other-worldly females, we could understand this plaque as being a schematic illustration to the "Gifts of the Dead" theory.

A grotto used as the stage-setting on the plaques of Athens, may be connected to a vision by Homer (Odyssee XIII-103-112) where the holy grotto on the Pheacian island is said to have two entrances, one for the human race and the other for the divine beings. Those ten verses remain mysterious and were the subject of many interpretations. The most famous of them by the neoplatonic philosopher Porphyrios which runs in many dark and enigmatic directions, also giving thoughts to the "mystic rapture" and the "final elevation of souls." But the very fact that the Homeric vision was widened to include many districts, could be a hint that this grotto of the Nymphs – which originally had no connection to Afterlife – could well have been chosen, in funeral art, as the ideal meeting-place between the mortals and the Celestial Brides.

All those images point, of course, to the inflow of Oriental-Asiatic visions, as no Nymphs received the souls in the Greco-Roman realms of the dead, so that we may discern here once more the gentle blending-over from the Eastern dogma into Mediterranean figures of the nebulous Nymphs, who lent themselves to this transition, because of their everchanging spheres, patronates and outlines which they assumed already in their homelands.

Another example of the same idea is a small plaque [NM 2011] showing the three Nymphs in a mellow mood facing with a certain fascination a naked male figure before them, presumably the soul of the deceased, as one of the females reaches for this apparition with a gesture of tenderness and comfort. The scene is surrounded by rocks which look like clouds and may thereby suggest a divine realm of magic softness and uncertain borders between heaven and earth where the miraculous takes place. An amorous tinge, hinting at the further stages of his encounter, is given to the scenario by the person of Pan, appearing larger than any other figure and presiding over this otherworldly event.

118

A relief [NM 1449] which was often copied, represents the same three females within an environment which could be a grotto, and where they seem to stride towards a Pan with obviously sensual accent, playing the Syrinx of carefree dalliances, as if to indicate that they are votaries in his realm of amorous felicity. On other copies of the same scene the females are inscribed as "Horai" – the servants of Aphrodite, goddess of love, which would qualify them for the reception of the souls in the Orientalized Beyond, as stand-ins also for the heavenly Huries, promised there to please the True Believers.

119

A partly broken plaque [NM 1448] shows a young man, resembling the ennobeled and rejuvenated image of the deceased, so often seen in the company of celestial females on the Etruscan mirrors.

Here he is shown leading the usual three Nymphs into the sphere of the great unknown, characterized by a giant Olympian mask, probably denoting the realms of the divine Above, – (as opposed to Hades) – under the patronate of Pan.

120

The reappearance of Pan on all the plaques of Athens, hints at the amorous relation between the apparition of the soul and the celestial Nymphs, which was not clarified before on the plaques of Naples. The presence of Pan makes reference to the atmosphere of sensuality due to his priapic accent, while his flute hints at the joy promised in the paradise of the East, where the multitude of Apsarases provide love without attachment. The idea of having several loving brides at the same time was so foreign to Greek thinking, that the sculptors staged those Nymphic Brides, stark in appearance, but puppet-like lined up, like a purely theoretical inventory.

The prominence of Pan on all those plaques invites us to look more closely at this figure: Like his father Hermes [Homeric Hymn XIX.28] he was originally an Arkadian rustic deity of the shepherds, while his parentage is very differently given. One legend makes him the son of the shepherd Krathis and a she-goat, – another names his mother Hybris, meaning "Wantonness," – another relates him to Nymphs of the Wilds, so that we can understand that the sculptors made him on those plaques the symbol-figure for free love in the realms of the Blessed. This atmosphere was then projected onto the image of the Nymphs, who were thought to be partly servants to Aphrodite, dangerously close to Hierodules in her temple at Corinth, but partly also the innocent Love-spirits of nature, as stand-ins for the all-embracing Apsarases.

The fact that the plaques were found in the "Sanctuary of the Nymphs" may suggest that the donor wanted to beg for the benevolence of those heavenly spirits, to grant a loving reception to him, or to someone close to him.

121

We finally see on a relatively late and formal stela in an architectural setting [NM 1966] the three Nymphs or Graces, presented in an almost theatrical lineup of the "deus ex machina" type, possibly arising from a well, maybe symbolic for Water-Nymphs. The principal figure is an Apollonic apparition in a languid pose as if awakening from his death-sleep, so often seen on Etruscan presentations. Next to him is a little Pan blowing his pipe as the traditional inspiration to involvements of love. The mediator between that Apollonic apparition and the three females is, as usual Hermes Nymphagogos. A number of people in smaller scale resemble the souls shown on other pieces of funeral art, awaiting their ascent to the Above and giving the religious salute to the personages of the celestial spheres.

INSCRIPTIONS AND MEANINGS OF PLAQUES

The inscriptions on the plaques classify them into two types:

One of them are plaques dedicated to the memory of the deceased, in the sense of funeral stelae. They say: "so-and-so gave it to Apollini and the Nymphs" – (whereby sometimes V.S.L.M. is used as abbreviation-formula for "dedicated," or "dedit.") – This thought might be related to our formulation "der Verewigte" – (The Eternalized) meaning, that the dead has changed into a being of eternal outlines, comparable to the metamorphosis into the Apollonic epiphany. It is also said in our time, that the dead is now "with the Angels" or is recommended to "Heavenly Graces" – which is in this sense parallel to the vision of the dead with the heavenly Nymphs, or the "Three Graces" seen on sarcophagi, plaques and mirrors.

We have in those cases plaques which are dedicated by some donor to the memory of the deceased and are showing him as being received by celestial apparitions in the Beyond. This is a trend of thought reaching back to the Pharaohs shown to be received by divinities . . . to Greco-Roman presentations of the departed, or his metamorphosed soul with butterfly-wings, welcomed by otherworldly genii.

The other type of plaques are: "Dedicated by so-and-so to the Nymphs" – which could be understood as a donation to the Nymphs, to induce them to be mercyful to the deceased and to receive the dead in good graces. Such donations to the figures of the Above would then be classified as "Ex Voti" . . . given in return for favors asked. They are dedicated "ad majorem gloriam" as an endearment to the heavenly figure, to the sanctuary or to special altars. We have parallels in some of today's churches, where many donations, great, small, in pictures, in statues etc. are addressed to protector-figures to ask for their favors . . . interceding for the deceased, in begging on his behalf for a kind reception. It is obvious, that not the dead is addressed or emplored in those cases, but the protective mights, the mercyful, the kind and the loving ones, as in our case the Water-Nymphs.

Both types of plaques are then found in sanctuaries and shrines, either in memory of the dead in the sense of a "funeral stela" or else addressed to the spirits of protection, in the sense of an "ex-voto."

122

THE SEAFARER NYMPHS

There are some other plaques whose inscriptions are not, like those of Naples in Latin, but are instead in Greek, and above all they show some Water-Nymphs, but no Apollini. They are plaques expressing "Thanks" and "Supplications" for "Life."

It seems possible that the Water-Nymphs of the Greek district were thought to be protective Spirits of the Waters and that those plaques are "ex voti" given as thanks for the rescue from a calamity at Sea, together with supplications for further protection.

The fact that no Apollini appears on them seems to be a hint that those Greek plaques are not memorial-plaques but objects dedicated in thanks and supplication to the female protector-figures.

Samples of inscriptions:

"TO THE MISTRESSES, THE NYMPHS"

"TO THE DIVINE NYMPHS IN THANKS"

"EPYEKETHOS BECAUSE OF HIS LIFE, A SUPPLICATION"

"P. . .ENTIS BECAUSE OF HIS LIFE, A PRAYER"

"THE LORDLY NYMPHS DONATED IN THANKS"

"ONTO THE NYMPHS A SUPPLICATION"

On some of the plaques the three females are characterized as Water-Nymphs by the pitchers emitting water at their feet, while the poses of the Nymphs obviously are a primitive copy of the plaques of the "Three Graces." We therefore may speculate that the idea of those Nymphs — (originally "Those of the Waters" or the Celestial Brides) — was transplanted from the South of Italy to Greek-speaking districts, and that they changed their meaning on the way, representing then in those eastern lands, some protective Genii of the Waters.

We have also some rather gaudy representations of those celestial females, which somehow do not fit in their mood the solemn inscriptions and resemble more the original Oriental visions of the charmers of Paradise.

It seems possible that we deal here with a split between the garish appearance and the solemn meaning, reminiscent of the females in gay nudity and bright colors on the prow of Mediterranean ships, believed to protect the sailors from disaster and death – or akin to the frankly sensual amulets in the south of Italy or northern Africa, which are believed to be an antidote against misfortunes, as totems of "bonheur" counteracting "malheur."

Some other plaques from Capo d'Istria, still with Latin inscriptions, seem to have retained more of the original meaning of the three females, showing them in the company of a Satyr, thereby still connecting them to the environment of sensual pleasure.

In reconciling the Nymphs as protectresses from maritime disasters, with the Nymphs receiving the soul in the Beyond, we may speculate that the Nymphs – coming as a foreign element from the East – were associated by some maritime people with the waters of the seafarers – while by others, more given to eschatological thoughts, those very same figures assumed a relation to the celestial waters of Paradise, so that we may think that on all plaques where Nymphs appear with Hermes Psychopompos we deal with visions of the celestial spheres, reinforced by the presence of Pan or Priapus, as a hint at the amorous felicity of the Oriental Above . . . while we notice that on all plaques with the "Seafarer's Nymphs" the figure of Psychopompos is missing.

LOCATIONS

Some of the plaques in the museum of Naples are said to have been found in Ischia, an island South of Naples, which had been occupied by so many different tribes, that it is difficult to determine who imported those ideas. Many similar plaques were, however, found East of the Mediterranean, in what we may call the districts of the Thracians, who at times under Persian rule, were greatly influenced by Eastern ideas, and back-influenced, in turn, the Greek religious visions of Afterlife, of the Below and the Above . . . of Dionysos, Orpheus, the Nymphs, the Muses and the celestial females. The museum of Sofia contains many interesting pieces to that effect and above all the Museums of Athens and Istanbul.

CONCLUSION

As to the general spread of ideas, it seems important to remember, that all of those diverse objects, found in those different regions, show again and again the very same figures – (prominently Apollo and the Nymphs) – so that we must realize, that we deal here not with local cults, but rather with a very general and important belief within the Etruscan eschatology. We see, in short, that the Apollo- and Nymph-complex is based on three types of evidences: Plaques, Sarcophagi and Mirrors, which are distributed from the North to the South throughout the Etruscan enclaves of Italy, but having its roots in Eastern lands.

The figure of Leda seems to have two different meanings in funeral art:

The older symbolism, found on grave monuments in the Aegean spheres, appears to compare the Soul with Leda, in showing her embraced by the divine spirit of Zeus, in the shape of the swan, in the sense of a Hierogamy, the union of the soul with the Divine.

A later symbolism, found in the Roman sphere, reverses the meaning of the figures, now comparing the Soul with the swan, who is lusting for Leda, while Leda impersonates "the Female in the Beyond" – who is shown on stelae and sarcophagi in a coquettish mood, leading-on the "Soul-Bird" – making use of the old allegory of showing the soul in the shape of a bird.

Leda, Dioscuri and Helen, in short:

Leda, due to her adventure with Zeus, in the guise of a swan, laid two eggs. From one sprang Pollux and Helen, from the other Castor and Clytemnestra. Castor and Pollux were called the Dioscuri, meaning "young Sons of Zeus." During a quarrel Castor was killed, but his twin, Pollux, asked Zeus to be permitted to take turns with his brother, of living alternately in Hades and in Heaven. Thereby they became Symbol-figures for the process of going down to Hades – (Death) – and for arising to Heaven – (the Resurrection).

One of the many examples for the earlier "Soul is Leda" equations, we have a sarcophagus of Arles, France, [Reinach II.213] where Leda in her Hierogamy with the divine swan is closely flanked by the classical death-angel mournfully holding the traditional inverted torch of life . . . while Medusa and Griffins protect the sepulchre.

207

A most elaborate specimen of the earlier Aegean version is the sarcophagus of Kephisia – [Reinach II.344] – which shows Leda with the swan on one side panel, and on the other side, a winged Eros with bow, while on the main panel of the sarcophagus we have a stately female, probably Helen, holding an egg in her hand, the symbol of Rebirth, – so often seen on Etruscan tomb paintings.

What is suggested here seems to be that the Soul – (shown as Leda) – in union with the Divine – (shown as Swan) – causes the rebirth of the soul – (in the Egg) – to re-appear in the image of Beauty – (shown as Helen).

We may notice here a certain similarity with the Tefnut-procedure, where as the first phase we have the union of the Soul with the Divine, – (represented by Tefnut) – and thereupon the rebirth of the soul, as a consequence of that union . . . (possibly with a faint echo in the ideology of the Mysteries of Eleusis).

On the sarcophagus of Kephisia the figure of Helen is flanked by the Dioskuri to indicate the symbolism of Death and rebirth, projected onto the deceased, who might be a lady, suggesting that her alter-ego may reappear in the glorified epiphany of a mythological figure. This idea conforms hereby to the pattern set by the epiphany of the dead in the image of Apollo, as seen on sarcophagi, plaques, and mirrors, which demonstrates the very broad basis of the belief in the re-appearance of the alter-ego of the dead or his spiritual substance in the image of a mythological personage, even if the deceased is a female.

The Dioskuri may be a hint at still another symbolism, by being the patrons of the sea, which could be understood as the all-devouring sea to which all living return, – as well as the Ocean of eternal rebirth, – or even as the "Celestial Ocean" the scenario of the Eastern Paradise.

125

Another example of Leda being the "Female in the Beyond" who is persued by a bird, representing the soul of the deceased, is a late Roman sarcophagus – [Messina, Museo Nazionale] – having in its center, as its only ornament a Leda who is quite reminiscent of the celestial Brides, posing before some drapery as the promise in the Beyond, while being followed by a prancing Soul-Bird with the typical sinuous neck, known to us from other funeral monuments as indicating lustful attitudes. The fact that this image appears on a sarcophagus makes it obvious that Leda, as the image of female attraction, was connected in funeral art to the Eastern version of the Thereafter.

209

The same rather erotic atmosphere prevails on many plaques and images of those times, which were so greatly influenced by the Eastern and Etruscan visions of a sensual Afterlife. Reinach [II.11] for instance, shows the same type of an Orientalized female in the act of disrobing before an animal which again is rather a Soul-Bird than a swan, as she marches towards a Priapic figure in a paradisial setting. The active attitude of those females calls our attention to the Eastern influences, where especially the paradisial maidens are shown to offer their favors rather emphatically to the males, as if their livelihood depended on it – possibly as an upward-projection of the professional temple-girls, or the dark-eyed beauties of the streets – while in Greco-Roman art the male is the pursuing partner.

For archaeological purposes of "quick recognition" we may therefore establish the rule that, in earlier times, we have "Leda the Soul" – while in later times, under the influence of the East, we have "Leda as the Female in the Beyond" . . . Equally, we may also tentatively say that in Greek thinking, the swan represents the divine spirit, – in contrast to the Etruscan visions, where the swan represents the deceased, as the "Soul-Bird" which is encouraged by "Leda, the celestial Maiden" to otherworldly amorous adventures.

Here we want to repeat in short the position of the artists and follow their desperate search for solutions, which seem so obvious when found and so confusing and perplexing when missed. They worked according to a verbal transmission from the East, without having any visual or manifest Oriental-Asiatic samples of how to express those foreign doctrines, and had to use locally known symbol-figures to act-out those outlandish conceptions of the Thereafter.

We give here some examples of this process:

One is the Cyprus Sarcophagus of 600 B.C. in the Metropolitan Museum of New York. There the sculptor attempted to illustrate the saying of the Mahabharata that the Blessed in the Beyond make love and drink milk . . . while it is also proclaimed that there are many and joyous lovemakings in the next world.

To illustrate that, the Egyptian sculptor used the only symbol for amorous embraces known to him: the lovemaking-divinity BES. Consequently we see on the main panel of this sarcophagus many BES-es dancing, the plurality of them indicating the "many" of the lovemakings, – and their dancing, to show the "joyousness."

126

On the side-panel of this sarcophagus the sculptor attempted to show the "Milk-Drinking" – for which he had only the Egyptian symbol-figure of Isis, feeding Horus on her breast, as a model. However, it must have been reported to the artist that the females of the Beyond were free lovers to all. In combination of those factors and using "local actors" and local moral judgment applied to those celestial apparitions, he showed a number of North-African girls of pleasure, richly decked out in their well-earned coins, compressing or offering their breasts in an obvious effort to give milk.

127

Egyptian females are not shown to wear jewelry when otherwise naked and are never seen with coins on their ears – while the milk-girls on the sarcophagus conform to the typical Apsara-representations which depict them as being entirely nude except for their most elaborate neck-chains of that bullae-type, while the earrings of coins are, as we said, worn by the girls of easy virtues in North-Africa.

Another example of an Egyptian artist, illustrating the Eastern saying in the Mahabharata, that "the Blessed in Paradise will drink Milk from milk-yielding Trees" – shows the dead – (a Pharaoh) – straining to drink milk from a breast growing on a tree. This proposition seemed highly improbable to the Egyptian painter and he, therefore, again reverted to the well-known Isis-figure reaching her breast with the typical gesture of her arm to Horus, only this time it is the tree which sprouts a human arm to reach the breast, which, most surprisingly, grows on a branch of that tree.

128

The hieroglyphic inscription says that this is Menkheperre (one of the names of King Thutmosis III.) who drinks from the breast. To connect somehow this improbable situation to local figures, the tree is called in this picture Isis, his mother, justifying the arm of the tree – (although Horus is really the son of Isis) – so that Isis becomes a stand-in for the female element in the Beyond, as mother figure . . . (possibly connected to the mysterious remark, "I have seen my Mother") in the Pyramid Text – and elevating the King thereby to the son of Isis – while illustrating the Indian promise that the Blessed in the Beyond will drink milk from trees.

Thutmosis III. is of the *XVIII* th Dynasty, while the Hyksos were of the *XV* th to *XVI* th Dynasty, which means that the Eastern visions, imported by the Hyksos, had more than 200 years time to leave an impact on Egypt's imagery of the Thereafter.

129

A third example of illustrating the Oriental-Asiatic vision of the Females in the Beyond, we see on the panel of a sarcophagus, now in the Museo delle Terme in Rome: Here we have above "the Rushes of Hathor" – meaning the joyful Above – (indicated by the marsh-Ibises) – a group of big and small masculine souls clamoring with outstretched arms to get at some Bajaderes in transparent veils flouncing their most ample Oriental and non-Egyptian figures. To make sure that we deal here not with the purely artistic admiration of the dance-girls, on the part of the clamoring male souls, we see enthroned above those girls Bes, the lovemaking god, as the reigning spirit over the scene and realm, who is flanked by the double-monkeys, the insignia of the pleasure-girls . . . aptly approached by a bull, the symbol of masculinity to repeat in symbol-language the constellation shown below of the eager souls attracted by girls of easy virtues. This upper register, representing the spiritual patronship over the actual happening, is also flanked by a priapic Herm, to leave no doubt about the atmosphere here depicted. The clamoring male figures stand on, or arise from a sarcophagus with Etrusco-Roman insigniae of sanctification. The workmanship of that panel is Italian, but the symbol-language is Egyptian and the souls wear the Egyptian loin-cloth . . . so that we have here a case where an Italian sculptor expresses an Oriental-Asiatic doctrine of a love-encounter between the souls and the willing females, by means of Egyptian actors and symbols.

The Ibises on the lowest register are quasi forming the basis of the upper development and are a determinant for placing the sphere of action above it, as occuring after death, in the Above. The Ibis-hieroglyph AKH, stands for the "indestructible spirit of a privileged person" – and is thereby an important symbol-figure for Resurrection and Afterlife. In addition the Ibis is an incarnate of the god Thoth, who is the score-keeper in the "Weighing of the Heart" procedure and is therefore again related to the admission of the Soul to the realm of the Blessed . . . which obviously is shown in the upper register.

THE CHTHONIAN DOG

The figure of Apollini appears each time on the stelae in the company of a strange animal which could be a griffin or more often a chthonian dog, either showing the wandering soul the way to the Above, or because he was charmed by the lyra of Apollini so as to let him escape from the Below . . . as the subterranean dogs appear in both functions, as guardians and as guides in various mythologies.

A short digression be permitted here because the origin of the chthonian dog is very surprising as it appears to be a direct outgrowth of the idea of "Lustration" – that is the blessing of a field or building by sprinkling its four corners with water of magical properties.

This ritual is related to Water as the symbol of Purity and Cleansing, and by the word "Lustration" to Lux, the light, and thereby opposed to the region of eternal darkness, the world of the shades in the Below.

Both of those connotations seem reversed by the dog, as urine was symbolic for un-clean and thereby tarnishing all with the odium of anti-light, that is darkness, related to death.

The dog was considered a chthonian exponent, because he was seen all day busy, scandalously desecrating monuments of gods in open places and also showing the same contempt for the dwellings of the living. Just because the four corners of a house have a special magical significance when sprinkled, and the dog is the only creature doing that, he seemed to act due to a macabre mission from another region, to counter-act or persiflage any sanctifying effect. As the Netherworld was thought of as the antipode of the earthly existence and the divine sphere of the Above, the dog seemed to belong to the contrary of it, that is to that underworldly nihilism . . . also hinted at by the name for the all-denying philosophers as the "Cynics" – from "Kynos" the dog, and his shameless disregard. Even later, in Doctor Faustus, the black dog appears as an embodiment of the infernal regions.

In the magic recipes of India and Egypt it is said to practically wipe out the "numen" of a dead person, by making water on his grave, and dogs were seen doing just that. In the Mediterranean this was understood to be an effort on the part of the dog to keep the souls down in Hades. And this may be the reason why the dog got the reputation of serving the chthonian establishment – even before he was associated with the bourgeois notion of a "watch-dog" – which in itself hints at a later time, when the escape from Hades became a fashionable speculation.

A certain governor in the Mogul empire regularly made water on the graves of his enemies to keep their ghosts from "re-sprouting" – (maybe inspired by the observation on sprouting plants which get killed this way and never revive again) – but this very usual jinxing practice, related now back to the nihilistic magic of the dog, was finally outlawed by the Avesta. ["Laws against Daimons" by Zarathustra]. The fact that this practice had to be prohibited by law, shows the importance ascribed to this magic.

We see on very many funeral monuments dogs, which may sometimes be interpreted as symbols of mourning by the faithful friends, as dogs are known to follow their master to his grave, while at other times those funeral dogs seem rather related to their chthonian connection.

SEA SARCOPHAGI

THE PROBLEM

We deal here with Etruscan sarcophagi which depict scenes taking place in the water.

They are so fascinating because nobody could understand their meaning. Despite the dramatic beauty of their reliefs, showing enigmatic figures in emotional interactions, the significance of these scenes, and especially their environment, their very sphere of action, remained until now a complete mystery.

The difficulty is that nothing shown on those sarcophagi can be reconciled with any Greco-Roman mythos . . . and no connection whatsoever can be reconstructed between the visions shown on those sarcophagi and the ideas of death or Afterlife, as known in the Mediterranean . . . and yet, it is obvious that those scenes carved on so many sarcophagi, must depict something very important pertaining to death or the next world.

Because of the fact that those sarcophagi were made in the heart of Italy, the question arises: What Extra-Mediterranean "Next World" is it, which seems so joyous and full of mysterious embraces?

THE TRANSPORTATION THEORY

For some time there existed an attempt to explain the Sea-Sarcophagi as depicting the voyage of the souls over the waters to the island of the Blessed, the Elysium.

Although this theory has great appeal and a winning charm, many inexplicable contradictions were found and very little evidence could be provided to support that proposition.

The disturbing factors were that nowhere was a drift of action shown, nor a hint that the company of figures was en route to somewhere, nor do we ever have a sign of a happy landing.

The obvious embracements of the females (supposedly the souls) with the male figures of the sea (supposedly giving them transportation) did not fit into this scheme, because that amorous involvement would be comparable to some females, on the way to their sanctification, making love to their pilots . . . and yet, the scenes of sweet embraces, surrounded by Amorettes, form the main subject presented on the Sea-Sarcophagi. And what about the females clinging with incredible swoon to diverse animals with intimate kisses? And who are the babies, upheld by the males and females? Were they the results of flirtatious relations of the females with their transportation-guides? . . . an offspring conceived en route?

According to the "Transportation Theory" there is technically no other time or place for the babies to be conceived, except in those rather sacrilegious unions between the souls of the dead with their oceanic escorts, which at times are monsters . . . and why are all "Souls" female? Where are the souls of men? . . . should they suffer the indignity of being transformed into amorous Fräuleins after death . . . in scandalous affairs with animals or gay young men of the sea?

It is true that the "Soul" is mostly called by the female article, like "Psyche" – "anima" and "Seele," similar to abstractions in general, as "Idea" – "Invention" etc., but it was never thought that a male would have a female soul.

The support of the "Transportation Theory" is derived from images showing the soul as travelling into the next world, via a chariot or on horseback and in some cases riding on sea-creatures. But this combination with sea-creatures would rather hint at the return of the soul to the "Pool of Nature" that is: to the eternal Ocean into which ultimately all living is streaming, and out of which all is reborn.

This thought is amply demonstrated on early sarcophagi where the dead person is shown as being flanked left and right by sea-creatures in an heraldic manner and certainly not as travelling to somewhere, but being instead in a static position and at his final destination – and also showing him to be re-born right there, Venus-like in a shell, out of the eternal sea, the "Pool of Nature," or re-appearing out of the grip of the Deep and its devouring monsters, in radiance to a new light, the dawn of life eternal between the Blessed.

We see the idea of a voyage of the dead over the waters to an "Island of the Blessed" sometimes vaguely hinted in some Etruscan tomb-paintings – (Tomba dei Tori, at Tarquinia, ca. 550 B.C. etc.) – the Hippocampi being possibly a feed-back from the earlier types of Sea-Sarcophagi, – but all those representations making reference to the "Transportation-Theory" can not help us to explain the powerful images we have on the mysterious Sea-Sarcophagi, which are here the subject of our examination.

42

44

130

133

THE EARLIER SARCOPHAGI

The earlier school or tradition shows only sea-creatures, flanking a head or a circular disk. Those heads seem to suggest the deceased, as they show a rather happy expression, a condition which, it was hoped for, would now surround the departed – this, in contrast to the rendering of the dead, as often shown on the cover of the sarcophagi, where that person is depicted with grave and tragic features – as it seems shortly before his death, while those visages on the container of the sarcophagus may suggest the rather glorious extra-terrestrial sphere in which the departed exists after death. In some cases the face of the dead person seems to be metamorphosed into an Apollonic vision, vaguely emerging from the roughly hewn stone. The assumption that the central head on the sarcophagi wants to represent the dead person, is suggested by the fact that later sarcophagi – (which are made with greater skill and clarity) – definitely show the portrait of the deceased person in this very position in the center of the sarcophagi, and also flanked by attributes of the sea. (The fact that some later Roman sculptors, who copied the earlier sarcophagi, mistook the head in the center as representing the Lord of the Sea, should not confuse the issue.)

The assumption of a metamorphosis of the dead into an Apollo-like mask or vision is based on the Apollo-like hairdo of that apparition on the relief, which is in strict contrast to the hairdo on the portrait of the deceased, as shown on the cover of the sarcophagi. Supporting that assumption, are the parallel cases of the metamorphosis of the dead into the alter-ego of Endymion, used as a symbol for eternal sleep in supreme beauty, as seen on other sarcophagi. There are some more symbol-tie-ins with Beauty and Light-Eternal, superimposed over the dead-person, including the extended symbol-districts of Apollo, who was later also merged with Mitra, the Lord-Protector of the souls of the departed in the celestial realm. We also have the parallel of the dead person being identified with a divinity in Egypt, where the dead is addressed as Osiris so-and-so and is depicted with the beard of Osiris, to slip, so to say, into the personality of Osiris, the death god. That metamorphosis in Egypt is especially stunning, when even a dead woman is pictured with the Beard of Osiris (Queen Hatshepsut, 1504 to 1485 B.C., daughter and wife of Thutmosis I. – Met. Mus., N.Y.) or the soul of a dead person, traditionally shown as a bird with a human head, is depicted wearing the beard of Osiris (that is: a bird with human features, Egyptian haircut and a long and pointed beard), thus representing the soul of the dead person, assuming, as we see, the facial features of the divinity Osiris, – which is quite similar to the death-mask on the early sarcophagi assuming the facial features of Apollo. Curiously, we see in both cases the dead assuming the typical hair-style of the respective divinities, which is

131

132

22

130   possibly connected to the magic which in old times was ascribed to hair and hairdo in general to indicate the change of personality in particular, as applicable to the case here in question, of Apollo and Osiris, respectively.

In later Roman times the deification of the Emperors was not understood as transmutation of the Emperor into an existent divinity, but was thought to concern the divine element or genius within his person, because the genius was considered divine and the separable spiritual double of man. (See Cicero concerning the deification of Augustus.)

It could therefore be assumed that the "Spiritual Double" of the dead re-appears in excelsis with the features of Apollo, Endymion, Osiris, etc. – as a metamorphosis, which is suggested by all visual evidences as seen on sarcophagi, stelae and Etruscan mirrors where the Apollo figure, appearing in the Above is identified as such by inscriptions, as "Aplu."

THE LATER SARCOPHAGI

135   The later school or tradition of the Sea-Sarcophagi modifies the originally rather indistinct sea-creatures into Sea-Centauri, showing the upper body, face and arms of young men of considerable beauty. From the hip down their anatomy blends over into the body of a horse, on whose forelegs grow fins, while the hind-legs are replaced by a dragon-like structure.

136   We now see females appearing who are making very definite advances to the males of the sea, shown at times upholding the image of the deceased person, clarified as being no longer a symbolic mask, but instead represent the portrait of the departed.

137   As a scenario we find all the figures apparently floating over the waters as if they were weightless and also showing no sign of getting wet as compared to the Nereids in Greco-Roman art, who clearly demonstrate the wetness on their clinging draperies and hair.

A further addition are some babies who are tenderly received by the company of males and females alike, so that we may assume, on first sight, that they are the offspring produced by the females of the sea, in conjunction with their obvious lovers, the Sea-Centauri . . . but this is not so, as we will see later on.

138   In some cases we see the babies eagerly reaching out for the females, and at times resting confidently cradled in their arms and actually being nourished on their breast, while we may notice that those females with unmoving facial expressions, act rather like theatrical symbol-figures in a mysterious pantomime.

In many cases, those babies are sprouting out of blossoms which seem to grow quite improbably in the salt waters of the sea and are of a botanical kind never seen in Italy, but reappearing on Etruscan mirrors. As nobody seems concerned about the babies falling down into the wildly whirling eddies of the Ocean, we are again left with the feeling that we deal here not with realities, but with the staging of outlandish symbols.

140

The most stunning sight, however, are the females in gestures of passionate swoon, embracing not only their human-shaped companions, the young lovers, but throwing themselves upon Sea-horses, bulls, and even rams of the sea, sometimes kissing them mouth to mouth . . . All of those happenings seem so entirely non-Roman and disquieting that we long to know at least the sphere in which those improbable scenes take place.

141

All of those new figures having been added to the early sarcophagi do not help to clarify the most basic question concerning the stage of action and the scenario which is presented on those reliefs, but rather create more problems in reconciling any of the figures and actions with any Greco-Roman mythological material known to us.

LOCATIONS AND NUMBERS

The earlier and primitive types of the Sea-Sarcophagi – which do not show aquatic females and Centauri, or babies – were mostly found around the city-state of Tarquinia, especially the so-called Nenfro-Sarcophagi in that region. Many of that type of Sea-Sarcophagi were discovered near the city of Tuscania, in the north of the state of Tarquinia. Remarkable are five of those primitive sarcophagi, located in a family-grave, two kilometers west of Rusa Veccia, which were made or inspired by Tarquinian workshops. Two of the early sarcophagi, showing only masculine sea-creatures – (without any human-like visages) – were found in Norchia and Musarna, respectively.

131

All together we may see at least twenty of those primitive examples in collections, which is a relatively small number, as compared to the great number of the later type of Sea-Sarcophagi, of which there might be a hundred.

The higher developed Sea-Sarcophagi, showing a great many personages with emotional involvements in accomplished craftsmanship, are found pretty close to that initial region of primitive development, that is: north of Rome in the old Etruscan settlements, provinces, or city-states of – (naming them from Rome northward): Veii, Caere, Tarquinia, Tuscania, Viterbo, Orvieto, and in the north Volterra, nearing today's Florence.

THE TRANSMISSION

Because of the relatively small number (100) of the Sea-Sarcophagi, as compared to the very great number of other sarcophagi – (for instance, those showing battle-scenes or subterranean happenings) – and because of their regional confinement, it can be assumed that we deal here with a specific sect or religious group of people, within the ethnic tribe of the Etruscans, who had especially exact information regarding some religious doctrines of India, because, as we will see in the following, all the odd and mysterious elements shown on the Sea-Sarcophagi are actually mentioned in full detail in Indian religious texts. The process of that transmission from India to Italy is not documented but many signs point to the probability that some Indian religious groups, or preachers, or holy men, migrated to Italy and there spread their beliefs, in the ways missionaries do. We have, from that time, in this region, many examples of such activities, starting with Buddha himself and his most extensive wanderings, his preachings and his conversion of peoples in far-off lands. We have the stories of Dionysos, his priests and votaries, and their partly fabulous, partly historical travels from the Mediterranean to India and their return to the Greco-Roman lands and their attempts, successful or otherwise, at converting the diverse peoples to the Dionysian doctrines. We have, further on, the many wandering prophets, to which Amos already in 700 B.C. makes reference, as a considerable and well established tradition of great men with powerful words who brought news about extra-terrestrial things to the people. It was about 600 B.C. when the contacts between the Mediterranean and Asia achieved their greatest degree of expansion. Paralleling this were intensified contacts among the traders, which helped to bring about an eager discovery of "New Worlds" on both commercial and spiritual levels. This can be clearly traced on art-objects produced at that time, as they show a very definite flow from the East to the Mediterranean, not only in artistic style but, more importantly, in broad human conceptions as well. A soul suddenly springs up among the otherwise semi-ornamental marionettes – a soul which seems so important that it is credited with wonderful sweeter-than-life adventures in another world, after having been freed from its mortal hull.

Much later, during the Christian era, missionaries (such as St. Paul) travelled to other continents too, converting the inhabitants to North African doctrines – again demonstrating the East-to-West flow of ideas.

The exact plotting of a chart locating the earliest Christian monuments show the same general system and pattern of enclaves, forming in certain regions, as did the earliest Etruscans within the Italic tribes.

In both cases those enclaves were created by missionaries of a sort, coming from a far continent; and in both cases the native population embraced those foreign teachings and visions, though at various times, and to different degrees, among the several regions.

But just as the Europeans did not become North-Africans because of the new Christian creeds, so the Italics did not become Indians in an ethnic sense, – which explains the clearly Italian faces on some of the Etruscan sepulchral covers. However, some of those faces are most definitely Asiatic, which would account for the Indo-Asiatic missionaries, or members of those religious groups, which immigrated from the East to Italy.

The missionary-like flow of doctrines from India via the Etruscans to the Italic people seems therefore well within the normal pattern of cultural enclaves at that very time and locale, in which the Etruscans seem to have been the spiritual leaders of the native population.

More than anything else the Etruscans were following the Indian death-cult, probably in the hope of entering in this way into the marvelous Indian-type paradise. Before 750 B.C. the Italic aborigines, called the Villanovans, buried the ashes of their dead in cinerary urns, covered with a helmet. More or less after 750 B.C. the igloo-like tombs of India, called "Stupas" and consisting of cupolas covered with earth, reappeared exactly in the same configuration in Italy, being now the tombs of the Etruscans. Also the Linga grave-stones used in India, representing the generative emblem of Siva (being symbolic for resurrection) – are found as grave-monuments of the Etruscans in Italy, in exactly the same shape, but made in Italy of Italian stone . . . although the Etruscans neither knew nor venerated Siva.

We also see on Etruscan cult-vessels and sarcophagi gradually appearing the fabled chimeras of the East, unknown to Italy, as well as griffins and equally foreign lions and panthers (painted in graves). Even coconut-palms and lotus blossoms became subjects of Etruscan ornamental art. All of which may be called cases of "visual transplants."

6

ASIATIC PERFUMES IN ETRUSCAN GRAVES

There are, however, many other objects pointing to a transfer from the East to the Mediterranean. Among these are great numbers of Corinthian perfume-bottles found in Etruscan graves of 800 B.C., especially at Formello near Veii. Why were they brought from Corinth, in Greece, to the middle of Italy? What is the connection?

It seems that the use of perfumes came from the Indo-Asiatic Orient to Egypt, because Olibanum and Terebinth, the two plants most often mentioned in death-rituals, grew on the shores of the Red Sea and to the east of it. Papyri of Queen Hatshepsut and Ramses III show that great expeditions were sent to the East to bring back those precious aromatic substances. Religious texts praise the divine fragrance of certain celestial personages, as their perfume is said to be more powerful than the perfumes of others — thereby implying its magic power. Small flasks of perfume found in Egyptian graves were labelled as "Bring-along gifts" (denoted as such by a special hieroglyph) — tokens from the dead to the assembled celestial divinities (not to the subterranean judges).

As Corinth was the great terminal of the Asia trade, it was thereby the port-of-entry for Indian traditions — one of them being the heavily perfumed temple-girls, available to the public, who duplicated in the sanctuary of Aphrodite at Corinth the function of their Indian counterparts. The girls were so highly perfumed because the "divine fragrance" was associated with the heavenly realm, of which the sanctuary with the girls was supposed to be a replica. The perfume, i.e. the "Divine fragrance," was actually used as a means of spiritualization. (This perfumed oil later developed into the holy ointment with which emperors were consecrated; later still it evolved into the "Extreme Unction" for the anointment of the dying, and the "holy water" used for blessings and purification in the modern Church.) The Etruscan dead of Veii were therefore given the "original" Indo-Asiatic perfumes, "bottled in Corinth," to aid in the purification and sanctification of their souls. They were a kind of "patent medicine," exported from Corinth to all believers in the Etruscan Afterlife, and were thought to "guarantee absolutely" the acceptance of the dead among the Beati.

Perfumes and unguents for funeral rituals and other ceremonies were often manufactured in laboratories connected directly to the sanctuaries. (Such a laboratory exists intact at one temple of Edfu, where recipes for the manufacture and use of the holy fragrances are still written on the walls.) The demand for these holy oils was so great that, besides making enough for temple use, the perfume factories supplied additional quantities "for export to foreign lands" — a phrase often found in Indian texts, pertaining to the perfumed oils and to the girls as well.

In Egyptian inscriptions it is remarked that the body of the dead one is made pleasing by perfumed oils for its reception among the gods. It is crudely said in the oldest Mithraic texts that the bad ones stink, while the divines are fragrant. The divine fragrance of Buddha is often mentioned and becomes synonymous with a state of holiness and elevation. Thus, for their love-bouts, the temple-girls of India were drenched in perfumed oils, to signify their temporary transformation into semi-divine figures. It is stated in manuals of the training-schools for temple-girls in India, that the aim of their education is to make the girls saleable to foreign lands. It is therefore possible that those exported girls, indoctrinated with Indian thinking, also contributed to the spread of the Indian paradisial visions from Corinth to the Etruscan settlements. It was, of course, in the interests of those girls to convert the Mediterraneans to Indian beliefs in which the heavenly damsels – (and thereby their earthly stand-ins) – were of great importance and highly priced. Consequently, those Indo-Asiatic girls played very active roles in "converting" the native population to Indian patterns of thought.

The traditional idea of the dead bearing perfume as a gift – (or perhaps a bribe) – to the gods is also an old Sumerian custom. Perfume bottles have been found in graves from the Mediterranean to the borders of Asia. They were inscribed as gifts and addressed to the judges of the next world, and were affixed to statements which recommended the deceased. Those texts were especially explicit in Egypt and were called "The Negative Confession," as they did not mention the sins, but only the good deeds of the deceased, and enumerated the bad deeds not committed.

Example:

> "HOMAGE TO YOU O YE GODS WHO DWELL IN HEAVEN.
> I HAVE BROUGHT TO YOU PERFUME. I HAVE MADE AN
> END TO ALL SINS COMMITTED. I HAVE BROUGHT TO
> YOU WHAT IS TO YOUR PLEASING" – etc.
> [Papyrus of Ani, Chapter LXXIX]

More in detail:

> "Hail to thee, great god, Lord of Right and Truth!
> I have never bidden any man to slay on my behalf.
> I have not stolen the offerings made to the
> blessed dead. I have not snatched the milk from
> the mouth of the babe" (hieroglyph of breast-milk)
> "I have not snared water-fowl of the gods"
> (belonging to the clergy) "nor turned away the
> cattle set apart for sacrifice. May no evil
> happen to me in this land" (of the dead)
> "in the Hall of Right and Truth" (of judgement).
> [Translation W. Budge, Brit. Mus.]

Also to the question of the transfer from Asia to the Mediterranean, the following seems important:

In Book V, Paragraphs 4, 5 and 6, Herodotus talks about the Thracians, a people which seems to have linked the Indo-Asiatic sphere with the Greco-Roman world, as he tells of typical Indian customs trailing out towards the Mediterranean along the "upper route" of transfer, that is, along the North of the Mediterranean – and not via Persia to North-Africa.

The Thracians lived where Asia borders on the Mediterranean, that is: from the Bosporus and south of the Black Sea to the West and extending into Greece. As we see on the examples of Samothrace, a fusion of the people of the Greek Samos were the half-Asiatic Thracians seems to have influenced Greco-Roman customs to a large extent.

In V.4, Herodotus speaks of the belief of those people in the immortality of the soul. He says that if a child is born, the family sits around and weeps because of the suffering this creature will have to endure, while if somebody dies they celebrate his liberation from the earth with rejoicing and merriment.

In V.5, Herodotus talks about the custom of letting the widows follow their husbands into death, which is a typical Indian custom, hardly practiced by other people and therefore a clear sign of that flow from India to the Mediterranean, especially where death-cults are concerned. All that in support of the theory that the Etruscans came from India, maybe as missionaries or religious groups, who, on the way from India to the Mediterranean, converted several tribes which were located in their path and left, so to say, their mental footprints along that road, in the form of Indian visions and customs.

> "It is customary for a man to have a number of wives; and when a husband dies, his wives enter into keen competition, in which friends play a vigorous part on one side or the other, to decide which of them was most loved by the deceased. The one on whom the honor of the verdict falls is praised by both men and women, and then slaughtered over the grave by her next of kin and buried at her husband's side. For the other wives, not to be chosen is the worst disgrace and they suffer accordingly."
>
> [Herodotus V.5]

The next paragraph talks about the selling of girls, to be trained by monks or travelling acrobats for the services in domestic or foreign sanctuaries – which is also a most typically Indian feature, now appearing on its way to the Mediterranean.

> "The Thracians carry on an export trade in their own children. They sell their daughters partly to foreign lands. Their virgins they do not guard, and they can have intercourse with any man. Their wives, on the other hand, whom they purchase at a high price for themselves, they watch strictly. . . .
> They consider tattooing a mark of high birth, the lack of it a mark of low birth."
>
> [Herodotus V.6]

This last feature too is typical Indian not only because of the tattoo-marks they wear on their foreheads, but also concerning the idea of "high" or "low" castes.

INTERPRETATIONS

THE CELESTIAL OCEAN

According to the Indian scripture the universe is such that far above all other things, there is a Celestial Ocean, also called the Heavenly Sea. In its center stands Mount Meru with Indra's Paradise. Below that Celestial Sea is a great layer of air, and under that is our earth with all its profane creatures.

The odd notion of an Ocean above the atmosphere of air is derived from the blue color of the sky, and as blue was thought to be the color of water, due to the observation on earth, and as the air was assumed to be colorless and transparent, it seemed to follow that one can see through the medium of the air a celestial body of water, high up, extending from horizon to horizon, and thereby, as it seems, enclosing our planet. Of all the earthly substances, water is the only one that appears to be blue and therefore this rare color seen high above the air was believed to be a Celestial Ocean.

The Sea-Sarcophagi obviously show this Celestial Ocean as their stage of action, being now the scenario of all the happenings which faithfully illustrate the Indian vision of the Beyond. This topmost sphere is also the realm of the Paradise, to which the souls of the dead revert after their earthly departure.

Although the Celestial Sea is consistently the scenario of the Sea-Sarcophagi, we also see it, at times, more vaguely suggested in other sepulchral art.

The mural on the end-wall of the "Tomb of Lionesses" in Tarquinia, for instance, is divided horizontally. The upper part shows the usual gay atmosphere; in the center a giant drinking-bowl, possibly containing the drink of immortality festively draped with ivy, symbol of everlasting life and flanked by two musicians, a beautifully dressed female to the left, and at the right a male dancing with a quite undraped and light-skinned girl . . . (light-skinned often means "other wordly").

Underneath all that is the sea, represented as a bluish mass, in a quasi cross-sectional elevation, thereby showing on its upper edge the waves and diving dolphins. It seems probable that this sea is the "Celestial Ocean" above which there is the euphoric region of the departed souls shown now in paradise according to the Indian topography of the heavens which exactly describes this arrangement. To denote the luxury-living in those upper spheres, some figures rest on soft and ornamented pillows and an elaborate carpet seems to cover the floor, with artful fringes hanging down.

The Lionesses shown on the highest register above, are the emblems of the protective divinity Durga, the "Slayer of Demons" and wife of Siva. She was the beautiful defender of the righteous, with bow and sword in hand. In time the protective Lionesses became the Sphynxes, as we will later see.

FEMALES IN THE SEA

141

Some of the most inexplicable creatures on the Sea-Sarcophagi are the amorous and seductive females in what we identified as the Celestial Ocean. They are less mysterious, however, if we remember the Apsarases, the heavenly damsels of love, promised in the next world. To repeat here in short: The Apsarases are of wonderful beauty; they are the daughters of Indra and are fulfilling all the wishes of the souls elevated to paradise, which is the realm of eternal sensual love and pleasures. In addition to enchanting the souls of the departed, the Apsarases also have their lovers, the Gandharvas, and, at times, also are in charge, on Indra's orders, to seduce earthly saints who endanger the sovereignty of Indra, through their severe penance.

Now, in keeping with the conception of the Celestial Ocean, the Apsarases were, in their oldest form, visualized as existing in those heavenly waters and to be, in fact, aquatic beings, as shown on the Sea-Sarcophagi. In later times the same Apsarases were pictured as Cloud-Maidens and still later as Nymphs of Vegetation.

Numerous Indian mythological stories depicted them involved in fabulous terrestrial adventures with Kings as their paramours, and conceiving children from them. Those children must not be confused with the babies shown on the Sea-Sarcophagi, who have a very different provenience.

SOULS REPRESENTED AS BABIES

According to Indian tradition, the souls of the dead reappear in the form of babies in the next world, the celestial paradise.   **138**

This process of re-birth of the soul into the realm of eternal bliss is very elaborately described in the holy scriptures of India and is found in the initiation ceremonies re-enacted with astonishingly realistic symbol-pantomimes, in which the Neophytes actually assume the position of an embryo to be transformed into the status of the Epoptes, those who see the light eternal.

The sacred texts of India also mention that the souls of the departed   **140**
spring of Lotus-blossoms in paradise, as the Lotus-blossoms are symbolic of purity and spirituality . . . (Buddha is addressed as "Jewel in the Lotus" in the endless turning of the prayer-mills). As a consequence of those Indian texts we then actually see on Etruscan Sea-Sarcophagi Babies sprouting out of blossoms within the Celestial Waters.

The idea of being re-born into the sphere of the blessed became so deeply embedded in the fantasies concerning the paradisial Other-world of the souls, that it still appears on sarcophagi of 100 B.C. to 100 A.D. where the deceased is pictured as re-appearing in the next world in a rejuvenated   **40**
condition . . . even on Roman sarcophagi which no longer show the waters of the Celestial Ocean as their stage of action. In all fairness it has to be

admitted that another thought from India corrupted that initially pure and sweet apotheosis; namely, that entering the next world as rejuvenated, would help those who are old and feeble, at the time of death, to better enjoy the beautiful Apsarases in the Beyond. Those later versions of the re-juvenation-thoughts are important to keep in mind, because they show that the Sea-Sarcophagi reflect a very early date of transmission of the Indian doctrines, still showing the next world in its oldest version, as the Celestial Sea, and the archaic form of the Apsarases as aquatic beings, and the earliest Soul-Babies sprouting out of blossoms.

The Etruscan sarcophagi do not show Lotus-blossoms, but some fantasy-plants, not found in Italy, which points to the fact that the Italian sculptors were not given samples of Indian art to copy, but that there must have been a verbal transmission of the idea of a baby emerging from a blossom of some foreign and marvelous sort, never seen on Italian soil: an idea to which the Italian artists conformed, as it seems, with some puzzle-ment.

On very early Sea-Sarcophagi we sometimes see in its middle, as its main-issue, only a plant without a baby, while the scriptural proposition of a baby coming out of a blossom was skipped as being too improbable to the Mediterranean sculptor – to whom the traditional image of Buddha, born out of a Lotus-blossom, was not known.

SOULS BREAST-FED

139

We see on the Sea-Sarcophagi the Soul-Babies at times being fed at the breasts of the females of the Celestial Waters.

Breast feeding, like eating, is very rarely shown in Greco-Roman art, which prefers to be directed towards nobler visions. But here, in the center of Italy, we see the breast-feeding demonstrated as a very important feature in the foreground of all actions, related to the solemnity of the death-thought.

The idea is, that the babies represent the souls newly arriving in the sphere of the Blessed, the Celestial Sea, and are shown to be welcomed there with tender care, which is expressed by the females taking those Soul-Babies to their breasts. The females are, of course, the aquatic Ap-sarases.

At first sight there seems to be a discrepancy between the vision of nursing as shown on the sarcophagi, and the Indian scripture in which the function of the Apsarases is not to suckle the souls of the departed, but to make love to them. However, to be breast-fed and to be also the lover of a female is no direct contradiction in India, where children were occasionally suckled beyond their age of puberty – or took a sip of milk here and there from a passing woman or animal.

Several stories tell of little boys who became the lovers of their wetnurse, and those relations were considered to be of sublime charm and beauty, so that it seems not impossible that a similar situation was thought of in the celestial spheres.

Although those sarcophagi were not made in India but in Italy, even there some connection between nursing and love – that is: love-returning for life-giving – seems to have existed, as Tacitus and Suetonius report that Nero publicly kissed the breasts of his mother as a sign of filial thankfulness and tender devotion, at the end of a great banquet given in her honor, – while his relations to her were well known.

It also must be said that we deal here not with a mother-and-child situation (similar to the Tefnut pattern), but rather of the wetnurse type, and above all, with a symbolism depicting the excarnate soul in relation to a semi-divinity. The humble terrestrial gesture was chosen, because a newborn baby was by no means sure that it would be welcome and that efforts would be made to sustain its life, as especially female infants were drowned on arrival – a practice ascribed to the Apsarases in their celestial environment on many accounts, as well as being customary in actual life – to which the Koran makes reference in a later insert of the seventh century.

In contrast to that deeply felt anxiety of the soul of being rejected, the females of the Sea-Sarcophagi demonstrate that the souls of the departed . . . (shown symbolically as babies) . . . are most tenderly and joyously received in the paradisial sphere of the Blessed. This impression is underlined by the attitude of the Sea-Gandharvas who are also shown upholding the Soul-Babies with tender joy and welcoming them with outstretched arms. This is remarkable, because the Gandharvas, being the official lovers of the Apsarases, are represented in all sagas as being very jealous of any liaisons between the Apsarases and strangers, of which the babies would be proof, as the Gandharvas produce no offspring with the Apsarases. The Gandharvas are therefore never pictured as being kind to babies. The situation, shown on the Sea-Sarcophagi is therefore a renewed demonstration that we deal here not with normally conceived babies and not with babies born by Apsarases due to their flirtations, . . . but instead with

Soul-Babies, who thereby fit exactly into the psychological layout of all personages in the Celestial Ocean, and into their pattern of behavior as shown on the Sea-Sarcophagi.

The emphasis on the loving reception in the realm of the Blessed is understandable, as this was about the only comfort and hope of the dead and the bereft alike – for if the soul departed and could not find asylum with the Blessed, what then? An erring soul was considered a formidable specter and menace. One of the reasons for solemnizing the funeral was therefore, in part, also defensive, to pin it down, to finalize the act with all available ceremony. Because to dispatch the soul to its abode was to rid those left behind of a restless, homeless, haunting ghost, who may not have been well disposed towards some. On the other hand there was no greater comfort for all than to think of the departed as being received with infinite tenderness and love, as expressed so abundantly on the sarcophagi. They had besides their solemnity also the function of the heavy stone, which acted almost like a paper-weight, holding down volatile matter to prevent it from fluttering away. The sarcophagi also possessed the quality of "Picture-magic." In the sense that one could harm a person by sticking a needle into his effigy, one could also give a person a magic direction by making a picture of him in the act of his elevation, or by picturing his soul in the process of being received in love. The vision of the Soul-Baby as being adopted by the celestial company is, by the way, also expressed in Egypt, as it is said in the death-prayers that Isis will adopt the soul of the departed as her child. Re-birth in the form of a child into the company of the Blessed appears also in prayers to Tefnut, the Door-Figure to the celestial spheres.

Concerning the importance of the joyful reception of the soul in the celestial sphere, and also concerning the strange similarity between the Egyptian and Indo-Asiatic visions of the dramatics in the ascent to a celestial abode, here follows a short digression into the Egyptian doctrine:

In earliest times the Egyptians believed that the floor of heaven formed the sky of our world. This floor was made of an immense plate of metal on which lived the gods and the souls of the departed. This plate was so close to a certain sacred mountain that the deceased might almost reach it, but not quite. To actually clamber onto that platform of heaven, the dead needed a Ladder. The divinities Set and Horus were thought to be the guardians of the Ladder (the Ladder was probably something akin to a draw-bridge in function, so as to let only the deserving souls into the realm of the Blessed). The deceased King Pepi I, ca. 2200 B.C., is made to address the Ladder in these words:

"Homage to thee, O divine Ladder!
Homage to thee, O Ladder of Set!
Stand thou upright, O Ladder of Horus,
Whereby Osiris came forth into heaven."

(now addressing Osiris, who too came via the Ladder into heaven): . . .

"For Pepi is thy son and Pepi is
Horus" (son of Isis and Osiris)
"and thou hast given birth unto Pepi
even as thou hast given birth to Horus.
. . . and thou shalt give
unto him the Ladder whereby this Pepi
shall come forth into heaven . . .
Ye, who are on the brethren of the gods,
rejoice ye that Pepi journeyeth among
you. And the brethren of Pepi who are
all gods, shall be glad when they meet
Pepi, and every god and every spirit
stretcheth out his hand towards
Pepi when he cometh forth into heaven
from the Ladder, and they shall
feed him and nourish him when he
appeareth in heaven from the Ladder
and every god and every spirit
stretcheth out his hand to Pepi
on the Ladder." . . .

As a postscriptum to that request, the result of the incantation is given as accomplished fact, projected by magic power ahead of events to guide the proceedings:

"they take him by the hand and lead
him towards Sekhet-Hetep" (i.e. the
celestial paradise) "and let him take
his seat among the stars which are in
the sky."

[Papyrus Pepi, Line 192f.,
translated by E.A. Wallis Budge, Brit. Mus.]

231

Very touchingly, a little model of the Ladder was in earlier times placed near the mummy in the tomb. Later the Ladder was only hieroglyphically painted on the papyri that were given to the dead and were buried with them.

Besides the structural similarity of the Egyptian Above with the Indo-Asiatic concepts, we see the great urgency and intensity in the wish to be admitted to, and the exuberant joy of being received in, the celestial sphere.

We further see in the magic death-prayer the idea of being accepted as a Child . . . (Soul-Baby) . . . by the personages of the Above.

And finally, in similarity to the breast-feeding, shown on the sarcophagi, there is the invocation: "Feed him and nourish him when he appeareth in heaven."

Maybe not connected to the vision of breast-fed babies on the sarcophagi, are, nevertheless, very old Vedic texts, stating that the souls of the departed would drink Milk in paradise and enjoy the love of women, first motherly, then otherwise.

Milk has, of course, the connotation of the primeval "Fluid of Life" which becomes of great importance in questions of re-birth and life-eternal, the same as the "Ocean of Milk" has the connotation with the "Ocean of Life" (limitless life) in excelsis, as mentioned in some other Indian texts.

In a possible transmission from India to Egypt, Hathor, the divinity of Joy, Beauty, and Love, was in later times shown comforting the dead in the next world. Hathor was represented as Divine Cow, thereby uniting in her person the component of "milk-giving" with the image of female charms and joys in heaven, Indian style. The fact that a Vedic concept could infiltrate from India all the way down to Egypt, makes a similar transmission from India to the Etruscan-Italic enclave more conceivable.

SEA-CENTAURS ARE GANDHARVAS

The last puzzle on the Sea-Sarcophagi are the Sea-Centauri in the Celestial Ocean, who are often shown with a Lyra in hand and who are embraced by the females of the sea, the aquatic Apsarases.

The traditional paramours of the Apsarases are the Gandharvas, who were in oldest times shown as images of virility in the form of Man-Horses, but however impressive their sex may be, the front hoofs of the horses were not fit for tender embraces, and therefore human arms were given to them, so useful for all the gestures of love – and because the stage-setting is the Celestial Sea, those Man-Horses were also equipped with fins and fish-tails.

Moreover, the Gandharvas were the heavenly musicians . . . as the word Gandharva actually means Music. We therefore see them in the celestial waters, embraced by the aquatic Apsarases and with the Lyra in hand as their symbolic emblem. The Indian string-instrument was here translated into a Greco-Roman Lyra, which is again a hint that the Sea-Sarcophagi were not copied from Indian visual art, but that the gist of the doctrine was verbally transmitted from India, via the Etruscans to Italy.

Another detail might be of interest: In Greco-Roman art we see the male person in amorous encounters as the active partner, and the female as the passive. This in contrast to Indian art, where the Apsarases, in particular, develop all their seductive efforts to enchant the men, and at times are even shown running after them in the heavenly spheres, indicating that theirs is the pursuit of a love-mission. On the Sea-Sarcophagi, though made in Italy, we see the females surprisingly acting-out the Indian pattern of behavior towards their love-mates, the centauric Gandharvas, as another hint that they are derived from the Apsarases.

136

According to the Indian tradition, probably influenced by the Harem-situation (in whose hierarchy the females advance by means of their endearments), we see the aquatic Gandharvas in a lordly and languid attitude towards their licentious mates, the Apsarases, who are the ones to display all of the amorous elan as shown on Indian reliefs of the Mamallapuram type.

5

To underline this extraordinary relationship we see those females almost invariably on top of their centauric paramours, and mostly clinging to them with the arms around their bodies.

134

This attitude conforms to some rock-carvings in India, but as the mountains in which those images are carved could not have been moved to Italy, it must again be assumed that this coinciding behavior-pattern was established via verbal transmission.

2

This is not too surprising, because we have many texts reporting back to Rome fabulous things about India at that time and also sculptures, made in Italy, which illustrate those texts, dealing often with psychological constellations, very accurately and factually.

The male character of the Sea, as an element, is shown by the females not only embracing the Man-Horses but also even more ardently throwing their arms around Bulls and Rams of the sea, as Bulls, Horses and Rams are the classical male symbols which are associated here with the sea.

As to the question of the transplant of those ideas from the East, it is of interest to note that Poseidon was the national-god of the Ionians who imported his image when they emigrated from Asia to the Peloponnese. Corinth, as the terminal-harbor of the Asia-trade, bore the most immediate influx of Indo-Asiatic patterns. There, in Corinth, Poseidon was called "Genethlios" – (the Creator) – and overshadowed local Greek divinities.

In a further similarity to the imagery of the Sea-Sarcophagi and the identification of the Male with the Sea, and Bulls and Horses as the power and fertilizing aspects of Poseidon, it seems significant that festivals called the "Taureia" were celebrated in Corinth in his name where black Bulls were thrown into the sea to supplement the creative energies of the sea by the potency for which the bulls were symbolic – and horse-races were held in honor of Genethlios as a glorification of the male energy, symbolized by the triumph of the winning horse.

We have further manifestations of the Sea-and-Horse identification in the myth of Poseidon pursuing Demeter who, to escape him, metamorphosed herself into a mare, whereupon Poseidon made love to her, taking the form of a stallion – from which union resulted a Man-Horse of the Sea, with the gift of speech and endearment – (the Gandharva-vision). (It is an open question whether Poseidon had a priori the image of a horse and Demeter changed into a mare to please him.) However, the whole story seems to have the purpose of explaining the existence of the Gandharvic Man-Horse of the sea which appeared in older Asiatic sagas as the traditional mate of the aquatic Apsarases. In the Mediterranean, any mythological story involving a horse can not be very old as the horse did not exist there in very early times, while it was most common in Asia.

Demeter (otherwise a noble and sedate figure) is also said to have had intercourse with a bull (Zeus disguised as such, to lend some magic dignity to the matter). However the real substance of those stories is that the Bull and the Horse represented the Male element, in conjunction with the Female, which was represented by Demeter, not as a lover, but as the embodiment of Fertility and Motherhood, being the patroness of the grain that nourishes the creatures of the world and has to be fertilized as such by divine creative powers inherent in the eternal sea as well as the mother of Kore, (also called Persephone when married to Hades) and thereby being on the other end of the life-and-death-spectrum the liaison-figure to death.

IONIAN ORPHIC

(Heavenly Females)

The Ionian culture is said to have come originally from Central Asia to Greece. Their Civilization was foreign, spiritual and antedated that of Greece proper, whose inspiration it became. The rise of the Ionians was often called "the Spring of Greece." Ionia was the land of Homer, of Xenophanes and Pythagoras, but most importantly for us, – it was the first center of Orphism from where its teachings advanced Westward to reach the Italic people via Magna Graecia, and eventually permeated the Etruscan sepulchral imagery. The Orphics (greatly helped by the authority of Pythagoras) spread the originally Indo-Asiatic doctrine of a blissful extraterrestrial existence after death. It is interesting that Plato's speculations about immortality, as such, found no expression in funeral art, because the Ionian-Asiatic element of the Heavenly Females was missing. Those females, however, provided an aspect of "human interest" in the esoteric speculations coming from the Asiatic homeland. The Queens of Heaven, formidable as they were, had no relation to the souls of the dead until their Seraglio was opened to the simple mortals.

In the hot and brewing Eastern corner of the Mediterranean, since time immemorial, some awesome "Queens of Heaven" held their majestic sway. The wild Sumerian Inanna rejoicing with blood-drenched hands, the Assyro-Babylonian Ishtar, the Syro-Asiatic Lady Ashtart of the heavens, feared and venerated by kings from India to Iran, the Anatolian Cybele of gruesome sexual mutilations – and many more.

37

36

As a premordially nebulous but majestic conglomeration of all those exalted visions of sombre opulence and lust in pre-Hellenic times, from Cyprus there arose the primitive-sensual figure of Aphrodite, who was so exotic and dazzling that she was split – like most Asiatic divinities – into many Avatars or aspects, some of them contradicting each other.

Several of those images of Aphrodite radiated to Greece and rose there to an extraordinary importance due to her newly found connection to After-life, the extraterrestrial great adventure of love, whose most glamorous patroness she became.

Her exalted role was, as we saw, re-enacted on the secular level by swarms of temple girls in the sanctuaries of Aphrodite, at first nearest to Asia, especially at Cnidus, as the Cnidians were Greco-Asiatics, and at Corinth, the first foot-hold of Asiatic traders. Those Hierodules were called priestess-servants of "Aphrodite Hetaera" who was herself pictured as riding on a he-goat or ram (symbolizing the male element), – as the inscription says, over the waters on the back of the lascivious ram – (super aequora dorso lascivae caprae).

The similarity to the Females of the Sea is evident, as they are shown riding on top of the aquatic Centaurs, who are representing the male character of the sea. Similarly also in both cases the females are embodiments of active love, be it the Apsarases of the sea, or the "Aphrodite Hetaera," patroness of the Hierodules pursuing men.

134

அக்கினி.   நிருதி.   யமன்.

2

142

The traditional pose of a female riding on a male was derived in the East from the idea of the Apsarases "pouncing" upon men, as frequently shown in visual art, and also derived from the Indo-Asiatic term of one being the "Vehicle" of the other, expressed in showing certain demons or divinities actually "riding" on diverse symbol-creatures – (Indra on his elephant, Durga, his spouse, on a lion etc.) – whereby the Vehicle was the "Determinant" of status and personality. This in contrast to the Mediterranean tradition where divinities are never shown as riding. An exception seems Dionysos riding on a sexy donkey, but he was shown as such returning from India, which exactly proves the point. Be it that riding became a typical mode of living due to the Asiatic horse, which was missing in the Mediterranean, or the dialectical pattern of the "Vehicle" — whatever the reason, we should be alerted in all cases where we see any allegorical personages riding, to check their provenience as to their possibly Asiatic background.

Considering those contrasts between the Asiatic and the Mediterranean attitudes, it therefore seems important to notice that the Sea-Sarcophagi conform to the Asiatic pattern, concerning both the riding of the females in general, as well as the Orientalized attitude of the females actively involving men. The females are shown on those reliefs consistently in the foreground, that is, in the sculptor's jargon, as the dominant figures, tentatively "defiling" the males of the sea, who in turn are pictured most obviously as the "Vehicle" — illustrating thereby this Indic religious-philosophical parlance.

ஈசானன்.   இந்திரன்.   குபேரன்.

As to the anatomy of those Oriental-Asiatic heavenly females, who now suddenly appear on the Sea-Sarcophagi, generously displaying their ample backsides, it can be said that before the influx from the sensual Ionians, all females were shown traditionally so small-hipped, that fragments of their statues were hard to distinguish from male figures — (see the famous "Girl from Attica" 820 B.C. — "Girl from Ephesus" 650 B.C. — "Artemis from Rhodes" 625 B.C. etc.).

139

Another aspect of interest is the male-female relation shown in art: Here we see the Indo-Oriental female as the dominant figure in male-female combinations ... possibly derived from the Indo-Iranian visions of "Love-Demons" subjugating man and the scriptural "Whore-Demons" of the Avesta defiling men ... while in Mediterranean art we see the male as spiritually glorified by the association with the female figure, as we have it, for example, in the surprisingly female embodiment of Victory, or of Athena, standing for Wisdom ... etc. used as epiteta ornans elevating those graced by their presence. On Egyptian monuments too – (belonging to the Mediterranean cycle) – we see female divinities enhancing the prestige of the Pharaoh and protecting rather than subjugating him, or any other male.

MISTAKEN RAPES

Later artists were often puzzled and perplexed by the love-bouts shown on earlier sarcophagi and understood them as the RAPE of mythical personages, – which in reality only depicted the PLEASURES of paradise, – Indian style. In this way it came about that a whole tradition of late sepulchral imagery showed famous mythological stories of rape – (like those of Demeter, Persephone, etc.) – which in turn was misleading later interpretations into the "Rape of the Souls-Theory" believing the Sea Creatures to represent the devouring Chthonian powers of the Deep, – or the "marriage" of the departing soul to the divine, the hierogamy in its most dramatic acts, of abducting the souls of the living by force in a lovebout with the genii of the great Above or Below.

143

Especially the story of Hylas was often misunderstood by artists to be the subject of the Sea-Sarcophagi, in an effort to understand what the aggressive female lovers were doing with the males.

> The story in short: Hylas, a most handsome youth was sent to fetch water from a well, but the Well-Nymphs were so charmed by his beauty that they pulled him down to their domain and he was never seen again.

We see, of course, the vague connection to death in the waters in the company of ravishing nymphs, as a pretty death-allegory, – but the failure of that myth to explain the love-scenes on the sarcophagi becomes evident by the fact that we see on the sarcophagi SEVERAL male creatures who are all oceanic and centauric with fins, which definitely cancels out the person of Hylas; also there are the dolphins, which do not live in wells but are symbols of the Sea, and thereby indicate that even the setting is incompatible with the Hylas story.

Later sculptors – (still not knowing what the Sea-Sarcophagi really mean) – were looking for mythological events which seemed on first sight compatible with the oceanic background, with Amorettes and embraces. As such, the "Nuptial of the Nereid Thetis" could qualify, and was thereupon depicted on several later sarcophagi – leaving out the babies – (so embarrassing at weddings) – and several other items which did not fit. And this is how Thetis got mistakenly mixed up in death-cults.

> The story of Thetis in short: Zeus and Poseidon loved the
> Nereid Thetis, but after she underwent several rather
> forbidding metamorphoses, she was taken in love (raped ?)
> by Peleus and their marriage was witnessed by all the gods
> in great assembly. – This scene of the assembled gods is
> intermixed at times in funeral art, with that of the soul
> meeting the divinities after its ascent to heaven (which was
> a very vivid Egyptian vision, and was then newly
> accentuated by the Persian Mithras, as a scene of blazing
> light and tremendous excitement).

According to Ovid, Peleus caught Thetis asleep and awakened her to love – as Ariadne was awakended to love by Dionysos. The awakening from sleep to love, at times through gruesome metamorphoses, was taken as symbolic for a hedonistic re-awakening of the soul after the extrinsic trauma of death and became a favorite motif on sarcophagi as late as 200 A.D. On those basically misunderstood works we may nevertheless still discern the faint afterglow of the original idea: of seeing the dead now festively "married" or consecrated to the spirits of the Ocean, – really the "Celestial Ocean" – but here, however, projected onto the "mare nostrum," the Mediterranean Sea, and its Greek Olympian figures as its cast of actors.

The fact that the majority of the sculptors and people did not understand their real meaning – at the very time those Sea-Sarcophagi were made – shows again that we deal here with enclaves of beliefs which were kept secret from the general public.

32

33

The old Indian texts ascribe to the aquatic Gandharvas a generative function, which is also shown drastically, at times, in their iconography.

It must be assumed that this feature is not merely to describe their relation to the Apsarases as their play-mates, because in the Indian mythological stories nothing is made of the offspring of the Gandharva-Apsara unions; but the generative function of the Gandharvas seems to make reference to the fact that the Sea was understood to be a patently Male element. Accordingly we already see on the earliest sarcophagi, Sea-Creatures with most prominent beards. The beard was a symbol for masculinity and power, especially in the Oriental Asia, connected to generative potency. The word 'ma'ashoom' denotes beard as well as phallus in the Asiatic Orient. We also have some astonishing connections between the Latin 'mentum' (chin) and 'mentula' (the male sex) . . . both converging in 'pizzo' the pointed thing in general, applied to the sex, as well as literally meaning the pointed beard. Supporting this symbol-connection are not only the formidable beards on the earliest sea-creatures, but also on later sarcophagi the bearded Horses and Bulls. As the sculptors knew perfectly well that Horses and Bulls have no beards in reality, we obviously deal here with this very symbol-connection.

The masculinity of the sea is a philosophical thought or cosmic speculation to the effect that the masculine sea was the beginning of all the evolutions. As a vague echo in Greek mythology of its primordial status, the sea, Okeanos, is called "the old one" and is shown as bearded. As to its generative function, Homer names Ocean and Thetis "father and mother of the gods" in the Iliad (XIV.201).

The daughters of Okeanos, the Nereids, are very many . . . the connection to the Celestial Ocean with the very many aquatic Apsarases, who were also the sovereign's daughters, might be very old, but not impossible. There we have to take into account that the Ionians considered the Ocean to be divine – (which is semantically close to being actually celestial) – and since the Ionians were thought to have come from Central Asia to Greece, it is not impossible that they transferred and implanted similar celestial characteristics into the Nereids from their sister-beings, the aquatic Apsarases of India's heavens.

The fact that on the earliest sarcophagi the sea-creatures are shown with Wings, is a hint that they were thought to exist in the ocean of the Above, that is, the Asiatic celestial sea.

In earliest times, since the horse was not known in the Mediterranean, the symbol for masculinity there was the bull. The fact that the earliest

131

Sea-Sarcophagi show the exclusively Asiatic horse as the generative symbol is one more hint that we deal here with an Asiatic influx. The Bulls and Rams appear only on later sarcophagi as an obvious absorption of local symbol-figures – who were, however, graced by anti-natural Oriental beards as a leftover from the previous Eastern tradition.

BEAUTY BORN OF THE SEA

In oldest times, for some mysterious reasons, females were associated with water. As the only hint at this connection we have the early mentioning of their "maritime smell." Astonishing as this trace may be, it must be considered that in very early or quasi-prehistoric times the faculty of the smell was extremely keen among men who made their living as hunters, so that this association may have been the true source of subsequent inventions. In earliest times the "Divine Fragrance" preceded the apparition of the halo (which is to say that recognition and identification by smell was at first predominant over the visual stigma); which might be another hint at the categorizing connotations evoked by the sense of smell. It was vaguely assumed that "those of the maritime smell" can be traced, as an animal is tracked by its scent – and must therefore somehow have come from the sea.

As to the ability of primitive people to recognize human beings by their still very keen sense of smell, there is a whole group of similar sagas in Milanesia, where it is said that some Swan-Maidens, or in other versions some Parakeets – (Love-Birds?) – descended on a lake, took off their feathery garments and went frolicking in the waters as naked girls; whereupon a young man crept up behind the bushes and stole the discarded plumage-hull of one of the girls, who called out to her sisters: "Whew! I smell Human Flesh!" At the end of those stories, the girl whose feather-dress the man has captured, becomes his bride. Those sagas seem to have the symbolic meaning that underneath the miraculously beautiful outer appearance of a woman, there is still secretly a purely physical human body . . . But for us the interesting part remains that nobody in the stories is amazed or considers it an extraordinary gift to be able to identify a fairly far off person by the odor of its body, a skill retained, as it seems, from the time when man, as a hunter, was tracking the scent of his prey – or his life depended on his early catching the smell of an approaching enemy.

In the animal world – our ancestry – hinting at our earliest and most deeply ingrained patterns, it is generally the male who is seeking out the female, whereby he is mostly guided by the sense of her smell. And as the survival of the species depends on their meeting, we can expect that Nature would give high priority to this "approach and guidance system."

In mythology and folk-lore we also find the female disproportionately often associated with moisture, the wet element and the sea, down to the Mermaid whose lower parts blend over into a fish, to make her a maritime creature, – the male seamonsters, the Hippocampi etc. relate (as the "hippo" indicates) via the horse to the potency of the sea, the still brewing multiform creature of the mysterious deep, in their combined morphology hinting at the drive of trans-species amalgamations in the twilight of the premordial swamps.

Concerning the typification and designation of creatures not by sight but by means of smell, it is interesting that in the "Negative Confession" of Egypt appear the sentences:

"Be praised, O gods who know the scent
of those who come from Egyptian land.
Be eternally praised, O divine spirits,
YOU can recognize those who stink
they have massacred others . ."

We further have, on the visual level, the association with the "Concha Veneris" based on the similarity of the female sex with the sea-shell, concerning its formation, its sometimes pink color and its moisture. Those connotations are then bridging over to the Venus of the Sea, but reflect back in an astonishingly direct way to women in general, called "Concha" or girls "Conchita" – as if their anatomical or maritime association would be their main determining factor.

The name Maria – (Marina) seems to mean "she of the Sea" – although there is a speculation that those names may be derived from a Hebrew root.

In a strange and certainly puzzling similarity to the story of Aphrodite, born out of the sea, we have the story of Lakshmi, the Indian goddess of Beauty and Love, also born out of the sea. The Indian story seems to be older and based on a core of actual observation and manifest technicality:

The Indian version speaks of an "Ocean of Milk" that was churned (with detailed descriptions of how this was done) and out of this churning resulted the formation of Lakshmi, queen of love and beauty . . . "at the sight of her the whole world is charmed, the sages sing her praise" . . . etc.

The idea that an Object can be formed out of a Liquid is derived from the actual experience of making butter. The act of Lakshmi's creation is thereby technically more soundly explained than the story of Aphrodite born out of the sea, where the transition from the liquid state to the solid is not explained, as if the fact of such a transition would have been adopted from a sounder story. This being the difference between the two stories. There is, however, also a common ground to both sagas: In both cases the goddess is born out of the sea; in both cases the sea is the MALE element, the generative substance. In the Indian version the sea is represented by male symbols: the bearded Sea-Creatures, the Bulls and the Horses and the aquatic Man-Horses, the Gandharvas, as actual lovers. In the Greco-Roman version the ocean is somehow tinted with spermatic substance, as a specifically male foundation for the creation of Aphrodite out of its plasmatic foam.

146

147

> To repeat here in short the Greek version: According to
> Hesiod, Gaia represented Earth, while Uranos was the
> embodiment of Heaven. They had several children, the
> youngest of whom was Kronos. Kronos castrated his father
> Uranos, as it seems, because of his sympathy for his mother
> Gaia, with a sickle she gave him . . . (see Freudian
> implications) . . . The severed manhood of Uranos fell into
> the sea and out of its "foam" – (uncertain translation) –
> sprang Aphrodite. Love and Desire (Himeros) attached
> themselves to her person.

This story could be understood to mean that the Ocean was made to be Masculine by way of a "symbol-transfer" of Manhood, whereby the sea actually acquired a male sex organ, and that out of its generative power sprang new life. The transfer of the male attribute to the sea seems to be the issue here, because no reference is thereafter made to the changed status or condition of Kronos. In other mythological stories similar incidences occur, but they report as its consequence some impact on the amputee – the least of it being revenge towards the aggressor.

Or, it could be understood, in a philosophical sense, that out of the male sexuality was born the vision of female Beauty.

Or else, that the prerogative of Creation, which was at first with the Heaven (Uranos) was transferred through Time (Kronos) to the sea.

VENUS IN SHELL

The idea of the "Birth out of the Sea" – originally derived from Lakshmi and Venus, – was later made symbolic for "Rebirth" of the soul after death – in both cases, out of the Ocean, especially in funeral art.

145

In the Museum of Naples we see very many little statuettes emerging from shells. Some of them are in an almost embryo-like position crouched in a semi-open double-shell; some others are tenderly kneeling as if to arise to a new life, out of the Celestial Ocean, or, maybe to the realm of the blessed, the Ocean of Eternity. Some others act as if joyfully liberated, in new-found beauty, almost victoriously ascending out of a shell. Those figurines, made by primitive hands and representing, no doubt, the re-awakening and re-birth of the soul after death, were possibly the first inspiration for the "Birth of Venus" stories, symbolizing at first, as ex voti of clay the rebirth of the soul after death, out of the Celestial Ocean.

133

The "Rebirth out of a Shell" became such a fixed symbolism that we see the portrait of the deceased in the middle of the Sea-Sarcophagi and Stele, as coming out of a shell – at times crouched in a shell – and on the very latest types of Sea-Sarcophagi, just framed by a big half-shell, embracing the whole portrait and thereby suggesting that the departed person is now to be thought of as "within the sea," no doubt the Celestial Sea, the Ocean of Eternity – quite similar to the Egyptian appellation of the dead as "in Osiris" – or the medieval "with the Angels."

148

To verify this assumption we also see gravestones where a figurine is enclosed in a sea-shell, and at times is arising out of a sea-shell, and sometimes seems to be happy there and being greeted by celestial genii. On another gravestone we see the dead person, in this case a little boy, stand-ing in a sea-shell, symbolic of re-birth, surrounded by a paradisial world, indicating that he should be thought of now as being reborn into the realm of the Blessed. The inscription tells clearly that he is dead, by the usual IN MANIBUS (with the Manes), that is: the shadows or ghosts of the dead. This grave-stele is, by the way, a very curious object, because the artist of that later period mixed the idea of the Celestial Sea with the vision of a terrestri-al paradise, as seen on different sarcophagi of that time, and shows the little boy enchantedly standing in the Sea-Shell of re-birth, but surrounded by birds, butterflies, and some other terrestrial animals, even a monkey as funmaker in that world of his pleasing – obviously attributes demanded by the family of the dead boy.

We see a similar mixture of Greco-Roman with Indo-Etruscan beliefs on some of the Etruscan tomb-paintings where the deceased are assumed to dwell partly under ground and partly happily in excelsis. In some cases we see the dead at gay banquets, as promised in the Indian scriptures, in the company of blond women with curly hair, who are definitely not their own women, who are shown on the covers of some sarcophagi together with their husbands, as being darkhaired and with long tresses of straight hair. But those encounters are set in the underworld presided over by Persephone, the wife of Hades. In some cases – (Golini Tomb II., the Tomb of the Augurs, etc.) – we see solemn priestly figures sacrificing with the palms of the hands down, meaning: to the subterranean gods. That mixture of ideas is not too astonishing, as we deal here with the spread of a new doctrine over an old and local tradition. The burden of compromise lay mostly in the hands of the artists, who sometimes showed most ingenious amalgamations of the two beliefs, but at times made intermixtures which shot way beyond the substance of both theories concerning the fate of the souls after death. To that group belong the sarcophagi where the figures of the aquatic Apsarases embracing an aquatic Bull are interpreted as Europa eloping with Zeus in the guise of a bull . . . etc. Also the Venus-like figurine in the shell, depicting the re-birth out of the sea, is at times confused with Leda and the swan, in remodeling one of the sea-creatures surrounding that figurine, into a bird of considerable size. In this process the aquatic fins of the sea-creatures were misunderstood as wings and their long necks as the neck of a swan, while the "Leda and Swan" symbolism belongs to another trend of thoughts in funeral art. We see in those cases a typical example of a transmission via seen art-objects, which could be misinterpreted as to their meaning, in contrast to a verbal or textual transmission, which mostly has the main idea correct, but permits the artist to express this idea in his own manner.

149

Although Aphrodite was never connected to death and funeral visions, and although Lakshmi was born in a sort of butter-churning process and not out of a shell, the two Queens of Beauty were nevertheless fused, because of their place of birth. As their common denominator was the ocean, (associated with the "Celestial Ocean" or Paradise in excelsis) both epitomes of Beauty and Love were fused to symbolize the celestial females and their love, promised to the faithful in the Beyond. We see then the original vision of the Apsarases slipping into the images of Lakshmi and Venus alike.

We therefore have on some sarcophagi as their only central ornament, a naked female in a shell, in a noble and dignified posture, as befitting a divinity like Venus, or a Queen of Heaven like Lakshmi. It probably seemed, in later times, more compatible with the idea of the majesty of death to ornament the coffin with a grand figure or vision, in contrast to the nymphic philandering Apsarases making their uninhibited advances.

150

THE THREE GRACES IN EXCELSIS

Then came the new branching off from the idea of showing the Venus-in-Shell as the general symbol of Rebirth.

This later version came even closer to the Oriental-Asiatic vision of a MULTITUDE of love-inclined females, promised to await the soul in the Thereafter. This staging was acted-out by derivatives of the Venus figure, splitting, so to say, the single manifestation into the "many" – and at the same time shifting from the general symbol of "Re-birth" to symbols of "Sensual Pleasures" in the company of beautiful females, illustrating the Eastern dogma in a Mediterranean version.

Consequently we see on a great number of sarcophagi, as their central ornament, the THREE GRACES in tender nudity, as if awaiting the soul, sometimes half-chaste before an open bed, to look like an Oriental dream come true. Conspicuous, however, is the fact that those figures are in all cases shown with no environment, as a medallion inserted in purely ornamental scrolls of a monotonous type . . . which seems to be a hint that the sculptors did not know in what sphere – the earth, the sky, or a dreamland – those apparitions occur, which have such dim roots in the Greco-Roman mythos. The Three Graces connected to Death or the There-after are in fact a transplant from another land and stand there totally isolated on Italian soil and outside of any Mediterranean thinking, where the Graces had no connection to Death, nor females of any kind to the Thereafter.

The monotonous scrolls may therefore be the visual expression of an ideological "blank" – a sign that the sculptors did not know the mysterious scenario surrounding those naked females and their extraordinary relation to the dead person in the casket . . . or else, that they preferred not to talk about it, as Herodotus often remarks in reference to foreign doctrines.

The fact is, that this very type of ornament is the same on all sarcophagi dealing with those female apparitions and that this very type of ornament is foreign to the Mediterranean repertoire of scrolls. However, it can be found in the Eastern "Arabesques" and with some imagination we may discern in it a suggestion of either Waves – (belonging to the Celestial Ocean) – or Clouds – (indicating the Above).

On Etruscan grave-frescoes an ornamental line of waves denotes the Celestial Ocean and thereby indicates that all above that wave-motif belongs to the sphere where the Beati encounter their celestial maidens.

This permits the speculation that there could be a symbolism attached to that ornament, which was well known to the initiated, but not to those who still believed in the official religion of Hades and who saw in all other beliefs a "dangerous foreign superstition" – (as Tacitus calls it).

The "Three Graces" were called the "Attendants" of Aphrodite, and sometimes her "Servants." In many shrines of Aphrodite there were Hierodules, who officially "served" the divinity by giving their persons to strangers and thereby collecting money for the temple. The attendants or servants to Aphrodite were called the Horai in Greek and Horae in Latin – which word was not too convincingly translated as meaning "the hours" and possibly "the seasons." The exact connection of "hours" or "seasons" to Aphrodite was never explained. However, there is a certain suggestive similarity between the words "Horae" and "Houri," who were the Oriental equivalent of the Apsarases. Not to overemphasize that phonetic similarity, there exists, nevertheless, the possibility that the "Three Graces" on the sarcophagi actually mean – mistakenly or not – the damsels of the Beyond, the Oriental Houries. The possibility for such mistakes is great because no exact demarcation exists between the Horai, the Charites, Dryads, Hamadryads, the Naids, and the diverse local Nymphs whose very name, at times, simply means "Bride" – celestial, semi-divine or terrestrial. We also have a relief in the Capitoline Museum of Rome, where the three Horai – (inscribed as such) – are shown with light steps and transparent garments to follow the figure of Priapus, marching ahead of them with erect staff, as their guiding spirit.

HORAI AND HURIES

The description of the Horai given by Homer around 800 B.C. fits amazingly well the vision of the heavenly females of the Eastern Paradise, while Hesiod, about 100 years later, and in a more moralizing time re-interpreted them as personifications of Peace, Justice and Order. In Hesiod [Theogony 15], they sing and dance at the wedding of Peleus and Thetis. Here it must be remembered that it was usual to hire girls whose profession was love, for such occasions from sanctuaries dedicated to Aphrodite, to dance at weddings draped or undraped, impersonating at times, the genii of the nuptial bed in provocative pantomimes inviting the newlyweds, quite similar to the Three Graces shown on sarcophagi of that kind.

The word "Houri" comes from the Avestan "Hawira" which means "black-eyed" with reference to the mascara of the Oriental love-queens and

247

their earthly representatives and servants, who were promised to the faithful in paradise.

After all arguments are presented, it could be said, in short, that there is the possibility that the Hierodules of Corinth introduced to the Mediterranean the Oriental-Asiatic temple practices.

Those temple-girls were devotees of the great Eastern divinities of Love, who were fused at Corinth with the Greek Aphrodite, and so were her servants, the Hierodules (as the earthly stand-ins for the celestial Houries) quite logically fused with the Horai, as their celestial counterparts.

The word-similarity between Houri and Horai may be incidental or not, but the fact that the word Houri itself was the result of a change from Hawira to Huriyah proves that such shifts actually took place, when words crossed the national borders.

There was no previous model in the Greco-Roman world of religious love-maidens in the Beyond or here on earth. At Corinth, where East met West, this vision became a reality for the first time, now facing the West, and it is therefore probable that the vague idea of the "Attendants of Aphrodite" absorbed the characteristics of the Hierodules – who in turn impersonated on earth the celestial Houries of Paradise.

THE SEASONS SARCOPHAGI

The beautiful but ideologically helpless sarcophagi with the three Graces, who tried to make the connection with the Orient, whose dream-image they bravely projected, while losing their hold or connection with their native land and mythos – in staging the Three Graces in the realm of the dead – later received a strange infusion of ideas, leading to the "Seasons Sarcophagi."

It is highly significant that the later re-interpretation of the "Graces" as being the "Three Blessings" was never shown on sarcophagi – despite the fact that it was, so to say, "the latest news" concerning those figures. This proves that the artists were well aware, or well briefed, concerning the true substance they had to show, namely: the Oriental sensual females waiting in paradise, and they therefore disregarded completely the moralizing interpretations of Hesiod.

But as time went on, nearing now the Christian era, there arose the magnificent figure of Mithras the chaste and first celibate divinity – (all other gods had mistresses, spouses, or female cult-partners) – and so it came that the voluptuous Oriental females of the Beyond, even when modified to the "Three Graces" of the Mediterranean heaven, and down to the representatives of the earthly "Three Seasons" – shifted away from the female body and lust and turned to ephebean boys to symbolize the seasons, in a pastoral mood with flowers, fruits and baskets. This transition from the languishing females to the males went, it must be admitted, through a twilight phase of quite sinful looking hermaphroditic boys, with the smiles of little girls, who later were blended over into Amorini, thereby still faintly reflecting the amorous spheres.

All the excitement of the next world is gone, and all hints of mysterious embraces, as we look now at the lyric interpretation of this world without any promises of a future life or luck in the Beyond. The only reference to death we see in the melancholic symbolism that life resembles the seasons, in having a spring, a ripening and then a wilting towards death.

FLOATING ON THE WATERS

Another strange sight on the Sea-Sarcophagi is the fact that all person-ages do not swim in the water, nor do they sink into the waters, or seem to be even partly submerged in the waters, nor do the diverse draperies of the females or their hair ever seem to be wet – this in a striking contrast to the Nereids on other monuments of the same time, who show wet and clinging drapery and hair. The creatures of the sea, be they Tritons or Nereids, are sometimes even marked on their bodies with scallops of waves to indicate their wet condition, as the water is running off their drenched bodies, or giving the illusion of braving the waves or having done so.

142

Instead, all figures on the Sea-Sarcophagi seem quasi weightless and most miraculously to float over the waters in an almost heraldic attitude of simply manifesting their presence in a staged pantomime.

143

The reason for it is that in Indian texts many apparitions belonging to the spiritual world are repeatedly and consistently said to "float" and only in specific cases said to sit or stand or swim. This probably came about as a

144

consequence of India's extravagant symbol-arrangement which disregards weight and gravity in their emblematic displays, the same as it disregards anatomy in their multi-limbed divinities and in the free dealing mixtures of animal and human shapes, shown in their diverse transitions during the transmigration of souls, from one creature to the other. Big figures stand on top of little creatures without squashing or even visibly compressing them, goddesses are shown to sit on flowers without bending their petals and scores of fat saints float through the atmosphere without visible support – because all of them are only embodiments of symbol-constellations. They are almost comparable to the charts showing the atomic or chemical structures which also disregard the notions of weight in their graphic presentation and want only to indicate symbol-connections. This extraordinary condition of the figures is one more hint that we deal here with the extra-Mediterranean imagery of the East.

However, it is especially said of the Apsarases and of the Gandharvas that they are weightless and whenever they are depicted iconographically, this weightlessness is clearly shown. The Gandharvas are not real persons; they have no genealogy and no cult, and are only symbol-images of the masculine sea, while the Apsarases are likewise only the psychological core of femininity and seduction, sketched, through the ages, on the most divergent backgrounds, – in the waters, in the air or on the ground, – in short: permeating all creation as Spirits or Genii of Love. The weightless condition of the Soul-Babies, being actually "Spirits" of the dead, can be easily admitted. All together we deal here with an epiphany of all the figures as opposed to their real and bodily presence.

AMORINI

132   A special case are the Amorini that fill the atmosphere; they are not weightless because they obviously need their wings to stay in the air and do not belong to the foreign symbol-world of those in the waters. They are Mediterranean creatures and are to symbolize the mood of mutual love – not only between the Gandharvas and Apsarases, the Love-Spirits of Heaven, but also their combined love towards the newly arriving Souls, shown as Babies.

The Amorini are a typical Mediterranean means for the sculptor to indicate the fluidum of love, which he was instructed to symbolize here. However, even the case-history of the Amorini is connected to India. There the mood of the main-figures was often indicated by little secondary figures, representing vanity or jealousy or victory or prudery etc. as so-called "determinatives" – either to indicate to us the identity or mood of the main figure; or to hint at a particular stage or adventure in its mythological saga. The Greco-Roman people took those little determinants for mis-formed dwarfs. Especially as the Greeks had an instinctive horror of any malformation, they represented those Mood-Figures, because they were small, rather as children, as gay and healthy and pretty children, mischievous at times. We see them on several Mediterranean sculptures, signifying different abstract notions, but the most famous of all became the Amoretti or Amorini, symbolizing love.

135

136

LATER DEVELOPMENTS

In later times the exclusively Etruscan features of their art and visions began slowly to wear off and started to amalgamate with the Greco-Roman religious and mythological conceptions surrounding them.

This process was no doubt a side-effect of the political depression befalling the Etruscans between 600 B.C. and 500 B.C. when they lost several battles against the Romans, which ended with the expulsion of the reigning Etruscan dynasty from Rome and their drop from power. In the period of their dominance it is natural for a people to proudly uphold their convictions which set them apart from all others, but in times of defeat the vanquished may at first doubt their own crumbling world and thereafter adopt many ways of those who had shown to be superior to them, at least in cunning and power.

In that time of Etruscan decline, a note of fear and horror crept into their funeral art and into their visions of the Beyond, which had been so full of joyous confidence before. There appear demons of the lower world out of the Greco-Roman mythology, but while in the local Roman vision those Chthonian figures were somber but majestic, the same personages reappeared in Etruscan art as horrible, cruel, wild and menacing. Especially the Etruscan Charun duplicating the Greek Charon, the boatsman who goodnaturedly ferries the shades over the river Styx, now appears in the Etruscan funeral art of 200 B.C. as the very image of the terror of death and decomposition, greenish in color and ugly of face. He swings a club or heavy hammer with fiendish pleasure to strike the mortal blow. Some other repugnant ghosts and demons appear with snakes to drag the shuddering mortals down into the fearful gaping mouth of the earth.

We see, mostly engraved on metal ash-urns, as a curious compromise still a banquet, but now underground, and gone is the exuberant joy of Eros in Paradise, and the open spaces of the Above.

As the death of a person was often compared to a voyage to another land, references to the Argonauts were frequently used as symbols for that adventuresome trip. In an echo of the involvements with females in the next world, scenes were preferred where the Argonauts have, – on rare occasions – some dealings with women.

On the Sea-Sarcophagi of later times the figures in the Celestial Ocean gradually become more completely Greco-Roman, while the sculptors take the real symbolism lightly and enjoy themselves in variations and innovations which make the visual contents of the artwork less and less reconcilable with its spiritual substance. But the main theme, that of a confrontation with a plurality of females, is still reflected on the sarcophagi, however thinly veiled by local mythos. For instance, "The Judgment of Paris" of the Antonine period (Villa Medici) whimsically adds Paris to the traditional three Nymphs of Heaven; and "Achilles among the Daughters of Lycomedes" (Capitoline Museum) is another version in a later period, just showing a man in the company of women, taken at random from the repertoire of mythology; while the truly aquatic scenes are often relegated to an "upper register," as if to indicate that they still prevail as a paradigm in the upper spheres, while the sea is often indicated as the basis above which the spiritualization and re-appearance of the dead takes place.

Some sculptors stripped the sarcophagi of figures betraying their Asiatic provenience, to create a more Romanized scenario of compelling mystery. They vaguely understood the maritime setting, the brewing eddies of the cosmic underground, as the basis of the Apotheosis; but they were, above all, entranced by the big sweep, the other-worldly elan, in which the soul is taken aloft to be united with the Female of the Beyond.

When compared to sarcophagi of this kind, it is the couple at left which is different from all the others, not in the idea expressed, but in the intensity of the gesture displayed by the female, which thereby makes the Dartmouth sarcophagus unique.

143

252

A similar, but more restrained gesture indicating the mood of eager expectation, is shown by the solitary Water-Nymphs on the cover of the ash-urn of Naples . . . and by those in the clouds of the Endymion sarcophagi where the celestial Nymphs, in a similar pose of readiness, are facing the approach of a male figure – however, from afar, and not in the closeness as shown on this extraordinary sarcophagus.

112

26

The sensual aura surrounding the celestial Water-Nymphs is otherwise symbolized by including a Priapic figure into their ambiance, or a Pan reigning over the setting in which they appear.

Because the horse is a symbol for the male, the maiden at right, guiding the Hippocamp, may suggest that the female is leading the male soul into paradise. The same idea is more drastically shown on the tomb-painting at Tarquinia, where an Orientalized girl in bridal dress pulls a man with her towards the Beyond . . . which is also hinted at by those female apparitions enticing their partners with Betelnuts, the symbol for loving intimacy.

59

56

The wedding band given by the Amorette to the central figure seems to suggest that she is in a nuptial relation to the male at the right, while this same male quite willingly follows the Nymph leading the wild horse, being the symbol of passionate maleness. As such philandering of a "married" male is not compatible with Italian thinking, – (especially not with the certain piety surrounding a sarcophagus) – it becomes more probable that we deal here with an import of an extra-Mediterranean vision, duplicating the Indo-Oriental paradise and the atmosphere of free love which seems to be the main feature of its scenario.

At the very end it can be said that the Sea Sarcophagi inspired the artists of later times – down to Cellini – with a very rich repertoire of elements which they used to embellish all sorts of vessels, elevating the sphere of the sea to a mysterious and grandiose realm of phantasies, vaster than all terrestrial imagery.

The old Sea Sarcophagi however, when discovered, often ended up as basins of fountains or in a melancholic finale as drinking troughs for animals.

144

In the atmosphere of swelling power and splendor of the Roman Empire the sarcophagi became increasingly adorned with magnificent scenes of battles, as uplifting mementos, almost suggesting that success and glory here on earth could easily dispense with rewards thereafter. Various mythological scenes still appeared on sarcophagi but rarely with any relation to death or metaphysics. They were considered as impressive showpieces like tapestries with evenly worked surfaces, whose size and workmanship made them costly and thereby a demonstrative monument to the importance of the departed.

SUMMARY

We see now that all personages on the Sea-Sarcophagi can be explained by way of the Indian doctrine of Afterlife and the Beyond, and that, in fact, all of those personages shown, exactly illustrate their relationship as given in India's texts, and that not only their groupings conform to the Indian scriptures, but also the individual pantomimic gestures of all of its participants reflect the psychological profile and condition described in the Eastern teachings. This means that we have no questionable or inexplicable appearances or gestures left over, which the Indian texts fail to reveal and to clarify.

To sum this up in the shortest terms, the following review can be made:

133   THE SCENARIO is the "Celestial Ocean" high above the air of the sky, which is the abode of the departed souls, also called "Indra's Paradise."

134   THE FEMALES are the aquatic Apsarases, Nymphs of Love, promised to the souls in excelsis. On early sarcophagi and sepulchral imagery, they still wear the Indian hairdo and earrings, but are otherwise nude, conforming to the Indian models. On later sarcophagi they are shown in their Mediterranean version as Water-Nymphs displaying, in their originally Oriental tradition, their prominent bellies and heavy backsides intentionally framed by drapes in the Indian manner.

138   THE BABIES represent the souls of the departed who reappear, according to Indian texts, in the form of Babies in the next world, the "Celestial Ocean." The idea of the Babies is based on the doctrine of re-birth. A side-issue is the rejuvenation, thus expressed, which is also promised in the Indian scripture. This is to put the faithful, who may be old and sick at the time of death, in a better position for their encounters with the heavenly nymphs. Some sarcophagi illustrate an early stage of Afterlife – namely the arrival of the souls in the Beyond. There are, however, more ancient sarcophagi which depict a later stage in the adventures of the souls, where they are shown fully enjoying the charms of the heavenly Apsarases, faithfully illustrating the promises of the Vedic scriptures.

THE FLOWERS are the immediate vehicle of re-birth, as it is said in the Indian texts that the Soul-Babies sprout out of Lotus blossoms in Paradise, which is a very usual sight in India's iconography. Buddha is called "The Jewel in the Lotus" and is depicted as such. Numerous divinities are said to be Lotus-born, so that the birth out of the Lotus-blossom indicates "birth in purity." As the souls of the departed are not thought to be re-born into paradise by a gynecological process, the Lotus-birth signifies the miraculization and sublime condition of those so born. However, the Lotus-Blossom was not known in the Mediterranean and therefore the artists of Italy showed the babies at times sprouting out of a fantasy-plant, not to be found in real life – satisfied, as it seems, to denote thereby the supernatural of the event.

140

THE BREAST FEEDING of the Soul-Babies should show that those newly arrived souls of the departed are cared for by the heavenly hosts, that they are received in love and are nourished with the "Fluid of Life" or, according to some texts, "The Fluid of Life-Eternal" which those heavenly creatures are able to exude and to dispense in this manner to the Blessed. The welcome between the Beati in excelsis is a very urgent concern of the wandering souls, as most touchingly shown in some parallel texts. Those visions are totally absent in Greco-Roman thoughts and thereby show the influx of Eastern doctrines, now depicted by Italian sculptors on Italian soil.

139

THE SEA-CENTAURI are actually Gandharvas, who were in early times thought to be "Man-Horses" but as they appear in the "Celestial Ocean" as the male counterparts and lovers of the aquatic Apsarases, they show fins and fish-tails as nautical insigniae to set them apart from the Greco-Roman Centauri who have a very different background. They are often seen with a Lyra in hand, as they are called in India's scriptures "The Musicians of Heaven" – (the name Gandharva actually means Music). The Indian string instruments look very different, so that we can assume that there was a verbal transmission of the request to show those Sea-Centauri with the symbol for music in hand. If the Italian artist would have been ordered to copy an Indian model, he would have shown an instrument of the mandolin type. This could be regarded as one of the hints that the Etruscans came not from India with household-goods and statuaries to Italy, but that we deal here with a verbal transmission, by missionaries or preachers or holy men wandering about to spread their doctrines, which was the great vogue at that time. Several other features too, point to a verbal transmission of Indian doctrines, instead of a copy of Indian art.

135

132 THE AMORINI who fill the atmosphere are Mediterranean symbols to denote the "Celestial Ocean" as a region of love and felicity, which is so glowingly described in India's eschatology. They make reference partly to the amorous relationship between the Apsarases and the Gandharvas – in which we see the Apsarases as the active partners, clinging with romantic elan to the rather lordly Gandharvas, conforming to the Indo-Oriental pattern and description of those nymphs, in contrast to the Mediterranean tradition according to which the males, especially the Centauri, are shown as the pursuing element in relation to all females. Also this very noticeable change in attitude would point to a verbal indoctrination of the Italian artists.

The other relationship the Amorini make reference to is the loving reception given to the Soul-Babies in the sphere of Paradise by all its inhabitants, the aquatic Apsarases and Gandharvas. The dolphins, the Mediterranean symbols of the sea, are shown on some of the sarcophagi as playfully elated by the arrival of the cherished souls, and as if giving them a welcome to their element, the Celestial Ocean, here identified with the Mediterranean Sea.

THE PORTRAIT of the deceased is often shown within a sea-shell, indicating that the departed is now within the realm of the sea, the Celestial sphere of re-birth. The idea of being surrounded by the sea is suggested by the shell, enclosing halo-like the image of the dead, and by the fantastic creatures representing the multiformed production of this "Pool of Nature." Sometimes this portrait of the dead is upheld by majestic Sea-Gods – (of Mediterranean coinage) – which should, no doubt, convey the idea that the loved-one is now cared for, upheld, honored and protected by the lords and masters of the Ocean. But this later version is an elaboration by artists who lost the contact with the original meanings and substituted for them their own interpretation. Working backwards from those late sarcophagi, we can guess that the simple heads which are placed on the early sarcophagi in the same central location between creatures of the sea, were thought to represent the dead person too, although possibly at times as a metamorphosed allegory.

Before looking at the historic development it may be of interest that there was also a later phase where a strict portrait of the dead was requested in just this central location. From that period we have some prefabricated sarcophagi which are finished to the last detail except the features of the

137 dead, which are still left a blank ...

Sometimes on the very earliest Sea-Sarcophagi we have a face with the hairdo of Apollo, ever so weak and vaguely emerging from the rough stone

– but this mere "suspicion" that this could be the glorified or canonized dead, re-appearing in the likeness of Apollo, is later verified beyond any doubt on the stelae of Naples and the death-mirrors, where we see the alter-ego of the dead re-appearing with the lyra in hand or in the more archaic version of Apollo, with his insignia of the bow, and even inscribed, in Etruscan lettering to be, in fact the image of Apollo. There he is, as we said before, confronted with the Three Graces, or derivatives thereof, representing the Females of the Beyond, promised in the Eastern scriptures, – and depicted on the Sea-Sarcophagi – (in direct translation of the Apsarases) – as "Those of the Waters."

It can be repeated in short that the re-appearance of the dead in the image of a divinity, or with its emblems and characteristics was a very widespread practice – (also in Egypt, where the dead reappeared with the beard of Osiris – even when the dead was a woman). In later times this metamorphosis of the departed was extended to include hero-figures, like Achilles, showing that epiphany of his alter-ego then surrounded by admiring celestial females – or else as Paris, making his choice between an assortment of Celestial Brides.

As a final note it could be said that the Sea-Sarcophagi, when seen in the perspective of time, stood in splendid isolation away from all attempts of interpretation, possibly because their symbolism was kept silent, already at the time when they were created, so that we have no texts, no hints in contemporary documents as to their meaning – possibly because of their reference to a foreign and "dangerous" doctrine, contradicting the official local creeds.

Their originally wild and eery scenario was, however, gradually blended over into the imposing splendor of the Olympian divinities to add, in the end, only here and there some mysterious figures out of the earlier visions from the East – like the Water Nymphs floating in the Above over the metamorphosed dead – or the animals embraced by aquatic females, the babies in the waters sprouting from flowers – all of them later relegated to border-figures only, but intriguing enough even there, to spread the atmosphere of secrecy and the magnetism of the enigma over those pieces of funeral art.

130

80

61

79

INDEX

The page numbers do not list passing references made to subjects,
but indicate where those topics are more specifically treated.

LIST OF ILLUSTRATIONS

1 SCULPTURE. The male Gandharvas and their paramours, the Apsarases, are the images of free love in India's heaven. Vaishnava Cavetemple No. 3, Badami, India.

2 SCULPTURE. The Apsarases are often shown as riding on their male counterparts as their "Vehicle" or basis of operation. Philadelphia Museum of Art, Philadelphia – 56.75.23.

3 SCULPTURE. The Apsarases with "Determinant" figures indicating the mood and aura of the princesses of lust. Philadelphia Museum of Art, Philadelphia – 56.75.12.

4 SCULPTURE. Stand-ins for the celestial brides are statues of heavenly females, receiving the homage of pious men. Temple site Sanchi, India.

5 ROCK CARVING. Paradigma of females pursuing men, to become their lovers in India's celestial spheres. Mamallapuram, India.

6 PHALLIC MONUMENTS. India's symbol of Resurrection and the insignia of Siva, re-appear in Italy as Etruscan Gravestones. Museo Archeologico Nazionale, Naples.

7 CIPPUS. The Sivatic monuments gradually change on Italian soil to the images of sprouting plants. Museo Archeologico Nazionale, Naples.

8 CIPPUS. The Indian gravestones later assume the less anatomical and more Mediterranean shape of Columns. Museo Archeologico Nazionale, Naples.

9 GRAVESTONE. Two Rams and the Cup of Immortality symbolize "Everlasting Manliness" in paradise. National Archaeological Museum, Athens.

264

10 GRAVESTONE. Harpias changing to Sirens on top of a grave represent the promise of the Eastern Paradise. National Archaeological Museum, Athens.

11 GRAVESTONE. Later monuments formalized the idea of Resurrection by representing a re-sprouting plant. National Archaeological Museum, Athens – NM 1028.

12 GRAVESTONE. The bull on its base was meant to symbolize everlasting manliness in Paradise. National Archaeological Museum, Athens.

13 SKYPHOS. The painting shows a column for the male and a hut-like monument for the female. Museum of Fine Arts, Boston – 97.372. (Detail).

14 COVER OF ASH-URN. The soul is guided by two Priapic emissaries with torches in hand to a sensual next world. Villa Giulia, Rome.

15 COVER OF ASH-URN. The soul of the dead is gently lifted from the ground by a Faunian spirit. Villa Giulia, Rome.

16 COVER OF ASH-URN. The soul making first steps, supported by an otherworldly spirit with torch. Museo Archeologico, Palestrina, Italy.

17 SARCOPHAGUS. The soul already dressed in Bacchian Nebris is received by Pan and Dionysian spirits. Museo Archeologico Nazionale, Naples.

18 FUNERAL FRAGMENT. The soul supported by a Dionysian Spirit, is embraced and kissed by a celestial bride. Museum of Fine Arts, Boston – 00.325. (Detail).

19 FUNERAL MONUMENT. A female soul is tenderly welcomed by a heavenly apparition of love. Campo Santo, Pisa.

20 FUNERAL STELA. The Hermaphroditic soul with Nebris is supported and guided by a Panian spirit of the Above. Palazzo Braschi, Rome.

265

21 SARCOPHAGUS. Banquetting on a couch with a female in the Beyond. Death-angels with torches of Resurrection. Museo Nazionale Romane, Rome – 115174.

22 SARCOPHAGUS. Selene rushing to Endymion representing the deceased in his epiphany as being merely asleep. Museo Archeologico Nazionale, Naples.

23 SARCOPHAGUS. The still unfinished facial likeness of the dead as Endymion, visited by the anonymous Selene. Musée du Louvre, Paris.

24 SARCOPHAGUS. Endymion with ancestral figure and Water-Nymph in the Above, approached by Selene. Metropolitan Museum of Art, New York – 24.9713.

25 SARCOPHAGUS. Endymion asleep dreams of an Apsara as Water-Nymph with pitcher floating high above him. Casino Rospigliosi, Rome.

26 SARCOPHAGUS. Endymion and vision of love-scene in the above while Selene is guided to him by Amorini. Basilica San Felice, Cimitile.

27 SARCOPHAGUS. The Nemean Lion is shown in enormous size. Selene and Endymion are depicted with tragic expression. Metropolitan Museum of Art, New York – 47.100 4 A-B.

28 SARCOPHAGUS. The Nemean Lion devouring creatures. The deceased Lady in medallion, her soul received by genii. Villa Doria, Rome.

29 SEPULCHRE. Two giant Nemean Lions are overporing a collapsing bull, the symbol of Life overcome by Death. Museum of Fine Arts, Boston – 86.145.

30 SARCOPHAGUS showing Heracles, who killed the Nemean Lion, guiding a woman out of the doors of Death. Museo, Valletri.

31 SARCOPHAGUS. A dead person escapes out of the doors to the Netherworld to join other famous immortals. Museo Campano, Capua.

32 SARCOPHAGUS. Ariadne awakening from her death-sleep
to the realm of sensual pleasures in the Above.
Museo Nazionale Romano, Rome.

33 SARCOPHAGUS. Ariadne awakened to the Dionysian
Pageantry of Fauni and Maenads, leading to Priapus.
Vatican, Belvedere, Rome.

34 SARCOPHAGUS. Replacing the wild revellers, wine harvesting
putti are now serving Dionysos, the image of Priapic joy.
Museo, Tipasa, Algeria.

35 STELA with an Oriental dance-girl as the promise in the
Thereafter on the grave of a Roman Legionary in Carinthia.
Fraunkirchen, Carinthia, Austria.

36 STATUE of Cybele, one of the Eastern Queens of Heaven, with
music players as her determinatives for Lust and Delirium.
Archaeological Museum, Ankara, Turkey.

37 STATUE. Lady of Byblos, Egypto-Asiatic amalgam of the
Beloved in the Above with monkey-emblem of free love.
The Brooklyn Museum, Brooklyn, New York.

38 PAPYRUS. Lady Anhai in Egypt's heaven, giving homage
to the great figures of Eternity in a pastoral setting.
Book of the Dead, Papyrus Anhai.

39 SARCOPHAGUS COVER. The deceased Lady as a Maenad envisioned
to join the joyous Dionysian merrymakers in the Thereafter.
British Museum, London – 1425.

40 SARCOPHAGUS. Lady in medallion received rejuvenated,
with same hairdo, by genii of Love in the Beyond.
Museo Nazionale Romano, Rome.

41 SARCOPHAGUS. Roman soldier received rejuvenated
as Achilles, with the insignia of Apollo, by Chiron.
Museo Nazionale Romano, Rome – 124737.

42 SARCOPHAGUS. Couple in horse-drawn cart travels to the
Above, as a break with the dogma of the dreary Hades.
Museum of Fine Arts, Boston – C 6307.

43 FRAGMENT. A female looking aghast, is revived by a compassionate Nymph and a paradisial apparition. Museo Gregoriano Profano, Vatican, Rome.

44 FIGURE ON SARCOPHAGUS. The Etruscan garland of sanctification has the same meaning in India. British Museum, London – 60.3573.

45 INDIAN MINIATURE. The same "Garland of Elevation" is bestowed on a highly deserving person in India. Kalpasutra, Gujerat, India.

46 SARCOPHAGUS. The Begging Bowl of Buddha, the oldest Indian symbol of sanctity, re-appears in the hand of the Etruscan. Museo Archaeologico, Chiusi, Italy.

47 ETRUSCAN TOMB PAINTING. The Garlands and Scarves on bushes hint at lovemaking in the realm of the Beyond. Museo Archaeologico, Florence.

48 PAINTING. Holy men bathing with haloes over them, parallels the suspended Garlands of Sanctification. Terry Gallowhur, Reading, Vermont.

49 SARCOPHAGUS. Garlands of Sanctification handed out by the Three Graces, representing the Celestial Brides. Museo Bardo, Tunisia.

50 STELA. Harpia cradling the soul in a motherly manner, blending over into the Eastern Females in the Beyond. British Museum, London – 60.3635.

51 STELA. Harpia in union with a man whose death is here interpreted as sleep in which he becomes her partner. Museum of Fine Arts, Boston – 08.34C.

52 SCULPTURE. Harpia awaiting the ascending soul with open arms and wings for the protective embraces of her love. Museum of Fine Arts, Boston – 96.680.

53 STATUE. Harpia, the femininity of her body overflowing the bird-like appearance of the original conception. National Archaeological Museum, Athens – NM 2583.

54 SCULPTURE. Harpia with humanlike soul seems to cry over the death or destiny of a mortal beloved. Museum of Fine Arts, Boston – 03.757.

55 MIRROR FRAME. Harpia on top, the image of Death towards which all living streams, shown as Cocks and Rabbits. Badisches Landesmuseum, Karlsruhe, Germany.

56 STATUETTE WITH BETELNUT. An Etruscan female of the Beyond holds out this symbol of love to a soul as an enticement. Cleveland Museum of Art, Cleveland, Ohio – 53.124.

57 STATUETTE WITH BETELNUT. A winged female with this symbol in hand, tempts the soul to come with her to paradise. British Museum, London – 491.

58 MINIATURE. The Betelnut as symbol for "Loving Intimacy" is shown by Krishna, ready to insert it in the lips of Radha. Kanoria Collection, Calcutta, India.

59 TOMB PAINTING. A Celestial Bride intices a man to follow her with the same gesture as seen on the Statuettes with Betelnuts. Tomb of the Bacchantes, Tarquinia, Italy.

60 FUNERAL RELIEF. The amorous Thereafter of the Etruscans with Asiatic Girls, Faunian men and Death-Garlands on ceiling. Musée du Louvre, Paris – MA 3603.

61 BUST. Emperor Comodus as Heracles. This glorification of the dead was greatly condemned by Seneca and Plinius. Galeria Orti Lamiani 12, Conservatori, Rome.

62 STATUE. Empress Faustina is shown as Venus with her paramour Mars, following the Eastern idea of amorous encounters in the Thereafter. Museo Nazionale Romano, Rome. Edition Leipzig (DDR).

63 - 65 MIRRORS. The soul carried off: Winged females of the Beyond take the souls of men lovingly to their realm. Gerhard, Etruskische Spiegel, Reprint, De Gruyter, Berlin.

66 - 69 MIRRORS. The Fate of the Soul decided: Such decisions are often made by the scrutiny of a liver in the Above. Gerhard, Etruskische Spiegel, Reprint, De Gruyter, Berlin.

70 - 73 MIRRORS. Mirrors as Gifts to the Females: Those objects are frequently shown to be given by the souls to celestial maidens. Gerhard, Etruskische Spiegel, Reprint, De Gruyter, Berlin.

74 - 76 MIRRORS. Reception in the Beyond: The soul of men is mostly shown as being lovingly received by celestial females. Gerhard, Etruskische Spiegel, Reprint, De Gruyter, Berlin.

77 - 79 MIRRORS. Reception as Hero: The dead re-appears as being honored in a sumptuous setting between otherworldly females. Gerhard, Etruskische Spiegel, Reprint, De Gruyter, Berlin.

80 - 83 MIRRORS. Reception as Apollo: The deceased is glorified in the image of Apollo, often shown ascending from the sea. Gerhard, Etruskische Spiegel, Reprint, De Gruyter, Berlin.

84 - 87 MIRRORS. Heracles and Death: Heracles became the hero of Resurrection by overcoming the Lion-symbol of Death. Gerhard, Etruskische Spiegel, Reprint, De Gruyter, Berlin.

88 - 90 MIRRORS. Paris and the Three Graces: The deceased is given a multiple choice of females in the orientalized paradise. Gerhard, Etruskische Spiegel, Reprint, De Gruyter, Berlin.

91 - 93 MIRRORS. The Eastern Brides: Conforming to Eastern visions, exotic maidens are shown awaiting the souls in the Above. Gerhard, Etruskische Spiegel, Reprint, De Gruyter, Berlin.

94 - 95 MIRRORS. Nuptial Washing: This ritual procedure is the preparation for the embraces by the Celestial Brides. Gerhard, Etruskische Spiegel, Reprint, De Gruyter, Berlin.

96 - 99 MIRRORS. The mysterious Strigilis: The shape of this scraper may symbolize a gift of the arriving soul to the females. Gerhard, Etruskische Spiegel, Reprint, De Gruyter, Berlin.

100 - 102 MIRRORS. Reception of earthly Women: It seems that promises are also made to women of finding Love in the Thereafter. Gerhard, Etruskische Spiegel, Reprint, De Gruyter, Berlin.

103 MIRROR. The Cistae are toiletry containers, but are often found in graves of men as their gift to the celestial females. Gerhard, Etruskische Spiegel, Reprint, De Gruyter, Berlin.

104 CISTA. The left figure holds a gift mirror with the image of a Soul as donor. The maidens at right perform the nuptial hairwash. Badisches Landesmuseum, Karlsruhe – F 1859.

105 PLAQUE OF NAPLES. The same hairwash scene as shown on the Cista, appears on this Plaque, in the company of Apollini. Museo Archeologico Nazionale, Naples.

106 PLAQUE OF NAPLES. Apollini as the avatar of the dead with celestial maidens, represented as Water-Nymphs. Museo Archeologico Nazionale, Naples.

107 PLAQUE OF NAPLES. The Water-Nymphs are the verbal translation of the Indian Apsarases into "those of the Waters" (apsa=aqua). Museo Archeologico Nazionale, Naples.

108 PLAQUE OF NAPLES. Water-Nymphs, shown by Italian artists sometimes with Sea-shells and sometimes as Well-Nymphs. Museo Archeologico Nazionale, Naples.

109 PLAQUE OF NAPLES. The Nymphs show their maritime provenience by appearing with Okeanos and the Dioskuri, the symbols of rebirth. Museo Archeologico Nazionale, Naples.

110 PLAQUE OF NAPLES. The deceased as Apollini appears rejuvenated according to Eastern beliefs, to enjoy best the heavenly maidens. Museo Archeologico Nazionale, Naples.

111 PLAQUE OF NAPLES. Apollini is shown in the stillness of a mythological apparition and the Nymphs in a static pose. Museo Archeologico Nazionale, Naples.

112 ASH URN. A Water-Nymph with pitcher emiting water shows here for the first time a gesture of readiness for embraces. Museo Archeologico Nazionale, Naples.

113 PLAQUE OF NAPLES. The Water-Nymphs are here depicted as Horai, the servants of Aphrodite, rushing to a male lover – (Apollini). Museo Archeologico Nazionale, Naples.

114 PLAQUE OF NAPLES. Apollini flanked by Water-Nymphs, their shells possibly symbolic for the Concha Veneris offered to him. Museo Archeologico Nazionale, Naples.

115 PLAQUE OF NAPLES. Later, the Nymphs still with Sea-shells in hand appear as a promise offered in a paradisial garden. Museo Archeologico Nazionale, Naples.

116 SARCOPHAGUS. On Roman Funeral monuments the three Nymphs change over into the Moirai, goddesses of Fate and Doom. Municipio, Velletri, Italy.

117 PLAQUE OF ATHENS. The suppliant as donor, Pan as Mediator, Nymphagogos and the Celestial Brides. National Archaeological Museum, Athens – NM 4466.

118 PLAQUE OF ATHENS. Pan as the protector figure over the encounter of the soul with the Nymphs in a grotto. National Archaeological Museum, Athens – NM 2011.

119 PLAQUE OF ATHENS. The three Horai as the devotees of the Love-goddess Aphrodite, dance to the tune of a Priapic Faun. National Archaeological Museum, Athens – NM 1449.

120 PLAQUE OF ATHENS. A rejuvenated man with three Nymphs under the patronate of Pan appears in the Olympian Above. National Archaeological Museum, Athens – NM 1448.

121 PLAQUE OF ATHENS. The Apollonic dead awakening. Pan, Nymphagogos, three Nymphs and miniaturized donors. National Archaeological Museum, Athens – NM 1966.

122 STATUE. The Water-Nymphs became in some of the Greek maritime districts the protector figures of Seafarers. Museum of Ancient Corinth, Corinth, Greece.

123 SARCOPHAGUS. Apollo with the Muses later replaces the oriental vision of the deceased surrounded by females. Galeria Doria, Rome.

124 APOLLO SARCOPHAGUS. Confirms the connection of Apollo to death, first made by the earliest "Grave Apollos." Basilica San Gavino, Porto Torres, Italy.

125 LEDA SARCOPHAGUS. Leda with the soulbird shown as a swan hints at the amorous relation of the soul to the females. Museo Nazionale, Messina, Italy.

126 CYPRUS SARCOPHAGUS. Egypt's dancing Lovegod Bes here symbolizes the many lovemakings promised in paradise. Metropolitan Museum of Art, New York – 74-51.2453.

127 CYPRUS SARCOPHAGUS. The milk drinking in the paradise of India is staged by Odalisques offering their breasts. Metropolitan Museum of Art, New York – 74-51.2453.

128 PAPYRUS. India's promise of "Milk-yielding Trees" in its paradise is illustrated stunningly by an Egyptian artist. Tomb of Thutmosis III, Valley of the Kings, Egypt.

129 SARCOPHAGUS. Souls are clamoring to get at Oriental dance girls in the Above, presided over by lovegod Bes. Museo Nazionale Romano, Rome.

130 SEA SARCOPHAGUS. Earlier versions show an Apollo-like mask in its center, which is flanked by two Hippocampi. Museo Nazionale Tarquiniense, Tarquinia – 1419, Italy.

131 SEA SARCOPHAGUS. Earlier model with the Apollonic mask and Sea-creatures with beards, symbolizing the male sea. Museo Civico, Viterbo – 239, Italy.

132 SEA SARCOPHAGUS. The bearded creatures now change to aquatic males, the mask in the center to the portrait of the deceased. Museo Archeologico Nazionale, Naples.

133 SEA SARCOPHAGUS. Females are added shown in most tender interaction with males who become lordly Sea-Centauri. Musée du Louvre, Paris.

134 SEA SARCOPHAGUS. Females in intensified embraces or riding on males, in the Indian pattern of "Vehicles." Campo Santo, Pisa, Italy.

135 SEA SARCOPHAGUS. Females embrace Bulls, symbols of masculinity and are playing with a sensual monkey. Museo dell'Opera della Cattedrale, Siena, Italy.

136 SEA SARCOPHAGUS. The unfinished portrait of the deceased in the shell of rebirth. Embraces with animals increase. Museo Nazionale Romano, Rome.

137 SEA SARCOPHAGUS. Unfinished portrait of the deceased. The love scenes with animals become more stereotyped. Palazzo Venezia, Rome.

138 SEA SARCOPHAGUS. Babies appear, representing the re-born souls, clamoring for the females as "Those of the Waters." Conservatori Palace, Rome.

139 SEA SARCOPHAGUS. Soul-Babies breast-fed, the Lyra of the Gandharvas, wedding-band given to female with Bull. Conservatori Palace, Rome.

140 SEA SARCOPHAGUS. Babies sprouting out of flowers, as the "Lotus-Born" according to India's holy scriptures. Conservatori Palace, Rome.

141 SEA SARCOPHAGUS. Later, the symbolisms of the celestial ocean were no longer understood and became formal poses. Vaticano, Belvedere, Rome.

142 SEA SARCOPHAGUS. Still later the meaning of the figures gets confused, males tame horses, Nereids play the Lyra. Church S. Francis, Trastevere, Rome.

143 SEA SARCOPHAGUS. The exotic lovestory between the soul and the celestial females is Romanized as hierogamy with the sea. Dartmouth College Museum and Galleries, Hanover, N.H.

144 SEA SARCOPHAGUS. The sarcophagi, when later found empty, were used as ornamented drinking-troughs for animals. Villa Spigarelli, Anzio, Italy.

145 STATUETTE. The birth of females out of the sea is often equated with the rebirth of the soul out of the sea-shell. Museo Archeologico Nazionale, Naples.

146 LEGIONARY SARCOPHAGUS. The soul in the image of a female is lifted out of the premordial waters and greeted by Amorini. Palazzo Mattei, Rome.

147 POSTAMENT. A young female either arises out of the waters, or sinks into the devouring "Pool of Nature." Galeria Borghese, Rome.

148 SEA SARCOPHAGUS. Venus in shell of rebirth is flanked by a male and female, now representing "Land and Sea." Galeria Borghese, Rome.

149 POSTAMENT. A soulbaby is mysteriously received in the shell of rebirth by a Venus reminiscent of Leda. Conservatory Palace, Rome.

150 SEA SARCOPHAGUS. A Grand Finale mood of all elements is presented by an artist who disregarded their symbolism. Lateran Museo Profano, Rome.

151 SARCOPHAGUS. The connection of the Three Graces to Death is shown by their triad, flanked by genii of the Beyond. Palazzo Mattei, Rome.

152 SARCOPHAGUS. Detail of frontice piece. The Three Graces set in relation to Death, as the promise to the soul in Excelsis. Museo Nazionale Romano, Rome.

1

The male Gandharvas and their paramours, the Apsarases, are the images of charm and passion and the prototypes of lovers in India's heaven. The idea of a romantic atmosphere in the Above gradually infused the Mediterranean lands from about 600 B.C. onward and eventually displaced the native visions of a dreary Below in Hades. This development is the subject of the following sequence of illustrations.

TO PAGE 6

2

The sphere of action is the Celestial Ocean, the Paradise, the realm of felicity, and eternal rebirth. The Gandharvas were first pictured as Centaurs in raw masculinity, as personifications of the generative "Pool of Nature" and the Apsarases, being "those of the Waters," as their passionate playmates, often riding upon them, as their "Vehicle" – their basis of operation. Later the Gandharvas changed to princely creatures, bewitching the females with the spell of their music – (Gandharva means Music).

TO PAGES 7, 233, 236

3

The Apsarases are the daughters of the main-god Indra and the sweet
princesses of Paradise and Lust. The Heavens are full of them and they give
their favors to the Gandharvas, at times also seducing earthly males, but
mainly fulfilling all amorous desires of the souls of the Blessed in the great
Above . . . as promised in the holy scriptures. Their Oriental counterparts
are the Houris, who also consort with the Faithful in Heaven.

TO PAGE 8

4

The earthly replicas of the Apsarases are the Temple-Girls who, oiled, perfumed, and with acrobatic skills, give samples of paradisial bliss to some men. Although Buddha, in his early writings, forbade bodily unions, with stand-ins for the Celestial Brides in the temples, there were sanctified images to receive the adoration of the Believers.

TO PAGE 25

5

The many erotic sculptures on the temples were a grand display, manifestly showing the population the attractions of the otherwise vague vision of Paradise, to which the temples were able to elevate the souls. The above relief suggests that the Celestial Females are pursuing the souls of men. This thought is repeated on Etruscan funeral monuments, in contrast to the Mediterranean imagery where the male is the pursuing element.

TO PAGES 17, 233

6

The symbols of resurrection were well established and plentiful in the
Greco-Roman sphere, as Hermes Psychopompos, who guided the souls
from the Below to the Above, or as the voyage and elevation of the deceased
by carts, or by winged horses or genii. It is therefore especially remarkable
that the Etruscans – (living in Italy) – used a definitely Indian symbol of
resurrection, in the form of the phallic column, the insignia of Siva, a
divinity not known in the Mediterranean.

TO PAGES 37, 221

7

The Sivatic columns were used in India as grave-stones, denoting the presence of divine protection and were the symbols of Resurrection, the raising upward, of youth eternal and the "everlasting manliness" in paradise, so frequently mentioned in India's scriptures.

TO PAGE 38

8

The original meaning of this monument gradually shifted its appearance when used by the Etruscans in Italic lands, and assumed the shapes of re-sprouting plants, still symbolic for the idea of resurrection. Those markers became less clearly anatomic and from their surroundings absorbed the form of Dorian columns.

TO PAGE 38

9

In the National Museum of Athens there are several grave-stelae of vaguely phallic outlines, illustrating the idea of "everlasting manliness in Paradise" as promised in the scriptures of the East. They show two rams, the symbols of male procreative powers, in copulative positions, and a vessel, known to us from other representations, as being symbolic for the drink of immortality.

TO PAGE 40

10

Another funeral stela of more lyric-ornamental outlines, shows two smiling Harpies with oriental hips in graceful, almost longing poses, as the
Females promised in the Beyond. Similar to some engravings shown on
Etruscan mirrors, we see here again the fusion of the once horrifying
soul-snatchers with the Sirens, charming the souls to their death, – but now
following the shift towards Eastern visions, blending over into angelic
creatures, promising sweet celestial encounters. The stem in the center
may symbolize here the re-sprouting power of the male.

TO PAGE 40

11

We finally see a highly sublimated stela, but still in phallic outlines, where the once so drastic resprouting-power is subdued into symbols of vegetation. The strange upshooting center of the plant is reminiscent of the 'Flower of Sensuality' on the Etruscan mirrors and the sinuous accents on Priapic figures. Beneath it we have the greatly formalized begging-bowl of Buddha, now turned into blossoms, hinting at the resprouting of the soul, and below it the traditional hand-shake of farewell from the living.

TO PAGE 40

12

It is not only the tip of those grave-stones which hints at the sensual involvements in the orientalized next world, but we see also at the base of such funeral monuments symbols of "everlasting manliness" in the form of a bull, the most archaic image of masculine energy, be it in the sense of the secular Power-and-Passion-complex, or the irrepressible break-out of the soul from the grave to the everlasting life in the Above. The same contradiction to death, which is also expressed by the impudent Hermae.

TO PAGE 40

13

In former times the Sivatic column was used as a grave-stone for men and women alike, but later, when the Indo-Asiatic component in the Etruscan enclave wore off, and the local Italian feelings became more prevalent, the monument for the male still remained the column, while for the females a hut-like domicile for their souls was considered more appropriate, as this painting suggests.

TO PAGES 38, 159

14

On the cover of an ash-urn we see the Apollonic image of the dead,
supported by two emissaries of the next world, which is hinted to be the
realm of sensual pleasures by the fact that those figures are Fauni. Their
vivid emblems of generation are not only the symbols of joy in the Beyond,
but also are the counter-aspects of death and destruction and thereby the
images of life protracted beyond the grave.

TO PAGE 40

15

Also on the cover of an Etruscan ash-urn, we see the soul of the dead, as if still in its eternal sleep, being lifted up from the ground, the sensual component, now symbolized by a Faunian spirit of the next world, again suggesting the joyful realm to which the dead will be re-awakened.

TO PAGE 41

16

Atop another ash-container is a figure of the next world with a torch, to indicate that he has brought the barely reawakened soul from the Dark to the Light of the Beyond. The soul of the dead, with Apollonic hairdo, seems still supported while daring its first steps towards its future existence, looking thankful and maybe questioningly at its guide, who appears strong and confident.

TO PAGE 41

17

On a sarcophagus there appears the resurrected soul, as a promise to the dead of a next world of joys. While still in the company of a chthonian animal the soul is received now by a Faunian figure representing sensuous pleasures and by an apparition from the train of Dionysos. The re-awakened soul is clad in the Bacchic Nebris as a sign of his initiation into the spheres of eternal bliss.

TO PAGE 41

18

Here we see the soul, still supported by a Pan-like creature, already embraced and kissed by a female of the Beyond, who is heavily dressed, as compared to similar scenes shown on Etruscan mirrors, where the celestial Brides joyously abandon their garments to please the arriving soul.

TO PAGE 41

19

In the solemn magnificat of an Apotheosis we have the rather rare view of an earthly female being welcomed by a heavenly apparition. To differentiate between the genii of the Above and the soul of a mortal, the heavenly being is shown with feathery wings, while the liberated soul – (based on an analogy with a cocoon?) – wears butterfly wings. In a strange uniformity of movements, the female souls touch the lower belly of the otherworldly figures, which are mostly shown to be of the male sex.

TO PAGE 42

20

The soul, possibly thought as Hermaphroditic, seems to have come from the Deep in the company of a chthonian animal, but is received by an emissary of the joyful Above, in the person of a Priapic Faun –(known to us as the symbol of sensuality leading the Horai) –. The soul of the deceased is dressed in the Nebris of the Dionysian Fauni to indicate that he is now initiated into their happy celestial clan.

TO PAGE 42

21

The torch bearing symbol-figures of Death and Resurrection on this sarcophagus – (here holding the torches upward as a sign of re-awakening) –
frame the completely Romanized version of the Indo-Oriental doctrine,
showing the deceased on a couch with a celestial bride, waited on by
females with fruitladen plates, as described in the Koran, chapter 44 . . .
"they will be served every kind of fruit . . ." while of the souls it is said . . .
"we shall wed them to darkeyed Houris."

TO PAGE 43

22

Now abandoning the Etrusco-Asiatic visions and returning to the Greco-
Roman world, we see the dead person here in the image of Endymion in his
eternal sleep, which is equated with Death. However, he is visited by a
Female of the Beyond in the person of Selene, the moon-crested queen of
the night, as his celestial beloved, and as such a reasonably good stand-in
for the celestial Brides, promised by the Eastern scriptures. Amorettes
illustrate the amorous drift of Selene towards her otherworldy bridegroom.

TO PAGES 44, 217

23

The interesting disclosure on this sarcophagus is the fact that the faces of
Endymion and Selene are not finished, while all other figures are executed
in great detail. This proves that the features of Endymion were intended to
be a portrait of the deceased to be finished after the sarcophagus was sold.
Hermes Psychopompos touches Endymion with his magic wand to awaken
him to his love-encounter with Selene.

TO PAGE 46

24

Selene descends from her chariot with one breast bared to indicate her readiness for tender embraces and is guided to her encounter by a spirit of love, while another symbol-figure holds the burning torch of her affection. However, Endymion, watched over by an ancestral figure, still seems to dream of the original Indo-Oriental Apsara, now represented as a Water-Nymph with pitcher, high in the clouds of the Above.

TO PAGES 44, 47, 49

25

*The strange persistence of the Apsaratic Water-Nymph in the exotic Above
as the ultimate wish-dream of the soul, seems to indicate that the replacement of those celestial brides by Selene was only a concession to the local
population not in the know of a secret and much more exciting phantasy of
the adventures, promised by the Eastern dogma, of those heavenly princesses "fulfilling all desires."*

TO PAGES 46, 48

26

The *Apsaratic Water Nymph* in the *Above* appeared, so far, as the static
emblem of a dream-vision. But here we see the same figure in the same
location above Endymion, ready to be embraced by a male, representing,
no doubt, the soul of the deceased. The more advanced stage of the dream
phantasy seems also supported by the animated figure in the back of
Endymion, replacing now the calm ancestral apparition.

TO PAGE 46

27

This sarcophagus leads us over from Selene to the Nemean Lion. As Selene
was the Queen of the Night, and Night-Eternal was equated with Death, it
was said that the Nemean Lion was her offspring, or earthly emissary,
symbolizing Death and was depicted on Sarcophagi and Etruscan Death-
Mirrors as devouring all the living and is in this superior role, shown to be
larger than all the other figures, as the Majesty of Death, crashing abruptly
into the scenes of life.

TO PAGE 49

28

Here we see again the Nemean Lion, larger than life, as the image of the cruelty of Death, befalling and devouring innocent creatures. Forgotten by now are the local ideas of Hades, while the far off Eastern visions of a love-filled scenario in the Thereafter seem totally accepted. The original Idea of love-bouts in heaven are modified in the case of the matronly lady, by showing her rejuvenated – (according to Eastern ideas!) – and caressed by male celestial apparitions of love.

TO PAGE 50

29

Two horrible Lions, as symbols of Death, are falling upon a bull, the image of vitality and power, associated with the deceased. While in former times Death was accepted with gentle melancholy as pre-ordained by the noble figures of Fate, we see now its representations, like the Nemean Lion, hinting at its cruelty and injustice, and at the same time we notice ideas brewing in the Mediterranean of how to escape from the Below, other than by means of the Eastern phantasmagories.

TO PAGE 51

30

As the revolt against Death, there arose a local hero in the person of
Heracles. Although the Nemean Lion was said to be invincible, like Death
itself, another saga tells us that Heracles killed that formidable beast. In
this totally Greco-Roman scenario we now see Heracles freeing some souls
and guiding them out of the door of Hades, – shown here is an old woman,
greeted by her husband. Heracles the Hero, is also often seen on Etruscan
mirrors in the role of the liberator from Death.

TO PAGE 50

31

In a later refinement it is suggested that great men, like poets, philosophers and statesmen, made themselves immortal by their own great works and thereby joined the ranks of the immortals, ideologically and without anybody's help. Sometimes we see a shrouded figure with scroll in hand, leaving the ornate door to the "Palace of Persephone" to join the illustrious company of other celebrated immortals "outside of death" and acclaimed by the Muses.

TO PAGE 50

32

The Ariadne sarcophagi seem to contain a double allegory, usable for male and female alike. In one version the soul of a female is compared to Ariadne, at first cruelly abandoned, but then re-awakened from her death-sleep to a new existence of love and joy by Dionysian figures. Consequently Ariadne is shown half awakening and in a pose of receptiveness towards the Priapic figure which, in the other version, now symbolizes the male deceased.

TO PAGES 58, 239

33

This other conception of the Ariadne sarcophagi dealing with the otherworldly adventures of a male soul, shows this newcomer entering from the
left, dressed in the familiar Nebris and received at once by a voluptuous
female and a miniaturized Pan who lifts some drapes, to show him
Ariadne. Various figures in the train of Dionysos lead to images of transition between Death and Rebirth — till we see the snake of sensuality coming
out of the basket and sacrifices brought to the altar of Priapus, being the
protector of the realm.

TO PAGES 58, 239

34

Grapes and Vines often decorate grave-chambers, sarcophagi and Etruscan mirrors, as a symbol for Dionysos, who in turn was the symbol-figure
for the Eastern doctrine of Joy and Priapic felicity in the Thereafter. In later
moralizing times the sensual figures of the Dionysian pageantry were
replaced by decent wine-harvesters and innocent or angelic Babes, while
Priapus himself remained in the background.

TO PAGE 61

35

Many Roman legions were recruited from the Asiatic borders of the Empire and brought the Eastern visions of the Thereafter along. The grave-stone of a Roman soldier in the northern province of Carinthia shows an Oriental dance-girl shedding her veils, as the promise of Afterlife. We also see the Soul, as little "Wanderer" marching with gifts towards that otherworldly apparition, while another dance-girl with lifted tunic above him seems to be on his mind.

TO PAGE 62

36

The grandiose Anatolian goddess Cybele came from Asia Minor to Greece in Cretan times. This statue in the Museum of Ankara shows that from earliest times the "Queens of Heaven" were associated with Joy, symbolized here by the two music players, as "determinatives" explaining the patronate of the main figure. The ecstatic and blood-drenched aspects of this divinity can be understood as expressions of the delirium and rapture connected to the sensual complex.

TO PAGE 235

37

As a consequence of the Asiatic inflow into Egypt, men wanted to be united
in the next world with a celestial female, instead of descending to the
Below of the tragic death-god Osiris. They also wanted to be converted into
a "Bull-Husband" of Asiatic origin, to become the beloveds of Idols like the
"Lady of Byblos" being an amalgamation of the Eastern "Hierodules of
Heaven" and sweet Hathor, holding here 'Horus the child' Isis-like in her
hand but wearing the "Double-Monkeys," the insignia of Egypt's harlots.

TO PAGES 83, 235

38

Many thoughts were given to the amorous adventures of men in Egypt's Beyond. Here we have the rather chaste and solitary vision of an earthly female in the Above. We see dark haired Lady Anhai in a pastoral setting with currents of water, where she reverently stands before great figures of the Beyond. She plows the fields, attends the harvest; we see the Bennu-Phoenix of resurrection and the barque of the soul with the seven steps to heaven, miraculously lifted from the waters.

TO PAGE 110

39

*As a total break with the local dogma of Hades and as the adoption of the
Eastern visions of a love-oriented next world in the Above, however, in
Mediterranean guise, we see on the cover of a Roman sarcophagus a lady in
her late years dressed as a Maenad with the traditional Tyrsos and lamb.
This seems to be a bold hint that this matron should be changed into a
Maenad, to join − (probably in a rejuvenated condition) − the Dionysian
train of lustful Fauni and intoxicated Bacchantae.*

TO PAGE 111

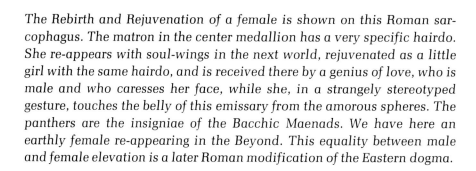

40

The Rebirth and Rejuvenation of a female is shown on this Roman sarcophagus. The matron in the center medallion has a very specific hairdo.
She re-appears with soul-wings in the next world, rejuvenated as a little
girl with the same hairdo, and is received there by a genius of love, who is
male and who caresses her face, while she, in a strangely stereotyped
gesture, touches the belly of this emissary from the amorous spheres. The
panthers are the insigniae of the Bacchic Maenads. We have here an
earthly female re-appearing in the Beyond. This equality between male
and female elevation is a later Roman modification of the Eastern dogma.

TO PAGES 112, 227

41

In obvious similarity to the previous picture we see here the sarcophagus of a male, probably a soldier. The portrait of the deceased, in the central medallion, shows him at the time of his death, while he again re-appears at left and right rejuvenated in the Beyond in the features of Apollo, as usual for a male . . so often seen on mirrors and plaques. His otherworldly guide seems to be the wise Centaur Chiron, the teacher of Achilles – suggesting that this soldier would re-appear as the young Hero . . but it seems that his alter-ego first has to go through the Apollonic epiphany, before the glorifying thought of Chiron is added.

TO PAGE 114

42

In this apparently classic Roman conception, showing husband and wife on their voyage into the next world, by means of a horse-drawn cart, watched over by a winged apparition, . . we already discern a first break with the local doctrine of Hades, and the turn towards the Eastern visions of an elevation to the Above in the company of a female, although being his own spouse, but still contradicting the classical dogma of Hades.

TO PAGES 114, 216

43

It seems that a female is reawakened here from her death, helped by a
sensuous otherworldly apparition, while another more regally dressed
figure with a classic hairdo and possibly divine rank, takes her hand and
greets her in a formal manner. The atmosphere of a tender compassion
prevails in a setting where a tree may give a hint at a paradisial surrounding to which the female is now admitted.

TO PAGE 114

44

On the sarcophagus we see the deceased on the way to the Beyond travelling in a cart, and as it seems joyously urging the horses on, which are
guided by a winged figure, while mourners follow in a procession. Our
attention shifts now to the cover of the sarcophagus where the deceased
appears wearing a Death-Garland as the only ornament which has a very
special meaning in the funeral art of the Etruscans – but amazingly also in
the iconography of India, as a symbol of sanctification.

TO PAGES 119, 216

45

The inscription to this picture says that it shows the "Consecration" of the great teacher Mahavira at the hands of Sakra. The holy man is naked except for the garland, which attests to the importance of the decoration, but it also shows that the divinity has many of such insigniae, to be handed out to the deserving. This very feature of the many spare garlands re-appears again on Etruscan tomb-paintings depicting the celestial spheres.

TO PAGE 119

46

The influx from the East is confirmed by the re-appearance of the same garlands with the same meaning decorating the images of the deceased on the covers of Etruscan sarcophagi. The very shape and falling of those garlands often seem a direct copy from India's iconography. The Begging Bowl of Buddha became in India a general symbol of the Blessed and is often seen in the hand of Etruscan grave figures.

TO PAGE 119

47

The astonishing sight of discarded scarves and loinclothes hanging on shrubs indicates, according to Athenaeus, the readiness for lovemaking. Exactly the same scarves with the same fringes and knotted tassels appear on Etruscan mirrors, which are depicting the euphoric Beyond, while the garlands, suspended from the ceiling, are shown on sepulchral monuments, visualizing the pleasures of Paradise. The combination of those scarves with the garlands suggests that the idea of Elevation and Lovemaking is synonymous for denoting the world of the Blessed.

TO PAGE 116

48

A most peculiar feature of the Garlands of Sanctification is that they often appear hung up in the Above. The idea suggests itself that they might be physically in the way of the souls shown in dalliance, or else, that the idea of consecration may not be compatible with the very bodily pursuits. A hint in this direction might be provided by a picture showing holy men bathing, whose haloes seem to be suspended above them, either because they were practically in their way, or they seemed ideologically not compatible with their profane preoccupation.

TO PAGE 118

49

One of the most convincing documentations showing the inflow of Indian symbols and visions into the Mediterranean sphere are the "Three Graces" – on a sarcophagus, representing the Eastern "Females in the Beyond" – who are seen here handing out the "Garlands of Sanctification" – the purely Indian insigniae of the Elevated, – while the heavenly Nymphs promise the fulfillment of all desires in Paradise.

TO PAGE 121

50

The Harpies were the horrid "Soul-Snatchers" of Greek mythology. They were thought to be not only greedy – "with faces pale with hunger" – but also malicious tormentors. Due to the influences from the East, they took on a more mellow attitude, cradling the soul in a motherly manner, as the idea of loving "Females after Death" penetrated more and more the Mediterranean imagery.

TO PAGE 136

51

Sometimes the Harpies were melting into the image of Sirens, who also had the claws of birds and were in older times highly dangerous, because of their seductive bewitchment, ensnarling the souls of men. Here a Harpia, bordering on a Siren, seems to receive the "Soul-substance" of a man in physical union, whose death is interpreted as sleep.

TO PAGE 136

52

As the image of Death in the Deep changed from the idea of horror to the
visions of sweet promises in the felicitous Above, so changed the figures of
the Harpies to fit the enchanted establishment, inviting, as it seems, with
opened arms the ascending soul, their wings not used for flight, but rather
for protective embraces.

TO PAGE 137

53

The very feminine body in all its softness seems to offer its consolation in the eery spaces of the great Unknown. The menacing birds-claws dominate no longer the basis of the figure, but appear gently overflowed by the warmth of the epidermis, extending more and more downwards from the upper part of the anatomy. Those creatures often bear musical instruments, as if hinting at the "Harmony of Spheres" in the celestial realms.

TO PAGE 137

54

The scavenger-like Harpies of earlier times not only go through bodily
changes, but their mental attitudes too seem to soften and assume the
feelings of compassion. While their faces showed mask-like features before, they appear now infused with a soul, so that we see them cry over the
death of a loved and a mortal.

TO PAGE 137

55

This mirror-frame shows on its top a Harpia, towards which all living streams. Cocks, rabbits and dogs are here the symbols of life, all of them drifting to the image of Death. The human figure below might be the soul, about to be received by the winged genii. Such mirrors suggest not to be objects of daily use, but rather of sepulchral significance.

TO PAGE 139

56

As a still deeper penetration of the Eastern visions into the Etruscan
imagery, we see an otherworldly female with turbanette and round earrings holding a Betel-Nut to entice somebody – (the soul) – to follow her . . .
which later is clarified on an Etruscan tomb-painting, showing a most
similar figure as a bride, guiding a man to her realm.

TO PAGES 141, 253

57

The symbolism of holding out a Betel-Nut is repeated by a winged apparition of the next world, who seems to gesture downward, tempting a soul to
come with her to a blissful Above, modifying thereby the image of a Harpia,
carrying off the soul, into a figure of seduction, possibly accentuated by the
motion of her left hand.

TO PAGE 141

58

Here we see the symbolism of the Betel-Nut explained, as Krishna is about to insert it into the mouth of Radha. The labial penetration by this object, indicating "loving intimacy," being a signal between India's lovers, now re-appears to our surprise on Etruscan figurines made in Italy.

TO PAGES 126, 141

59

The striding forward, while looking backwards, seen on the bronze
figurines, is explained by the otherworldly bride in the same turbanette,
dress and position, enticing a man to follow her into an amorous Thereafter. The aura of death enshrouding the group is shown above by the classic
symbol of the ambushed gazelle, the image of life.

TO PAGES 141, 253

60

How the amorous Thereafter was imagined, is shown by the females with the same turbanettes and earrings as seen on the metal-statuette (picture No. 56). Those nymphs of paradise characterized as Indo-Orientals by wearing nothing but the Tutulus, also seen on the celestial females of the rock carving (picture No. 5), are illustrating now the promise of the Mahabharata that "all desires shall be fulfilled." The garlands hanging from the ceiling are known from the Etruscan tomb-paintings to indicate the sphere of the Beyond.

TO PAGES 118, 141

61

We now turn to another subject dealing with the dead reappearing in the
likeness of various symbol-figures. We see, for instance, Emperor Comodus
as Heracles. The allegorical epiphany in the image of a mythological figure
or divinity started with the "Funeral Apollos" in early times and was later
condemned by Seneca and Plinius as being contrary to classical Greco-
Roman thinking. It never-the-less existed for a long period in funeral art.

TO PAGES 150, 257

62

The Empress Faustina the Younger is shown as Venus, together with Mars.
We see here again the glorification of a person and its elevation to the rank
of a divinity or mythological figure. As Venus was married to Hephaistos,
but had Mars as her paramour, it seems that the deified Empress is thought
to meet – (after death) – her celestial lover . . . conforming thereby to the
Oriental idea of an amorous encounter in the Thereafter, but extended here
also to female mortals.

TO PAGES 111, 150

63

This mirror shows a winged Lasa, possibly melting into the image of Eos
with one of her lovers, carrying off a youth. He asks with a typically Italian
gesture of hand, about his early departure, while holding in the other hand
the mysterious Strigilis, whose amorous implication is underlined by the
interest it evokes in the pigeon, being the insignia of Aphrodite.

TO PAGE 159

64

A Lasa, whose wings indicate the heavenly scenario, is carrying off a dead
warrior in full armor, the monogram "I E" probably identifying him with
the deceased in whose grave the mirror was found. In the lower register we
see, as usual, a parable of the above: A larger creature, symbolic of Death,
who wants to carry off a hare, which is the image of life and propagation.

TO PAGES 159, 162

65

A strange Lasa of early Eastern styling has wings attached to her hips as seen on Assyrian demons, but wears winged boots, reminiscent of Hermes Psychopompos, who brings the souls from the Below to the Above. She carries away an emaciated male, who might be related to a certain moralizing saga. Of great interest are the dolphins in the lower register, as a hint at the Eastern idea of the Eternal Waters of Rebirth.

TO PAGE 160

66

The Haruspex Calchas is divining from a liver, presumably the Fate of a soul, whether or not it should be elevated to the realms of the Blessed. The famous seer of the Iliad is shown with wings, suggesting that such decisions are made in the Above, for which Calchas became a symbol figure.

TO PAGE 161

67

The central figure is scrutinizing a liver, probably to foretell the fate of a newly arrived soul, which modestly appears with a branch in hand from the left. It is called "Rathlth" – (possibly the personal name of the deceased) – reappearing here in the traditional Apollonic glorification. Watching the procedure is Tarchon, the master of haruspex and a divinity of destiny. At the right, with spear in hand, is the "Lord of the sacred Grove" guarding the sanctuary of the chosen. The quadriga of the goddess of Resurrection foretells the glorious outcome of the deliberation.

TO PAGES 159, 161

68

The goddess of Fate, "Athrpa" – (from Atropos, the inflexible) – drives in the "Nail of Destiny" which was done to finalize an event, which seems to be the death of Adonis "Atunis" by the wild boar, seen at the upper right. Also shown is the sad mother of Adonis, really Aphrodite, but called here, as her Etruscan equivalent, the Love-goddess "Turan." There are further the lovers Meleagos "Melicar" and Atalante "Atlenta" involved in the boar-hunt story. In this allegory the deceased is – as it was done so often – equated with Adonis, the image of beauty and beloved by Aphrodite, so that the most splendid of the celestial Females becomes his in Excelsis.

TO PAGE 163

69

Athrpa, the winged goddess of Fate, being, according to Hesiod also a death-goddess, is shown here with her writing equipment, as having kept the record of the life of the deceased, which should influence the destiny of his soul in the Beyond. Between the genii of Fate it is also Vanth, the winged Death-Lasa, who is most prominently shown on mirrors and ash-urns. She stands for the "Fulfillment of Destiny" and her alabastron serves to write the necrolog, – which suggests that we deal here with "Death-Mirrors" – as such memento mori cannot be assumed to be a gift to a living lady.

TO PAGES 143, 163

70

The little naked figure, assumed to be the soul, brings a mirror and an apple
on a stick, as an endearment to the big and orientally dressed female, who
in turn makes the soul sniff a blossom, related to the "Divine Fragrance" by
which the soul is supposed to recognize her as a celestial being. Reminiscent of the Eastern vision of the Females in the Above, this woman wears an
Asiatic turban, round earrings, and the cloak with pointed ends and the
typically oriental tassels.

TO PAGE 164

71

The recipient of this mirror seems to be a Lasa, one of the winged females who carry away the souls in a gentle manner and act as their protector. The other female, and the donor of the mirror, may be the deceased lady with the "Corona Immortalis," who came up from the Deep with a chthonian dog. The plant and blossom at the bottom of the mirror could be symbolic for the re-sprouting of the soul.

TO PAGE 164

72

This picture mainly shows the fact that otherworldly females receive a mirror, presumably as a "Gift of the Dead." The person at left, inscribed as "Tipanu," is an Etruscan equivalent of Persephone, the hostess of the dead, whose arising in spring, is symbolic for resurrection. The figure at right, inscribed as "Thanr" is a servant of Aphrodite, with her emblem, the Dove in hand, hinting at an amorous Thereafter. The person with pointed cap is the alterego of the deceased, reappearing as Adonis – (based on the similarity with other mirrors) – who is wooed by a celestial female with an apple on a stick, a "Hedone," the symbol for the sweetness offered in the Beyond.

TO PAGE 165

73

This mirror generally repeats the idea of the otherwordly females receiving mirrors, supposedly brought along by the dead as an endearment. The right figure, being a servant of Aphrodite, actually uses the mirror hinting at the idea of beauty, while the figure at left, of the Persephone type, holds an egg, again being a symbol of rebirth. The central figures — (as if in continuation of the scene on the previous mirror) — show a more intensified embrace and a kiss, bestowed by the celestial female on the Apollonic image of the deceased.

TO PAGE 165

74

We have here the most basic element of a "Reception in the Beyond:" We see an aged man, not metamorphosed into another apparition, blessed by a Lasa, who brought him up from the Deep. While he is still gratefully or lovingly occupied with this spiritual being of protection and elevation, he is already swiftly approached by a "Female of the Beyond" who seems to urge him, with the gesture of her right hand, to come with her into the paradisial realms.

TO PAGE 165

75

*To amplify the basic idea of Reception, we see here more elements added.
The re-appearing male is rejuvenated and bears in his hand the disk of
sanctification, shown on funeral monuments in the right hand of the
deceased. The "Female of the Beyond" is transposed into a Maenad with
Thyrsos. Between them sprouts the bough of Resurrection and at their feet
we see the intertwined Snakes of Sensuality. The fish miraculously floating through the scene hint at the Celestial Ocean as the sphere of this
blissful encounter.*

TO PAGE 165

76

This mirror shows the usual attempt of staging, with Greco-Roman figures, the Eastern vision of the "Reception in the Beyond." We see Semele holding a Thyrsos and thereby impersonating a Maenad, — being the Etruscan equivalent of the celestial pleasure-girls, — embracing her son, who brought her up from the shades. "Apulu" (Apollo) — with the re-foliated Staff of Resurrection watches, while the little Pan with flute should convey the atmosphere of celestial felicity.

TO PAGE 166

77

The reception of the dead as a Hero in the Above is shown here in its simplest form. A winged apparition, holding the palm of victory, bestows the laurel of fame upon the soul-image, which wears the Corona Immortalis. A Female of the Beyond reaches out for the Hero, to which he responds with obvious affection. The Celestial Female appears on top of a line of waves, hinting thereby at the Indian Apsarases as "Those of the Waters" and promised in the Thereafter. As the line of waves continues throughout the picture, it suggests the "Rebirth out of the Ocean" as the scenario of the Above, in similarity to the stage-setting shown on the Sea-Sarcophagi.

TO PAGE 167

78

Developing from below upwards, there is a Lasa at the handle of the mirror, pointing to the scene above, to show what happened after death. On the lower register are the waters of Death and Rebirth, as the first stage of the development, while on top there is the symbol of Dawn, suggesting the Resurrection as the final outcome. The inscriptions "Menle" (Menelaos) and "Turan" (Venus) — are hinting at the re-appearance of the deceased in the image of the mythic hero and his reception by the most beautiful of the Celestial Females and their entourage.

TO PAGE 167

79

To make sure that we deal here with the dead re-appearing as Hero, the deceased is inscribed as "Achle" (Achilles), the very model of the Hero-figure. Of the first sketchy hint at "Those of the Waters" we still see another amplification: The winged Lasa is this time inscribed as "Thetis" the most lovely of all the Nereids. Thereby we have here an amalgam between the Lasae and the Eastern Apsarases, the loving creatures of the eternal waters re-appearing not only on the Sea-Sarcophagi, but also on the Plaques of Naples.

TO PAGES 167, 257

80

As a further tie-in with the Plaques of Naples where the deceased is glorified in the likeness of Apollo in conjunction with Water-Nymphs, we have here a mirror where the revenant dead is not only clearly described as Aplu, with bow in hand, but where also his relation to the sea is forcefully underlined by Neptun (Nethuns) who is handing him over to the goddess of Dawn (Thesan). The idea of Resurrection is expressed by the radiance appearing around the head of the auroral emanation of the soul. The "arising out of the sea" is also emphasized by the still multi-formed apparition of the eternal waters at the root of the mirror.

TO PAGES 169, 198, 257

81

Here we see again the soul in the image of Apollo (Aplu) received by three females of the Above, reminiscent in their number of the three maidens, which he faces on the Plaques of Naples. The females here are named, from left to right as: "Muira" daughter of Night, spirit of Fate and Doom – (so as to make us sure that we deal here with a Death-Mirror) – furtheron "Lethun" (Leto) who gave birth to Apollo in the darkness of the Waters – a hint at his re-arising from the deep of the sea, – and finally "Thalna" divinity of Rebirth with a blossoming staff in hand. Showing the destiny of the dead as being reborn out of the sea and his eventual apotheosis.

TO PAGES 171, 199

82

Artists, impatient with the monotony of the Apollo-Mirrors invented some charming variations. "Apulu" (Apollo) is shown here with his sister "Artumes" (Artemis). However, the scene is not as innocent as it seems, as above them hangs the Death-Garland of Sanctification, known from the Etruscan sepulchral art, to denote the Beyond. As both of them arose from the Darkness of the waters to ascend to divine splendor, they became a symbol for the Resurrection of the soul. The "sister" is dressed according to her origin, in an Oriental costume, as a stand-in for the Eastern Females.

TO PAGE 171

83

As the last of the Apollo-Mirrors we see Apollo with Lyra, already fused with Dionysos, who awakened Ariadne to Love, as an allegory in which the deceased is resurrected from his death-sleep to a new existence of sensual joy. "Phuphluns" is the Etruscan name for Dionysos – "Areatha" for Ariadne. "Semla" for Semele, at the right, is the witness of that union, while at the left a "Sime" (Satyr) with pointed goat-ear and sharpened Thyrsos whispers to the bride with his hand at her shoulder, who is in the Eastern fashion, the more active partner of the pair.

TO PAGE 171

84

The Nemean Lion was the gruesome offspring of Night-Eternal, equated with Death, and is shown as such, invincible and larger than life on Sarcophagi, devouring all the Living. However, Heracles conquered the formidable beast and thereby became a special symbol-figure for overcoming Death, and is glorified in funeral art as the great Hero of Resurrection.

TO PAGE 172

85

On the rim of the mirror we see the devastating Nemean Lion as the symbol
of Death, but on the handle Heracles emerges, ready to club the beast. The
main picture shows Heracles surrounded by three females, one of them
ready to confer upon him the palm of victory, hinting maybe at the idea
that it was the deceased, who overcame death, and equating him thereby
with Heracles, while Psychopompos with his refoliating staff looks on.

TO PAGE 173

86

Parallel with his images on Sarcophagi, where Heracles is shown freeing the souls from the Below, we see him here, in the company of a chthonian dog, being crowned as Hero by "Mean" the goddess of Fate, in the company of sad "Leinth" – (from "lein" = to die) – the messenger of Death, ominously pointing with her finger. It seems again that the rejuvenated soul of the deceased reappears in the image of the hero who overcame death eternal and is now received by celestial females.

TO PAGE 173

87

A rather enigmatic Mirror shows Heracles near the handle, by convention
as the beginning of the development, which seems to end in the Above,
with Dawn, the symbol of Resurrection. The scenario in the middle is
reminiscent of the "Sea-Sarcophagi" where the re-born souls appear as
Babies, who are received by the company of celestial apparitions. As
actions start at left, it is Hermes Psychopompos who may have brought the
Soul-Babies to the celestial spheres.

TO PAGE 173

88

Parallel with the development which we notice on the Sarcophagi and on the Plaques of Naples, reflecting the news slowly trickling in from the East, that there are more than one Celestial Female to be expected in the Beyond, the artists abandoned figures like Selene and Ariadne as the Greco-Roman stand-ins for single lovers, and turned instead to the "Three Graces" and the "Judgement of Paris" to represent the deceased as given a multiple choice of otherworldly females. Here we see the Hero-figure blending over into the image of Paris, surrounded by maidens wearing the typically Oriental crossbands of trinkets.

TO PAGE 174

89

The struggle of coming from the dread Below of eternal Death to the Above seems to be over and the miraculation of the dead reappearing in the celestial spheres becomes an accepted fact. The soul re-appears no longer as Apollini or as the Hero. The setting of the Above is conforming now to such a degree to the Eastern-Oriental visions of Paradise, as to become entirely love-oriented. Because Aphrodite promised Paris "Lust" if he would chose her, she appears as the ideal symbol-figure for "amorous felicity" promised in the Beyond.

TO PAGE 174

90

The Females of the Beyond, in later times, are no longer winged like the
esoteric genii from before, as the Lasae or the messenger foreboding doom
and brooding destiny, but, instead, became women, only thinly disguised
as mythological figures. The chosen female, however, as the winner of the
contest, is often shown crowned, as the last vestige of an enchanted realm.
The grapes framing the Mirror, as well as the winged creature on the grip of
the Mirror, gesturing to the above, remain a clear hint at the idea of
Resurrection.

TO PAGE 174

91

The winged Lasae sometimes seem to take the place of the pearl-studded Eastern brides. On this picture we see Hermes Psychopompos facing such a creature who appears to make the first move towards him with her right hand, suggesting maybe a readiness for an amorous encounter. (He once seduced a Lasa, or her mother Lala, which he had to escort from the Above to the Below.) Here he seems to motion at a symbolic blossom, of extraordinary size and importance, usually denoting sensuality by its united members of generation, while he opens his great-cape of the divine messenger towards his heavenly bride.

TO PAGES 143, 174

92

Possibly as a hint at the "plurality" of females in the Beyond, promised to the souls according to the Eastern doctrines, we see some "double" dance-girls in Asiatic attire, making motions which could mean the salute of welcome. Symbolically hanging in the background are two fringed scarves, which we know from Etruscan sepulchral paintings to mean readiness for love-encounters in the Above, which is made still clearer on the following picture.

TO PAGES 115, 175

93

Here we have no doubt, two Assyro-Asiatic Females of the Beyond. The fringed scarf hanging on the vegetation is well known to us from the description by Athenaeus as the preliminary to lovemaking. One of the girls holds out a bridal twig, seen also on the little oriental Houri pulling the man with her to the pleasures of paradise on the fresco in the "Tomb of the Bacchants" at Tarquinia. The opened bed hints boldly at the intentions of the females. On the lower register, there is a reference to the Celestial Waters, to indicate that the above scene takes place in the Beyond.

TO PAGES 115, 175

94

Leading over from the soul as Hero, to the idea of the "Nuptial Washing,"
we see "Achle" (Achilles) with two females belonging to "Those of the
Waters" (Thetis). The most important hint, however, is the wash-basin
which appears greatly amplified on other Mirrors, as well as on Cistae, and
is clarified on the Plaques of Naples, where the females are understood as
"Water-Nymphs" being the Romanized version and verbal translation of
the Apsarases, who are the pleasure-girls of the Eastern paradise. The
"Flowers of Sensuality" are strongly sprouting on the frame of the mirror.

TO PAGE 175

95

The "Nuptial Washing" is understood as the preparation by the Celestial Brides for their meetings with the soul in excelsis, according to the promise of the East. Here we see the classical three figures, reminiscent of the "Three Graces" or the "Judgement of Paris." One of them holding a pigeon, the symbol of the Love-goddess. A dancing Faun in the background foretells the priapic joy of the atmosphere. A Lasa, near the grip of the Mirror, holding the fruitbearing laurel of the "Corona Immortalis" confirms that the vision takes place after death and in the Above.

TO PAGE 176

96

The scene of a "Nuptial Washing" at a fountain is of interest, because it
shows the females highly reminiscent of the Waternymphs with pitcher or
urns on the Plaques of Naples and the "persistent Waternymphs" on the
sarcophagi. Newly added is a male figure, assumed to be the soul, which
holds an oil or perfume alabastron and a "strigilis" which is a scraper to
remove oil and dust from the body. The fact that this male takes part in the
nuptial washing confirms the notion of an impending mutual adventure
with the females.

TO PAGE 179

97

This scene of "Nuptial Washing" shows the pigeon-symbol of Aphrodite and the swan, famous for his love-involvements, looking at the females, as one of them uses a gift-mirror, while holding a stilo in her hand to beautify her hair. The male figure, known to us from the funeral plaques to represent the soul facing the Waternymphs, is holding a "Strigilis" of most unusual shape, which may, or may not, be symbolic for his "bring-along-gift" to the females, in similarity to the mirror gift, as he seems to address one of the maidens with this object in hand in a tender gesture.

TO PAGES 143, 179

98

The mysterious "Strigilis" almost forces upon us the idea of a second connotation on this mirror which shows an Eros-like apparition, clearly unveiling his maleness and holding with both hands this enigmatic object, which, by the way, is never shown on any of the mirrors in actual use and is therefore especially prone to be taken as a symbol, possibly as his gift to the females. This notion is supported by the Blossom of Sensuality with protruding generative parts, as the only attribute supporting the meaning of the main figure.

TO PAGES 143, 179

99

This truly puzzling picture shows on first sight the usual "Judgement of Paris" slightly reminiscent perhaps of an unfinished sketch by Picasso. But just the rather experimental idea-sketch may reveal more clearly the enigma of the "Strigilis" where the woman who is chosen seems to hold symbolically as the price of victory, the strigilis in her hand, while another female seems to have the same object tentatively, in the sense of a grafitti drawn upon her lap. The same composition was copied several times, each time showing the soul being confronted with a choice of females in the Beyond.

TO PAGE 179

100

Here we have an interesting connecting link between the Mirrors, the Cistae and the funeral Plaques of Naples, explaining each-other by filling-in meanings which are less completely shown on either of the single embodiments. Specifically as to this mirror, it seems possible, that it is this time the soul of the earthly female which finds in the Beyond a heavenly youth to fulfill her wishes for bliss in paradise, because it is not clear if the Corona Immortalis is his, or if the wreath in his hand is hers, which he is just holding while she arranges her hair to please him.

TO PAGE 180

101

The remarkable feature of this Mirror is that the Corona Immortalis is given to the female designating her as the dead person and especially that no name is given to her, being the main figure, while the others are identified by inscriptions. This in similarity to the prefabricated Sarcophagi where the identity of the deceased is not defined. It therefore seems possible that this may be one of the Mirrors to be given into the grave of any lady, wishing her that she should encounter a lovable young man in the next world.

TO PAGE 181

102

The present mirror suggests more clearly the possibility that the next world may be populated by Bacchian spirits, offering the souls of females amorous pleasures – to conform to the sensuous scenario awaiting men. The scene is reminiscent of Ariadne, who was awakened out of her death-sleep by Dionysos to a new existence of eternal love. The female here seems to open her drapes voluntarily and wears the Corona Immortalis, not the wreath of the Maenads, indicating that she is the deceased.

TO PAGE 180

103

The fact that most Cistae show scenes from the next world and the figures on their covers are depicting the dead person or his soul as being carried away by kindly spirits, leaves no doubt that the Cistae, being basically containers for female toiletry, were eventually addressed, as bring-along-gifts, to the Females of the Beyond, as an endearment. They were frequently found in graves of men, which excludes the idea that they should serve the deceased himself in the Thereafter, and tend to confirm the notion of a gift to otherworldly maidens.

TO PAGE 184

104

The theme shared between the previously shown Mirrors, the above Cista and the following Plaques, is the washing of hair, a Nuptial ceremony. Here we see two females in this symbolic gesture, while a third, with a stilo to part her hair, upholds a mirror, presumably received by her as a gift of the dead. This mirror seems to bear the image of a winged soul, an appropriate portrait of its donor, who possibly could be shown next to her in heavy drapery, usually associated with the death-shroud of the deceased. On the upper register, we see the Nemean Lion – the symbol of death – with creatures of the Deep, hinting at the rebirth out of the eternal Waters.

TO PAGES 186, 196

105

Surprisingly, we see here on a Plaque of Naples the same theme of Hair-Washing as on Mirrors and Cistae which make reference to Death and the Beyond. But as they are found in northern Italy and the Plaques in the south of Italy and as they show almost identical subjects we must assume a very broad and general conception of afterlife in the minds of the Etruscans. While the Plaques picture Apollini in "breathless silence" – only the Mirrors have told us about the further adventures of the soul with the celestial females.

TO PAGES 176, 196

106

There is a whole series of dedicatory or commemorative Plaques in the Museum of Naples. They show the epiphany of the Dead re-appearing in the image of Apollo, then called "Apollini" to distinguish him from the divinity Apollo. The idea that the dead re-appears in another "Avatar" or embodiment comes from India, where the transmigration of souls into other manifestations was a basic assumption. This "transfiguration" of the dead was severely condemned by Seneca and Plinius, but persisted in funeral art.

TO PAGE 196

107

The Alterego of the Dead, now re-appearing as "Apollini" is shown as being confronted by Water-Nymphs. They are the original Apsarases, in their verbal translation, as "Those of the Waters" – ("apsa" in Avestan cognate with "aqua") –. As the Apsarases are depicted in their homeland quite differently, we have here the proof of a verbal transmission from the East to the Mediterranean. The Italian artists, uncertain as to their role or identity, show those females sometimes as Well-Nymphs on a rock, or scooping water from a fountain, or simply as water-carriers.

TO PAGE 197

108

"Those of the Waters" were thought, in the East, to exist in the Celestial Ocean, the Paradise in the Above. In Mediterranean lands they were sometimes interpreted as Well-Nymphs, that is sweet-water-Nymphs. On the Plaques, however, they are shown in most cases with sea-shells, meaning, salt-water-Nymphs or Oceanic creatures, again pointing to the fact that the rumor must have reached Italy that those otherworldly females exist in the "Ocean." When the confused artists attempted to be more specific, they erred the most, depicting the females as Well-Nymphs between the rocks, producing from a cornucopia the bounty of the land.

TO PAGE 195

109

The notion that we deal here with Oceanic females is verified by a Plaque showing Okeanos on the lower register, as the basis of the scene above, suggesting that the maidens arose from the sea, which is understood as the "Waters of Death and Rebirth" towards which all living drifts, and out of which all is reborn. The females are not Well-Nymphs, nor Nereids, but a tribe unknown until now to the Mediterranean. The Dioscuri left and right are archaic symbols for rebirth and the elevation from the Below to the Above.

TO PAGE 195

110

We see the deceased in the image of *Apollini* each time as a young man.
The idea of reappearing rejuvenated after death is contrary to the local
conception of Hades, as rejuvenation in the dreary realm would serve no
purpose, where the shades exist "without midriff" – meaning: without food
or sex. However, the rejuvenation becomes very important in the Eastern
doctrine, where the departed wants to enjoy to the fullest the heavenly
maidens.

TO PAGE 194

111

Apollini and the Water-Nymphs are shown on the Plaques as a static constellation of elements, without interaction between them. On this plaque Apollini even looks away from the Nymphs and the "static" character of the position is underlined by the postaments separating the figures. Only the scenes on the Etruscan grave-mirrors explain that the soul, in the image of Apollini – (there inscribed as "Aplu") is handed over by the lord of the Sea to the goddess of Dawn for his final apotheosis and that he then enters a nuptial relation with the celestial Nymphs.

TO PAGE 197

112

The original Apsarases, re-formulated as Water-Nymphs in the Mediterranean, were later typified as females with water-pitchers. But their heraldic appearance on Plaques gave no hint that they were embodiments of Love in the Above. Here, however, on the cover of an Ash-urn, we see such a Nymph with water-pitcher, ready in mood and gesture to yield to embraces. Almost exactly the same figure later appears as "The persistent Water-Nymph" on Sarcophagi, as the ultimate dream-vision of the deceased in the Above, while the Mirrors confirm their nuptial relation to the soul of the deceased.

TO PAGES 197, 253

113

Sometimes the artists try to understand the elusive Nymphs as the Horai,
the embodiments of loveliness and graces, and servants of Aphrodite. They
appear then rushing to a male idol, often in the person of Priapus, or a
Faunian creature on Greek plaques, but here taking the shape of Apollo.
Those females are – in their function as Celestial Lovers – related to their
Oriental sisters, the Houries, while they are still wearing the seashells as
their emblem, thereby connecting them back to the Water-Nymphs, as the
equivalent of the Apsarases, their Indian sisters.

TO PAGE 197

114

In later times, the sea-shell seems to have lost its connection to the Celestial Ocean, and became a stereotyped emblem held by the females with bare breasts in a decorative manner, similar to the Karyatides, in a theatrical setting, in which Apollo takes the center of the stage. The shells, because of their position relative to the body of the females, may be symbolic for the "Concha Veneris" offered to Apollini.

TO PAGE 197

115

In a further reduction of their initial meanings, the Water-Nymphs become smaller as compared to the richly ornamented frames of the memorial-plaques. The relation of the females to Death and Afterlife seems here reduced to decorative marionettes in a landscape with fruit bearing-trees, as if offering refreshments in the gardens of paradise, be it to the vegetation in the function of Well-Nymphs, or to the souls of the Blessed, only faintly suggesting thereby their intention of fulfilling their desires.

TO PAGE 198

116

On the late Roman Sarcophagi a triad of Water-Nymphs still appears, but
in a subordinate role. They are now fully clothed and are shown contribu-
ting water to a large container and seem to have assumed a totally different
meaning, reminiscent of the Parcae or Moirai, the daughters of Night and
embodiments of Fate, the abstract powers of Destiny, measuring and ter-
minating life. The running or flowing of time is sometimes symbolized by
the flow of water and the "fulfilling" of life by the filling of a measuring-
container.

TO PAGE 198

117

The Plaques of Athens introduce three new personages to the Nymphs: One is the suppliant being the donor of the plaque – here at right – receiving the drink of everlasting life from an ephebe. Another is Nymphagogos – in the center – who guides him to the Nymphs, or brings the Nymphs to him, and the third is Pan, hinting at the amorous relation between the donor and the otherworldly females in excelsis.

TO PAGE 200

118

Pan appears as the protector-figure over this scene, foretelling thereby the amorous outcome of the encounter between a male apparition – probably the soul – and the three heavenly Nymphs, who seem to be in a gently receptive mood. The surroundings, in a vagueness between clouds and rocks, may suggest the legendary grotto where mortals are said to meet celestial spirits.

TO PAGE 201

119

To clarify the character of the otherwise rather sedate three classical maidens, we see them here dancing to the tune of the priapic Pan, suggesting that they are in fact the Horai, or servants to Aphrodite in her sensuous aspects, and as such related to the Oriental Houries and their mission in the Eastern paradise which is said to be the embracing of souls in the celestial spheres.

TO PAGE 201

120

*A princely young man, or the rejuventated image of the deceased, appears
in a scene which could be a solem hierogamy under the aspects of a priapic
Pan, who is uniting him with the three celestial maidens, known to us by
now as to their character and mission from Plaques, Mirrors and Sarcophagi. The giant Olympian mask seems to denote the realm of the divine
Above, in contrast to the abandoned visions of the soul in Hades.*

TO PAGE 201

121

The largest figure here, is the Apollonic apparition, half awakening as it seems, conventionally impersonating the soul of the deceased, but already inspired by the Panian spirit, the emissary from the realms of celestial felicity, so often seen on ash-urns. The wing-footed Hermes Psychopompos, in the role of Nymphagogos, introduces to him the three heavenly brides. The small figures at right traditionally represent the donors of the plaque, who also are the suppliants, wishing for a similarly miraculous reception in the divine Beyond.

TO PAGE 202

122

The sweet daughters of Indra's paradise assumed in some other Mediterranean lands the aura of venerable genii of maritime protection, invoked by people who were depending on the mercy of the Sea. This marble figure of Corinth holds the sea-shell and drapery exactly in the position as seen on the Plaques of Naples, and reappears paraphrased on many other dedicatory reliefs where the Water-Nymphs blend over into the image of the "Three Graces" and thereby return to their original meaning of representing the females, promised in the Oriental Afterlife.

TO PAGE 203

123

Later, in a return to a Greco-Roman scenario and in a trend towards spiritualization, the dead person is staged as Apollo and the mysterious Nymphs of the Beyond as his subordinate Muses, the adoring females around the apotheosed male, as a faint echo from the Eastern conception, where the soul of the dead is promised a multitude of celestial females, fulfilling all desires.

TO PAGE 154

124

The dedicatory Plaques of Naples do not make it clear that Apollo was
actually connected to funeral art. It is this Sarcophagus, with Apollo in
paradise as its center, which clarifies without any further doubt that this
relation of Apollo to sepulchral visions exist. The glorification of the dead
in the image of Apollo is confirmed by Sarcophagi and Mirrors where a
variety of maidens is shown receiving the soul of the dead in its Apollonian
Avatar.

TO PAGE 154

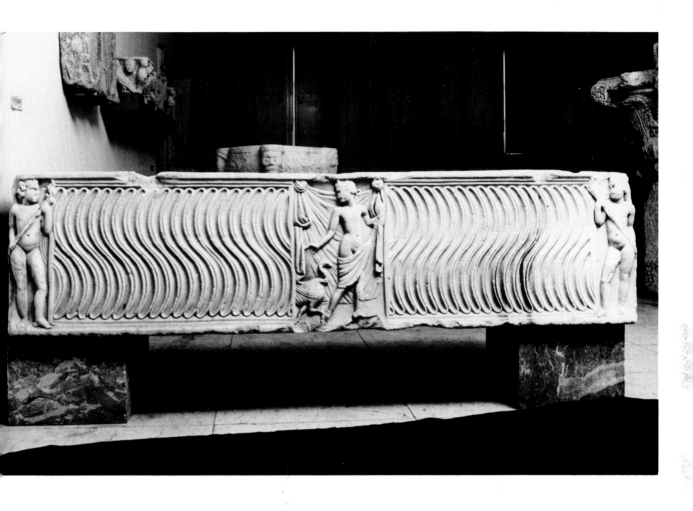

125

We could not be sure that the "Three Graces" on Sarcophagi were related to lovemaking, until we see one of them on this Sarcophagus, of the same time and type, coquettishly involved with a swanlike bird, repeatedly used as symbol for amorous adventures with Leda, whereby the deceased, in the image of a swan or soul-bird, approaches now the Female of the Beyond, allegorically shown as Leda, to indicate her eventual consent to that encounter.

TO PAGE 208

126

*Artists of foreign lands expressed the Eastern beliefs in their own symbol-
language. The restaging of foreign doctrines with local actors often leads to
grotesque imagery. On this Sarcophagus of Cyprus of 600 B.C. the many
joyous lovemakings promised in the Indo-Oriental paradise are expressed
by many dancing figures of Bes, the lovemaking god of Egypt.*

TO PAGE 211

127

The milk-drinking in India's paradise is here illustrated by many females
offering their breasts. The fact that the Apsarases were thought to be
promiscuous lovers is translated now by characterizing those celestial
brides as North African girls of pleasure, richly decked out with their
typical head-gears and coins.

TO PAGE 211

128

The Indian scripture states that the souls of the Blessed in Heaven drink milk from milk-yielding trees. An Egyptian artist showing the drinking of milk in paradise paints a breast on a branch, which the tree reaches to the soul of the Blessed in the next world. This tree also sprouts an arm, conforming thereby to the traditional gesture of Isis, the supreme milk-giver, nourishing Horus. This most improbable image is one of the many curious cases which illustrate the Eastern doctrine of Afterlife by means of Egyptian symbols and components.

TO PAGE 212

129

India's paradise, as depicted in Egyptian symbol-language, shows above the premordial swamps the souls in the Thereafter clamoring with outstretched arms, in a gesture between longing and supplication for the celestial females, pictured as broad-hipped odalisques, while above them the lovemaking god Bes is enthroned, flanked by the double-monkeys, the emblem of Egyptian pleasure-girls, meant to be the equivalent of the Heavenly Brides.

TO PAGE 212

130

On the earlier or more primitive sarcophagi we see in their center an
Apollo-like mask, characterized as such by its classical hairdo, that in
some cases seems even to have been transferred to the deceased who is
portrayed on the cover of the sarcophagus, which suggests, at first quite
vaguely, the metamorphosis of the dead into the apparition of Apollo. The
assumption is later verified on Mirrors and Plaques which now show
clearly the alter-ego of the deceased in the image of Apollo with Lyra and
Bow and identified as such by Etruscan inscriptions. Further on he is
depicted in the company of celestial Females, thereby conforming to the
Eastern conceptions of the Thereafter.

TO PAGES 216, 218, 257

131

Still belonging to the primitive sarcophagi we see some sea-creatures with beards, flanking the apparition of the dead. The beards want to be a hint at the Maleness of the sea, as the "Pool of Nature" to which all of the living return and out of which all life is re-born, making thereby reference to the idea of Resurrection. The Sea has a twofold meaning: One is the premordial element of eternal Death and Rebirth, on a rather Mediterranean level employed on the sarcophagi; the other is the Eastern vision of the Celestial Ocean, as the paradisial spheres of loving embraces, which notion becomes increasingly clearer on later sarcophagi, as we will see in the following.

TO PAGES 217, 219, 240

132

On later, or more eloquent sarcophagi we now see the person in the
center-medallion clearly defined as the deceased shown in the portrait of
the old lady. We also notice that the "Male Creatures of the Sea" took the
shape of men, however, hinting at their representing the Sea by their
blending-over into aquatic beings. There appears the suggestion that the
old lady has arrived at the "Pool of Nature" and is protected and upheld
there by the Lords of the Ocean. The Waters of Eternity and the Amorini
symbolize the joyful atmosphere of the Eastern Thereafter.

TO PAGES 217, 250, 256

133

The vague suggestion of earlier sarcophagi are here more eloquently clarified, as well as the stronger influx of Eastern visions concerning Afterlife. Females are added to the scenario in tender inter-action with the "Males of the Sea" who now become aquatic Centauri, melting into the vision of the Gandharvas of India's celestial ocean, while the Females seem to be a Mediterranean version of the heavenly Apsarases, the paramours of the Gandharvas. We also notice the Lady in the center as being rejuvenated, which is the Indian conception of re-appearance in the Beyond, while the shell becomes increasingly the symbol of Rebirth.

TO PAGES 216, 244, 254

134

Here we see in the left corner a more intensified embrace of the Gandharvic
Males of the Sea with their paramours, and the Females "riding" on the
males, which is a typically Eastern mode of expressing the "Vehicle" in a
relationship. We also see the mood of exuberance expressed by the Amorini raising the deceased person out of the eternal waters to a love-oriented
next existence. The waters, as such, which formally conveyed the heavy
aura of the unfathomable Deep, appear on later Sarcophagi more and more
as the swirl of rebirth, populated by new life in the form of Amorini bobbing
about and intermixing in springlike joy with all figures.

TO PAGES 233, 236, 254

135

A distinguished lady appears reborn out of the Eternal Sea which is now understood as the Celestial Ocean, the paradise of Love in the Indo-Oriental sense. We notice for the first time Females upholding the deceased, possibly suggesting that the noble lady would not enter a close relation with the amorous males, and would instead be sisterly received by the female apparitions of the Above. We discern, however, at first quite vaguely, embraces of the females with symbols of Masculinity and Love, at left represented by a Bull, the image of "Power and Passion" – and at the right by the Monkey the arch-symbol for playful embraces. The Amorini stride forward like heralding the arrival of the great lady.

TO PAGES 218, 251, 255

136

The intention of showing the dead person as being re-born out of the sea
and now appearing in the shell, is made clear by the fact that on some
Sarcophagi the face of that center-figure is left un-finished, obviously in
order to complete the portrait of the deceased, as soon as the sarcophagus
is sold, while all the other figures are finished in great detail. We also notice
the theatralized bravado in which the females embrace the male symbols
of the sea, which calls the attention of the other figures shown here. With
the exuberance of a newly found idea, the covers of the Sarcophagi display
even more male symbols, like lions, horses, and rams, blended into aquatic
formations, representing the sea as the spermatic "Pool of Nature."

TO PAGES 218, 233, 251

137

We encounter the same un-finished portrait of the future inhabitant of the
Sarcophagus, but it seems that the excitement, the piquantry and gusto of
the idea, has worn off and that we deal here with the mere copy of the great
and flamboyant idea. Instead of the mouth-to-mouth kisses of the females
with animals, we see lukewarm pantomimes, where it was not clear to the
sculptor whether the females are chasing or embracing the aquatic beings,
while the attention paid to those scenes by the other figures seem to have
cooled considerably.

TO PAGES 218, 256

138

The souls of the dead re-appearing in Paradise as Babies were a problem
for the Italian sculptors, especially the question of how to set them in
relation to the deceased person, so that we see at times the attempt to
understand the Oceanic male, although being a Centaur, as the father and
the aquatic female as the mother of the baby which reaches for the
motherly breast . . . as a most uneasy replica of an Italian family-picture,
following the myth from foreign lands, that the Soul-Babies are fed and
cared for by the celestial company. As the act of re-birth is presented by the
baby, the deceased lady is no longer shown in a shell, but framed instead as
an ancestral memento.

TO PAGES 218, 227, 254

139

The portrait of the deceased in the center has lost its importance and is now replaced by a votive inscription. But there is a new element to be seen, most probably due to a new wave of information reaching the Mediterranean from the East: The Eastern Gandharvas are the paradisial musicians and the aquatic centaurs are therefore shown with a muscial instrument, the Lyra, which does not fit at all the visions of any Mediterranean mythos and should alert us again that we deal here with a foreign doctrine.

TO PAGES 228, 237, 255

140

The Indian scripture actually says that the souls in Paradise are born out of
Lotus flowers. To be Lotus-born means to be born in purity. The supreme
image of it being Buddha the "Lotus-born" addressed as the "Jewel in the
Lotus" in the endless prayers of the Prayer-Mills. The difficulty for the
Italian stone-carvers, however, was that the Lotus flower was not known to
them and therefore they made do with some exotic flowers which are
sprouting babies – also falsely assuming the Gandharvic Centauri together
with the Apsaratic Waternymphs as the loving parents of that astonishing
offspring.

TO PAGES 219, 227, 255

141

Now we come to a slow return from the Eastern visions, blending back into the Mediterranean imagery. After 600 B.C. when the Etruscan power was on the wane, the exotic Eastern scenario was increasingly invaded by the surrounding Greco-Roman world of figures, displacing the ideas of the "Celestial Ocean." Some of the former motives, like the females embracing Bulls and Rams, were still retained as time-honored curiosities, which were no longer understood, as they seemed not connected to Death or Afterlife, nor to the domestic notion of the voyage of the souls to the Island of the Blessed.

TO PAGES 219, 226, 241

142

There came a new surge or vogue in the sarcophagi-fashion, to transfer the sphere of action into happenings within the Mediterranean, involving figures of the Greco-Roman mythology. We prominently see Aphrodite riding on the "lascivious ram" in an entourage of Nereids, some of them in an arbitrary mixup of symbols, holding the Lyra, which belongs to the Gandharvic Centaurs, — "the Musicians on the court of Indra" — who in turn, hold babies, who really belong to the care of the Celestial Females, while the oceanic men seem to tame horses and bulls, in a totally lost symbolism.

TO PAGES 234, 236, 249

143

The Dartmouth Sarcophagus shows an interesting amalgam of Italian iconography with the Eastern iconology. The exotic love-story between the soul and the celestial females is projected onto a Mediterranean setting. The central Nereid represents the theme of a hierogamy with the Sea, supported by the wedding-band in the hands of the cupid, which is shown on another Sarcophagus (Illus. 139) uniting her as the bride with a bull, representing the procreative powers of the Ocean. The celestial Female on the left displays an intensity of embrace which does not exist on any other Sarcophagus, while the Nymph at the right alludes to the drift into paradise quite often seen on sepulchral images of the East, dramatized by her pulling a violent horse, being the symbol of masculinity.

TO PAGES 238, 249, 252

144

After the Sea-Sarcophagi became a mysterious tradition of unfathomable meanings, we are faced with free compositions which at random show scenes of frolicking Nereids embraced by Tritons, and a host of figures of Mediterranean coinage, without any reference to Death or Afterlife. Sometimes however, there is a hint that the deceased is under the protection of Okeanos and some Sarcophagi resemble containers of water, watched over by Olympian lords of the sea, together with various monsters, while even later newly made water-troughs were ornamented with aquatic creatures copied from Sea-Sarcophagi, —which, in turn, when abandoned, were used as water-basins.

TO PAGES 249, 253

145

The Idea of the birth out of the sea was by no means confined to the Mediterranean. The notion of females originating in the maritime element is elaborately explained in Indian mythology by the story concerning Lakshmi, goddess of Beauty and Love, who was produced in a butter-churning process, whereby the liquid was converted into a solid state and body. The birth of Aphrodite is technically much less convincing, but her miraculous story took never-the-less deep roots in the Mediterranean due to the elevation of this vision by the greatest sculptors and poets.

TO PAGE 244

146

Wherever it may have originated, the female arising out of the sea became an important feature on the Sea-Sarcophagi, symbolizing the re-birth of the soul in general. This very weatherbeaten, votive-relief, probably of a legionary, represents the soul, in the image of a female, lifted out of the premordial waters, which are characterized as such by the males of still undetermined morphology, while a hint at the "Birth of Venus" is made by the two Amorini flanking the epiphany.

TO PAGE 243

147

The birth out of the sea is also suggested on a postament where a female
seems to arise out of the headless bodies of aquatic creatures, as if she
would have had her roots in the still brewing life of the premordial waters.
But we may also think, in reverse, that it symbolizes death by showing that
lovely image of life sinking down to the mysterious Deep.

TO PAGE 243

148

Here we see the female in the shell, well defined as Venus, with an Amorette representing the idea of Himeros or Priapus attached to her. The flanking females, whose original model, the Apsarases, are long forgotten and who, in fact hold strands of grain in their hands, now mean to represent together with the aquatic centauri "Land and Sea" – an allegory often repeated, to show the levitation of the soul above that sphere. We thereby see the originally celestial figures now suggesting the earthly scenario.

TO PAGE 244

149

Another postament shows in a slightly eery mood an almost motherly
female in the shell of re-birth, framed by dolphins and upheld by male
creatures of the sea. We may discern here, however vaguely, the return to
the Eastern idea of the "Soul-Baby" which is lovingly received in the next
world. This hint is made by the Amorette inspiring the female, while the
Baby arising from a swan-necked bird evokes the uneasy memory of Leda's
visitation by the divine male, a vision repeated more explicitly on Leda-
Sarcophagi and Stelae.

TO PAGE 245

150

Here we have, in the mood of a Grand Finale, all the elements seen before, gloriously united. The Venus in the Shell of Resurrection, the little Amor with bow on one side and the soul-baby victoriously reborn on the other. The maidens riding on the aquatic Centaurs as slightly amused observers of the females embracing the galloping animals with the smooth bravado of circus performers, while the babies, sprouting out of the exotic flowers are considered mere ornamentations. The only hint at extra-Mediterranean influences are the extremely heavy bellies of the females, modelled after the Oriental Odalisques, now clinging to the animals.

TO PAGE 245

151

The connection of the "Three Graces" to Death and Love is shown on sarcophagi where they are flanked by souls of the dead – (with butterfly wings) – in embraces with Love-Genii of the next world, (wearing feathery wings). The souls received by Genii of Love seem to be of principal interest, while the "Three Graces" appear small, like a distant fantasy.

TO PAGE 246

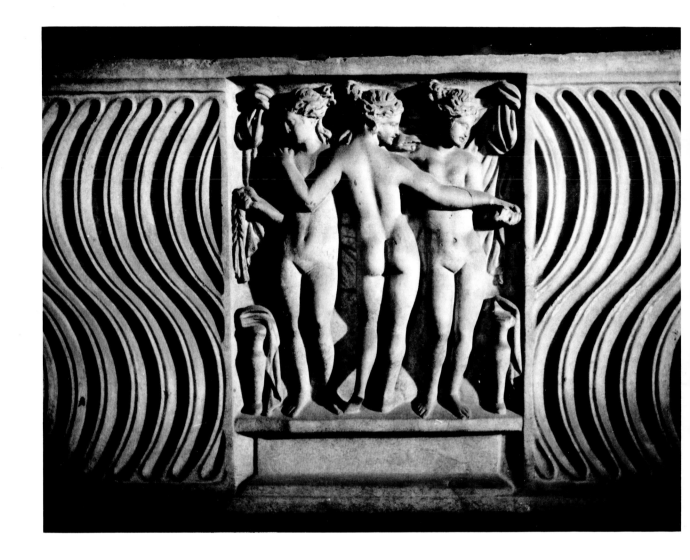

152

Enlarged detail of the Frontispiece: The central ornament of a Roman
Sarcophagus shows the "The Graces" clearly relating them thereby to
death. They are the stand-ins for the Eastern "Females of the Beyond"
fulfilling all desires of the souls in the next world. This role of the Celestial
Brides is here hinted at by the Wedding-band in the hand of one of the
maidens, and the pitchers with towels, suggesting the idea of the "Nuptial
Washing" so frequently seen on Plaques, Cistae and Mirror-engravings, as
the preparation for the tender encounter of those brides –(nymphae)–with
the epiphany of the soul.

TO PAGE 246

THE CELESTIAL BRIDES IN FUNERAL ART
THE DEVELOPMENT

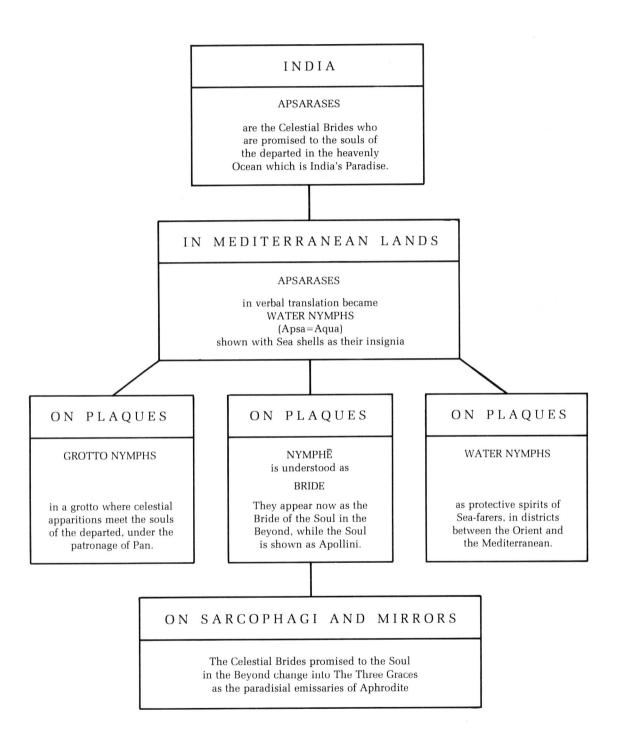

INDIA

APSARASES

are the Celestial Brides who
are promised to the souls of
the departed in the heavenly
Ocean which is India's Paradise.

IN MEDITERRANEAN LANDS

APSARASES

in verbal translation became
WATER NYMPHS
(Apsa=Aqua)
shown with Sea shells as their insignia

ON PLAQUES

GROTTO NYMPHS

in a grotto where celestial
apparitions meet the souls
of the departed, under the
patronage of Pan.

ON PLAQUES

NYMPHĒ
is understood as

BRIDE

They appear now as the
Bride of the Soul in the
Beyond, while the Soul
is shown as Apollini.

ON PLAQUES

WATER NYMPHS

as protective spirits of
Sea-farers, in districts
between the Orient and
the Mediterranean.

ON SARCOPHAGI AND MIRRORS

The Celestial Brides promised to the Soul
in the Beyond change into The Three Graces
as the paradisial emissaries of Aphrodite